THE PROGR… UNDERGROUND

KEV ROWLAND

Vol 1

Edited by Jonathan Downes
Typeset by Jonathan Downes
Cover by Martin Springett
Internal Layout by Jon Downes for CFZ Communications
Using Microsoft Word 360 Microsoft Publisher 360, Adobe Photoshop.CS2

First edition published 2018 by Gonzo Books

c/o Brooks City,
6th Floor New Baltic House
65 Fenchurch Street,
London EC3M 4BE
Fax: +44 (0)191 5121104
Tel: +44 (0) 191 5849144
International Numbers:
Germany: Freephone 08000 825 699
USA: Freephone 18666 747 289

ISBN: 978-1-905723-84-5

Dedicated to my amazing wife Sara: without her support, Feedback would never have kept going for all the years it did. It is also dedicated to my incredible daughters Nicola, Elizabeth, Hannah and Amanda, who grew up thinking that having a dad stuck at a computer all the time, while playing strange and often unusual music very loudly, was the normal thing to do.

Foreword

Many years ago in a galaxy far, far away there was a young band ploughing their own very unfashionable furrow, namely 'progressive rock', which at the time, i.e. the late 80s and early 90s, was really not very cool. However, they persevered and against the odds gradually managed to build up a reasonable fan base by playing hundreds of local gigs. They then decided to record a proper demo at a local studio containing state of the art recording equipment, the resulting EP was called 'In A Moment of Madness': this was initially released on cassette only and sold at local gigs.

'Madness' seemed to go down well so the band decided to release a full album 'Nothing Is Written', self-written, produced, funded and distributed, not bad for a very young band, three members of whom were still teenagers or thereabouts at the time! Yes, it is hard to believe how young we were at the time.

The band set up a post box at their local Post Office sorting office from which they would collect mail every day. Of course this was long before the days of email, the internet or social media and communication took a little longer and wasn't instant like it is today, but that was part of the buzz. Moreover, there was something very exciting about receiving actual letters, written by hand by very enthusiastic followers and fans. I always replied to every single letter, which was very time consuming, but worth it for the goodwill alone.

The majority of mail was from fans interested in buying our albums, T-shirts etc. but much of the interest was also coming from a burgeoning network of fanzines that began to increase noticeably by the week. It seemed that we weren't the only ones interested in this very uncool music, there appeared to be a healthy underground scene if you knew where to look. As time went on the band even managed to garner interest from mainstream 'rock' magazines such as Kerrang! and Metal Hammer.

However, one such fanzine who wrote in to ask about the band went by the unusual name of RockSIG which caught the eye of myself and which turned out to be a rock fanzine for members of Mensa. This magazine was compiled and written almost exclusively by one Kevin Rowland. RockSIG eventually changed its name to Feedback, the name of the band was Galahad.

We began corresponding on a regular basis; it was great to know that there were likeminded people out there. Kevin was incredibly supportive of the band for which we were very grateful in those, somewhat naïve early days, and I'm proud to say that we became firm friends and have remained so over the years, even though Kevin now lives on the other side of the Globe in New Zealand! Kev also wrote the booklet notes for our 'Other Crimes and Misdemeanours II' in 1997, twenty years ago now. How time flies when you having fun!

I was always struck by Kev's unerring enthusiasm and incredible passion about music and the amount of time he must have put in to what was essentially a hobby, and the fact that he has had the patience and found the time to listen to literally thousands of releases over the years. In addition, I am grateful that we stood out a little bit from the crowd for him, and of course, the fact that he also had a demanding full time job and was raising a family at the same time, along with Sara of course. :-)

He has also turned me on to a great deal of new music plus we also got to know many other rock and prog aficionados such as Artur Chachlowski in Poland who is a dear friend of both of us plus various musicians such as Mark Colton, Clive Nolan, Karl Groom to name but a few.

I thank you Kevin for your friendship and support over the years, not just to Galahad but to hundreds of other bands for whom in some way you have helped to spread the word, the gospel according to rock and prog.

Stu Nicholson, Galahad

Introduction

At the end of the Sixties, musicians realised that they were no longer constrained by having to fit into defined musical forms and the three-minute single. Instead, the only limits were their musical ability and imagination: this led to an explosion of music as styles as diverse as jazz, blues and classical crashed headlong into electric and eclectic instrumentation. Progressive rock was born, and not only was it embraced by fans worldwide but also by critics (at least for a while) and bands as diverse as Jethro Tull, Genesis, Pink Floyd, King Crimson, ELP and Gentle Giant among many others found huge success and sales. However, 1976 was year zero for prog, with punk supposedly sweeping away the 'dinosaurs' of music.

As far as the clear majority of critics (and it must be said many fans as well), this was the end for the prog scene, although some bands from the Seventies still found huge success in both albums and ticket sales. The only newer prog band recognised as such to gain major success within the UK was Marillion, but once Fish had parted ways they also suffered the same fate and died, (as far as critics were concerned). One wonders if anyone had been brave enough to tarnish Radiohead with the 'progressive' label if they would have had success.

After leaving university in 1984, I soon found myself working in London, and I thought that if I joined Mensa I might be able to make some new friends. Although I felt I had little in common with many of the 35,000 members, I soon discovered that there were small sub-clubs called Special Interest Groups, and in 1988 I saw an advert asking if there was anyone interested in rock music. Enough people replied, and there was soon a new group called RockSIG. I wanted to be involved, and having written an article on Carmen for the Jethro Tull fanzine 'A New Day' had the taste, so inundated the secretary with reviews and pieces for inclusion. The first RockSIG newsletter came out in October 1988 and at 28 pages was respectable enough but inside #5 (April 1990) the secretary announced her resignation. I had enjoyed writing and thought that I would give it a shot. After all, it couldn't be much hassle, right? I produced #6 in Nov 1990 - it came in at 60 pages and I soon realised that this length could not last. I was right. It got bigger!

I was out with another Mensan one night, and he asked if I was aware of the underground progressive rock scene? This was 1991, when the music press refused to acknowledge that such a thing dared to exist, and was pre-internet. He lent me some music by Galahad and Twelfth Night, and some copies of a fanzine called 'Blindsight'. I loved the music I heard and wrote to Galahad to buy a copy of their CD and cassette, and was soon corresponding with Stu Nicholson. Shortly thereafter, a demo tape arrived, 'From The River To The Sea' by Big Big Train. I knew nothing of the band, but they were sending me music. What would happen if I used the addresses in the back of Blindsight and wrote to bands to see if they wanted me to write about what they were doing? I could never have imagined what would happen.

A reader poll in #11 gave our newsletter a name and over the years 'Feedback' grew until it reached a peak with #50, which gave postal workers hernias in August 1998 and was some 284 pages long! I became very involved with some bands, trying to get gigs for both Freewill (and running their newsletter) and Credo, and writing the blurb for a Galahad compilation. In 2006, some sixteen years, 80+ issues and more than 11,000 pages of print later I stepped down, as we moved to New Zealand. I still wrote about music of course, but I will always look back on those days with many fond memories, back when the prog world seemed to be a club that was for a select few, but those of us who were members were fortunate enough to hear some incredible music.

The support of my amazing wife and family over the sixteen years I ran the SIG must be recognised, as I could not have done it without them. Sara became used to our bedroom being awash with CDs, photos, press releases etc., and by the end I was on my fifth computer, having started running the mag using an electronic typewriter with 1K of memory!!

This book documents the progressive rock scene of the time, with all the progressive reviews and interviews I wrote during that period. Many of these bands are no longer in existence, while others are still going strong, but very few ever reached the wider success and acclaim they deserved. As Feedback was produced officially as a "newsletter" for a closed group, it did mean that those who were members were treated in my writing more as friends than public, and that they all knew something about the scene either through direct involvement or from reading what I had written previously. This book captures a time gone by, and one that now we have ready access to information can never exist again, but back then it was very special indeed.

Album Reviews

A.C.T.

TODAY'S REPORT

This is the debut album by Swedish outfit A.C.T., a band that clearly have been heavily influenced by Saga. The result is an album that while mostly melodic rock has huge swathes of progressive keyboards, along with highly structured songs and great vocals. It is hard to believe that this is a debut album as the band are obviously on the top of their form, and very confident in what they can achieve. It is also well produced, and gives the impression of a band that has been around for years. Ola Andersson's guitars give the music the balls, but often it is the keyboards of Jerry Sablin that provide the melody and the lead runs. Peter Asp (bass) and Tomas Erlandsson (drums) hold it all together while singer Herman Saming has a very melodic voice, although sometimes just a little too bland. While not as good as Saga, and while the band are not copyists, it is to Saga that they will be compared to, based on what I am currently playing, this is still an album that will appeal to lovers of that style of pomp/prog. *#56, Jan 2000*

ABARAX

CRYING OF THE WHALES

Abarax are a new progressive band from Enger in North Germany, and are a side project of Taste Of Timeless, who have been around since 1993. However, only four members of TOT have taken part in Abarax: Udo Grasekamp (keyboards), his son Dennis (lead guitar, drums, bass), Howard Hanks (guitar, spoken words) and André Blaeute (vocals, acoustic guitar, e-bow). This concept album was two years in the preparation, and the band state that it is "a rock music fantasy describing the imaginative truth about the whales and the reasons for their existence". This is symphonic prog with strong melodies and vocals and the obvious point of reference for many will be Pink Floyd, but although there are elements of that style, they have taken that as a starting point and moved away.

Maybe this should have been given to the IWC at their most recent meeting where they passed a declaration calling for the eventual lifting of the 20-year global moratorium, but while this is obviously raising important and relevant issues, it does not come across as being overly political. There are some wonderful guitar breaks here, which do reference Gilmour, as they are just beautiful with loads of passion. The arrangements are many layered and at times it is like sinking into a warm dark place as the music just surrounds and envelops the listener. It would have been very easy for the guys to put in lots of samples of whale song but they have managed to keep away from it, although there are times when the keyboards do mimic this, and it works very well indeed. If you are interested in 'traditional' progressive rock music then this is an album that you will enjoy, choral vocals on the beginning of the epic "Whale Massacre" and all! There are some nice photos in the booklet as well and this is worth investigating. *#88, Jun 2006*

ABBFINOOSTY
THE WIZARD

Abbfinoosty are Asif Ali (27) on guitars and vocals, Bob Low (30) on drums, and Tony Norton (23) on bass and vocals, and they gig consistently in the London and Surrey area, recently playing a couple of dates at The Marquee. 'The Wizard' is worth picking up, and the opening title song is a stunning example of how a tight outfit can sound together. As with other power trios the bass is kept high up in the mix to knock you back while the others spread their wings. It certainly starts with riffs heavy enough to bring a smile to any Iommi fan, but these get faster, then change into peaceful tranquil acoustic guitars, before reverting again, all the time with wonderful harmony vocals. Also, guesting on the harmonies is Sam Brown, daughter of Joe, who adds an extra element with her soaring voice.

Throughout the ten minutes the song is constantly changing, either developing new ground or reverting to previous themes. At the end of "The Wizard" the group leave the studio and one says to another "three pieces are still the biggest sounding bands aren't they?". On this evidence that is certainly the case. "Capture A Dream" is far more accessible on first listen, a slower start with again some great harmony vocals, then the guitar kicks in and we're off again as the bass drives the song along, allowing Asif to deliver some soaring guitar.

It calms down again for a while, but does not stay that way for long. "Dream of Undisturbed Places" is a nice quiet finish which allows the listener to gently wind down before turning the tape over to play "The Wizard" again. This is well worth discovering, and I look forward to hearing some more material and seeing Abbfinoosty live. *#11, Dec 1991*

ABBFINOOSTY
FUTURE

Way back in the distant mists of time, in fact all the way back to #11, I reviewed the new tape by an unknown (at least to me) band. That band was Abbfinoosty and the tape was 'The Wizard'. The title track was, I felt, brilliant, and I was most annoyed when I lost the tape (along with Tarrasque's first demo). Still, here they are at last with their debut CD. The first thing I did was check out the track listing and there it is, closing the album, so all is right with the world. Looking through the tracks I recognise a few from old demos, especially "Arabian Sales Markets" (now called "Arabic Sales markets") and "Wake Up", which were on their 12" EP, and "Capture A Dream" which was also on 'The Wizard'. Abbfinoosty are a trio comprising Asif (guitar, vocals), Tony (bass, vocals) and Robert (drums); the name comes from putting the letters from their names in alphabetical order, in case you wondered, Abbfinoosty have been lumped in with the 'progressive' bands but they have little or nothing in common with the current crop as they are far more of a rock act, with guitars in abundance. The album is very guitar-oriented, but although there is the danger of becoming a heavy rock outfit, they manage to avoid this by incorporating many different styles. Perhaps they are the truly progressive ones? So, having played the whole album finally you get to "The Wizard" which is nine minutes and thirty-five seconds of brilliance. To my ears, it is the same recording as it was on the tape, but I may be wrong. It starts with Iommi-style riffs but it builds on this as the guitars give way to vocals. The bass is high up in the mix, providing more of a rhythm guitar feel as the guitar becomes sparing. Harmony does not last too long, and there is a real impression of menace as the song develops. The guitar solo gives Sam Brown (yes, Joe's daughter) the chance to harmonise with some very high vocals. This gives way to the gentle acoustic and vocal section that makes you think that the song is ending. No way, they have not finished with you yet. Having lulled you into a false sense of security, it is time for all hell to break loose again. And it does. At the end of the track the group leaves the studio and one says to another "three pieces are still the biggest sounding bands aren't they?" Very true.

#24, Jul 1994

ABEL GANZ
GRATUITOUS FLASH

ABEL GANZ
GULLIBLE'S TRAVELS

ABEL GANZ
THE DANGER OF STRANGERS

Abel Ganz were formed in 1980 by bassist Hugh Carter and keyboard player Hew Montgomery as a vehicle for writing and performing songs in a progressive rock style. They were joined by guitarist Malky McNiven and drummer Kenney Weir, with Hugh and Hew sharing vocals, and it was this line-up that recorded the first demo tape. By 1983, vocalist Alan Reed had joined them and together they recorded 'Gratuitous

Flash', which was released in 1984.

Right from the off, 'Gratuitous Flash' is an album of strength as "Little By Little" commences proceedings with a wealth of power chords and fine keyboard playing. The song changes themes and styles before Alan makes himself heard. I have long been a fan of Alan's pure clear vocals, and here he shines as the song settles down so that Alan is very much at the forefront. It is extremely commercial and accessible and even now, ten years on, stands up very well against the current crop of material being released. The guitar solo and heavy chording from Hugh shows that the band were very much a rock act, rather than just a meandering prog outfit. Some of the keyboard sounds used show very definite nods towards Tony Banks, and there are hints of late Seventies Genesis. "Kean On The Job" is totally different, being dependent very much on piano and although the lyrics on this leave a little to be desired, the melody is certainly insistent and I have found myself singing this around the house. However, the highlight of the album is the rocking "The Dead Zone" which is seventeen minutes in length. Powerful and atmospheric, this starts off as a real belter, most unlike many of the 'epics' of recent years and live this must be a showstopper. This album gained Abel Ganz quite a bit of publicity, and fellow Scots Pallas got to hear it. They had just parted company with vocalist Ewan Lawson and snapped Alan up for the gig. Malky McNiven decided to leave, and Hugh Carter stepped down to manage the band. Paul Kelly joined as guitarist and vocalist and they recruited Gordon Mackie on bass.

Having played many gigs, the band went back into the studio and came out with 'Gullible's Travels'. Although Paul Kelly was taking on many of the songwriting duties, the album still sounds like a logical profession from the first. Opening cut "The Unholy War" is every bit as powerful and rocky as the name suggests, although to me a downside is that it is faded out during a guitar break instead of being finished off properly. The title track again harkens back to the days of 'Trick' era Genesis, although yet again Abel Ganz are far more of a rock band than Genesis ever were. Some extremely strong drumming lays the backdrop for the guitar solo, which lets the song develop through keyboards. Favourite track is probably the Western tale "The Hustler", which is extremely strong lyrically as it tells the tale of a card sharp who kills the boy who sees him cheating, and is later cut down in a hail of bullets himself. Music and words combine perfectly to create a very strong image. Overall, 'Gullible's Travels' is a very good follow-up to the debut, quite an achievement when you consider the personnel changes that had taken place in between time. Paul Kelly's voice is quite a bit lower than Alan's, but carries the melody extremely well. The album was received positively, as were the live gigs, but changes were yet again happening within the Abel Ganz camp. Drummer Kenny Weir left to be replaced by Alan Quinn, then the band reverted to the original songwriting team of Carter, Montgomery and McNiven as Paul Kelly and Alan Quinn left to pursue other interests and Gordon Mackie moved away from Glasgow. Still, in 1996 the band reformed to record a track for the compilation 'Double Exposure', namely "The Danger of Strangers". 1988 saw the band back in the studio recording an album of the same name with the line-up now comprising Hugh

Carter, Hew Montgomery and Malky McNiven along with former members Paul Kelly and Alan Reed with session drummer Dennis Smith.

'The Danger of Strangers' proved to be the band's most successful release to date. The songs were again of the highest order, and they even provided Jadis-like harmonies on the ballad "Rain Again" where Alan again shows why he is rated as one of the top prog vocalists around. The song is in three distinct parts, and the middle part bounces along very happily indeed – and could even have been a hit single! Well, in a world where music is played by musicians and not computer programmers. There is a sequel to "The Hustler" in the imaginatively titled "Hustler II". This again shows the rockier side of Abel Ganz and tells the tale of the posse looking for the hustler, but failing to catch him before he killed yet more people. Vocal duties on this are by Paul, linking back to the original song.

It was after the release of this album that the band signed to MSI, who re-released all three albums on CD with new artwork. After a few years of inactivity, the new-found success prompted the band to start gigging again and Carter and Montgomery were joined by Robert Wilson on guitar and Colin Johnson on drums, Vocalist in '92 was Billy Duff, who was replaced by Graham Strachan in '93. During this period, they wrote new material and set up their own recording and rehearsal studio. 1994 sees the band with a new album, 'The Deafening Silence', which is due for a September release. It has been recorded with new boys Chris Forsyth (vocals) and Stewart Clyde (keyboards) while Hew Montgomery has stepped down to concentrate on the rehearsal studio and a new solo project. Abel Ganz cannot be said to be one of the most prolific bands of recent years, and they rival Fairport Convention for turnover of personnel, yet all the albums are extremely strong and worth further investigation. I know that Hugh is very proud of the new album, and I look forward to hearing it. If you are wondering which of the three to sample I would suggest the debut, but that is only because I have been playing it far more than the others. It got locked into the CD player and I could not bring myself to take it out as it was just so good! *#24, Jul 1994*

ABEL GANZ
THE DEAFENING SILENCE

Yes, the Scots proggers are very much back! With their first album in more than six years, and only bassist Hugh Carter remaining from 'The Danger Of Strangers', it was always going to be interesting to see if they could recapture the glory days. Abel Ganz are probably best known for originally having current Pallas vocalist Alan Reed in their ranks, and a decision has been taken to go for a totally different sound with new boy Christopher Forsyth. Christopher sings in a far gruffer manner, yet suits the music perfectly. 'The Deafening Silence' is one that grows the more it is played. There is a harder edge to the proceedings this time, as Abel Ganz turn up the guitars, but the melody and great keyboard playing that characterised their earlier works is still there. The first time I played it I was not sure if it could match up to the other three, but now I am sure that it does. It is one that will appeal not only to the progger but also to those into good melodic rock. The keyboards are never allowed to totally dominate proceedings, yet neither does the guitar. All in all, a good mix of hard and soft, with good songs and melodies to boot. Not as immediate as 'Gratuitous Flash' (still their best), but a great album to return with. Nice to have you back lads! *#27, Feb 1995*

ABIOGENESI
IO SONO IL VAMPIRO

This is the fourth album by Abiogenesi, which means multi-instrumentalist Toni D'urso along with a rhythm section and keyboard player. Toni is very much the leader and has obviously been influenced by early Seventies dark progressive and rock music such as the band this Italian label is named after, Black Widow. This is a soundtrack album to 'I Am A Vampire' and consequently not all the songs work as well on their own as they might otherwise. There are many instrumentals, and I got the impression that Toni was being restrained due to the purpose of the music, yet it manages to remain interesting and extremely atmospheric. It is also nice to see artwork that is carried through to the back of the booklet, and of course, as this is on Black Widow it has also been released on vinyl where the album artwork is carried through. With all the lyrics in Italian this may not be as accessible as it could be, but there is a good use of acoustic instruments within the basically hard rock setting and if you are interested in what Uriah Heep may have sounded like if they were involved with vampires then this is probably a good place to start. *#86, Feb 2006*

ACID MOTHER'S GONG
LIVE TOKYO

Whatever you may think of Daevid Allen, no one can doubt that he is an unusual person to say the least. Born in 1938 he has been a mainstay of the avant-garde for many years and this album captures the latest incarnation of Gong, where they joined forces with Acid Mother's Temple, a Japanese band performing a similar style of music.

This is the second album to be released from the 2004 tour and captures a band that is kicking together producing music that is at the very limits of that definition.

My wife tells me that the simple way to describe this album is just to say that it is crap, and I know where she is coming from. This is music that is out there, way out there, and if you want to see a photo of a naked 66-year-old hippie strutting his stuff onstage then just look inside this digipak. *#89, Sep 2006*

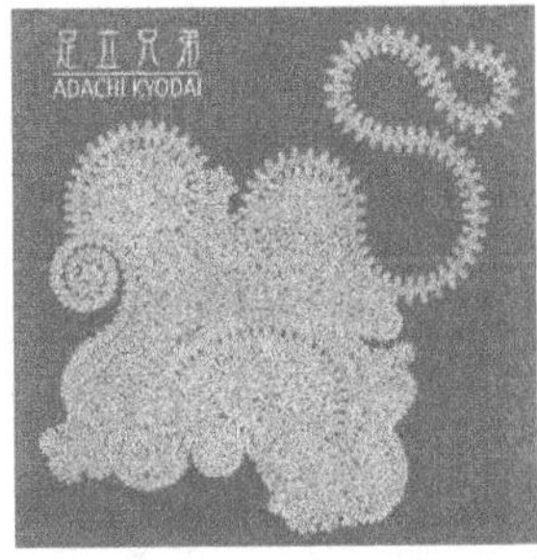

ADACHI KYODAI
ADACHI KYODAI

There are quite a few Japanese albums reviewed in this issue, which not only are available from Poseidon but also in Europe from Musea, which makes them a lot easier to get hold of. This first album is a strange beast, in that it features the Adachi brothers on acoustic guitar and, um, nothing else. Okay that is not strictly true as while Ryusuke plays guitar his brother Source "K" does also provide some vocals.

But, this is a mostly instrumental album that any fan of acoustic, classical guitar will want to have. There are passages that just cause the jaw to drop with the techniques being displayed while at others the sheer beauty of what they are performing is just wonderful. But there are also some covers on the album, which will be of interest to progheads. First up is a frantic and very enjoyable cover of Tull's "Mother Goose".

They also cover King Crimson's "I Talk To The Wind" although while the music on this is beautiful the vocals do suffer from the Eastern pronunciation of certain words, and the other cover of note is "Cheap Day Return" which again takes on a different interpretation to the original. Overall, this is a very interesting, enjoyable and wonderful album that I will be playing time and again.
#78, Apr 2004

ADACHI KYODAI
XIANSHI

This is the second album from brothers Ryusuke Adachi and Source 'K' Adachi, who apart from the odd vocals from Source K are a duo dedicated to shred on acoustic guitars.

Most of the songs are instrumental, and sound as if the brothers have been listening in equal parts to Jethro Tull, Roy Harper and Yngwie Malmsteen. Hearing music like this played on acoustic guitar is very strange indeed and when it works it is incredible, but sometimes they do get lost inside their own technical ability so that although it is very clever it may not be musically all that it could be.

There are a couple of covers on the album, as there were on the debut CD which I reviewed a while ago, and this is where Source sings. This time around we have a very unusual take on Roxy Music's "Chance Meeting" and they return to Tull (there were two Tull covers on the debut) and this time give us "Wond'ring Aloud". This is much more of a straightforward take, although there are some interesting arrangements taking place under the surface. I enjoyed the debut, and this is again a very fine attempt although it certainly is not essential – if they were playing on electric guitars there would certainly be a much larger audience but as it stands then this is for those who want to hear some very nimble fingers on acoustic. *#86, Feb 2006*

ADDISON PROJECT
MOOD SWINGS

Richard Addison is a bassist who first became known through his work with Mystery, so it is probably of little surprise that this album has been released through Michel St-Père's label, and that Michel is one of the musicians to feature on the album. This is instrumental jazz, and as the title suggests is designed to capture different types of moods. Richard may be a bassist but he has brought the musicians together as a whole, not as a place for his own instrument to shine. Take opener "Sleepwalker" – the sax and keyboards combine to provide something that is complex yet laid back at the same time. This can be contrasted against the sax-led "The Muffin" which in its' opening sequence has some extremely dynamic and rhythmic bass, but all in the background. This is music that works well both when being listened to intently, but also as a background to create a feeling. It is not New Age, and there are some extremely dramatic pieces on here, but the title does the album justice. There is some great musicianship, and any fan of jazz or prog will get something out of this. *#76, Oct 2003*

AD INFINITUM
AD INFINITUM

After the break-up of Cathedral, keyboard player Todd Braverman set out to recreate what he felt was missing from the current progressive scene, that a lot of majesty and melody was missing in an ever-growing pursuit of "Aren't I the clever one?" attitude. He was soon joined by Craig Watt and together with some guest musicians set out to solidify the dream. It took them four years, but they have managed to produce an album that has far more in common with the sound of Yes and Genesis than it has with the current movement.

Whether this is due to the heavy use of 'traditional' instruments such as Mellotrons, Hammond Organs and Moogs or the fact that they treat structured songs as being the mainstay I am not sure. The first time I played it, I listened to it from the next room while doing something else and my initial reaction was that it was very like Yes. When I next played it in a more focussed fashion, I found that it was more in line with Genesis than I would have believed. Possibly Yes were put into my mind as they managed to convince THE artist of the Seventies to not only provide the sleeve but also provide them with a logo. Roger Dean has very much put his seal of approval on the whole project, working with them over the last two years. Only one song is under five minutes long, with three over ten, and throughout this is a delight. I find it hard to believe that the last thing recorded was the drums! Feel sympathy for Don DiPaolo who had three days to record over the top of the original samples that had been used throughout the recording! If anyone is a fan of Seventies prog (and who is not?) then this is an album that you will want to discover. *#50, Aug 1998*

ADVENT
CANTUS FIRMUS

This is the second album from Advent, only nine years after the debut (mind you – still better than Credo). The band has quite an unusual line-up in that Alan Benjamin provides guitar, bass, stick, mandolin and recorder, Drew Siciliano is on the drums and then there are two keyboard players. Henry Ptak also provides lead and backing vocals while his brother Mark also provides backing vocals. Listening to the multi-tracked unaccompanied vocal opening that is "GK Contramandum" (I can't believe that many songs are dedicated to GK Chesterton) it is obvious that the band have been very heavily influenced by Gentle Giant, but as the album develops they keep some GG nuances while very much bringing in early Collins Genesis with distinct styles of their own. This is a prog album that is fresh and inviting, music that embraces the listener and brings them warmly in instead of throwing strange time signatures and musical complexity at the listener and daring them not to enjoy it. I first listened to this album when wide-awake at 4.00 in the morning being extremely jet lagged after returning from New Zealand and as soon as it finished it got put straight back on again as this is such a delight to listen to. Whether it is with short numbers or longer epics ("Ramblin' Sailor" is over eighteen minutes long and has been taken from a sea shanty) Advent manage to draw the listener into their world with music that is captivating and just so damn good. There are also two bonus numbers on the album, 24 track versions of songs that only appeared as 4 tracks on their debut. This is a very solid, very enjoyable prog album. *#88, Jun 2006*

AELIAN
THE WATCHER

Originally known as Strobo, Aelian came together in 1990. They are an Italian band, but it would not be possible to ascertain that from listening to their great new album, 'The Watcher'. Aelian display wonderful musicianship, but their greatest asset is their three-part vocal harmonies that remind the listener very much of the work of Nineties Yes or Asia. They are not copyists, but a band with their own identity and ideas. 'The Watcher' kicks off with the title track, which is wonderful unaccompanied layers of vocal harmonies. Mark Aixer (vocals, bass) has a clear voice reminiscent of Jon Anderson. This leads well into "Dragon's Land" which is a laid-back number using acoustic guitar to some effect. After the first song, which puts Mark's vocal prowess firmly in mind, this one does nothing to dispel the thoughts of Yes. The others are no slouches either, with Max (guitar, vocals), Maurizio Antognoli (keyboards, vocals) and Paelo Negroni (drums) working hard to provide great musical accompaniment to go with the vocals. Of the nine songs on the album, my favourite is possibly the most commercial, "You Don't Touch Me", which is a rock song a la Asia. Great lead vocals, ably assisted with harmonies, and a driving bass to boot, makes this song a sure-fire hit in America. The album is a delight to listen to, with wonderful melodies and those superb vocals. Very much at the commercial end of the prog field, almost stretching into AOR, it is a great album to listen to,

very polished production together with well-crafted and arranged songs means that this is one to augment any collection. Well worth discovering.
#16, Dec 1992

AESCULUS HIPP
MASTER OF ILLUSION

There is a definite dearth of bands from the West Country so it is nice to be able to review this mini-album from recently formed East Devon trio Aesculus Hipp. They describe their music as moderately strident guitar based rock, and it is certainly no surprise to see that the one cover out of the six songs is "Sunshine Of Your Love". These guys want to be Cream, except not quite so blues based.

Although it does not say as much on the sleeve, I get the impression that this was recorded live in the studio and has been engineered so that it sounds live as well. If you go to see these guys, then this is exactly what you will hear. All of them have been playing in bands for a while, and know what they are doing. The impression is that the band are in a state of development and while they would be fun to see at a gig, the songs as of yet do not stand up to repeated hearing. But watch out for these guys over the next few years.
#61, Feb 2001

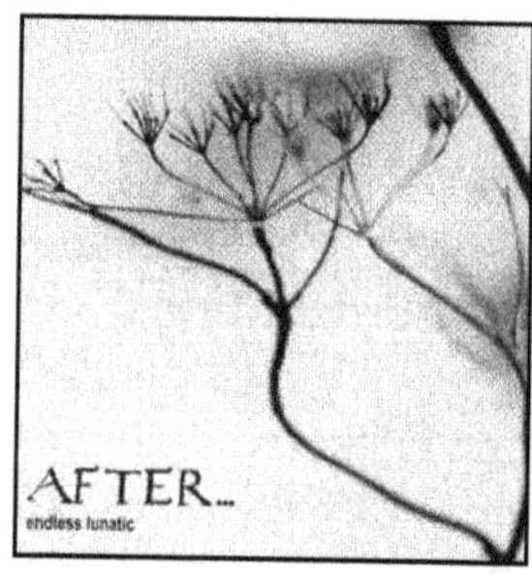

AFTER
ENDLESS LUNATIC

This is the debut album from yet another Polish prog band – it is a vibrant scene over there. Even though they have two guitarists, they are not approaching music from a hard rock angle but more something that is flowing and inventive with nods to bands such as IQ and Pendragon but in the lighter fashion so that early King Crimson also gets a look in.

They have even managed to get some noted guests on board, not bad for a debut, with Colin Bass (Camel), Josef Skrzek (SBB) and Jacek Zasada (Quidam) all making an appearance here and there. After have been playing with Quidam recently, as well as with Riverside and even appeared at ProgFarm, so even though not much has yet been heard about these guys even within the progressive underground outside of Poland it can surely only be a matter of time. There is a depth but also an ethereal beauty to what they are producing so that at times it feels that with one good gust of wind the whole thing would be blown away.

Somehow, they also find room for a cover of Systems Of A Down's "Spiders", which shows that even though they may be looking backwards for influences they look to current music as well. Overall, this is a very impressive debut and I am sure that we will be hearing more of them. *#86, Feb 2006*

AFTER@ALL
A.C.I.D.

This must be the heaviest prog album that I have heard from the Hungarian Periferic label. To be honest, it is prog metal that moves more into the rock area than it does into the prog arena: there are prog touches, but for the most part this is about heavy guitars and a sense of adventure. All the lyrics are in English and there is no indication that it is not their native tongue, and it is the most Western sounding release that StereoPeriferic have released. On some songs, they even come across like Alien Ant Farm! Favourite tracks are seven and eight, which segue into each other (the first is "_dust_in…" while the second is "_…hoffman") which show that being in a prog band is about exploring different musical areas and putting them together, as well as having fun. It is a very immediate, forceful, album that should get them many friends in Europe. The label describes it as "psychedelic, heavy, alternative and sentimental at the same time"; while I would just say that this is one to seek out. *#66, Feb 2002*

AFTER CRYING
STRUGGLE FOR LIFE

Available as both an "essential" single CD or as a full-length double (which also contains three MP3 songs as well as plenty of other stuff to download), this captures Hungary's top prog band on the road, and this really is progressive rock at its' very best. While in some ways like King Crimson (the one cover is of "Starless" which features guest John Wetton on bass and vocals), they are much more diverse than that. Songs veer from the very short to the very long, from the simple to the incredibly intricate. During the opener "Viaduct" there is a breath-taking trumpet run (yes, trumpet) competing with the electric guitar for dominance. It is not an album to be played in the background, but rather one that demands total attention and if the listener is prepared to give the time then they will be much rewarded. Hungary has a lot to offer in the way of music, and After Crying has already performed at Baja Prog in Mexico. This is their eighth (and ninth) album on Periferic, and all that I have heard of theirs I have most enjoyed. If you like 'proper' prog, and not 'neo-prog' then search these guys out.
#57, Mar 2000

AFTER CRYING
BOOTLEG SYMPHONY

Hungary's foremost progressive rock band was probably always one of the prime candidates for working with a modern orchestra, given that they already use brass instruments within the band. This concert was recorded at the Liszt Fernc Academy Of Music on 2nd October 2000, where they were joined by an orchestra and performed songs that they had especially re-arranged for this format. Again, they have

shown their love of King Crimson, with the one cover being an excerpt of "The Great Deceiver". They have pushed progressive rock music right over the boundaries with this release, as this is much more a classical piece of music than rock. The result is that if you enjoy dynamic classical music, then you will like this as much as the fans at the sell-out gig. After Crying have shown that they can move their music into other areas and achieve success.
#63, Jul 2001

AFTER CRYING
SHOW
After Crying are probably Hungary's best-loved progressive rock band, but with this album they have moved a long way from how they have sounded in the past. Although the title gives the impression that this is a 'live' recording, it is very much a studio work, with many layers. The album starts with the much-repeated line "A new world's coming and the old one's gone". Is this a statement about their new musical adventures or it is a reference to their new singer? After Crying have always had a more orchestral feel to their music than many, but with this album they have managed to keep that intact yet also bring in a much more modern commercial element to their music. I kept thinking of Styx and 'Kilroy Was Here' as this has some similar musical threads. The music is the important part, with most of the album being instrumental, and it swirls and drives around so that the listener is always interested and intrigued to see where it will lead. It is an album that I have enjoyed playing when I have the time to listen to all of it quietly, not being distracted, as this is an album to get lost in. They may not have as much impact in the UK as some, but fans of prog need to search this out.
#76, Oct 2003

AFTERGLOW
YGGDRASIL
Afterglow are a French band, singing in English, who have the attribute of being the only neo-prog band I know who employ the services of a full-time conga player. This adds a different edge to their music as it seems at times a little drum oriented, as the congas and drums are both kept high up in the mix. The guitarwork can be heavy, and there are some interesting keyboards, while the overall musical style leans heavily on IQ with some nods to Marillion and Genesis. They are not afraid to use acoustic guitar to good effect, and the songs range in length from three minutes to nearly seventeen. For a new band, I was very impressed with this their debut and in fact the only drawback is that they are singing in English as it appears as if the songs were originally written in French and then translated, something that never seems to work very well. Afterglow are a band to look out for, and if they can produce more music of this standard then they could make real waves not only in France but over here as well.
#28, Apr 1995

AFTER THE FALL
IN A SAFE PLACE

This is quite a strange album in many ways. It is recorded by one of those rare things, a prog rock trio (Mark Benson (guitars, vocals), Ken Archer (keyboards) and Rich Kornacki (drums)), and musically they are all over the place!

Some numbers sound as if they are a commercial rock outfit, while others sound as if they had been recorded by ELP, while yet others sound as if they are a strange hybrid of the two distinct styles. What you can be sure of is that this is a very good album indeed.

There is never any room within a trio for a poor musician to hide and these guys are all very good. There are a lot of instrumental passages, of course, and they are carried off with great panache. Mark has a great rock voice but it is not needed, as they are just as good at playing long instrumentals, as they are 'proper' songs.

I must contact them as this album is from 1997, and although I know that there are two earlier ones available, I do not know if the band is still going. Hopefully, they are and if you like instrumental passages which are heavily reliant on keyboards but also feature wonderful interplay with the rest of the band, then you should seek this out post-haste.
#55, Sept 1999

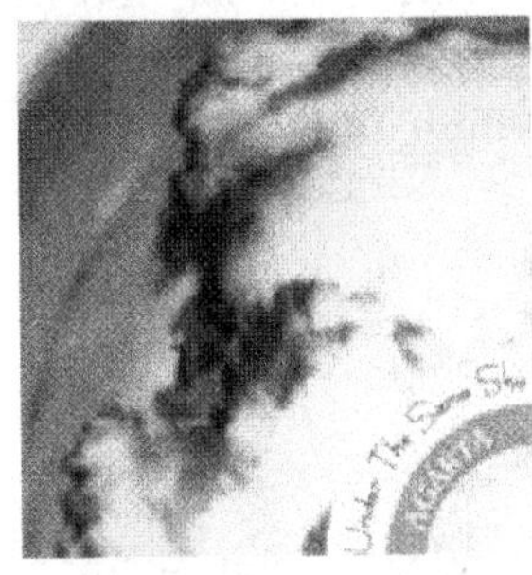

AGARTA
UNDER THE SAME SKY

This is one of a few albums that I have been sent by the Russian Starless label to review this issue. The band was created when Svyatoslav 'Miff' Opritiv (guitar, guitar synth) joined forces with three members of The Force, who are the in-house band for the musical theatre in Irkutsk. It probably is not surprising that these guys know how to play together given the amount of shows that they must perform.

The label describes this music as progressive/fusion and that is probably a good description. All the songs bar one are instrumental, with the emphasis very much on the guitar, and there are times when it is quite Hackett-like, while at others it is just gentle noodlings which if the listener is not careful can just drift into the background. It is an enjoyable album, but whether it is one that I would recommend trying to search out from Russia then that is another matter altogether
#85, Nov 2005

AGENESS
SHOWING PACES

AGENESS
RITUALS

Ageness is a Finnish band, formed in 1991 by Tommy Eriksson (vocals, keyboards) and Kari Saaristo (drums). They attempted to reform Scarab, a band they had both previously been members of (a single album was released in 1983), but after this failed they were joined by Jari Ukkonen (bass) and Vesa Auvinen (guitar). The line-up was completed by the arrival of another keyboard player, Jari Laasanen, in 1992 and the debut album 'Showing Paces' was released in December the same year. It is of little surprise that with two keyboard players in the band that Ageness shows a distinct nod towards the music of classic Saga, and Tommy's vocals are very clear and melodic while Vesa's guitarwork is superb. This means that the album is very accessible, showing influences of IQ among others. It is high quality prog with more than a good dose of AOR, and can be enjoyed on first hearing and certainly does not suffer with repeated playing. During the recordings for the follow-up, 'Rituals', guitarist Vesa Auvinen moved to Washington and he was replaced by Mike Hella (a founder member of the aforementioned Scarab) to complete the album. From the symphonic opening cut that is "Forever Returns" the Saga influence is still very much in place, again with a heavy AOR feel, but there is more depth and feeling, probably brought about as the band had been together for a few years now. I have no hesitation in highly recommending both Ageness albums for your prog collection, but if you are only going to get one than I would favour the second but they are both worthy of your attention.

#35, June 1996

AGENT COOPER
BEGINNER'S MIND

It may have taken six years for the guys to release their second album, something to do with losing the rhythm section and having to get new guys on board. They recorded enough material for two albums, picked the very best of it and then put together the album that contains ten songs and is only approx. 45 minutes long. Surely these guys can't be a prog band I hear you cry, well yes and no. This band are built around strong well-constructed numbers that are technical and filled with lots of complex twists and turns, and in some ways, are reminiscent of a heavy Arena, or a very heavy Asia. These guys are a rock band first and foremost with guitarist, singer, songwriter Doug Busbee driving things from the front whether it be through his guitar or through his vocals. This is immediately accessible well-crafted music that is crossing through boundaries, as melodic rock fans are going to like this as much as progheads into

bands like those already mentioned or Tiles and possibly Echolyn. What makes this so fresh is that they are playing well-crafted hook-laden songs that are there to be enjoyed for their own sake instead of pandering to the 'look how clever we are' school of prog. This is a great album from start to finish, without a filler in sight, but with plenty of dynamics and different styles to make this an essential purchase.
#87, Apr 2006

AJALON
ON THE THRESHOLD OF ETERNITY
Ajalon is found in the book of Joshua 10:12 and the paraphrased meaning is 'Grace in the midst of the fire.' This group is another of the growing movement in the USA of Christian Progressive rock bands, of which the most well-known is probably Neal Morse, and Ajalon features his bassist Randy George. Except on this their second album Randy shows himself also to be a fine guitarist and keyboard player with the line-up completed by drummer Dan Lile and singer, tin whistler Wil Henderson (who sometimes adds bass and guitar). The album starts with a relaxing complex drum pattern with Randy coming in with the backing music and doing a Gary Chandler solo over the top – but as with all prog music what you hear is not what you get so although the band do keep returning to themes there is a lot going on as they prove that a tin whistle can work as a lead instrument in this setting. There are a great many styles on the album and Randy may frantically strum an acoustic guitar or take the lead with some keyboard runs and the music is always developing and changing. Ajalon are also not beyond looking to friends for support so Phil Keaggy joins for one number, while Rick Wakeman is here for a few. Mostly the songs are short, but the closing title cut is an epic to be proud of as it powers its way in at sixteen plus minutes. Of course, if you are going to produce an epic then somehow it seems only right that Neal Morse guests on vocals. This is yet another song where Randy provides all the music apart from the drums, but this does sound like a band performance – complex, driving and hard but also uplifting with quieter spells this is superb. But wait, there is a 'hidden' song which is not listed, a cracking take on The Moody Blues' "You And Me" which is distorted and heavy, and just right.
#85, Nov 2005

JAN AKKERMAN
C.U.
Jan Akkerman probably needs little in the way of introduction as he has now been in the music business for forty years but will probably always be best remembered for his time with Focus. This is not a rock album, mixing together soul, dance in a jazz in a fashion that although undoubtedly very clever just is not the sort of thing that I listen to. I managed to keep my interest going through the opener "See You" but to listen to Jan then play some (admittedly stunning)

guitar to a dance beat as he worked his way through The Isley Brothers' "In Between The Sheets" made me want to start flicking through the tracks. Unfortunately, this is an album that people will buy out of interest (it is his first album for four years), will play once and then let it gather dust….
#80, Jul 2004

ALASKA
ALASKA

Alaska has a possibly unique line-up in progressive music, as they comprise Al Lewis (vocals, drums) and John O'Hara (keyboards). On the CD Kent Wells also provides some guitar, although it is sparing, and they have the proud boast that "Alaska performs live without the use of pre-recorded instrumental tracks or sequences". If they can get away with performing the music totally live, then this must be an awesome experience. The first band that most people are going to compare them with will be Yes, on the basis that Al sounds uncannily like Jon Anderson. True, the complexity of the music and the style does lend itself to that comparison, but without the use of guitar then it comes across more as a Yes/ELP/Rush hybrid: rather pleasing on the ear I thought. Unsurprisingly there are some long instrumental passages, but not as many as would be imagined given the line-up. They are both fine musicians with some interesting ideas and two of the songs are over eleven minutes long, "Tiananmen Square" and "Wellsbridge". It is the former of these that is the best song on the album as it starts very powerfully, and then calms down into almost a ballad to allow the vocals the opportunity to take centre stage. The little trick of repeating "It Will Never Be!" in three languages (German, Chinese and Arabic) and using shouted lines above the music adds a heightened tension.
#53, May 1999

ALBION
SURVIVAL GAMES

Artur Chachlowski of Art Rock in Poland recently discovered this young band and has released this tape, the first on the Art Rock label. It is not yet available in the UK, and is only on cassette, but he is hoping that both will change soon. Vocals are in English, sung by Anna Batlo. She has a rather strange vocal style, very high in range but managing to sound quite like Clare Grogan (remember "Happy Birthday"?). I can't say I enjoyed the tape as there was nothing to pick up on, it was all a bit easily listening prog to me: alright, but nothing special. Possibly it was the vocal style that put me off as I never did like Altered Images. With repeated playing it may have grown on me, as there is some fine guitarwork, but time is something I seem to have little of these days.
#24, Jul 1994

AL-BIRD
SODOM & GOMORRA XXI

Underneath the name of Al-Bird it states "A solo album from one of the three of X Religion", and underneath the title it states "Progressive Symphonic Poem". On turning the CD over to find that it was a four-part epic which was further sub-divided into another twenty pieces, and had been presented as a 'scenic version' as well, I was ready to fall asleep. But, and it is a very large 'but', this is a damn fine album. It has been recorded by the three members of X Religion, a progressive rock band from Uzbekistan, but has been released as a solo album. The only thing that is a pain is that although it states that it is in separate sections, and indeed these are musically obvious, it has been loaded onto the CD as one data track so the only way to listen to it is by playing it through in a complete sitting. The press release mentions bands such as Pink Floyd (definitely) and ELP (I can see where they are coming from with that one), but in truth there is a lot more going on here. There are sections that with just a small amount of mixing could belong on Chemical Brothers while at others it is quite hard rock. One of the joys of this album is that it is not just possible to deduce what is going to happen next, yet at the same time it does seem to fit together as a whole. Musea state that the album "is as ambitious in its conception as it is successful in its production" and I wholeheartedly agree with them. Not an album that I thought I was going to enjoy but it is very good indeed.

#71, Dec 2002

ALIEN ON MY MIND
ALIEN ON MY MIND

I think Alien On My Mind was formed in 1993, and that they have played gigs with Soulcages and Threshold. I say, "think", as unfortunately the record company has only sent me a press release in German! They are hitting into a similar musical area as Threshold, with twin guitars and strong keyboards. Michael Kinzel is an excellent vocalist, not unlike Damian, and I would imagine that a gig featuring both bands would be quite an event. While always melodic, and at times extremely heavy, Alien do have more than one musical string to their bow and they are not afraid to mix and match styles. I am sure that if you like your rock melodic yet at the same time with plenty of energy and enthusiasm then there is plenty here for you to enjoy. This is hard rock that may be too heavy for the average prog fan, but should appeal to the rocker who would not be seen dead at a prog gig. During "Life Is Eternal Morning" Michael lets out a scream that would make Rob Halford proud, and there is even a Rodney Matthews cover to admire while listening to some great sounds. If you like Threshold or Queensrÿche you will love this.

#42, July 1997

ALIAS EYE
A DIFFERENT POINT OF YOU

Sometimes one just puts on an album and immediately falls in love with it just because it is so different and that is true for this record. As I listened to opening song "A Clown's Tale" I was wondering just how a band could come across so much as Threshold with all the heaviness and power that means, but at the same time mix in some Moroccan influences. Next up was "Fake The Right" which was Glenn Hughes doing his most soulful Wet Wet Wet impression although of course far heavier than they ever managed. By the time "Your Other Way" started with classical acoustic guitar I was far beyond trying to second guess what these guys were either trying to achieve or to do next (of course there is also some accordion on this song!). The one truth is that these guys can all play, and they can play whatever they damn well want to and certainly do not feel that they need to be restricted to just one genre. Of course, the problem with that is that someone who likes one style may not like another but that is obviously a risk they are prepared to take as this German act are out to produce good music and they should be admired for that. Me, I sometimes find an album containing many different styles to have highs and lows but this time it is all highs, possibly because I have such a very wide taste in music and someone with more conservative views may not get as much out of this as I did. But the way that the band can go off on tangents within a song that is already far removed from the one before may not be what people normally think of when they discuss 'progressive', but if that is about breaking down musical barriers then these guys have laid them flat and stomped all over them. *#84, July 2005*

ALIENTAR
ALIENTAR

One of the great things about being involved in the music business is that sometimes I hear albums from bands that make me sit up and take notice and the debut from this Santa Cruz outfit is one of these. This is Space Rock with heavy psychedelic influences, so in other words if you like Hawkwind then you will think that Alientar are producing some of the finest songs around. Opening number "Sonic Wave" sounds as if it was lifted straight from one of Hawkwind's classic albums like 'Quark', it is that good. But this is not an outfit that has just one musical string to their imaginary bow, they are out to experiment and bring in jams and improvisations with funk and a groove but all with this space rock feel about it. Some of the sounds are clear while others are heavily distorted and full of fuzz; some are literally full of space and are laid back while others are there in your face and dominant. This album certainly gets me excited and anyone into this genre will also feel the same way, of that I am sure as songs such as "Kraz-e Naybr" show that the band are not content with just being influenced by one band as they also bring Floyd into the equation. It is a great debut and I can only hope that it will get the publicity that it deserves and that that the follow-up is as good.
#84, July 2005

ALKEMY

DA 63 PROJECT

Putting on the album and listening immediately to some finger popping bass I knew that I was heading deep into jazz territory, something that was not totally unexpected given that the release was on the Canadian Unicorn label. The rest of the band joined in and I was struck by the tightness of what I was listening to. But that guitar seemed a little heavy to be jazz, and ever so slowly the song turned from jazz rock to highly complex prog that had jazz influences. The vocals are good, but a little laid-back and not as dominant as they could be, with the focus very much on the instruments. When these guys fly, they do not need wings, and the result is an album that is immensely enjoyable and interesting. They say that their main influences are Dream Theater, Queensrÿche, Chick Corea and Pat Metheny which is certainly an eclectic mix to say the least. They appear to be happiest when meddling with jazz in one form or another but they are fusing it with rock in a way that makes the music more intense and heavier than one would expect from Metheny. I can understand when they state the heavier influences because there are times when there is no doubt at all that this is a rock band, and not four guys bent over their instruments in pain playing trad. An album that is certainly diverse, and worth investigating for those who are looking for something a little different but certainly with plenty of strong musicianship.

#80, Jul 2004

DAEVID ALLEN

STROKING THE TAIL OF THE BIRD

Here Daevid Allen was joined on this 1990 release by Gong member Gilli Smythe and Mothergong member Harry Williamson. It is ambient meanderings that I am sure has a market somewhere, just not on my player.

#56, Jan 2000

DAEVID ALLEN & RUSSELL HIBBS

NECTAN'S GLEN

The cover for this CD only credits Russell Hibbs (The Invisible Opera Company of Tibet), while there is a flash saying that it features Daevid Allen (Gong) and Mark Robson (Kangaroo Moon). The spine credits Russell Hibbs & Daevid Allen while the press release is for Daevid Allen/Russell Hibbs. Confused? The result is an album immensely more listenable than Daevid's last solo album and is basically acoustic, but with a lot of harp. It is strangely reminiscent at times of early Seventies Tull, and I feel that the high-profile use of Daevid's name, while gaining the album some publicity, will probably cause it some harm. This is an album that while enjoyable, will probably be dismissed by all those who do not share Allen's vision,

while those who do may be disappointed and this deserves more than that. This is an enjoyable acoustic album with a great deal going for it, as Russell's melodic vocals contrast in nicely with the higher harmonies of April Galetti.
#56, Jan 2000

AMAROK
NEO WAY

This album was kindly sent to me by Artur in Poland, and I could find out virtually nothing about it on the web. I think that this is their second album on Ars Mundi, but I do not think that either band or label have a web site (which is unusual, to say the least). What I can say is that for the most part this is an instrumental album featuring the talents of just one man, Michael Wojtas, who seems to be as happy on guitar as he is on keyboards. Listening to some of the finger picking on "On The Road" it is hard to imagine that this is a prog album at all as it just bounds along without a care in the world. But, this is an album that has taken influences by bands like Camel and brought them in with other styles to create a prog sound that at times is quite Eastern in its' approach but is always restful and relaxing. The Camel influence is taken further by guest Colin Bass who sings on the three songs that contain vocals. His warm tones add a further depth to the music. It is an album that is very pleasant and just right for the end of the day. Not sure who is carrying this album in the UK but try GFT in the first instance.
#73, Apr 2003

THE AMBER LIGHT
GOODBYE TO DUSK

This is the first full length album from German quartet The Amber Light. This is music that is built more on soundscapes and the use of emotion than many standard prog epics. They appear to be interested in Radiohead and possibly Pineapple Thief but I must confess that for me the jury is still very much out, as I can't make up my mind whether this is a good album or not. I enjoy the gentle acoustic "Devil Song" which has some delicate touches and is always building yet restrained, but some of the others just do not work for me. There are two songs at over thirteen minutes long but I have found it hard to get excited about these either. They are supposed to be the new future for German progressive rock – of that I'm not too sure. *#80, Jul 2004*

AMBERVOID
DEMO

Not many unknown bands send me a CD (3 songs), a video, professionally taken band photo, stickers, and reams and reams of comments from those who have seen them playing. Over 50 gigs last year, so all in all they are going for it. They have been in the studio recording their debut album and for an extreme band; they have a lot going for them. They themselves feel that they can be called Heavy

Progressive and maybe that is a true description as they bring together many different styles. Power and new ideas are often lacking in UK bands so I look forward to the album with great interest.
#62, May 2001

AMORPHIS
MY KANTELE
This is a mini-album from Finnish outfit Amorphis, following on from the debut 'Elegy' and commences with an acoustic version of the title track, which originally appeared on the debut. This is followed with "The Brother-Slayer" which is divided into two parts and has a weird hybrid of Tull-style guitar and Uriah Heep Hammond mixed with Hawkwind-like keyboards and loads of Seventies styles. The vocals are more Nineties in inflection, but apart from this the song could have been recorded more than twenty years ago. They show their influences more readily with the fourth song, which is a hard rock version of Hawkwind's "Levitation" where they have the sound to a tee, and it could be the original band in a live environment. The final song is another cover, "And I Hear You Call" (originally by Kingston Wall) and is another space rock workout, this time with some Indian influences. Overall this mini-album has whetted my appetite and I hope to hear more of them soon. Of course, being a Finnish band they have signed to an American label and I do not know who is distributing this in the UK.
#43, Aug 1997

ANABIS
HEAVEN ON EARTH
Imagine Genesis, about twenty years ago, add a touch of Eloy and you will have a very good idea as to how Anabis sound. Some of the guitar lines sound as if they have been lifted straight from Steve Hackett's catalogue. Now, it's not a bad album in any sense, but there is not any impression whatsoever of originality. If you like Seventies-style Genesis then the chances are you may enjoy this, unless of course you find the similarity all too much. If you do not like Seventies-style Genesis, then you will of course hate this.
#31, Oct 1995

ANATHEMA
ETERNITY
This is Anathema's third album, and it has been creating quite a stir in metal circles. This is because they are known as a heavy metal outfit, and have been touring with the likes of Bolt Thrower, Paradise Lost, Cathedral, At The Gates and Cannibal Corpse yet here they have produced an album that could well be deemed to be progressive!

Although doom-laden music often incorporates some Hammer House

of Horror-style keyboards to create a certain mood, on this album Anathema have taken it a stage further and have ended up with doom crossed with Pink Floyd! The inclusion of Roy Harper's "Hope", which he wrote with Dave Gilmour, adds a certain weight to this. This is an album that may be too much work for those into straight forward hard rock, but if they choose not to persevere with it then it will be their loss. This is an album that proggers also may find strange because it is outside of their normal sphere of reference, but anyone into music that is at times challenging, and certainly never peaceful or romantic, will find that this is a masterpiece.
#39, Jan 1997

ANDEAVOUR
ONCE UPON A TIME
I have long been a fan of Chris Rodler, and his work with Drama (later renamed RH Factor) and Leger De Main, so I was intrigued when he sent me this CD. Andeavour is a band where he is only playing keyboards (quite a surprise when I have always thought of guitar as being his main instrument, although he has also plays keyboards in his other bands).

The other guys in this project are Steve Matusik (guitars), Douglas Peck (vocals, bass keyboards) and Steven J. Starvaggi (drums, harmony vocals). It did not take to long for me to realise that although the music they are playing is extremely complex technical rock, so therefore something I should like a great deal, there is a problem. The problem is that they had a singer who was not as good as he thinks he is (sorry guys). The long notes, and some of the short ones, go off key and do not quite make it. He is extremely inconsistent and sometimes sounds great but there are too many places where he lets the music down.

It got to the point that I was cringing as I was listening to it. Perhaps I am being too harsh, but bearing in mind I have loved all of Chris's past projects then maybe I was too disappointed in this one and am too overly critical. That is possible, but I know that out of all of Chris's projects this is the one that I will be returning to least. A shame, as the musicianship and ideas cannot be faulted.
#55, Sept 1999

ROBERT ANDREWS
AN AMNESTY…
The full title of this album is 'An Amnesty For Bonny Things On Sunny Days', and is Robert's first album for Cyclops. He already has over ten solo albums and more with the rock band Land Of Yrx (no, I have not heard of them either) to his credit.

Robert provides all the guitars and bass while David Gates is on keyboards, and the music is mostly instrumental. It is visual, and as well as creating pictures for the ear, it creates and fashions feelings. The highlights are 'songs'

such as "Indian Summer", where Robert shows that for all the flash guitarists in the world there is little to match an acoustic guitar in the hands of someone who really cares. This album must be listened to intently, just to get the best out of it. I found that playing it in a darkened room with no interruptions was the best way to hear what Robert is trying to achieve. If you are a fan of artists such as Anthony Phillips, then this must be heard.
#59, July 2000

ROBERT ANDREWS
THE HOST
Way back in #59 I raved about Robert's debut album on Cyclops so I was looking forward to hearing his new one (even though label boss Malcolm Parker is the drummer….). He does not feature on all tracks on this instrumental album which is mostly keyboards and guitars, which has seen quite a shift in direction from 'An Amnesty For Bonny Things On Sunny Days".

There is not nearly so much reliance on acoustic guitars on this album, and the feel is much more of a New Age slant, dreamy and 'airy-fairy' at times. There are sections that are quite rocky, and bits of songs that are very good, but my overall impression was of an album that was too long and in need of serious editing, almost as a 'work in progress' rather than the finished article. There are two quite long pieces on here and one of these, "The Saboteur", neatly sums up all that is good and bad about the album.

The keyboard introduction is poor and is not at all representative of the piece and should have been cut altogether. This gives way to some powerful and rhythmic drumming which leads into a powerful rock guitar section that is very good indeed. It is the inconsistency that detracts from the album which is real shame as I was looking forward to this. Congrats to Malcolm for waiting until his 112th (!!!!) release before playing on an album himself (and he's not bad), but overall I felt that this was a disappointment.
#69, Aug 2002

ANEKDOTEN
VEMOD
In February 1990 Nicklas Berg (guitar, Mellotron) and Jan Erik Lijestrom (bass, vocals) discussed forming a prog rock band in Sweden. Along with Peter Nordin (drums), they called themselves King Edward and started off as a King Crimson covers band. Anna Sofi Dahlberg saw them at a gig in May 1990; she had been playing classical and folk music on cello, but wanted to be in a prog band. She approached Nicklas and joined in August 1991, so to celebrate the band changed their name to Anekdoten. 'Vemod' was recorded in April 1993, and although eleven labels expressed an interest in releasing it, Anekdoten were inspired by the success of Änglagård's CD so decided to release it themselves. 'Vemod' came out in September, and the first pressing of 1500 sold out in three days. They are now on their third

pressing and it has also been released on vinyl in Norway on the Colours label. The music is very different to most of the prog around now, as while they are heavily influenced by King Crimson and VDGG they combine these together with classical forms: the use of cello obviously also gives them a distinctive sound (Anna also plays Mellotron). The bass sound is also very heavy (like Chris Squire), which gives the music a 'Yes' edge to it at times. "Karelia" is the opening track, and is an instrumental, and right from the off it challenges the listener to get into the music. This is not stuff to sit and relax to, there is far more to it than that, just what prog music used to be about at one time. The lyrics are in English, and although sung reasonably well, I do get the feeling that the band are happier without vocals. This is very much a CD for the person interested in the more "progressive" side of "prog rock", who wants to listen hard to get the most out of it. 'Vemod' will never work as background music, but it is not intended to be. *#22, Mar 1994*

ANEKDOTEN
NUCLEUS

When Anekdoten released 'Vemod' at the end of 1993 they created quite a storm and everyone seemed to be talking about the band from Sweden who sounded quite unlike anyone else around. Instead of using Genesis as a starting point, like many progressive acts, they had instead looked to King Crimson and an unusual line-up. That line-up and musical style has survived onto the second album, which is bound to make them many new friends. The unusual element to Anekdoten is Anna Sofi Dahlberg who provides cello (along with Mellotron and vocals), and the result at times is extremely mournful as she coaxes notes that are sad and lonely, yet totally in keeping with the music. Overall the album works very well, from the bombastic hard rocking opener which is "Nucleus" to sad, stark, songs such as "Here". Anekdoten have a lot to offer, not least that progressive rock is a term that covers a multitude of sins and while they sound nothing like IQ they will be grouped together. If you like challenging music that is often depressing and always enthralling, then Anekdoten has again produced the goods. *#33, Feb 1996*

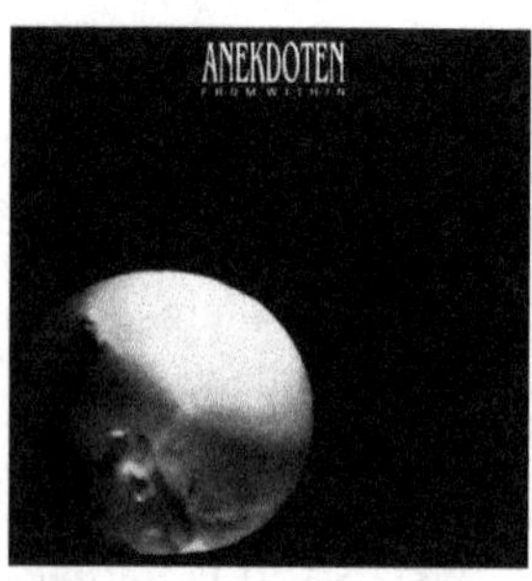

ANEKDOTEN
FROM WITHIN

Anekdoten's debut album 'Vemod', took the progressive world by storm when it was released, and the follow-up, 'Nucleus', was a totally different but no less impressive work, but I had lost touch over the years so when I saw Jan Erik's email address on a distribution list I did not hesitate to get in touch. To my delight I discovered that they had just finished recording a new album, which is now playing. Yet again Anekdoten appear to have made a dramatic change in direction, as for the most part this sounds nothing like their earlier work (although "Slow Fire" starts life as if it belonged on 'Nucleus'). One of Anekdoten's strengths lay in the unusual line-up (a four piece, one of the main instruments was cello). Cellist Anna Sofi Dahlberg is still in the band but these days concentrating much more on keyboards. It is an album that would

probably gain them radio play in the States, as they had moved far away from the threatening challenging style of music for which they were renowned. Overall it is an enjoyable album, and one that I have now played many times, but it did take me quite a while to get over the fact that this was indeed Anekdoten who were playing. If you have heard either of the two previous albums then be prepared for a departure, and while they are still in impressive outfit and this is a good album, I would much rather play the debut. Sorry guys.
#56, Jan 2000

ANIMATOR
GALLERY

Animator are a band that are beginning to make a definite mark for themselves on the UK prog scene, with rave reviews in fanzines. What is a little more unusual is the fact that they are American, and not British at all. They have been likened to an American version of Jadis, and while no-one can dispute their outstanding musical ability most of the audible influences come from the other side of the Atlantic, namely bands like Rush, Kansas and Shooting Star. Animator were formed in December 1988 out of the ruins of two Champaign Illinois bands, Ex Nikilo and Cinema. Stacey Krejci (keyboards, backing vocals) and Tim Brooks (vocals) were in the former, while John Hawkins (drums, backing vocals), Kay Hawkins (bass, backing vocals) and Rik Ruzga (guitar) were from the latter. They all loved the same kind of music and as nobody played it in their area anymore, they decided to learn some of their favourites themselves. These included "In The Cage" and "Starship Trooper", as well as various songs by Rush, Kansas, Pink Floyd, Peter Gabriel etc. Their initial feelings were that the music would not be appreciated, but they were proved wrong and soon began to build themselves a following. After live success, they started working on the original material that was to find its way onto 'Gallery'. There was no intention at the time to release an album, so they took their time writing the songs, introducing a new one onto the live set every so often. After about a year most of the songs on 'Gallery' were written, and fans were requesting a tape. It was decided, after some discussion, to record a demo to send to record companies, but in the end, they released it as an album on their own Rotamina label.

The CD package is well put together with complete lyrics. It starts with "A First Impression", which is a beautiful piano instrumental which leads into "Cycles", where gentle keyboards and intricate bass lead into a rock number full of time and mood changes. Stacey is a phenomenal keyboard player, in the Martin Orford mould, sometimes providing backdrops for the others to play against and at other playing solos with amazing speed and skill. "Cycles" shows Tim's strong high vocals to good effect, and the harmonies are pure and clear. It is typical of many songs on the album that it is lengthy (more than seven minutes), but it passes in no time at all. I would be very interested in seeing this band live as on the CD there are many examples of songs with the guitar to the fore (the eight-minute "Choices" being a case in point), but it is never too heavy, too dangerous. It may be an accurate picture of what they are like, but it may also be a sound that was strived for only for 'Gallery'. Lyrically the album

is excellent, but a special mention must go to "Lady Splendour" where Tom is singing to his mother, who has died. The music and words combine to produce a song of real beauty. This album will be loved by all those into prog, or even American-style rock, as 'Gallery' is a careful blending of the two. It ends with another short piano instrumental which leads well into the first one as the album plays all over again. Since the release in 1990, Rik Ruzga has married and left the band, and after auditions they have just managed to get a replacement guitarist in Chris Carroll, who they are now getting up to speed with the material. Their first gig with Chris was set for 30th November, and they plan to be playing live as much as possible while beginning to write the next album.
#16, Dec 1992

ANNALIST
ARTEMIS
Annalist is a Polish band, and to my knowledge this album has only been released in Japan and Poland, but I do hope that it will be available over here as it shows a lot of promise. Annalist has managed to capture a sound quite unlike many of the bands around today, and have also avoided sounding like the other Polish acts. Listening to it, even if you did not know where the band were from, you would guess that they are from Eastern Europe as they bring their own heritage into the music. Songs like "Anoit I Duch" (the songs are split between Polish and English) have a Polish folk feel, which adds to proceedings. Still, this is not a wimpy acoustic folk outfit, as "Glebej w Biel" proves as it powers along. Great music can be appreciated, even if some of the words cannot be understood. With 'Artemis' Annalist have created an album that should see them appreciated by an audience not restricted just to Poland.
#34, Apr 1996

ANYONE'S DAUGHTER
REQUESTED DOCUMENT
This double CD contains live recordings of Anyone's Daughter from 1980 to 1983. They were surely the most well-known German progressive band of the time and this CD shows well why they managed so much success. In Harald Bareth they had a fine singer/ bassist in the style of Greg Lake while Matthias Ulmer (keyboards), Uwe Karpa (guitar) and first Kono Konopik and then Peter Schmidt (drums) were no slouches either. While they sometimes came across as ELP, they were in the main not nearly as dynamic and forceful, much softer in approach although they too can produce some very complex pieces.

The four tracks that form the title cut of their debut album, 'Adonis', is here at over 25 minutes, while their self-titled number also manages over eleven. But they prove that they are no mean slouches with shorter numbers either as "Moria" is a great song yet is under five

minutes long. They played over 500 gigs, and sold over 120,000 albums, something that many of the UK's prog bands would love to emulate. They are often ignored, but if you enjoy prog that is complex yet easy to listen to then this is a good place to start.
#64, Oct 2001

ANYONE'S DAUGHTER
DANGER WORLD

At one time, Anyone's Daughter were one of the most important prog bands in Germany and although I knew that they had broken up in 1984 I was not aware that a version of the band had reformed in 2000. They certainly sound different to how I remember them, which is probably due in large part to Harald Bareth not being involved. They are no longer a prog band, but have moved much more into song-based rock.

The vocals are extremely powerful, as are the tunes. I could imagine John Wetton or Glenn Hughes being very much at home with this album. Some songs have sparse backing, relying on the clear melodic vocals of André Carswell, while others are much more complex and belting.

The more I played the album the more I fell in love with it, and the longer it took to get it out of my car. It may be that the band are using the original name to get more publicity but with an album this strong then all I can say is the best of luck to them as an album this good deserves to be heard, through fair means or foul. If you want a great rock album that will certainly never get the kudos it deserves then contact the label.
#66, Feb 2002

ANYONE'S DAUGHTER
WRONG

Anyone's Daughter reformed three years ago (although 'reformed' may be too strong a word given that out of the five musicians only two are from the original line-up) when they released 'Danger World' and 'Wrong' is the follow-up to that. This music has moved a long way from the material that I had heard of theirs in the Seventies and Eighties, now this is a polished hard rock band with progressive tendencies. Keyboard player and founder Matthias Ulmer is at the heart of everything that they do, but this is a belting rock album that also relies heavily on guitars. To top it all there are the vocals of André Carswell (who is American, although he has been living in Germany for several years). He has a great set of pipes and although he is not in quite the same league as Glenn Hughes (apparently, he also has the moniker 'The Voice') he is a fine singer and his range and control from low register through to high also gives this music an extra depth. If Emerson Lake & Palmer had turned into much more of a hard rock

outfit, then they may have sounded something like this. The more I played this album the more I enjoyed it – this is a band reborn and rejuvenated and this album is not 'wrong', it is 'right'.
#81, Dec 2004

ARACHNES
IN PRAISE OF SCIENCE

Arachnes is band that was put together by the Caruso brothers Frank (guitars, vocals) and Vincent (vocals, keyboards) and with this their fifth studio album they have now been joined by Gabriele Baroni (bass, vocals) and Stefano Caironi (drums). Overall this is quite an eclectic mix as while the band have obviously been heavily influenced by the symphonic and bombastic over the top approach of Rhapsody and Stratovarius, there is also quite a progressive element to what they are doing. Take the first song, "Gothic Description"; this is a straight between the eyes power metal song with loads of pace, yet also containing some interesting keyboards where Vincent uses a Hammond instead of a normal synth. On playing the album one thing that is apparent is that he uses quite a variety of sounds and this does give the band more depth. But while there are also other bombastic numbers such as "Just Try and Hit Me" there is also room for much more in the way of experimentation. For example, there is a three movement "Mediterranean Suite" on the album, and the way the keyboards start it off it wouldn't sound out of place on any prog album while the guitar that comes in to duet with these could have come from Vai. There is also one cover on the album, a great rendition of ELP's "Blues Variation" which has some wonderful chunky keyboards, and just drives along. Overall this is a very interesting album, one worthy of investigation.
#87, Apr 2006

ARAGON
DON'T BRING THE RAIN

Okay, I know that there is a lot of great music out there, but the fact that 'Don't Bring The Rain' has been available since 1990 and Aragon are not a household name is a major crime. I first heard the CD when I was at The Red House in Whitchurch and Pete Martin put the whole CD on the jukebox for me to listen to (it is his pub after all). Unfortunately, we were talking, and the music was not loud enough for me to fully appreciate then, but I do now! This album is brilliant, a masterpiece, everyone needs to go out and buy it etc. etc. etc... The band are Australian, and I have very little information to go on: the line-up (if it hasn't changed) is Les Dougan (vocals, originally from Scotland), John Polyannis (guitar, born in Egypt to Greek parents), Tom Behrsing (keyboards, German parents), Tony Italia (drums, Italian parents) and Rob Bacon (bass, fourth generation Australian). There is a myriad of different influences, and it should be no surprise that their music is so rich and varied.

The album kicks off with "For Your Eyes", and the gentle acoustic guitar gives way to a pounding bass with the vocals gently laid over the top. There is no indication that the song is going to pick up into a commercial rocker with great guitar and keyboards. Have any of you seen 'Wayne's World'? Remember where they are all head banging in the car? Well, one of my most vivid memories of music will always be some mates doing the same the first time I played this in the car when returning from Winter the other night. Poor guys, yet another CD they must get. But I digress. The song speeds up, slows down, and ends with a wicked guitar break that show that prog bands can rock with the best of them. Follow that! After such a dynamite opener, the next song could be something of an anti-climax, so it is interesting that they follow it with a two-parter, "Company Of Wolves". The first part is an instrumental (which starts off in a similar way to "The Battle of Evermore"). Aragon again use a soft quiet introduction to a song that is much stronger in substance. The instrumental features some very upfront drumming, while the bass and keyboards provide a backdrop of melodies and counter-melodies. Gentle keyboards lead into the second part of the song as the guitar and drums start to drive the song along. Les has a similar voice to Geoff Mann, and he uses different cadences and sounds to great effect. Again, he is a vocalist who likes to take on the character he is singing about. The song takes on a very commercial bent and the thought comes to mind time and again that if they were European or American they would have a huge following.

Some of the influences are clear, such as Genesis, Pendragon and Zeppelin, but Aragon have a style all their own. The highlight of the album is easily "The Crucifixion", which clocks in at more than fifteen minutes. The initial energetic keyboard runs become instead a gentle backdrop to Les's voice and all is calm, with only the harsh edge on the vocals giving any indication of what is to come. The song becomes almost unhearable as it goes so quiet, but I think this is a ploy to get people to turn up the volume. This is not advisable, as suddenly the band are rocking at full pelt. Somehow the word "contrast" does not do it justice. As suddenly as it began, the rocking stops and the keyboards take over again: the song is an undoubted masterpiece. The album is almost fifty minutes in length, with eight songs, but it flies by and the only good thing about it coming to an end is that it is possible to put it on again. Aragon are putting the final touches to their second album as we speak, and there are plans to bring their live show (which features Les wearing a long black coat and a rodent's head) to Europe later in the year, which I hope will go ahead as planned.
#15, Oct 1992

ARAGON
ROCKING HORSE AND OTHER SHORT STORIES

Some of you may remember me raving over their debut album 'Don't Bring The Rain' in #15, but this is not actually the follow-up (which was 'The Meeting' – which I have yet to hear). What 'Rocking Horse' attempts to do, is to provide an outlet for material recorded by the band in their past, mostly in demo form, that has been lying around. Some of the material harks back to the formation of the band in 1985: "Rocking Horse" opens proceedings and was the first song that introduced the more theatrical side of the band's live performances. It clocks in at twenty minutes long and shows Aragon to be a prog band willing to try and match anything that their European counterparts were attempting. Loads of time changes, intricate passages and great vocals should all add up to a prog masterpiece, but unfortunately although it is good I found my attention wandering after a while. "Sequences" or "Supper's Ready" it is not. Now, this is the opening song on the album, and challenges the listener to play the rest. "Ghosts" was conceived, written and recorded on a four-track inside a day and broadcast on Melbourne's PBS radio station that evening. Quite some achievement, but I confess I found the repetitive nature of the keyboards very distracting after a while. "Secrets" was the first song ever written by the band: it shows. I will quickly pass over "Touch" as it sounds like an unfinished demo (which it is), and next up is a live version of "Ghosts". I did not like the studio version, and this is only improved by some great vocals from Les. "Changes' is the last song on the album, and at long last Aragon prove themselves with a great track. It was recorded at the Rocking Horse sessions, and although dated a little, it has energy, enthusiasm and life. 'Don't Bring The Rain' is a brilliant album, and I have been told that 'The Meeting' is as good, but 'Rocking Horse' is only for the diehard fan.

#17, Mar 1993

ARAGON

MOUSE

1990 saw the release of Aragon's debut CD, and like many others I fell in love with it on first listen (especially the brilliant "The Crucifixion"), and it is an album that I still turn to today. 1992 saw the release of 'The Meeting', the first part of the 'Mouse' project, but it has taken until now for the completion of this, due to loss of personnel and problems getting into the studio, but at long last the new album is here. Aragon is now Tom Behrsing (keyboards, programming), Les Dougan (vocals) and John Polyannis (guitars). The loss of a bassist and drummer has meant a reliance on programming, which is never a satisfactory affair, but in this instance Aragon has managed to produce the goods (although musicians are better than computers any day of the week!). What stood out on their other works was not only the extremely strong songwriting, but also the great vocals of Les Dougan who has a rough edge to his voice that provides for real emotion and strength. At the front of the booklet is the story of Mouse, broken down into the different songs, so that the storyline can be fully understood and there are also the lyrics for each. This is an interesting idea because it does not rely solely on the words to tell the story, but rather explains what is going on. Overall, Aragon has produced an album to be proud of. It is not designed to be background music, or broken up into component parts, but rather is meant to be played from start to finish and listened to intently, a novel idea these days where so much music is treated as wallpaper. The Aussies have done good, so give yourself a treat and listen to some great music (especially the dynamic "Tying The Knot")

#32, Dec 1995

ARAGON
THE ANGEL'S TEAR

If I look up at the top shelf of my CDs I can see a very battered, often played, copy of an album called 'Don't Bring The Rain'. It is one of my favourite prog albums, now some sixteen years old and it contains some truly wonderful songs, the best of which is the fifteen-minute epic "The Crucifixion". I did hear some of their other albums on SI but over the years lost touch yet again and it is only now that I realise that they have been releasing material on the Dutch La Bra D'Or Record label, albeit intermittently. This album was released in 2004, six years on from 'Mr Angel', and still contains the same three core members of Les Dougan (vocals, drums, and keyboards), John Polyannis (guitars, bass, keyboards, percussion) and Tom Behrsing (keyboards). These guys always had one major thing going against them, and that was geography. If these guys had been UK, US or even Europe based then I am convinced that they would have been major players – but no, they are Aussies! Of course, it may be that very separateness that has encouraged them to follow their own path as their branch of prog is quite unlike anything else around, taking bits and pieces from lots of different styles and genres. But what they seem to specialise in is creating a real sense of atmosphere, not only in their music but also in the wonderful vocals of Les. He is an incredible singer and these three create some very special music together. I have not had enough time playing this yet to gauge how it compares to 'Rain' but as soon as I put in the player I felt that I was very much back in the times of old and knew instantly that these guys hadn't lost the touch. If you ever had the opportunity to hear 'Don't Bring The Rain' then I can assure you that you will not be disappointed with another glorious album from Aragon, and if you have not heard them at all then now could not be a better time.
#87, Apr 2006

ARCHETYPE
HANDS OF TIME

This American band came together in 1997, and pursue an interesting avenue of prog/technical metal. No keyboards for these guys, just a lot of clever things going on with the melody, and plenty of riffing from guitarist Chris Maytus. It is the guitarwork that sets this album apart from many, as Chris proves that he is much more than a guitarist with his amp set on ten, while at the same time he is not a huge fan of the widdly-widdly either. The four-track debut CD offers a lot in the way of promise, and it will be interesting indeed to hear the new full-length album 'Dawning' when it is available. If I had to pick fault it would be with vocalist Chyle Vagner who seems to be struggling at times, but given that he only joined the band two weeks prior to going in to the studio he ought to be given the benefit of the doubt. Overall a very intriguing and interesting band with a lot going for them, occasionally reminiscent of Queensrÿche or Winter, this is a band that is worth discovering. *#58, May 2000*

ARDENCY
DEAR HUMAN

Ardency are a new British prog band, only forming in 2003, and have already got around to releasing their debut album. These guys have obviously been influenced a great deal by Pink Floyd, but have also got some Ozrics sounds around them and have been paying close attention to some Camel and Steve Hillage which gives the music quite a distinct feel. There are times when I wonder if they would be happier as an instrumental band, and there are leanings towards the trippier side of space rock, but the vocals do work as Nick Edgar has a very pleasant high voice although they do appear to be kept lower in the mix than one might readily expect. This is music that can easily fall into the background, as there is little in the way of dynamics to keep the listener consistently interested throughout; that is not to say that this is a poor album, far from it, but it does come across at times as being just too one dimensional for repeated playings. I do believe that the music would work very well indeed when combined with visuals, but as for sitting and listening to this repeatedly I am not so sure. But they have a well-constructed web site (click on the bassist's bio to see an animation of Dragons' Den, I found it funny) and it is possible to hear some of the music and make up your own mind.
#88, Jun 2006

AREKNAMÉS
AREKNAMÉS

If ever an album sounded as if it was recorded over thirty years ago then this is it. Slabs of Mellotrons and Hammond Organ combined with heavy guitars and psyche and prog mentalities bring forth an album that does show the influences that the band are drawing from. They mention Still Life, VDGG, Necronomicon, Quatermass, Monument, Czar, Bram Stoker, Black Widow, and Egg but The Nice should be in there, plus Atomic Rooster. In fact, imagine a more proggy Rooster and that is probably the closest you will get to an album that is extremely intense and at times almost overpowering. They do not play at full throttle all the time, and there are some very mellow and reflective moments but when they go for it then it can be almost overwhelming. This is not an album that could be considered pleasant background music, and while as for prog it is as regressive as it comes that means that it is a fresh sound as there are not many bands pursuing this style of music. Areknamés are a trio, but one plays drums, one plays bass, and everything else is performed by Michele Epifani so they can't perform many gigs unless they have extra players. With just six songs, but two of these being more than ten minutes long and the shortest being nearly six this Italian prog outfit (all lyrics are in English) have produced an album as intense at times as any extreme metal and for the adventurous this is quite some work.
#83, Mar 2005

ARENA
SONGS FROM THE LIONS CAGE

Once upon a time there was a drummer. This drummer gathered together like-minded souls and formed a band. This band had people come and go, but the drummer was always there. Eventually they had a recording contract and released arguably the most important debut album of the 80's. However, after the album came out the drummer left the business, never to return. Well, it's nearly true. After a period of more than ten years, Mick Pointer is very definitely back. Along with Clive Nolan (Shadowland, Pendragon, Strangers On A Train etc.) he has formed Arena and take it from me, ARENA ARE GOING TO BE MASSIVE. Bass is provided by Cliff Orsi, Keith More (ex-Asia!) is on guitars and John Carson provides vocals. I was, well, stunned when I heard this album. I have long been a fan of Clive's, and along with thousands of others I bought 'Script' the day it came out, so there was always the possibility of setting expectations too high, but I needn't have worried. This album has been seen by Mick and Clive as the follow-up to 'Script', and the songs have an early Marillion feel to them although to my ears there is more than a touch of the debut Asia album as well. Mick and Clive co-wrote all the songs, although the next album will be more of a band effort. Many of you will probably be aware that Marillion were originally called Silmarillion, and the idea was to shorten the name whenever someone left, hence the album title.

Opening cut is "Out Of The Wilderness", no prizes for guessing what this is about. "I'm breaking out of this wilderness, I've cut my way through all the sympathy and tenderness, a soldier of fortune I fell once before but I live again! I'm part of this once more!" "Quality" is the word that shines here like a beacon. The quality of the songs, the quality of the vocals, the quality of the musicianship, the quality of the production (care of Mike Stobbie from Pallas). Anthemic in its presentation, the song switches from one musical theme to another as it goes through its eight minutes. Sheer brilliance.

Follow that I thought. As a total contrast to the bombastic over the top opener, what follows is an acoustic guitar solo. This is part one of "Crying For Help", which develops in three more stages. It is the perfect piece to follow "Out Of The Wilderness" and leads us nicely into "Valley Of The Kings". This is one of the longer pieces (more than ten minutes) and features some brilliant guitarwork at the outset. One of the things that made this album for me are these touches of musical skill: never rammed down the throat, there are sometimes sudden bursts of speed from one or another that leaves the listener breathless and thinking "how on earth did they do that?" Because it is used sparingly, it has far greater effect than if it was happening all the time. Keith and Clive have developed a real understanding and I can't wait to see these guys live.

"Crying For Help II" has Clive developing the earlier theme with a harpsichord, overlaid with flute sounds, relaxing and beautiful. "Jericho" starts off with just John and Keith as a ballad, and it gradually builds into the most emotional piece on the album with some wonderfully restrained keyboards and soaring guitar. It is the final phase of the song, when it becomes a keyboard driven rocker, that the attention is grabbed. Uplifting and soaring, this part bounces along and with some judicious editing could be a hit single. "Crying For Help III" further develops the earlier themes. As well as building up from instrumental into a song on their own right, these pieces are breathing spaces for the listener to calm down and get ready for the next belter (memories of 'Aqualung' perhaps?). This song ends with the phone ringing and the answering machine saying "This is the problem line, we're not in right now but leave your message after the tone". Another nod to 'Script' where Fish slammed down the phone saying "I don't need your problems!"

"Midas Vision" sounds to me as if it could have originally been written for Shadowland as parts of it could belong there, but apparently most of this one was written by Mick and not Clive! The shortest actual song on the album, it is also the heaviest, with some wonderful guitarwork. "Crying For Help IV" develops the earlier themes into a full-blown song with some guest guitar courtesy of Steve Rothery. Mick is back and welcomed into the fold once more. Emotional, certainly, and one of the most Marillion-esque moments. It builds with John and Clive, but develops with Steve's solo which is beautiful, yet restrained.

The last number, "Solomon", is both the longest and the best, with nearly fifteen minutes of brilliance. A gentle repeated keyboard melody, like a child's toy, gradually leads into the vocals. A song full of anger, as it again returns to Mick's departure from Marillion, Gentleness is replaced with roughness, then gentleness returns. Swirling curtains of keyboards, along with the quiet bass, allows John to cry to the world. When the guitar break takes place, it captures all that has gone before, and cries out in pain. This is far more than just a ballad though, as suddenly we are up and running as Arena break free and guitars and keyboards vie for dominance.

Phew! I received this album on 30th December and it just must be my album for 1994, although as it is not released until February I think there is a major chance that it will be my album of 1995 as well. There is no doubt at all in my mind that this album is going to be huge, and with Mick Pointer in the drum seat Arena are going to get loads of publicity, which is just what the UK prog scene needs. You watch, after Arena crash through the barriers erected by the UK media many others are going to follow. If you like good strong melodic rock, then this album cannot fail to gain your support. Arena have released the most important debut album this scene has had for many a year. If you only get one album in 1995, it should be this one.
#27, Feb 1995

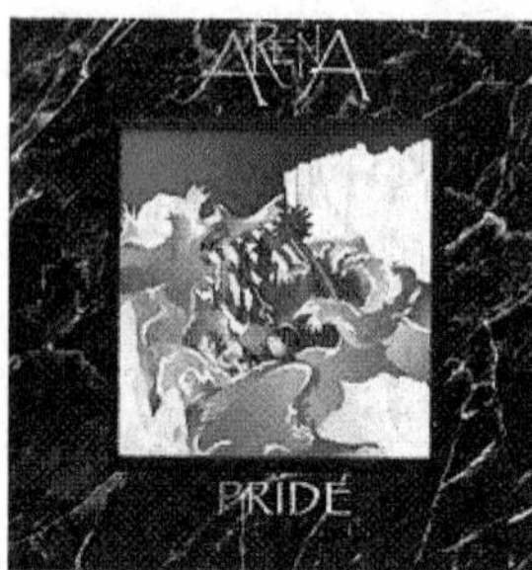

ARENA
PRIDE

'Songs From The Lion's Cage' has been quite rightly seen as one of the most important progressive debuts of the Nineties (although the players have been around for quite a while). It was always going to be a hard act to follow, and what hasn't helped in the interim is the much-publicised departure of vocalist John Carson and bassist Cliff Orsi. Paul Wrightson now provides vocals while Mr Bass himself,

John Jowitt of IQ, is in the fold. The album opens with "Welcome To The Cage" and I immediately became a little concerned, as while it is a cracking rock song, a perfect opener in many ways, it did not sound like Arena. What it did sound like was IQ in one of their heavier moments.

I am aware that the songwriters are still Clive Nolan and Mick Pointer, just as they were on the first, so I do not know if the addition of John has had something to do with it. "Crying For Help" is continued from the first album, here in another four parts (tracks 2,4,6 and 8). Apart from "Crying For Help VIII" these are all shorter 'songs', linking the album together. Paul must be commended for attempting an a capella song ("Crying For Help VII") but I do not think that it works, except for setting up the dramatic introduction of "Fool's Gold". "Sirens" closes the album, and at nearly fourteen minutes is the longest song. A gradual builder, it is dramatic and powerful. Overall this is a good album, but not nearly as indispensable as the debut. Possibly it needs to be played a great many times to be appreciated, but 'Songs' was immediate.
#37, Oct 1996

ARENA
THE CRY
'The Cry' is a mini-album bringing together all the "Crying For Help" series from the first two Arena albums along with some alternate and new versions to finish it all off. There are good sleeve notes, explaining the release of 'The Cry', and where each individual song came from and where it has been altered if that is the case. But, bearing in mind that most of the material on offer was recorded during sessions for the first two albums why is there no mention of John Carson (vocals) or Cliff Orsi (bass) who were members of Arena for the first album or Keith More (guitar) who played on both? I know that they have all been replaced but surely if they played on the songs then they should be credited whatever the circumstances of their departure?

Casting all politics aside, what about the music? It may be only thirty-five minutes long, but this mini-album does give a strong indication as to what Arena are all about. This is high quality music, with at times a very classical bent, as in "Isolation". New guitarist John Mitchell, who wrote that delicate instrumental, seems to have a real understanding of what Clive is about so I look forward to the new album with interest. It may be that Clive will hand over the songwriting reins a little as he has with Shadowland, which will provide Arena with a wider musical base. Although 'Songs From The Lions Cage' is still the album to buy first, this is enjoyable and well worth getting hold of even if you have the first two albums.
#42, July 1997

ARENA
WELCOME TO THE STAGE

Of all the UK bands, this is the one that has come most rapidly to the forefront of the underground scene, which is due not only to the excellent music but also to the publicity they initially garnered by having not only keyboard player Clive Nolan but ex-Marillion drummer Mick Pointer in their ranks.

Having released two albums this live album finds these two as the only ones on the band who played on both. This was recorded towards the end of a tour that saw them playing in twelve countries so it is of little surprise that the band are tight, with new guitarist John Mitchell slipping happily into Keith More's shoes. The album starts as if this was an actual concert, with a three-minute version of the "William Tell Overture". This is played to get the crowd going and to allow the band to leisurely get on stage, but whether the complete length works on CD is another matter and perhaps a faded in version might have been more appropriate. Two of the longer songs from the debut, "Out Of The Wilderness" and "Valley Of The Kings" kick off proceedings in the proper manner.

Arena have a delicate side as well as the much more up-tempo rocker songs such as "Welcome To The Cage" and all in all this is well balanced and if you enjoy "traditional prog" (if ever there was a contradiction in terms than that must be it) then you will enjoy this.
#45, Nov 1997

ARENA
THE VISITOR

At long last it is time for the third "proper" release from Arena, following on as it does from a live album and a mini album. Putting those two to one side for the moment, then this is the follow-up to 'Pride", which I was disappointed with after the brilliance of 'Songs From The Lion's Cage', so I viewed this with more than a little trepidation.

The line-up is now settled with Clive Nolan (keyboards), Mick Pointer (drums), Paul Wrightson (vocals), John Mitchell (guitar) and John Jowitt (bass), although only Clive and Mick remain from the line-up that recorded the debut. The fact that this line-up has been gigging across Europe shows, as there is a buzz, a sense of togetherness that was missing on 'Pride'.

It is an exciting album, one that every progger will be rushing out to get. Of all the progressive bands formed in the last five years, Arena are head and shoulders above the rest and this album shows why as it oozes class and shouts "brilliance" with every bar. I love this album, in case you hadn't realised, whether it is the blazing commercial passages in songs such as "Running From Damascus" which lyrically harkens back to opener "A Crack In The

Ice" as well as looking forward to "The Visitor", or the teasing guitars leads in the title song which are reminiscent of Mike Rutherford in "Burning Rope".

This is an album that is undoubtedly going to open a great many doors for them. No one can accuse them of going forward half-heartedly as they have utilised both designer Hugh Syme (Rush, Aerosmith, Whitesnake, Fates Warning) and co-producer Simon Hanhart (Marillion, Tin Machine, Yngwie Malmsteen, as well as the recent single "Perfect Day"). This is from a band signed to the label set up by Clive and Mick themselves.

They may not have the power of a large organisation behind them but they have still sold more than forty thousand copies of the first two albums. I am convinced that this marks yet another step forward for Arena in terms of musical ambition, and further success is sure to follow. If you enjoy top quality melodic or progressive rock, then this is an album that you cannot afford to miss.
#48, Apr 1998

ARENA
IMMORTAL?
Another album, another line-up change, but let's hope that this time there can be a long-term continuity in Arena's ranks as personally I believe this to be their best album to date. Joining Clive Nolan (keyboards, vocals), Mick Pointer (drums) and John Mitchell (guitars, vocals) are Rob Sowden (vocals) and Ian Salmon (bass). Those who follow Clive's projects, as he has been in Shadowland since their inception, already know Ian.

Each of the songs works extremely well, although they encompass a myriad of styles. Opener "Chosen" is very much an anthemic rock song, with power chords and soaring keyboards set against delicate vocals. It is one of the rockiest numbers ever undertaken by Arena, almost like a cross between Shadowland and Threshold. Contrast that to the following "Waiting For The Flood", which is all about acoustic guitars and a ballad style which is much more reflective in manner. Ian also uses fretless bass on this, which gives a warmer sound. I found it very hard to pick a favourite on the album, as they are all so good.

While sometimes looking backwards, there is a great impression of moving forward and looking outside of the normal progressive genre for ideas. Talking to Clive yesterday, he was telling me that this has had the most pre-orders of any of their albums and to my ears that is richly deserved. If you are a fan of Arena then this the album you have been waiting for, and if you have yet to discover the delights of the Clive/Mick partnership then now could not be a better time. Oh, and listen for the end of the album which works well.
#58, May 2000

ARENA

BREAKFAST IN BIARRITZ

Those with long memories may remember that when I last heard an Arena live album ('Welcome To The Stage') I was not over-complimentary. Now that was a few years, albums, and line-ups ago, so it was with an open mind that I put this double CD on the player. The first time I listened to it, I was alone in the house so I whacked it up while I concentrated on painting a bedroom. The time flew by, and being alone I could get increasingly into the music. This line-up is certainly the best so far. Clive Nolan is and always will be Clive Nolan, one of the very best keyboard player, composer or lyricist in any musical field. He has probably graced more stages than any other person in the prog scene due to his many other projects (including also the fact that he has been keyboard player in Pendragon for an awful long time), and knows what the audience needs. Of course, the other co-founder is still there, the one and only Mick Pointer. The line-up is completed by bassist Ian Salmon (who has been involved with Clive for years, most notably in Shadowland), guitarist John Mitchell who has a much more central role to the music these days, and vocalist Rob Sowden. Rob has also been developing his stage persona and this comes through on the album. A very strong double CD, with Arena showing that when it comes to symphonic prog there are few to match them. There is also a lengthy documentary on the band available as a CD-ROM track that is well worth watching. A good album.

#62, May 2001

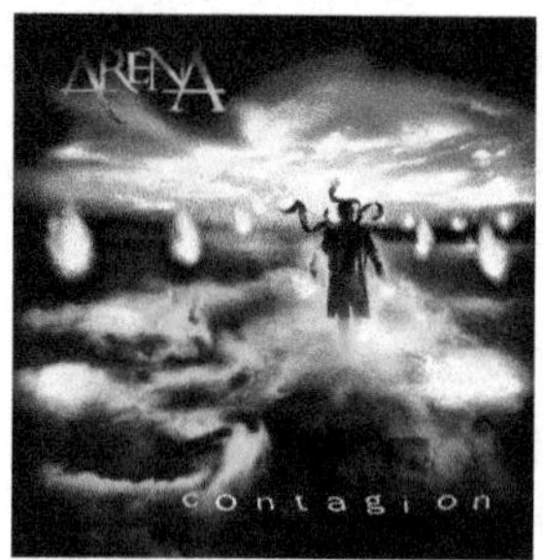

ARENA

CONTAGION

This album is the follow-up to 2000's 'Immortal?' and sees Arena with the same line-up of Clive Nolan (keyboards, vocals), Rob Sowden (lead vocals), John Mitchell (guitar, vocals), Ian Salmon (bass) and Mick Pointer (drums). It is a concept album concerning a search for salvation through a dark and foreboding vision of the future. Apart from the striking artwork by David Wyatt, the one thing that stands out on this album is the sheer intensity of the work. Some bands think that everything should be turned up to the max, but they often miss the dramatic edge which this album has in abundance. This is a step forward for Arena; they have raised the stakes and dare others within the prog field to follow. They have moved more into the prog metal area while at the same time staying far removed from bands such as Threshold. This is an album that is keyboard-led, as would be expected from one of Clive's bands, but when the guitars are there they are crunching and when they are not there is the anticipation and edge that they will soon be back. It gives the album a sense of drama which is heightened by the way that the music swirls and moves through themes, returning to ideas and moving on in different ways. It takes a strong vocalist to stand out against all that is going on and Rob Sowden knows when he must take control with strong soaring vocals or when the time is right to be more emotional. He is at home when singing with just a piano or when he is fronting an

all-out rock band. When Arena are in full flight they are a sight to be heard and the production by Clive Nolan and John Mitchell gives the sound the quality that it deserves. There are times when this album is multi-tracked acoustic guitars and pure venom from John while at others this is a prog band that have let loose the hounds and are running at full pelt. With 'Contagion' Arena have thrown down the gauntlet and are daring others within this area to follow. Intense, majestic, theatrical, powerful, full of visual imagery, I do not know how to convey the sheer wonder of this album.
#72, Feb 2003

ARENA
PEPPER'S GHOST
This album celebrates Arena's tenth anniversary, where the band have all been transformed into cartoon characters in a dark gothic Victorian age. This new image is part of Clive's intention of reinventing the band, but this is much more than just a new veneer, as the music has also taken a shift. It is almost as if Clive has decided to let loose the reins and to move wherever the music needs to, instead of being constrained in any way. "Smoke And Mirrors" sees the Shadowland sound being brought bang up to date and although Rob Sowden is very much the voice of Arena it is the backing vocals of Clive that come through. But this album is much more than just power and guitars within a prog environment, with not only a ballad but always music that shifts and changes direction. "The Shattered Room" starts off emotional, with just Rob and Clive, but when the guitars make their dramatic entrance the piece changes totally. In some ways, it is as if Clive has taken Twelfth Night but updated it and wrapped it in the Arena 'sound'. In great contrast is "The Eyes Of Lara Moon" with acoustic guitar leading the way to the climax. This is a very different sort of song for Arena, but one that works dramatically well. Or what about the piano and vocal ballad that is "Tantalus" which harkens back almost to Strangers On A Train? Highlight of the album is the closer, "Opera Fanatica" which at thirteen minutes is the longest song on the album, one that incorporates both symphonic and metallic styles in a way that could only be Arena. 2005 may be the tenth anniversary of the band but Arena show no sign at all of slowing down, and in 'Pepper's Ghost' have again produced an album that all progheads simply must have.
#82, Jan 2005

ARENA
LIVE AND LIFE
This triple disc set shows what Arena were like if you had managed to catch them on the 'Contagion' tour in 2003. Clive Nolan has been involved in the scene for more years than he would probably like to admit to, but it is with Arena that he is now best-known. With ex-Marillion drummer Mick Pointer they are the only two left from the band's inception (the joke always used to be do not stand on the

outside on a photo shoot as you will be the next to leave) but in more recent years there has been some stability with singer Rob Sowden and guitarist John Mitchell (The Urbane, Kino etc.) having been there for a long time while bassist Ian Salmon also now has a few years under his belt (and of course has been involved with Clive in other projects for many years). The two CDs capture a complete Arena gig, showing that this is a progressive rock band, with plenty of the emphasis on the word 'rock'. John Mitchell is one of the rockiest prog guitarists around, and Ian and Mick link up well to provide a strong base. In Clive, they have one of the finest keyboard players in modern progressive music, and the songs have been written to use all their skills. Add to that Rob's vocals and here is a band that is showing repeatedly why they are one of our top prog acts. Pick a song, any song, and there are loads within it to delight the listener with rock guitars and keyboards blasting out and Rob over the top of it all. But if the prospect of a double CD is not enough then there is also the 'Life' version of the set which is a 40-minute DVD capturing the band and crew on tour. There are snippets of gigs but this more about what happens on the road, and on the rare days off. On the first part of the tour they played 27 gigs in 32 days in 12 countries! This shows something of what happened, and the reaction of the fans. Overall this slip-sleeved package is a good introduction to those who have yet to discover the band as well as for the hardened fan.
#83, Mar 2005

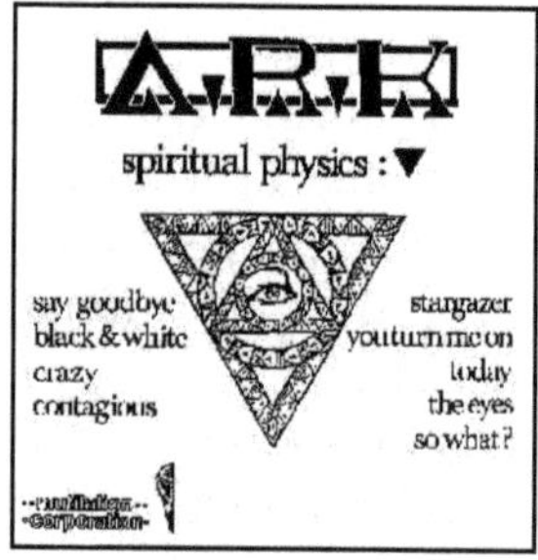

ARK
SPIRITUAL PHYSICS

Ark were formed back in 1986 by Ant Short (vocals, flute), Pete Wheatley (guitar), Steve Harris (guitar synth), Andy Harris (bass) and Dave Robins (drums). Initially Ark's output was several cassette singles, which culminated in the release of the limited-edition vinyl single "Communications". After the first heat of the Battle of the Bands competition in 1988 Andy left to be replaced by John Jowitt and the band went on to win the final and entered the studio to record the mini-album 'The Dreams Of Mr Jones'. Dave was replaced by Richard Deane in 1989, and Ark again went into the studio to record the 'New Scientist' EP, following this with a nationwide tour. Towards the end of 1990 John Jowitt decided to leave (he is now in IQ and Jadis) and was replaced by Gel Newey, then within four months Richard also left and was replaced by Paul Rodgers. Back in the studio in March 1991 to record songs for the 'Cover Me With Rain' CD EP, they also entered the 'Rock Wars' on Radio 1, and won with the highest number of recorded votes. This led to a session being broadcast on the Friday Rock Show. The release of the EP in 1992 was followed with a nationwide tour, after which they were back into the studio for the 'Spiritual Physics' sessions. The first album to come from these sessions, alternately titled 'The Black Album' was released in March, and a lighter album ('The White Album') should be out anytime now. I have seen reviews of Ark that have slated them for being more of a rock act than proggers, but is that a bad thing? What matters more to me, whatever form the music takes, is whether it is any good and what we have here with 'Spiritual Physics' is a very commercial rock album. True, there is some evidence of keyboards, but for the most part they are in the background. Ant has a great voice, reminiscent of Peter Gabriel, and it fits perfectly with the style of music they play. The album is also very immediate, being totally accessible on first hearing, but it is also a grower as the more you play it the better it gets. My personal favourite must be "Contagious" which starts off as a rock number, but rapidly becomes an acoustic song with (for the most part) just Ant and acoustic guitar. It is a beautiful number, where the electric guitar towards the end both demonstrates the restrained power of the band and the effectiveness of acoustic guitar in a rock environment. Ark are a superb live act and should be touring again soon, so catch them if you can and look out for 'Spiritual Physics'. *#20, Oct 1993*

ARKUS
1914

Arkus were originally formed in the late Seventies in Holland, releasing this their debut album in 1981 with a line-up of John Bouwman (bass, vocals), Frans Smits (lead vocals, rhythm guitar), Erik van Duin (drums), Ron Willems (lead guitar) and Jan-Henk Wiggelinkhuizen (synth). The album was well-received in Holland, USA and Japan, but a year later it became apparent that their manager was not very good and he departed leaving the band with loads of debts. Arkus kept going, but with not nearly the same enthusiasm as before. Jan-Henk and John left and were replaced, and a new spirit led to the band recording a new CD, 'Win or Lose', which was released earlier this year. SI have now decided to re-release the debut on CD, with some bonus tracks which were recorded by the original line-up for a radio session, and this is what is currently on the player. I could not get into this album at all. There is a very heavy BJH influence (who I like, honest), and while that may not be altogether a bad thing, the whole album grates after a while. The lead guitar has a distorted sound that is sometimes used to very good effect by other bands, but here it is on every single track of the original album. Unfortunately, there is also the use of electronic percussion on one song, and although it may have sounded very avant-garde twelve years ago, it now sounds simplistic and dated. Frans has a pleasant voice, but the music seems to lack bite and soul. It's not prog by numbers but there should be more to music than this. A mate of mine who I played it to described it as "lift music" and I can see what he means. It is music to relax and mellow out to, but there are many others in my collection I would turn to before this one. *#19, Aug 1993*

ARTENSION
SACRED PATHWAYS

They released their first album in 1996 but Artension have only recently started working with each other again. The press release describes this as 'Neoclassical Progressive Metal', and that is probably quite a fair description. The music is based very much around the keyboards of Vitalij Kuprij who met guitarist Roger Steffalbach when he travelled to Switzerland to further his studies on piano (as well as playing in other rock bands such as Ring Of Fire he has also recorded a solo classical CD). Vitalij writes all the music and loves nothing better than to show off his speed and dexterity, sometimes to the detriment to the music. But when it works, such as on "The Emperor", it can be awesome (possibly as this is one of the tracks where Roger also lets rip). John West (Royal Hunt) provides all the vocals but the feeling for much of the album is that although it has many good points, and some quite brilliant, overall the band could do with a few more tunes and less of the posturing. Not an album to totally dismiss, and one that I will play again, but bands like Stratovarius are more consistent to my ears. *#66, Feb 2002*

ARZ
SERAI

ARZ
THE MAGI

For ARZ read Steven Adams, a guitarist from Portland Oregon, and these two albums are his first releases (although a third, 'Mountains Of Madness' will be available shortly). What I particularly like about these two albums is the way that he manages to blend together so many different styles yet at the same time create music that is intensely enjoyable and easy to listen to (without of course ever managing to become easy listening). He is a fine guitarist of that there is no doubt, but the skill with these two albums is probably in the arrangement. If there is a need for a mandolin here, or a banjo there, or maybe a touch of synth then it is all put in so that it fits well together. 'Serai' starts life with many different melodies and sounds all vying together to be heard in "Jjinn" before a rock riff takes over. It is quite different to other guitar instrumental albums that I have heard (apart possibly from Jeremy), and there is a real feeling of a journey, of a story to be told. Not all the songs on here are electric, and there is room for a more classical Steve Hackett feel on songs such as "Spindleshank". He has obviously been very influenced by prog bands as opposed to straightforward rock shred and that very much comes through in his approach.

'The Magi' also came out last year, and shows Steve continuing along on the path that he started with 'Serai'. This album is probably even more prog oriented and again there are some wonderful arrangements and mixing of styles such as on opener "Futureman" which is all over the place stylistically but works extremely well indeed. There are only five songs on this album as opposed to the eleven of the debut, but given that the title cut is 24 minutes long and 'Ur' is also over fifteen minutes we should forgive him. This extra room allows Steve to spread out and show more than ever his prog roots but he also manages to bring in some very Eastern feelings and this album appears to have more depth then the debut, although arguably because of this the debut is the one that is easiest to listen to.

Overall these albums are certainly a very interesting find and progheads should discover more.
#87, Apr 2006

ASGARD
IMAGO MUNDI

Asgard were formed in 1986 in Treviso, north-east Italy. After various demos and recordings, they signed to WMMS in 1991 and 'Imago Mundi' is their fourth album with them. They are an Italian band that I have heard of, as they have worked with Galahad in the past. Prior to playing the album I read an excellent review in 'Raw' which I found amazing. I mean, a straight rock mag with good words for prog? Totally unbelievable. The title of the CD may be in Italian, but thankfully the lyrics are in English: complex and complicated, this concept album is the tale of a warrior travelling through many lands. The beauty of this album is that not only are the songs readily accessible to the casual listener with great melodies and hooks, but there are enough style and time changes to satisfy the hardened progger. Some are rock guitar based, while others allow the keyboards to take front role and many more just keep switching from one to another. "Justice", for example, has a keyboard lead that turns into guitar (with double bass drum pedals driving it along) then moves and melds into a different animal altogether. For total contrast, listen to "Virtue", which starts off with a hymn-like quality! There again this can be contrasted with "Courage", which commences with a devastating run down the frets. All in all, I found 'Imago Mundi' immensely enjoyable, and if you are interested in good melodic rock or prog with (at times) a very heavy edge then this is very much an album for you.
#23, May 1994

ASHADA
CIRCULATION

I had already decided that I really enjoyed this album before I took a closer look to see who was involved. The instruments and vocals are mostly shared between Tae and Midori but investigations of the booklet revealed that Akihisa Tsuboy and Dani has been involved on violin and bass respectively, both members of one of my favourite Japanese bands, KBB. This album is a mixture of instrumentals and songs, taking the music of Quikion and putting it into a more Western environment. At times I kept thinking of Mike Oldfield but the music does not have that depth – it is almost as if there is a deliberate shallowness so that all of the music is on the surface – what you hear is what you get. The accordion is an important part of the Japanese folky side of the music, but it often gives way to piano or violin. Tae's vocals are gentleness and innocence, all wrapped in purity – as if a small child was singing and not a woman. There is a naievety that is beguiling and enthralling – music that starts as a small voice that fills the room. I found this album compulsive listening – and it is hard to explain why. That it is in many ways quite beautiful is never in doubt, as is the fact that it it is hard to get this out of the player. There is a simplicity to this album that shows that it is not about note density or complexity, all you need are for the right elements to be in the right place and here that has easily been achieved. In many ways this is a stunning album. *#89, Sep 2006*

ASIA
ARENA

Here is the sixth album from Asia, and the sixth to have a short title starting with the latter 'A'. We went from 'Asia' to 'Alpha', 'Astra', 'Aqua' and 'Aria' but what seems strange to me is that they have chosen 'Arena' for this one. What is in a title? However, their last guitarist was one Keith More who, while recording an album with a new band, refused to re-join Asia. The name of that album was 'Songs From The Lions Cage' and the band was Arena. Strange, huh? Anyway, onto 'Arena'. Since 1992 Asia have been a duo, Geoff Downes (keyboards) and John Payne (bass, vocals), with added session musicians. Possibly this is why 'Arena' is far removed from 'Asia'. I firmly believe that 'Asia' is a classic, and one of the finest debut albums ever recorded, no matter what genre of music: 'Arena' sounds as if it was recorded by a totally different band, which I suppose it is, and has none of the dynamism or brilliant songs that made the former what it was. It would be very easy to dismiss this album, which would be unfair as it is not actually that bad. Rather, it is enjoyable, but one that does no justice at all to the Asia name (apart from possible "Heaven", which has some of the old magic). It is time that Geoff and John, if they are going to pursue this type of music, decided on a new moniker. *#34, Apr 1996*

ASIA
ARCHIVA 1

ASIA
ARCHIVA 2

On January 1st this year, John Payne and Geoffrey Downes returned to their studio to find that a burst water pipe had destroyed most of their equipment. They had to salvage what they could, and while doing so discovered a box of tapes that had been archived. These contained songs that had remained unreleased so a decision was made to make these available for the first time, on two CDs. They have been well presented with recording details, lyrics and other information. For example, "A.L.O." was originally written as a demo for ELO Pt. II and was called "Quest For A Key", it was then upgraded and recorded as a demo for 'Aria' (renamed "Asiatic Light Orchestra"). "Boys From Diamond City" was originally recorded by the aborted 'new' Asia of Downes/Wetton/Gorham/Sturgis (minus

Wetton), and both Max Bacon and John Payne provide lead vocals. I should say that although this song is basic it shines out because of Scott Gorham's guitarwork. As with all collections of this type there is the concern that the material may have been originally archived because it was not any good, but this easily stands up against their latest material (not nearly as difficult as once it may have been). They have great Rodney Matthews covers, with good information, and if you are an Asia fan then you must have these two albums. *#37, Oct 1996*

ASIA
ANTHOLOGY

Asia is probably one of the best supergroups ever formed, with Geoff Downes (Buggles, Yes), Steve Howe (Yes), Carl Palmer (Atomic Rooster, ELP) and John Wetton (King Crimson, UK, Wishbone Ash etc.). Their debut album is rightly seen as a classic and singles from it did very well, particularly in America and Japan. The second album 'Aqua' also did well but during the touring John left the band. He was replaced by Greg Lake (King Crimson, ELP) in time for the recording of the 'Asia In Asia' concert that was released on video, but by the time of the next album Greg had left to be replaced by John, and Steve Howe was also no longer in the frame (replaced by Mandy Meyer). It should be said that from here on in the plot gets very complicated. Basically Asia are now down to two, Geoff Downes (keyboards) and John Paine (bass, vocals) along with session musicians. I put on the CD and noticed that the first song was "The Hunter". It did not sound quite right to my ears so I checked in my collection and found it right where I thought it was, on 'GTR'; the band formed by Steve Hackett and Steve Howe after he had left Asia. Geoff has produced that album and provided them with the song. Strange, I thought, to have this on an Asia collection recorded by Asia. Still, the next song was "Only Time Will Tell', so nothing could go wrong with that. Funny, the guitars and keyboards do not sound quite right. Hang on, that is not John Wetton singing! A close examination of the box showed that all the songs featured from the early albums, i.e. the well-known ones ("Only Time Will Tell", "Don't Cry", "The Heat Goes On", "Go" and "Heat Of The Moment") have all been re-recorded with John Payne! This is a shame, as although the album has great songs I felt that somehow I had been ripped off by not having the originals (bearing in mind that I did not pay for this either!). I am sure that if I had bought it I would have been annoyed. Yes, there are some great songs on here but do not say that I did not warn you! *#47, Feb 1998*

ASTRALASIA
AWAY WITH THE FAIRIES

Astralasia released their first album as long ago as 1990, but this their tenth is the first for five years. They were one of the originators of the acid house rave revolution and were also very involved with the trance scene, and have also appeared at numerous festivals such as Glastonbury. This is music that has seen them stay fairly focussed to

their roots while also bringing in some different styles. There are times that they do come across as different version of Ozrics, but there are others such as on "Wave Of Probability" where they come across far more as being influenced by Alabama 3 (or could it be the other way around?) This is a double digipak and great care has been paid to the presentation as well as to the production so the result is something that is both enjoyable to listen to and to look at. The violin of Simon House swirls through the music, sometimes in the background and sometimes in the foreground providing an extra to the flute, guitars and sax that also take lead roles. This is not music to jump up and down to, but rather something that is designed to take your mind into different areas. Well worth further investigation.
#88, Jun 2006

ATARAXIA
ARCANA ECO
Ataraxia are a band quite unlike any other that I have come across while writing reviews – this is much more than just acoustic music, it is neo-classical, baroque even, yet bringing in folk sounds and styles at the same time. This release also combines a book which describes their albums through the images of a voyage that inspired them. It contains six chapters with Livio Bedeschi's photos, as well as the reflections of journalist Ferruccio Filippi and Francesca Nicoli's writings. It also contains an exhaustive interview; full discography and the lyrics to 'Arcana Eco' which has seven songs, four of which are exclusive and three older ones. This is quite an undertaking which shows just what a following they have, even though they are unknown over here. Unusual listening, but strangely compelling with some wonderful vocals and atmosphere.
#85, Nov 2005

ATON'S
CAPOLINEA
Apparently, this is going to be the last album by this Italian prog band who has decided to call it a day after 25 years, which surely must make them one of the longest lasting prog bands around. All the lyrics are in Italian, which means that this album will only have limited appeal which is a shame as this trio are creating quite a storm about something. The first number, "Star" begins life as an organ recital but it gives way to a bouncing rock number that contains some great finger popping on the bass, as well as some driving rock guitar that moves this band a million miles away from the normal neo-prog scene. They contain modern elements yet at the same time hearken back to a long-lost age when bands were quite prepared to go their own way and not worry about what others within the genre were doing. I think that is one reason why I have enjoyed this album, in that it is different from the norm and the listener is never quite sure what is going to happen next as it may be a peaceful acoustic guitar interlude or

something much more powerful. Aton's are never going to be fashionable and the language barrier will turn off quite a few people which means that many people who would enjoy this album will not even try hearing it. It may not be essential but it is enjoyable.
#70, Oct 2002

A TRIGGERING MYTH
THE REMEDY OF ABSTRACTION
This is the sixth album from the duo of Tim Drumheller and Rick Eddy, and following on from the success of their last album where they brought in drummer Vic Stevens and guitarist Scott McGill they have now also brought in the third member of McGill, Manring, Stevens with bassist Michael Manring. If that was not enough, they have also brought it my favourite Japanese musician Akihisa Tsuboy who adds violin to a couple of tracks. This is instrumental progressive rock music that has been heavily influenced by bands such as Soft Machine and National Health, and as one can deduce from that statement there are plenty of jazz influences within this. The music can be delicate, or it can be complex, and given that this is the band of two keyboard players it is somewhat surprising that they do not place themselves more to the front. But, this is music where the arrangements and overall feel is important – it is to be listened to carefully as if it was a classical work as opposed to jumping around and getting into it. This is often fairly laid back, but the wonderfully warm fretless bass offsets the almost clinical precision of some of the music. This is music that must be played many times to get the most out of it, as some of the melodies and styles are not as dominant as they might be, but will be of interest to those who prefer their music like this.
#87, Apr 2006

ATRIA
BOULEVARD OF BROKEN DREAMS
Atria are a French outfit comprising Jean Michel Paci (vocals), Martial Urnbanc (keyboards), David Jucan (bass), Gerard Larue (guitars), Stephane Pacini (drums) and Vincent Detoffoli (guitars). All lyrics are in English and the overall sound is one of very commercial prog rock. I know that the Dutch fanzine 'Background' raved over this album and it is not hard to see understand why. Although there are two guitarists, the sound is very much keyboard dominated for the most part; is very melodic and to my ears "safe". The guitars sometimes threaten, but never seem to manage to break through as perhaps they should. Apart from the instrumentals, all the songs are at least seven minutes long, with two being more than nine. The longest track. "Ghost Of A Child", has some nice changes and moods to it with acoustic guitars being used to good effect. I get the impression that this CD is a "grower", as the more I play it the more I like it and if you are deeply into prog then this well-produced sanitised CD may be for you, but I can't see it attracting the non-progger. *#19, Aug 1993*

ATTICA
YOU ARE IN DANGER

When I come across an album on the Carbon 7 label then I expect it to be full-on jazz, possibly with some rock, but not always, and often instrumental. Of course that does not apply to Attica who although containing large elements of jazz are using this as just one strand, while they do have a lead singer (who as well as playing trumpet also provides flugelhorn – not the only time I have come across that instrument in this issue). There is a delicacy to this album, as they mix the styles, and I have seen one review where they were raved about as being the new Jeff Buckley! I wouldn't go that far, but did find it interesting that the one cover on the album is a wonderfully atmospheric take on Nick Drake's "Riverman". The five guys know what they want to achieve, and use guests where they need some extra brass or violin, or a double bass where the mood is right instead of electric yet there can also be some electric guitar breaks when the music demands it. This is a fascinating album that brings together elements of classic Floyd with jazz but instead of the result colliding they mix together so that one can't hear the seams. Fascinating stuff.
#85, Nov 2005

AT WAR WITH SELF
TORN BETWEEN DIMENSIONS

'Torn Between Dimensions', is the debut recording of At War With Self, a project that has been put together by Glenn Snelwar on guitar, mandolin, and keyboards; Michael Manring on fretless bass and e-bow; and Fates Warning's Mark Zonder on drums and percussion. It is being released as a digipak on Free Electric Sound, which is a sub-label of The Laser's Edge. Glenn is best known for his work with Gordion Knot, while Michael is a Grammy-nominated bassist. The drumming is subtler than one might imagine, and a key part of the sound is the fretless bass, which has such a warm quality that it can sometimes become the lead instrument in its own right as well as providing tonal colour. But this is Glenn's band, and he provides most of the material and takes on the lead role either on electric guitar, keyboards or sometimes mandolin. This is a strange fusion of styles, so that it is hard to follow the actual flow of what is going on. That they are all fine musicians is never in doubt, but this certainly is not the most accessible album that I have ever heard. Glenn states that he is trying to open doors to listeners who may be unfamiliar with progressive rock, classical guitar or metal, but his very aim may find himself at odds with some listeners in that he is hitting so many musical bases that it is hard to work out where he is coming from and who he is going to appeal to. Will King Crimson fans want their eclectic music to contain so much in the way of power riffs, and will fans of Satriani and Vai understand what he is trying to achieve? I am not sure and I came away from this album musically confused.
#83, Mar 2005

AUSIA
KASA KASA

Ausia is a trio that has been put together by Akihisa Tsuboy (violin, KBB etc.), Source K. Adachi (guitar, mandolin, vocal, Adachi Kyodai) and Yukihiro Isso (recorder, shinobue and dengakubue). Although there are vocals, this is primarily an acoustic album where the band have improvised around a framework. The result is music that is alive with interplay, something that is vibrant and exciting. All three guys are masters, but with no percussion or bass to get in the way they can all have their turn at providing the main melody, although it is often left to Source to provide the backdrop for the other two as they literally duel it out. There is incredible energy as well as musical complexity and dexterity and the music is fresh and invigorating. The first time I played this I hadn't looked at the tray card and I kept thinking how close this was in many ways to Tull (Ian combining with Eddie Jobson), so I was not surprised to find a Tull cover creep in. However, I was surprised to note that it was "Mother Goose" again! Given that Source sang it on his own album I did not expect here as well but it is again a worthwhile version, here given some different emphasis with Akihisa and Yukihiro trying to find room where there is not any. A wonderful album that all fans of acoustic music need to search out.

#78, Apr 2004

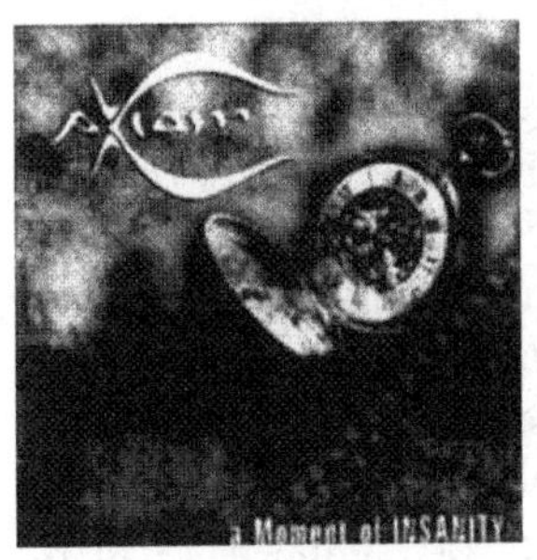

AXIOM
A MOMENT OF INSANITY

This is a new one on me, I must confess. This is the debut album by Axiom, and being a debut of course in itself is not unusual. But what is strange is that these guys are ALL in another band called Landguard. In other words, the band that is signed to Underground Symphony decided that they wanted to release something so different to their normal material that they had to do it under another name. Both bands are ongoing artists, so it must get a little confusing when they go out on tour etc. Anyway, I have not heard any of the other material so I can only concentrate on Axiom. There are some who are going to call this prog metal, but that does not do this justice as although there certainly are places where the keyboards take the lead role this is a guitar album with a few overlays. There are also some very HM vocals indeed as Marco Mangiapia shows that he can shout and scream with the best of them or growl when he wants to. This is metal with prog overtones, melodic technical heavy stuff with one eye on Savatage as well as Queensrÿche etc. This is crunching stuff that is obviously aimed at the metal head with a melodic bent as opposed to the 'normal' proghead (as if there is such a thing) and overall is interesting stuff. I will be intrigued to hear the Landguard material at some point to see what they are pursuing in that venture but for now this is a damn fine listen.

#84, July 2005

KEVIN AYERS

TURN THE LIGHTS DOWN

This album was recorded in West London on March 10th 1995, with Kevin supported by The Wizards Of Twiddly. Kevin has always been 'cult', and this has meant that the crowd there to see him there that night was hugely enthusiastic, as he went through a set that features songs from the length of his career. This is not about playing material at breakneck speed or at high volume, but more about reflecting and feeling the emotion. Kevin has a distinctive voice, and it is best heard on songs such as the superb "Lady Rachel". This sounds like a very personal and atmospheric gig, and it is a great introduction to his work. This is the first Market Square release that I have come across but hopefully it will not be the last. A very informative booklet, along with photos makes this a strong release.

#60, Oct 2000

AYREON

THE HUMAN EQUATION

This is a modern concept rock opera on a huge scale. The double CD only just manages to cram it all in, this is epic on an epic scale. Arjen Lucassen has outdone himself this time as the different singers and musicians create something magical. I mean, for starters look who is involved in this project with Arjen, who as well as providing electric and acoustic guitars, bass guitar, analogue synthesizers, Hammond, Mellotron and additional keyboards also sings the part of 'Best Friend'. He is joined on vocals by Devon Graves (Dead Soul Tribe) as 'Agony', Devin Townsend (SYL) as 'Rage', Eric Clayton (Saviour Machine) as 'Reason', Mikael Åkerfeldt (Opeth) as 'Fear', Magnus Ekwall (The Quill) as 'Pride', Heather Findlay (Mostly Autumn) as 'Love', Irene Jansen (Karma) as 'Passion', James LaBrie (Dream Theater) as 'Me', Marcela Bovio (Elfonia) as 'Wife', Mike Baker (Shadow Gallery) as 'Father' with the following musicians: Ken Hensley (Uriah Heep etc.) – Hammond Organ, Oliver Wakeman (Nolan & Wakeman) – keyboards, Martin Orford (IQ, Jadis) – keyboards, Ed Warby (Gorefest etc.) – drums, Joost van den Broek (Ayreon) – keyboards, John McManus – low flute, tin whistle, Jeroen Goossens – flute, Robert Baba – violins, Marieke van der Heyden – cello. You can see already that this is something that is out of the ordinary. When this rocks it does that in spades, and there are areas within this are that are pure beauty. This is a prog album that is setting new standards when it comes to imagination and construction. It is an album that is compelling, but each theme leads seamlessly on from the one before. This is more like a symphony ever changing and developing than a series of songs telling a story and the result is that the listener is truly transported into a new world. I have been listening to the double CD, but it is also available as a deluxe edition containing the double CD, a DVD and a book. Inside Out have put a lot into this release and I can see why. This is setting new standards for concept albums – superb.

#79, May 2004

AYREON
ACTUAL FANTASY REVISITED

AYREON
INTO THE ELECTRIC CASTLE

In 1996 Arjen Lucassen released his second album under the Ayreon name, 'Actual Fantasy'. At the time he used only a few guest musicians (just three singers) and apart from a couple of synth solos he played all the music himself. However, when deciding to go back to the album he brought in drummer Ed Warby to replace the drum machine used on the original and asked Peter Vink to play bass, replacing the parts originally played by Arjen himself.

The result is 'Actual Fantasy Revisited' which in many ways is the same album that was released eight years previously, but at the same is a different kettle of fish altogether. It is possible to see just how much this has changed as the album comes with a second disc which contains a video, a feature of Arjen in the studio and the process of re-recording, a 5.1 mix of this album and the album in its' original format. Two albums for the price of one! Within the booklet (which contains all the lyrics) there are also notes as to what each song is about, as these are linked as much as they are on other Ayreon albums. It is an enjoyable album, which those into the rockier end of prog are going to like. But in this issue, I am reviewing two Ayreon albums, and the other is a different item altogether…

Arjen's second album did not sell as well as expected, which put a lot of pressure on him to come up with a killer product for the third. Reading an old Acid Dragon the other night, I saw a review of the original version of this where the writer said that this had to be the album of the year, and I know just where he is coming from. This version has been reissued with a new booklet and interviews with Arjen, but pretty much this is as it was when it was released in 1998 and it has lost none of its power or majesty over that period.

With many guests playing parts (including Fish and Damian Wilson) this is very much a space opera, very much a concept work so that it is difficult to play just one of the CDs but instead this cries out to be played in its' entirety each time it is put in the player. Arjen convinced some top musicians to help him out with this album, including Clive Nolan and Thijs Van Leer yet this sounds like a band instead of just a group of players.

The music moves from hard rock through many different styles of prog and even brings in folk, and the result is something that is compelling and intensely rewarding. If you feel that you would like to investigate Ayreon then 'The Human Equation' or Star One release are probably the best place to start, but 'Into The Electric Castle' is extremely close behind and 'Actual Fantasy Revisited' shouldn't be dismissed out of hand either.
#82, Jan 2005

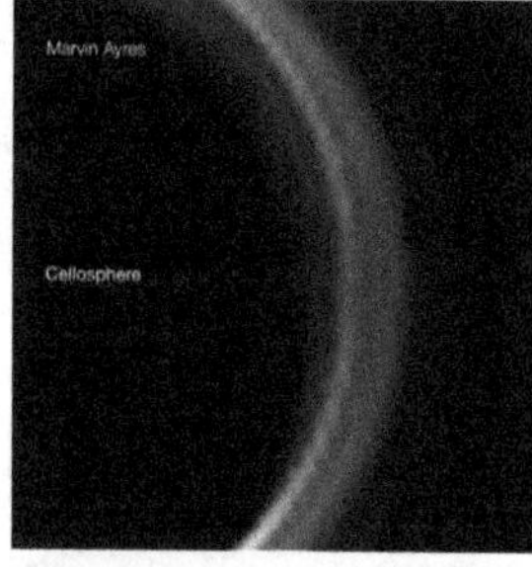

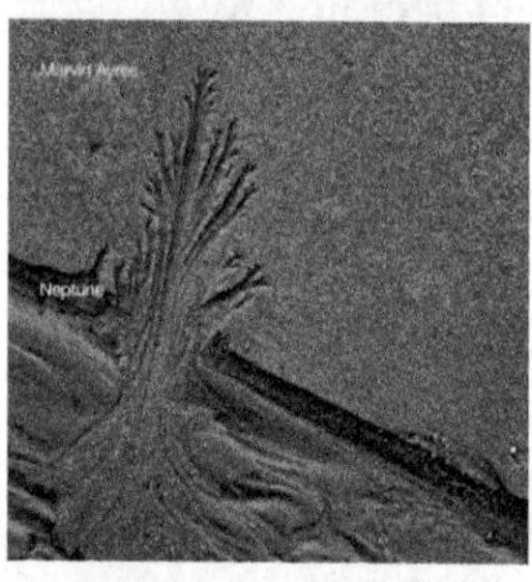

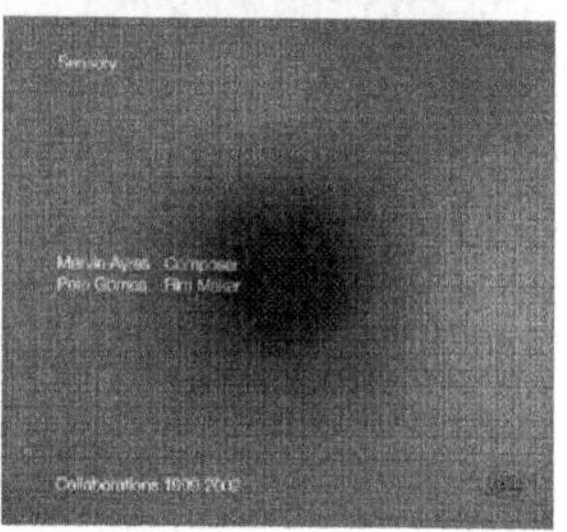

MARVIN AYRES
CELLOSPHERE

MARVIN AYRES
NEPTUNE

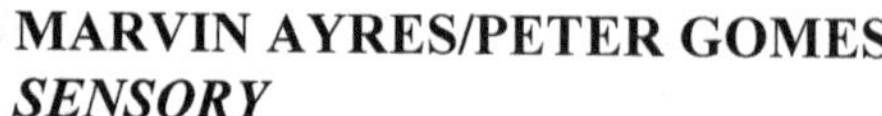

MARVIN AYRES/PETER GOMES
SENSORY

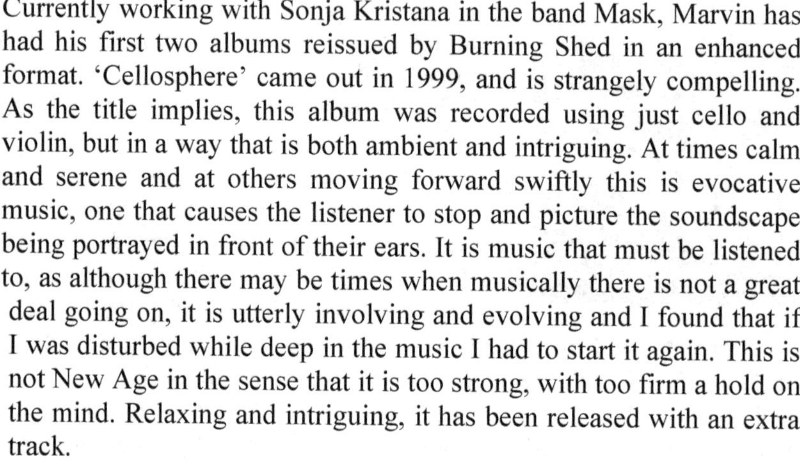

Currently working with Sonja Kristana in the band Mask, Marvin has had his first two albums reissued by Burning Shed in an enhanced format. 'Cellosphere' came out in 1999, and is strangely compelling. As the title implies, this album was recorded using just cello and violin, but in a way that is both ambient and intriguing. At times calm and serene and at others moving forward swiftly this is evocative music, one that causes the listener to stop and picture the soundscape being portrayed in front of their ears. It is music that must be listened to, as although there may be times when musically there is not a great deal going on, it is utterly involving and evolving and I found that if I was disturbed while deep in the music I had to start it again. This is not New Age in the sense that it is too strong, with too firm a hold on the mind. Relaxing and intriguing, it has been released with an extra track.

The follow-up was 'Neptune', which has been reissued with two films. As with 'Cellosphere' the majority of the music was created by strings (keyboards do feature on one track), although here Marvin stresses that all of the instruments are electric as opposed to acoustic, and he also uses violas. This is very much a continuation of the work on the debut with Marvin using his knowledge of the instruments to create music that is again intriguing, compelling and swirling, direct yet also very much at a tangent to what many people would imagine when being told that the album contains only strings. It is music that creates an atmosphere, something tangible that lets the listener into a world that is very much of Marvin's creation.

'Sensory' is a three-track DVD (yes, I know I normally review DVDs separately, but this just seems to fit in so well with the two CDs) and is a collaboration between Marvin and film-maker Peter Gomes. They combine computer-generated sequences with music to create installations that have been screened at many prestigious art galleries, including the Tate Modern. The songs can be played one after another, or they can each be set to loop continuously. The images are very different between the three songs, and although I could see what they were trying to achieve it was this one that I enjoyed the least. I think that this was because images were being forced upon me that were at a contrast with those that I was creating with my own mind. Overall the three releases are all intriguing and worth further investigation by those who enjoy their music a little gentler than most and who would like to experience something that is very different. *#82, Jan 2005*

AZAZELLO
BLACK DAY

If I had listened to this, but had not been told the country of origin I may just have guessed it, but by no means would it have been a certainty. Opener "Beginning Of The End" has a very brisk melody, and some good guitar work but there are also places where it is almost like a Gregorian chant. Yes, Azazello is a prog band from Russia! I do not know how Brian managed to hear about them in California, but this intriguing release is out on the Moonchild label. And a bloody interesting release it is as well. It is very rocky in places with the guitar being very much the lead instrument, while at others it is the keyboards, but what is so interesting about the whole album is the way that the guys keep switching styles many times, even within the same song. They have also brought to bear some Russian touches as well as the more obvious influences such as Dream Theater and Queensrÿche. It is an album that has a definite sound all of its' own and is one that many progheads are going to seek out just because it has a novelty which is all too rare in these days of progressive sound-alikes. I have thoroughly enjoyed listening to this most progressive of releases.

#58, May 2000

AZAZELLO
SEVENTH HEAVEN

In my package from Russia I was pleased to find the latest album by Azazello, as this is one band that I have come across before when I reviewed their debut 'Black Day' some years ago. Although one might think that this is the band's seventh album from the title, it is their fourth, with the same line-up throughout. All the lyrics are in Russian, but somehow that only adds to what is undoubtedly a progressive album, but an unusual one at that. Although it could be said that at times this sounds a bit like Pallas, there are far more influences than just the 'normal' ones, as they also bring in Russian folk and very Seventies keyboards sounds to make a sound that is very much of their own.

Alexander Kulak can play some mean guitars when he wants to but it is never to the detriment of the keyboards and there are some intricate drum and bass patterns going on as well. There are some longish instrumental passages which allow the band to show just what they are capable of, and progheads are going to be impressed with this as there are some fascinating styles being melded together in a way that is uncommon. I believe that this album has only been released in Russia so far, but it does deserve a wider market as it is something that most progheads will enjoy. The booklet has also been well put together but again it is all in Russian so I can only admire it as a piece of art!

#85, Nov 2005

MAX BACON
FROM THE BANKS OF THE RIVER IRWIN

Max Bacon is a vocalist that I have always admired, having loved his work on the GTR album, although I did cringe when he was on New Faces (something not mentioned in the booklet…). This album is named after the song which is sung at Old Trafford, as Max wrote the lyrics for it when he was but a child! This album brings together songs from different periods of Max's career from 1989 to the present day, and some of these will be of great interest to people for more than just the music.

The first five songs are all taken from a rock supergroup that never released the material – namely Geoff Downes (Asia – who also wrote all the material), Phil Spalding (GTR, Toyah), Scott Gorham (Thin Lizzy) and Michael Sturgis. These songs are very good, and it is something of a surprise that they were not released as it shows a band that while heavier than Asia were extremely melodic and would have gone down a storm in the States. Virtually any of these could have been released as a single with the rockier "Boys From Diamond City" my personal favourite. Also included in the collection is Mike Oldfield's "Earth Moving" for which Max contributed the original vocal. He was replaced for the version that appeared on Mike's album but here it is as was originally performed. With self-penned numbers such as "Carrie" bouncing along in an extremely pleasant AOR fashion it is some surprise not only that Max has not had a major career but also that this is only his second solo album. He has a great voice and this is an enjoyable collection.
#70, Oct 2002

VLADIMIR BADIROV
GREETINGS FROM NOSTRADAMUS

Vladimir is a drummer from Uzbekistan, and although he has been working in various bands and projects over the years this is his first solo album and it is quite different to anything that I have previously heard. As he is a drummer this is where the songs first come from and the result is music that is moving around on different rhythms. He is also trying to mix different cultures so as well as electric guitars there are also traditional Uzbek folk instruments such as nai, ud, tanbur, karnai and sato. With brass also playing their part (not all instruments are on every track) this is something very strange indeed. The guitars can be rough and dirty with heavy bottom end distortion, or they may be clear and clean or they not be on a track at all! Although it has been released by Unicorn, who are much more well-known for progressive and jazz rock, this can only be treated as world music as it is bringing in so many folk influences and to my Western ears this is quite difficult to listen to. Treat with caution, but you may be intrigued.
#82, Jan 2005

FRANCK BALESTRACCI
EXISTENCES INVISBLES

Recommended Records originally released this album as a CD-R in 2002, and it is now getting a full digipak reissue by the Belgian Carbon 7 label. This is a totally solo album by Franck, who originally trained as a drummer so at least the drums that are on the album are real as opposed to programmed. But, this is keyboard-based music by those who want something different. Although it does contain smoother passages, there are sections which are very jazz-like and the whole album is rather challenging to listen to as many times it does not appear to be making much musical sense. It is not one that a listener could sit down and play for pleasure as the music takes itself far more earnestly and seriously to be entertainment. For me this is not something to which I will readily be returning.

#84, July 2005

BAND OF RAIN
DEEP SPACE

BAND OF RAIN
GARLANDS

One could argue, and quite convincingly, that the debut album from Band Of Rain is space rock but that would in no way manage to convey just how good this (mostly) instrumental album is. One problem with space rock is that most people initially think of Hawkwind and then attempt to capture that sound, or something very close to it, but that is not the case here. Apart from vocals from Andy Fisher on two songs, the whole thing has been performed by Chris Gill who often appears to be approaching the music from a bassist's point of view, which gives the music a quite different angle. There are also fewer keyboards than one might normally associate with the genre, and when Chris decides to hit the power chords this album works. Yes there is a feeling of improvisation and there are times when the music does wander but it is soon pulled back in again and the feeling is of a very tight album with strong production (something else not always associated with the genre).

The second Band Of Rain album came out in 2005, and again (although this time I could very well be wrong) this is the work just of Chris Gill. Unfortunately, the CD does not detail the players, although there does now appear to be a band but I am not sure if that is for the third (currently unreleased) album. Anyway, solo or band, this is a strong continuation of the first album. Again what impressed me immediately is the strength of the production – the sound is very good indeed and that adds to the album. Those who feel that space rock should be virtually unlistenable should be sent this as an example. There are feelings of Gong at times and possibly small amounts of Ozrics but again Chris has gone his own path and is producing music that is of a consistently high standard without sounding like anyone else. Both albums prove that this genre can be a much wider style than one may normally expect and if you are into prog, psyche, space rock or just music to expand your own consciousness then these are a good place to start and Chris is British so support him and Band of Rain! *#88, Jun 2006*

PETER BANKS
CAN I PLAY YOU SOMETHING?

To be polite about this collection, while some of the songs are interesting, it is not for their musicality that people are going to be searching this out, but rather for the rarity of some of the pieces. Peter Banks was of course the original guitarist in Yes, but he had originally joined forces with Chris Squire in Syn, and later in Mabel Greer's Toyshop. There are five songs by the former and five by the latter, as well as one by Peter Banks' first ever band, The Devil's Disciples. This is one for the collector then instead of the pure music lover, but interesting all the same. *#57, Mar 2000*

BARCLAY JAMES HARVEST
REVOLUTION DAYS

When I was doing my degree I spent a lot of my time in record shops, and was intrigued by a double cassette of a band named Barclay James Harvest. I bought the tape, and 'Time Honoured Ghosts' and 'Octoberon' could often be heard blasting out from my room. I quickly purchased a lot of BJH albums and I was particularly taken by the fact that there were two songwriters who did not write together, but produced songs that were complimentary. John Lees played guitar and provided lead vocals on his songs, while Les Holroyd played bass and sang lead on his songs. It was not until I received this album that I realised that all has not been well in the BJH camp, as this album has been released by Barclay James Harvest (Featuring Les Holroyd). Apparently, there has been a major split and Les and Mel Pritchard (drums) are in one version of the band while John Lees and Stuart "Woolly" Wolstenholme (keyboards, who had retired from the band some years before) are in another. There is a stylised butterfly on the front cover (all BJH covers have a butterfly on them somewhere), but a bit like the record it is not the real thing. Les always provided the softer material, and while this is a good album it misses out by not having John's songs to play against. It is an album that obviously all BJH fans should buy but it is a bit like yin without the yang. I enjoyed it, but it is missing something, and that something is John. They have been together for many years and I sincerely hope that they will patch up their differences and yet again delight concertgoers the world over. It is not bad, but if you want an introduction to the band then pick up 'Concert For The People' or 'Live Tapes'.
#67, Apr 2002

BARROCK
OXIAN

This is the second album by Barrock, who hail from Pordenone in Italy. Comprising four musicians, together with two female vocalists, this album is unlike much music currently around. In fact, the group they have most in common with is The Enid. 'Oxian' is one that takes its inspiration from music of the past, most notably baroque and renaissance, but mixes these well with more modern ideas. The lyrics that exist are sung in Italian, but it is the instrumental quality of this album that makes it shine. They can switch from delicate, almost chamber music, to sweeping orchestral with punishing electric guitar without a pause for breath. Anyone who likes the more complex work of ELP, or maybe even The Nice (although with different keyboard sounds) would find something here for them. The diversity of the music may not appeal to those who want a more 'rock' based approach, but if you are remotely interested in classical music and are open to a new interpretation then this will be for you.
#27, Feb 1995

COLIN BASS
AN OUTCAST OF THE ISLANDS

This is the Polish release, but I am sure that this must have been released through the rest of Europe as well. Here Colin has been joined by his Camel bandmates Andy Latimer and Dave Stewart, so obviously Camel fans will be after this. But, it must be said that on the face of it this is quite a strange project with Colin being joined by members of the Polish band Quidam, and most of the album being recorded in Poland and featuring members of the Poznan Philharmonic Orchestra. If you like Camel, then you are going to love this mix of powerful instrumentals and more gentle songs. Yes, it is 'progressive', but again this is an album that shows just what vastly different styles of music that term covers. I know that Colin played a gig on the continent with Galahad last month, and they are totally different bands, with Colin approaching from a more symphonic gentle style while Stu and the guys power in from the more rock side. You must be in the mood for this as it is quite bland and atmospheric and it can be a lot to take in at one sitting but that shouldn't detract from what is basically a very good album. If you like prog rock from the gentler side of the spectrum, then seek this one out. *#54, July 1999*

ADRIAN BELEW
SIDE ONE

This is the first of three albums scheduled for release over the next year by King Crimson guitarist Adrian Belew (the others will be called 'Side Two' and 'Side Three'). Each CD will be musically very different and Adrian decided that a power trio would play the first of these so he has been joined on this project by Primus bassist Les

Claypool and Tool drummer Danny Carey. The result is a very eclectic mix of music that seems to have been influenced as much by XTC as it has by Frank Zappa, while there is also a huge slice of Talking Heads in there. This is art rock, and at times can be extremely commercial and hook-laden which is when the album works at its best, as there are others where it breaks down and the result is something that just is not pleasant to listen to. It can also be repetitive, particularly with the vocals. There is no doubt that Adrian is an incredible guitarist, and the guys he has brought into this are no musical slouches but I am not sure who would purchase this unless they are already fans of his work.
#83, Mar 2005

BELIEVE
HOPE TO SEE ANOTHER DAY
Even before playing a note this band are going to be getting quite a few progheads excited as it has been formed by Collage founder member and guitarist Mirek Gil. He has also brought on board Collage's original bassist Przemek Zawadzki and the singer who fronted the band on their debut album 'Basnie', Tomek Rózycki (who also provides guitar). So with other ex-members of one of Poland's finest ever prog bands now working as Satellite, we now have two bands working again but whereas Satellite have released two albums this is the debut for Believe. Keyboard player Adam Milosz and drummer Wlodke Tafel complete the line-up, while Japanese violinist Satomi helps as a guest. This is a very punchy album, with the two guitars being used to provide a lot of depth but at no times does this stray into prog metal territory. This is a prog rock album with the emphasis firmly on both words, not just the first as is common with far too many bands, with Mirek firmly in the driving seat. All the lyrics are in English this time (Tomek sang in Polish on 'Basnie'). It is an album that while influenced of course not only by Collage but bands such as IQ and King Crimson, but also with a rockier approach with the band themselves saying that they feel that Stone Temple Pilots have influenced what they are producing. It is not as directly accessible as some, but is still something that I have been playing a great deal

#87, Apr 2006

ROBERT BERRY
PILGRIMAGE TO A POINT
Robert Berry has worked with some of rock's greatest musicians, being in both GTR and 3, the latter being the band formed by Berry, with Keith Emerson and Carl Palmer. Although he did not record with GTR, two of the songs he wrote with Steve Howe are included on this album, along with one he wrote with Palmer and one with Emerson. A biography is provided, along with loads of photos and a family tree (as well as the lyrics, of course), making a nice little package for anyone interested in ELP, GTR or Yes. All in all it is a great album, which has

just been made available in the UK thanks to Cyclops. Unsurprisingly some of the songs carry with them the mark of the bands they were originally written for, such as "Shelter" which has 3 stamped all over it. (I liked that album '3 To The Power of 3' – must have been the only one).

Robert has good clear vocals, along with some nifty guitarwork, and he has put together his recent experiences in a way that will appeal to many. Sometimes albums are released that completists must get because of one track or another, and the album is rarely if ever played. However, GTR, ELP and Yes fans who search this out will be grateful that they have it as it is a superb collection. Favourite is probably "Shelter" which combines in the same song such delicacy and over the top bombast as to be a real winner.
#29, Jun 1995

BEYOND THE LABYRINTH
SIGNS

I have not come across a great many bands from Belgium, but I am glad that I have come across this one, as this is a fine debut. This is very approachable prog rock, but with the emphasis more on the melody and classic rock stylings as opposed to complicated complexity. In some ways they remind me of the long lost The Covenant, but with more keyboards. The vocals are powerful and much more in rock fashion as opposed to being anything extremely fancy. While the music is punchy and powerful it was the lyrics that caught my attention the first time that I played it. Guitarist and lyricist (and most of the music as well) Geert Fieuw has a way of grabbing attention on a myriad of subjects, whether it be about the first World War, media, or the story of a person who can see events in the future.

But for me the highlight is "Freak Show" where fairground music and an announcer lead us into the music world as they see it "Moving on from town to town, Gotta get the message heard, Gotta keep the music going on, Won't you spread the word? They say we're out of format, they tell us that we don't belong, insist that we are out of fashion, Gotta prove them wrong". In an email, Geert told me the following: "The Visionary" is about Nostradamus and his '99 prediction of the eclipse, seen from his point of view. Obligatory, we read one of his quatrains at the end of the song. (How Cliché eh?) But ... in "Icons", the same voice reads something too... in the second verse we sing "collapsing towers, as foretold"... And in the bridge the same voice reads out the so-called prediction for 9-11... However... that one is a hoax; it's not even a quatrain (3 phrases, not 4)... So beware of double hidden meanings meant to set you on the wrong foot". This is punchy radio friendly progressive classic rock that deserves to be heard by a much wider audience. It is a very accessible fun album and one that lovers of melodic rock would do well to investigate further – it is a goody.
#89, Sep 2006

BIG BIG TRAIN

FROM THE RIVER TO THE SEA (DEMO)

Well, what can I tell you about this new prog rock band from sunny Bournemouth? Not a great deal as it happens. The other day a tape and brief bio popped through my letterbox, and since then all attempts to contact Greg Spawton have failed miserably, so here is all I know. Greg (guitars), Ian Cooper (keyboards) and Andy Poole (bass) joined together as songwriting unit in February 1990. Vocalist Martin Read joined in March 1991 with Steve Hughes on drums completing the line-up soon thereafter, and they have just released their first tape 'From the River To The Sea': and very good it is too. I do not know what keyboards are used, but I suspect that there is a Mellotron in there somewhere. The keyboards give a very Seventies feel to most of the album, but this does not detract from it in any way. It kicks off with "To The Sea", which is a very upbeat song that allows Greg to dominate without ever going over the top. Andy has a chance to display his ability with some great bass runs, but always Martin's clear voice presides over proceedings. As the song changes into a different melody I found the name Galahad coming to mind all the time. Big Big Train are very much in similar vein, and I notice they thank Stu in the credits (I presume it is he who put them onto me). There are ten songs on this fifty-minute album and I enjoyed all of them. Many have changes of style within them, but I wonder if my favourite, "Downhilling", is a portent of things to come as it is far heavier than the other material, which includes at times the use of a piano and acoustic guitar with lots of contrast. If you like Genesis (prog not pop), Galahad or Marillion, then this is the band for you. The tape is available from Greg, and includes a lyric sheet.

#11, Dec 1991

BIG BIG TRAIN

FROM THE RIVER TO THE SEA (CD)

When I reviewed BBT's debut tape back in #11 I knew very little about them, only that they had sent me a tape with a brief bio and a photo to which I could not even put names. In recent months the band have gone from strength to strength, and as the album 'From The River To The Sea' is now out on CD (having been reworked and re-recorded in places and with two extra tracks), it is time to update you on the situation. It has been released on Galahad's own Avalon label, with an initial pressing of one thousand. At the time of writing it has been available for six weeks and has sold about a quarter of that, mainly abroad needless to say. The band are pleased with the initial pick-up, as they have only played one gig since release (supporting Jadis at The Standard). As they play more gigs in the summer then sales will increase as more people become aware of its availability. The tape was widely liked, and most of the fanzines had kind words to say about it, but what does the CD sound like? On first listen, it is clear that the overall sound has greatly benefited from the extra work BBT have put into the recording, and that Greg is an outstanding guitarist. There are passages with some great riffing, such as in "Jas", where BBT power along. In contrast, there are acoustic spots with gentle piano tinkling, such as at the beginning of "Full Head of Steam". The latter changes into a wonderfully catchy rock song, which shows just how tight the band is.

They work well together, especially considering that they have only been a unit since March 1991. I have only one small criticism, in that I would have liked the vocals to have been slightly higher in the mix in a couple of songs like "Downhilling", but it is still a great CD and well worth purchasing even if you already own the tape. Future plans include working on material for the next BBT album, tentatively called 'Landfall', which should be out in early 1993.
#14, Jul 1992

BIG BIG TRAIN

The Infant Hercules

BIG BIG TRAIN
THE INFANT HERCULES

It seems a very long time ago that I first heard BBT. Their first tape turned up one day, and I was extremely impressed with what I heard and gave it a glowing review. Since then they have released a CD, 'From The River To The Sea', on Galahad's Avalon label, and now we have another tape, 'The Infant Hercules'. In just one year it is surprising how much the band has grown in stature. True, they have played live a lot more, but now they give an impression of a band that really knows what they want to achieve. They sound really together, and on a purely musical level they have developed further than could have been imagined. With 'The Infant Hercules' they have produced a tape that really vindicates all the nice things I have been saying about them in the past.

It easily surpasses what has gone before, and I really liked that! Greg's guitarwork is exemplary, and is probably the biggest single factor in the band's improvement, but whether you concentrate on Andy's bass, Martin's vocals, Steve's drumming (some great fills) or Ian's keyboards, it is just not possible to find a weak link. The songs and lyrics are better, and the production is spot on. Yep, a sure-fire winner that is going to make them many new friends and certainly please all those who have bought their previous product. The band have a harder edge than before, just listen to the guitarwork on the instrumental "Red Five". Criticisms?

Well, there is only one, which is that this really should be out on CD. I question whether or not enough people will buy a tape to give the band the exposure they richly deserve. BBT should get into the studio, add some more tracks onto this, and get it out on CD now! There are seven great songs on here, and it comes complete with a lyric sheet. On the insert you will find a quote from yours truly that BBT have been using for a year. Here's another: Big Big Train are going to be a Big Big Band, and it would be a mortal sin for any prog rock lover to miss out on the joys of 'The Infant Hercules'.
#17, Mar 1993

BIG BIG TRAIN
GOODBYE TO THE AGE OF STEAM

BBT have returned with their second CD, which is their third full-length recording ('The Infant Hercules', their last release was only available on tape). It is their first release on GEP and features on backing vocals Martin Orford (IQ, Jadis), Gary Chandler (Jadis) and Stu Nicholson (Galahad) among others. I have been a champion of BBT since the release of their first demo, and must admit that I found all the 'extra' vocals initially disconcerting. I mean, it was something that BBT hadn't done before, and I allowed myself to be distracted away from the album as a whole. I felt that the album had been over Jadis-ised, due especially to the influence of Martin Orford. However, with more listening I realise that my initial views were incorrect and while BBT may have real problems recreating this in a live environment, the extra vocals have actually added to and not detracted from the overall effect. While Andy and Steve provide the backbone, the mainstay of BBT's sound is Greg's guitar. While never providing heavy rock chords, it has a real edge to it, prevalent in tracks such as "Edge Of The Known World". Martin's vocals have also come of age with this release, while Ian provides keyboards that swirl and wrap around. These last two elements come together best in "Blow The House Down" which starts off as a beautiful ballad with just Ian and Martin, but in the middle, there is some sterling guitarwork that transforms the whole piece. Near the end there are harmony vocals of the highest calibre, which work well within the overall context. Eventually it all slows down again. Wonderful. BBT have proved yet again that they really are a band to investigate, and now that they are on GEP maybe we'll be seeing a lot more of them. I hope so, because an album as good as this is crying out to be heard.
#23, May 1994

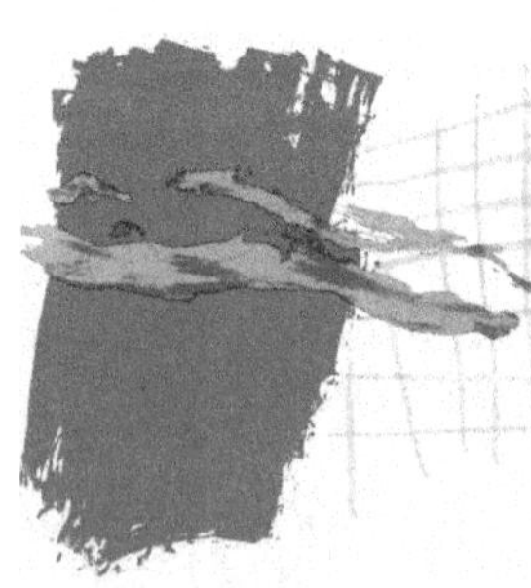

BIG BIG TRAIN
ENGLISH BOY WONDERS

I have always had a soft spot for the South Coast proggers, there hasn't been a lot to report recently as on the live front they are not the most prolific gig players (at last count it was twelve since inception), and it has been a while since 'Goodbye To The Age Of Steam'. I remember being cornered in a pub by guitarist Greg Spawton and bassist Andy Poole asking me what I initially thought of it, and having to admit that I was not too keen as to my ears it had been over-produced and the usage of many guest vocalists had taken the sound totally away from what I felt BBT were all about (although my views did change). I am glad to report that not only are BBT firmly back on track with their third album, but also that it is easily the best thing they have done so far, with a feeling of space that was sadly missing from previous efforts. One of the joys of their debut 'From The River To The Sea' was the naiveté of it all, but it was let down by the vocals of Martin Read, and I wondered at the time if he was up to the job. They have kept the faith, and have been amply rewarded as Martin shines, especially when accompanied by acoustic guitar and gentle piano, along with the lulling flute provided

by Martin Orford as on "28 Years". Many people will always view BBT as a prog band, but they have moved quite a long way from what is seen as the "norm", becoming more of an adult oriented songs band. This is not AOR, but good songs well-crafted and performed, which sadly will only ever reach a small percentage of those who would enjoy them. I am not sure what commercial success Big Big Train will find with this release, but they can be happy with the fact that this work stands comparison very favourably indeed with most of the music you are likely to find around at present. It is an album that will be appreciated by all those who have the good fortune to hear it.
#46, Dec 1997

BIG BIG TRAIN
BARD
The band has been through quite a shift since the last one and BBT are now just the two main members Greg Spawton and Andy Poole with assorted others. I had always felt that Martin Read's vocals were something of a weak point for the band but here he is sounding at his best, and the band have moved on by also using Tony Müller (who originally joined the band as keyboard player) and female singer Jo Michaels. Add to that a more fluid dynamic style and the result is an album that while staying within the realms of their musical past is a giant leap forwards. The production is top notch and the overall effect is of a band at the top of all of their powers, instead of one that according to their web-site is seriously considering packing it in. Big Big Train were never much of a live act, in fact I think that they have played less than twenty shows in their ten-year plus existence (I caught one of those at The Astoria, and they were much better than their confidence showed), and have relied on CD sales to keep their profile going. However, they are another act that has suffered through the downturn in the prog scene, but hopefully this album will do well enough to make them reconsider their position. It is full of depth and balance, well-produced and full of melody and soul that makes it an enjoyable jaunt. Nice one lads – you owe it to yourselves to keep it going.
#67, Apr 2002

BIG BIG TRAIN
GATHERING SPEED
Big Big Train have only ever had one weakness in their musical arsenal, that of vocals. For their fourth album they have definitely got to grips with that by bringing in singer Sean Filkins. Sean used to be in Lorien, whose SI album 'Children's Games' I reviewed some eleven years ago in #22 (by the way – I still have the press photo – blackmail can be a powerful thing). Although the music for this concept album was basically written prior to his involvement, it sounds as if he has been there from the outset. It is strange to think that apart from Sean and additional vocalist Laura Murch, the other four guys were all there at the beginning, some

thirteen years ago. Mind you, the only constants in the intervening time have been guitarist Greg Spawton and bassist Andy Poole, but the guys have come back together in order to produce their masterpiece. This album tells the story of a spitfire pilot who is shot down during the Battle Of Britain, and is easily their most musically complex to date. It has an extremely polished sound (due in no small part to the involvement of Rob Aubrey), but the layered vocals fit in with the different sections so that it is hard to imagine the band sounding any other way. In parts it is almost Floydian as the music moves like waves, with plenty of space for the music to get into the psyche. Starting with the roaring of merlin engines flying overhead, the gentle almost Genesis-style guitars soon become much harsher, showing that here is a band with their own musical identity – it goes back to the classic days of the early Seventies but is also very much for today. Even though the songs are not exactly short, there is the feeling throughout that there is definite structure which gives the music definition and purpose. There is just so many good things to say about this CD that by far the easiest is just that if you like modern progressive rock then this is an album to savour. This really is a million miles away from 'From The River To The Sea' (thinking about it, I probably have photos of the band from then as well – I must get them out of my file...). They seriously thought about ending the band after 'Bard' – that in itself was a great album, but this is even better. *#79, May 2004*

BIG PICTURE
BIG PICTURE

I am afraid that I know very little about this album, or in fact the band behind it, as I was sent it by Artur from Poland. However, I do know that they are an American five-piece and the album (presumably their debut) was released in 1993. It is quite a pleasant excursion into American prog with some stop offs on the way to visit Saga and even Pendragon. What lets the album down for the most part is the way that the guitars are muted and the keyboards given dominance. Now, that's not a bad thing per se, but with the songs written the way that they are, the impression is given that there is something missing. But, there are some songs where they do let the guitars take the lead and it is these where Big Picture really come through. I see that this is the only Big Picture album listed by GFT, so it is quite possible that it is the only one released. If so it is a shame as there is real promise and who knows, the next time they might have delivered. *#29, Jun 1995*

BLACK BONZO
LADY OF THE LAKE

This is the debut album from Black Bonzo, and it is hard to believe that these guys are from Sweden and that this is a new recording. Why? Because this sounds as if it is a lost Uriah Heep album from 1970/71. Given that Heep were prolific but did not have time to record an album and then discard it we have to take the evidence as read that this is indeed a new record. Heep are still going strong today

of course, but they had stopped making music quite like this the best part of thirty years ago, so these young Swedes have taken it upon themselves to resurrect a style of music that many of us thought was long behind us. There are swathes of Mellotrons and especially Hammond Organs, there are stacks of guitars and wonderful Byron style vocals but most importantly there are also some great songs. "Lady Of The Light" could be viewed as a classic Heep number, it contains all of the right elements in the right quantities to make any Heep lover to reach for the volume control to turn it up. Black Bonzo are not another of those annoying tribute bands as they have taken a musical style that they admire, have thrown some extra influences into it such as Purple and early Crimson, and have then developed songs around these. There are no covers on this album, they are all band originals, and whether they are ballads such as "Brave Young Soldier" or the blasting "Jailbait" this is a young band with a huge future in front of them. Can they keep it up with future albums? Only time will tell, but for now this is an album that every classic rock lover must obtain. It is orderable from Sweden and the US but I am not sure if it is readily available in the UK, but it is worth the effort.
#84, July 2005

BLACKFIELD
BLACKFIELD

One of the joys of writing about music is that sometimes you can be sent a CD which really blows the mind, and the debut album by Blackfield is a case in point. Given that it took them three years to record this one I wouldn't hang around waiting for the next one, but that may be something to do both with geography and schedules given that the band are Steven Wilson (Porcupine Tree, no-man etc.) and Israeli performer Aviv Geffen (plus various guest drummers). Aviv is well known in his own country, especially for his lyrics where he stands up against the military and for those with no voice. This album is so expansive that the only true term would be progressive rock, because this is music that is stretching the boundaries of what is expected and although it is going in a different direction I found that I kept being reminded of Neal Morse. But this music is somehow more expansive, more layered, still with plenty of Beatles and Pink Floyd references yet sounding like neither of them. Sometimes it is just the gentle notes on the piano behind the instrumentation that lifts it, sometimes it can be a few crunching riffs, the joy of listening to an album where there are obviously no rules is that one never knows what is going to come next. Gentle vocals can be the harbinger of music that is anything but, or it could just be the way that the whole song is constructed, one is never sure at the outset. Production of this album is extremely high class, as one would expect, and I found that sometimes I just wanted to listen to this quietly while at others it was played very loudly indeed. The album comes in a digipak, and it was only when playing it in the house that I found that hidden inside was another CD containing some more songs not on the main album plus a video. One of the strongest prog rock albums I have heard in a long time, it certainly does not fit into the neo-prog scene, but is an album that all progheads and lovers of good music should snap up immediately. *#81, Dec 2004*

BLACK JESTER
WELCOME TO THE MOONLIGHT CIRCUS
Another great Italian act, but quite different to Top Left Corner, as while Black Jester are a prog band they are firmly built around the technical guitar playing of Paolo Viani. Paolo is an outstanding guitarist, very fluent and quick, and happy in many styles. It is his guitar playing that sets Black Jester well apart from most other prog bands.

They are on the heavy side of prog, although more Dream Theater than Threshold. There are hints of Satriani in what they are doing, but they are much more than a one-man band. Black Jester are a very tight outfit, with each being a strong musician. There really is not a weak link in this album, as the vocals are also spot on and the melodies are interesting, although at times they do seem to be just carriers for some amazing guitarwork. This is an album I have been returning to, and can see me doing so again in the future. Anyone who is into technical rock must surely love this. *#31, Oct 1995*

BLACK JESTER
THE DIVINE COMEDY
I seem to remember reviewing one of the earlier albums by Italian outfit Black Jester, and they have now returned with their third, which is on Elevate but distributed by GFT. There is nothing like being ambitious and they have attempted to produce a concept album based on Dante's masterpiece. Does it work? Well, the CD is divided into three movements ("Inferno", "Purgatorio" and "Paradiso") and although there are twenty-one separate named sections it is only possibly to track to these three, and not the individual songs. This makes the album fairly hard going, but it is worth persevering with, as there are some touches of sheer brilliance. For example, the second song in "Purgatorio" is called "Harbour of Sinners" and it fairly belts along with some extremely strong guitarwork. Black Jester are often placed with the heavier prog bands, and certainly there are some breath-taking guitar runs that owe a lot to Dream Theater and even bands like Iron Maiden, but at the same time there is far more depth and subtlety than one might initially expect. I also ought to make mention of the CD booklet, which is very well presented and the cover artwork is superb. *#47, Feb 1998*

THE BLACK NOODLE PROJECT
AND LIFE GOES ON
The Black Noodle Project started life in 2001 as just one man, Jérémie Grima, who wished to record personal musical ideas from a solo viewpoint. In 2002 Jérémie released a demo, which Musea liked and he decided to set up a label called B-Smile Records to promote the album. The project soon became a band, with Jérémie (lead guitar and vocals) being joined by Arnaud Rousset (drums, Brainstore),

Antony Leteve, (bass, Spectrum of Oblivion) and Matthieu Jaubert (keyboards). The line-up has changed since the recording, but these are the guys on the CD. For a debut album it is certainly very polished, let down only slightly by the production but as this was self-produced due to finances this can obviously be corrected in the future. It starts gently enough; lulling the listener in with some background noise as the band gradually finds their way into the music. Although it can appear to be simplistic, it is actually constructed so that the listener concentrates carefully on what is going on and the Gilmore/Latimer/Chandler guitar solo that comes in makes total sense. There is a strong use of acoustic guitar and the result is music where Pink Floyd has been crossed with Roine Stolt in a way that makes for an album that is extremely enjoyable and open. Yes, this is prog, but it is easily accessible on first hearing, and is one that I have found that the more I play it the more I get out of it. This simply has to be one of the best I have heard from France; actually, I think it's the best I have heard since Minimum Vital's 'La Source' many years ago. After I had listened to and enjoyed the album I asked Jérémie about his influences and he responded as follows: - "I guess every musician in the band has his own, but I do not think I'm mistaken if I say that almost everyone has been influenced by Pink Floyd, of course. I like to work with open-minded people and everyone in the band listens to many different styles. For example, I really used to like metal when I was younger and I think it does influence my work now, but I like also movie soundtracks (I just LOVE cinema), folk music, pop rock and many different kinds of music. In fact, I'm interested in everything with true emotions and research... A band getting my admiration is The Gathering from Holland. They can do so many different things with so much emotion... So many styles and at the same time so much personality. Even if I do not want my music to look the same as theirs, it's a big influence in the way they handle their career and their music. About my guitar playing, I guess I always loved musicians who could forget technical stuff and only play real emotions even if it's one or two notes in a minute. I think Miles Davis (I think he did) said: "Why do a thousand notes when only the good one are necessary". I totally agree with it. It's for that reason that I like very much a guitarist like Slash from Guns 'n' Roses who could only have five notes solo if it's just melodic and emotional. David Gilmore too, of course, but also Tommy T. Baron from the old Swiss metal band Coroner..."

If you like Floyd, then you will love this.
#83, Mar 2005

THE BLACK NOODLE PROJECT
PLAY AGAIN

Formed in 2001 by guitarist and singer Jérémie Grima, The Black Noodle Project are already back with their second album, following on from 2004's 'And Life Goes On'. I enjoyed that album, and was in contact with Jérémie at the time, and am pleased to note that the second album continues in the vein of the first but is also moving forward into new directions. That the band is very influenced by Pink Floyd is never in doubt, yet there is much more coming into the music as the band continue to develop. There are some female vocals taking the lead at times,

some violin here and there, and the band have also moved into Muse and Porcupine Tree territory with some hard-hitting guitar. This is a band that is still moving onwards but this album is a step change on from the last one, and I enjoyed that! Here there is power and depth, so that the listener gets more out of it each time that is played – and it certainly does repay repeated listening. By going onto their website it is possible to play some of the songs, and is definitely worth trying out as the band move away from the pure Floydian emphasis (although that is here as well) into something that has more bite and edge.
#89, Sep 2006

TIM BLAKE
THE TIDE OF THE CENTURY
This is quite a different album to the ones I reviewed last time by Tim. There is no information whatsoever, but I get the impression that this is a new album as opposed to a reissue. Tim has used some guests, sparingly, and while the keyboards are stronger and more forceful than before it is actually a piano, vocal number that is by far the standout track. "St. Dolay" is beautiful, relying for the most part on simple piano and Tim's vocals. There is a delicate keyboard solo which adds to the ambience of the song as a whole, and I felt that this would definitely not sound out of place on an album by Dulcimer for example, or possibly early Chris De Burgh. The album is very different to his earlier work, and while the dreamy aspects of his keyboard playing can still be heard it definitely takes more of a back seat this time. Good.
#61, Feb 2001

BLURT
THE FISH NEEDS A BIKE
I presume that the title is taken from the old saying that a woman needs a man like a fish needs a bicycle. As well as being the title of one of the songs on the album it also was a single for Blurt twenty years ago! Blurt may only be known within certain circles, but Ted Milton formed the band in 1979 and has been going ever since. They are currently a trio with Ted on sax and vocals, with a guitarist Steve Eagles and drummer Paul Wigens. There are no details with this CD as to when each of the songs comes from, but checking Ted's website it appears to be pretty much from throughout his career. This is music that refuses to compromise – in some ways it could be termed jazz, or dance, or funk, but really it refuses to sit in neat pigeonholes and instead wants music lovers with broad minds to plug in and check out. It can be choppy and harsh, or rock based and more fluid, the music changes immensely from one song to the next. I found that the first few times I played it I really did not like it at all, but gradually I found that there were certain sections that seemed to make sense and the more I persevered the more I enjoyed it. Jazz-punk progressive with attitude? Maybe. Music to kill with when the surreal poems are being read? Possibly. Whatever this album is, it is not mainstream, and that in itself

can't be a bad thing and is definitely for the more adventurous. Having since been in contact with Blurt's management it appears that this CD has yet to be released, and indeed they may have to form a label just to get it out. But if you visit Ted's site you will find other albums from his career as well as tour dates. *#72, Feb 2003*

BLOW UP HOLLYWOOD
FAKE

This band are something of an enigma as no-one knows who is performing as from the beginning they decided that they would remain anonymous as they wanted to create an ego-less environment for the band to work in. Consequently, the booklet contains some arty shots of dummy's heads but little in the way of lyrics and nothing in the way of personnel details. Musically they are also creating an atmosphere that is quite sterile, musically bleak as opposed to being warm and inviting. Even the use of strings on the introduction of "Just Before Dawn" does nothing to improve this feeling almost of an apocalyptic event. It is almost as if Radiohead and Coldplay have got together with Japan and conspired to present something that is almost poppy in some respects, but quite different in many others. If it was being performed by them then I am sure that songs such as "Nde" would be in the charts, but of course it is not, and I doubt if this has even been made available in the UK which is a real shame. The strange thing is that I found out about this band from the Polish website of Artur Chachlowski, which is what led me to contact them and I am glad that I did. This may not be an album that is full of life and vitality but it is something that is very mature and well worth hearing, and you have to agree that it is a great band name. *#84, July 2005*

BLYNDSYDE
WHERE EXTREMES MEET

In #11, Keith Richardson reviewed this latest tape from Blyndsyde, saying "this is a very well packaged effort and comes the full KKK recommended". Well, who am I to disagree with him? I have just been sent a copy of the tape by the band, as a taster for the new CD, which should be available on November 2nd (expect a review next issue). The Lancashire-based band are a four-piece, playing what they describe as technical rock. Some of you may well be pleased to hear that there is not a keyboard in sight, and that the singer is female, Paule Van-Wijngaarden. One thing that is really noticeable about the tape is that there is one helluva amount of guitar, as Blyndsyde really rock. Many influences are apparent, but they really sound like no-one else. The music may well be too raucous for the standard prog fan, but for anyone who likes intricate rock ought to grab this with both hands. With a photo and full lyrics, the sleeve is very informative, and the music itself is loud and brilliant.
#15, Oct 1992

BLYNDSYDE

INTO THE STORM OF THE EYE

Well, here is a real rarity as far as SI Music are concerned. Not only is it a UK band that has no connection at all with Clive Nolan, but also there is not a keyboard in sight. This is because Blyndsyde are not really a prog band at all, but are increasingly being described as technical rock. Blyndsyde have always been associated with the prog scene, but there is real doubt as to whether this should be the case.

The music they play needs great technical ability, but they are far rockier and have more in common with Freewill than Galahad. Blyndsyde are only a four-piece, comprising Paule Van-Wijngaarden on vocals, Andy Whitehead on bass, John Brooks on guitar and Tony Doyle on drums. As anyone who bought their excellent demo tape 'Where Extremes Meet' can testify, they are a hard rocking outfit with clear vocals from Paule. The contrast between her soaring voice and the rest of the music is quite remarkable. First song on offer is "My Castle In The Green": with guitars riffing and bass and drums powering along, any thoughts that here is an album for the fainthearted are quickly blasted away. With Paule singing (as opposed to shouting) over the top, the differing styles meet and join in a sound that is instantly recognisable as their very own. No mean feat in this day and age. John has a guitar style that is very much his own, and although there are hard-hitting riffs in abundance he is no ordinary heavy metal workman, True, some of the passages could have been lifted out of the "I Want To Play Rock" textbook, but it is the way they are utilised that is important. There are some welcome respites from the bombast, such as with "Elysium", which contains restrained axework and double-tracked vocals from Paule.

There are also some dynamic instrumentals such as the title track, which starts with a killer bass riff which is copied and then transformed by the guitar. Heavy and menacing. "What It's Like" starts in a Sixties fashion, and just gets heavier and heavier, but still manages to retain its charm. The one thing I am a little concerned about is the ability for Blyndsyde to find the market they obviously deserve. They are being distributed by a prog label, yet they are not a prog band. They are heavy and furious, possibly too much for a melodic rock audience, but they have a polished edge, especially with Paule's great vocals, which may be too smooth for the metalhead. Their audience has to be one that likes and appreciates good technical skills, likes heavy guitars, and at the same time wants to hear singing as opposed to shouting or growling. If you feel that you fall into that category then this thirteen song, fifty-minute-long album, is definitely one for you. I realise that the mass media is very unlikely indeed to ever promote many of the bands in the current UK prog scene, but if Blyndsyde can break out of the prog market where they do not really belong, and into the hard rock arena (although not straight HR or HM) then they can do very well for themselves. And if someone can get "Kiss The Rose" released as a single they them might just find themselves with a surprise hit on their hands.

#17, Mar 1993

TOMAS BODIN
PINUP GURU

Tomas is of course keyboard player with The Flower Kings and this is his debut solo album. His aim was to produce an album that was similar in fashion to The Nice or ELP so he brought in band mates Jonas Reingold (bass) and Zoltan Csörsz (drums) to assist him in achieving this. While I agree he has gone some way to being able to do that, the album is still lacking in many respects. There are times when he has got it very right indeed, such as on "Harlem Heat" where he recreates the gospel atmosphere and vibrancy, but there are times when I was just wondering what was going on. There just are not enough melodies on the album to maintain interest throughout. There is no doubting that all of these guys are very fine musicians indeed but it takes more than skill to be able to produce a killer album and when it is an instrumental work it is even more difficult. Some of the Floydian touches are quite good and as a background album it is quite pleasant but certainly for me it could never be anything more than that.

#70, Oct 2002

TOMAS BODIN
SONIC BOULEVARD

Tomas Bodin is keyboard player with The Flower Kings, and this is his follow-up to 'Pin Up Guru' which came out in 2002. Initially his idea was to create a low budget album to sell through the internet where he could experiment with different styles without having to worry about budgets.

Having given a copy of the work in progress to Roine he was told that the album should be released properly. He has been joined by Roine and other musicians, so that it is not a solo album in all respects of the word. The result is an album of lengthy 'songs' which is quite dreamy and almost Floyd-like, with a lot of keyboards and some guitar. But while it works quite well as background music I can never conceive of it being any more than that. When listening to it intently the attention soon starts to drift and it is hard to overcome the urge to just eject the CD and put on something with a bit more bite to it. I am sure that there will be times when this will be the correct music for whatever I am doing, but it will not be just sat and listening to it.

#78, Apr 2004

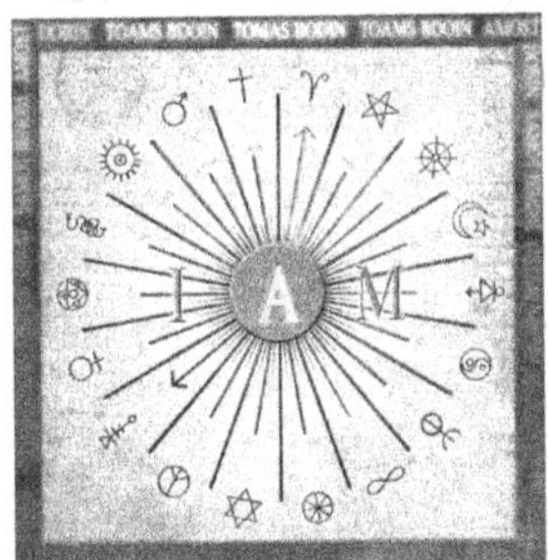

TOMAS BODIN
I AM

The fourth solo album from Flower Kings keyboard player Tomas Bodin shows him stretching out into new areas as this time he brings in extra musicians to assist in creating a prog rock opera in three acts. This is a huge leap for Tomas who previously only produced instrumental albums and here he has provided the words as well as the music. One of the major problems with his day job is that The Flower Kings can sometimes

go on for too long, producing songs that should have been edited down, but I did not feel that with this work and it did not take too long for me to realise that this is by far his best solo project to date. Jonas Reingold on bass, Marcus Liliequist on drums, and Jocke JJ Marsh on guitars have joined him and together they produce some very fluid, extremely complex music. The singers are Anders Jansson, Pernilla Bodin and Helene Schönning and they do a solid job of putting across Tomas's ideas. I am not sure if the overall concept of man's time on earth comes through as well as Tomas would have liked, but it is an interesting album if not essential, with some passages that are truly beautiful and others which are complex and complicated. This is an album that takes a lot of listens to fully get inside, and while this may not be to everyone's tastes with some very heavy riffs in places, it is something far more enjoyable than his solo works in the past.
#85, Nov 2005

JEAN PASCAL BOFFO
NOMADES

Jean Pascal Boffo's 'Jeux De Nains' was the first album ever to be released by Musea, and now seven years later 'Nomades' is the hundredth. To celebrate it has come out as a digipak, the first I have ever seen on Musea. Jean provides guitar and bass along with keyboards, and is joined by musicians on violin, soprano sax, keyboards and drums. It is quite a strange instrumental album in many ways, as although there is a lot going on there is also a sense of simplicity. The influence is mostly jazz, with rock taking very much a back seat, while the violin in particular is used in an almost Arabic way that gives a definite Eastern edge to the proceedings. There is no doubt that Jean is a fine guitarist, and the way he picks the guitar manages to give at times a Dire Straits feel, although of course it sounds nothing like Straits at all, it is an album that you have to sit and listen to, otherwise many of the nuances and intricacies just get way, but it is worth doing so. Although I was initially unsure, I found that by the time the CD was finishing I was hitting the repeat. A good 'un.
#24, Jul 1994

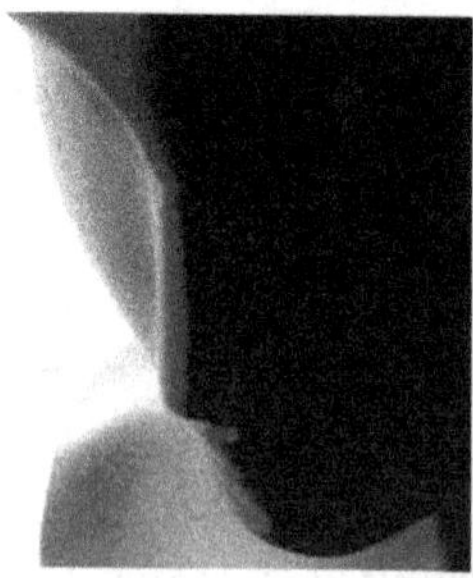

BOLT
MOVEMENT AND DETAIL

10T Records are a new progressive label from Georgia that have already signed some interesting acts such as Frogg Café, Man On Fire and Little Atlas and here they are with their debut release Bolt's 'Movement and Detail', the follow up to their 2003 'Circadian Rhythm'. All three members are credited with vocals but do not let that fool you as what we have here are a trio of musicians who are producing extremely complex instrumental music with nary a vocal in sight. This is extremely complicated stuff, with rhythms and melodies being intertwined, repeated and then take off into new tangents. In some ways it is unsettling music to listen to – they have obviously been paying close attention to Adrian Belew and Robert Fripp – yet there is also something strangely compelling about it. There is the feeling that this has been highly devised and designed, and little is left to chance or improvisation. They do bring in some jazz elements from time to time but mostly this is about creating music that is seeking to provide something that is outside of the norm with the rhythm section being as carefully crafted and organic as the melodic guitar which is always striving onwards. There are some keyboards, but these are often left behind as the trio get on with producing music for their own world.

#89, Sep 2006

THE BOND
WON BY ONE

THE BOND
PRINTS OF PEACE

The Bond were formed in February 1986, about the same time as the release of Geoff Mann's third album, 'Psalm Enchanted Evening'. Here he was joined by Dave Mortimer (guitars) and Steve Ridley (keyboards) with drums being programmed. By the time the first album was released Geoff was already training for ordination into the Church of England, so it is hardly surprising that lyrically both albums are very Christian oriented. The Bond was very much a vehicle for Geoff's outstanding song writing ability and there is not a weak track to be found: on the recent 'Mannerisms' CD a track was chosen from each of these for inclusion. By February 1989 The Bond was no more and Geoff formed the more rock oriented A Geoff Mann Band, and many people seem to look either to their albums or to Twelfth Night and miss these which is very sad as the songs on here are well worth investigating. Just listen to "New" or "Sob Stories" and discover what lyric writing is all about. These are great songs by a master of his craft.

#26, Dec 1994

ANDREW BOOKER
AHEAD

This is Andrew's first solo album, although he has been playing drums and singing in bands for many years. While at Imperial College London he combined his classical and rock interests by singing in the IC Choir and running the Jazz & Rock Society. He has been active as a jazz drummer, although his earliest compositions showed a more classical bent. So, it is not surprising that he is drumming as well as singing on this album, but he also provides virtually all of the rest of the instrumentation, namely keyboards in one shape or form. What lifts him out of the normal EM fold is not only the singing, which considering his background in choral is not surprisingly in that style, but also in the use of "live" drums. It is quite refreshing to hear keyboard music accompanied by proper drums as opposed to that bloody box! This is a pleasant collection of six songs, which brings together influences as diverse as Camel, Blue Nile and Underground. The songs are structured, and not mindless keyboard doodlings and overall there is a dreamy, almost New Age, feel to proceedings.

Andrew has managed to produce a thoughtful first effort that can easily be listened to and enjoyed.
#38, Nov 1996

CHRISTIAN BOULE
NON-FICTION
This is very much an album of its time, in fact it probably sounded dated in 1979 when it came out, as it really belongs firmly in the mid-70's. The first few songs are pure pop, and do not really display the guitar style for which Christian was more well known, namely glissando. Think of that and think of Gong, and Christian did tour with Steve Hillage for a while as second guitarist (and can be heard on 'Live Herald'). While numbers such as "Psychedlik" are much more jazz-oriented and interesting from a prog point of view, the overall feel is of an album that while fairly enjoyable is not one to be rushed out and purchased immediately. Accessible, with lyrics in English the reissue also contains two songs that were recorded in 1999.
#69, Aug 2002

TIM BOWNESS
MY HOTEL YEAR
The press release for this album captures the feeling behind Tim Bowness' debut solo work really well when it says "Calling all fans of Bowie, Sylvain, This Mortal Coil and the quintessential 4AD sound, Hammill, Walker, Drake, Tim Buckley, Eno, Marks Hollis and Eitzel, Portishead, Red House Painters and existential introspection set to a smorgasbord of 21st century beats - upbeat, downbeat or simply a heartbeat." This is an album that is full of emotion and passion, fully laden with atmosphere and a very different take on the musical world. Tim is of course well known for his work with Steve Wilson as no-man (I have a sampler containing a song from the band when they were known as 'no man is an island except the isle of man'!). Probably the word that best sums up this album is 'reflection', whether it is self- reflection by the listener or by the singer. This is music to drift along to, music that creates a certain ambience. One can imagine some of these songs being used in films, as there is a definite cinematic quality about them. This definitely will not be to everyone's tastes but when the latest shredder has taken away the wits and what was left of your ear drums then this would be the album to chill to.
#81, Dec 2004

BRASSÉ
PAWN
This is Marc Brassé's second album, which he has been recording over the last two years. Marc plays the keyboards, wrote all the material and contributes lead vocals on one song. The other musicians are ex-Egdon Heath vocalist Jens van der Stempel (who sang on their highly acclaimed 'The Killing Silence'), Maarten Huiskamp on guitars and keyboards, and Gregor Theelen who sings on "In The Presence of The Entaur". This is a

concept album, based around a fantasy story where the hero is an unwilling pawn who is used by the White Lord, Dinitrio, to kill the evil leader of the golems, The Entaur. After a while the pawn marries Indrisha but she is killed by the mad Dinitrio who wants to rule the world as a totalitarian hell. The pawn takes his revenge and the land recovers. The pawn ends his story as a bitter old man, feeling used and abused by both Dinitrio and The Entaur. The CD insert is well laid out with some great artwork from Marc, along with all the lyrics and the story. On a personal level I love fantasy novels (Tolkien, Moorcock and Gemmel in particular), I love concepts and I love prog, so what do I think of this CD? It works.

This is an album with a definite Nineties prog sound, but it is also wonderfully commercial at the same time. Some of the songs, such as "In The Presence of the Entaur" feature great hooks. Marc and Maarten obviously have a great understanding, and trade licks and runs with great skill and finesse. Very much an album for lovers of extremely melodic progressive rock: at times there are swathes of keyboards such as at the beginning of "Free At Last" while in others the guitar is dominant (e.g. "Pawn").

It is very accessible, enjoyable on first hearing: there are lots of high points, but I think that "Pawn" takes a lot of beating. It starts with a thunderclap and the guitar and keyboards gradually work together building up to the vocals. Jens' multi-tracked vocals rise up and gradually the song changes and drives along with a pulsing beat. Throughout the album the vocals are spot on and work well with the music to make the overall sound very commercial. 'Pawn' the CD has great depth and melody, and should claim a place in the home of any commercial progressive rock lover.
#18, May 1993

BRASSÉ
DANTE'S INFERNO

BRASSÉ
TURBULENCE

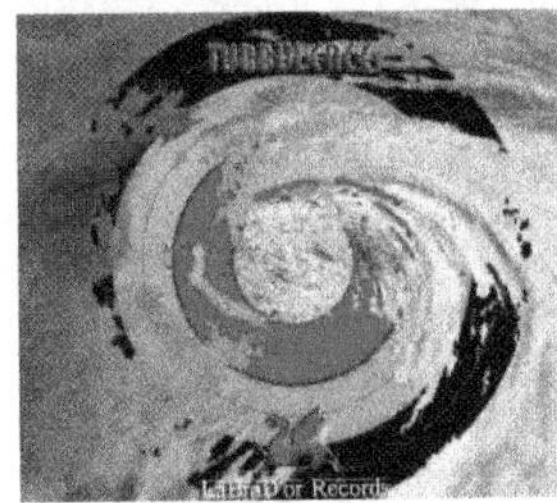

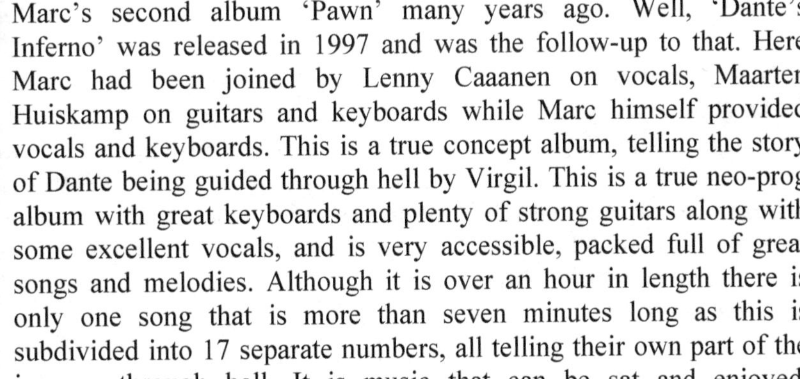

Those with a very long memory may just remember me reviewing Marc's second album 'Pawn' many years ago. Well, 'Dante's Inferno' was released in 1997 and was the follow-up to that. Here Marc had been joined by Lenny Caaanen on vocals, Maarten Huiskamp on guitars and keyboards while Marc himself provided vocals and keyboards. This is a true concept album, telling the story of Dante being guided through hell by Virgil. This is a true neo-prog album with great keyboards and plenty of strong guitars along with some excellent vocals, and is very accessible, packed full of great songs and melodies. Although it is over an hour in length there is only one song that is more than seven minutes long as this is subdivided into 17 separate numbers, all telling their own part of the journey through hell. It is music that can be sat and enjoyed,

preferably in the late evening, with loads of different styles being used to make the album as a whole and it does a strong job of telling the story. Four years on from 'Dante' and Marc was back with his fourth album, but although Maarten was very much on board Lenny was now only singing on one song and other musicians had also been brought in. It means that there is a much fuller sound and now with live drums driving it along there is a stronger sense of dynamic. Marc has also allowed himself to extend further so there is a true epic here with "Storm" managing to break the twenty-minute barrier. There are again lots of different styles in play and "Sinful City" steps over the prog boundary into melodic metal with a great hook in the chorus as it builds to a climax. But then comparing that to the next song, "Trickster", it sounds as if it should be from a different act altogether as this is much more keyboard based with some judicious guitar lines and the riffs not starting until the song has been going for a few minutes and there are times when I think that this may have been influenced by "Robbery, Assault & Battery" but only on a few of the vocal line. It is nice to be back in touch with Marc again after all this time, and I know that his new fifth album should be out soon. I have found it hard to pick between the two as the concept is so strong in the first but the overall musicianship and songs are better in the second.
#87, Apr 2006

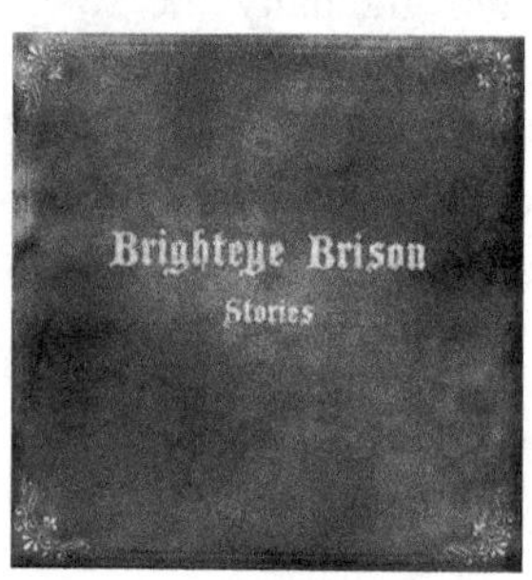

BRIGHTEYE BRISON
STORIES

There may be those people sat in their armchairs who bemoan the lack of good prog music around these days – but with just a bit of work one can find that there are some great albums still being released, and that is true of the second piece of work from Swedish band Brighteye Brison. Their debut was released on Rivel Records but surely it cannot be long until it as again made available as this is superb. The line-up is Linus Kåse (keyboards, saxophone, vocals – who founded the band after attending the Royal College Of Music in Stockholm), Daniel Kåse (drums, percussion, trumpet, vocals), Kristofer Eng (bass, Taurus pedals, theremin, flute, vocals), Johan Oijen (guitars) and Per Hallman (vocals). This is a very polished album with multi-layered harmonies and vocals – so much so that it brings to life the very best of early Seventies Genesis and Gentle Giant while also being very much an album of now.

It is accessible, it is lush, and is an album that progheads will want to play repeatedly – as although it is enjoyable on first hearing one just knows that the more that this is played then the more that the listener will get out of it. I am always on the outlook for obscure bands releasing stunning albums that I can bring to your attention and this is yet another goody that needs to be searched out. They say that their influences are from bands such as PFM, Genesis, Echolyn, Yes and Klaatu etc. and if you want multi vocal prog that is damn good fun and full of melody then look no further.
#88, Jun 2006

BROADCAST
HAHA SOUND
It is not often that I find myself at a total loss when attempting to review an album, but that is the case here. When I first played it I thought that it was quite interesting, but this is one of those albums that grab you and take you to places where you have never been before. This is not the sort of music that I normally listen to – but I just could not bring myself to pass it along. Is it the sweet charming female vocals, or the way that they often seem to reference early Pink Floyd, or the fact that this music which sounds so experimental can also seem compellingly poppy? I really have no idea – but I do know that I have enjoyed playing it a great deal and know that I will be doing so a lot more in the future. How can an album that is so left field sound as if it belongs most firmly in the centre? How can music that defies description be so much fun? All I can say is that if you enjoy music that is different, yet has sweetly sung Sixties pop over the top, then this has to be worth further investigation... *#76, Oct 2003*

BROTHER APE
ON THE OTHER SIDE
This is the debut album by a Swedish four-piece that is going to be gaining them a great many plaudits. Although it has been released on a progressive label, it could be argued that this is not really a progressive record at all, but much more an album based on songs and wonderful harmonies and singing. A lot of prog is 'in your face', with incredible amounts of complexity that almost scream out 'look at me – I'm clever', but that is not the case with this album at all. If you want some musical handles, how about Camel mixed with It Bites along with Steve Hackett yet at the same time is not really anything like these at all. There are great melodies here, but they just manage to avoid going too far into AOR and the result is something that is intensely listenable and enjoyable and at the same time is refreshing and immediate. These guys have managed to pull together something that is quite different to much of the rest of the scene, and due to the freshness of the songs is like a gentle breeze against the hurricanes of noise being created by those going heavier and deeper into weird time signatures. It is complex simplicity, and is one that I have really enjoyed playing time and again.
#85, Nov 2005

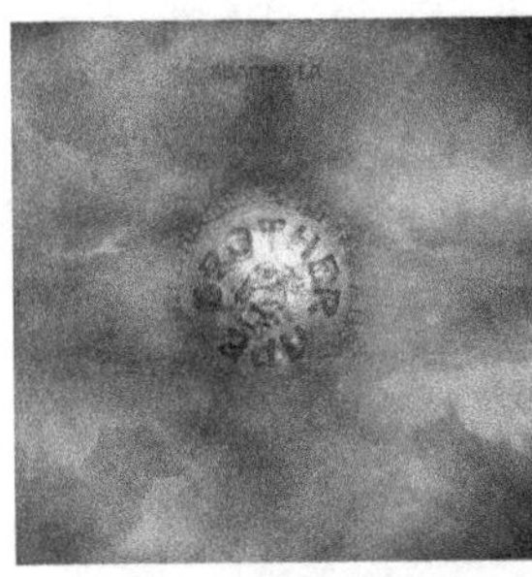

BROTHER APE
SHANGRI-LA
Since the release of their debut album singer Peter Dahlgren has left the band so composer Stefan Damicolas (guitars) has now taken on that role, with the band being completed by Max Bergman (drums) and Gunnar Maxén (bass, keyboards, harmony vocals). Still very melodic the album has seen a movement in some ways more into the progressive field, and the change in singer has certainly meant that

the band have lost the Styx element that was there on the debut. Although the album is quite guitar oriented, the keyboards play an important part, as does the bass playing – this is because the bass sound is quite deep like Chris Squire but it is on a fretless bass which provides a different tonal quality. This album does take a while to get into, just because there are different elements being used and I am not always sure that they are working as well as they could. The band is at their best when the guitars are rocking and the keyboards are riding right in behind, being driven on by the rhythm section. The vocals are still strong with lots of layered harmonies and the production (where the band have been assisted by Hansi Cross) is very strong. Highlight is probably "Lunatic Kingdom" where the vocals and music are spot on. I do not think that this is an essential prog album, but is one that should at least be heard. To be able to do that go to the label site where it is possible to download a complete song for free and see what you think of it.
#89, Sep 2006

BUDDERFLY
BUDDERFLY

Containing members of both Sixnorth and Strings Arguments (who have both released albums on Musea), this five-piece (two guitarists, one bassist and two drummers) recorded this instrumental improvised album on November 24th last year. Improvised music very much depends both on the players and the listeners – the players need to be able to follow leads being provided by others and build some sort of musical thread while the listener has to be able to comprehend what is going on. This style of music is loved by few and loathed by many, and while I wouldn't go quite that far, I must say that this is not something I can imagine playing again. Sorry guys.
#72, Feb 2003

TIM BURNESS
INFINITE OCEAN

Many moons ago I was given a tape to listen to, and contained within was a song that really captured my imagination, "Mumbling In The House of Commons" by one Tim Burness. After a while I managed to get a contact address for Tim and over the last few years I have written to him a few times but never had a reply, so I was surprised to receive this his new release the other day. Fudge Smith (Pendragon) is now in his band, but did not play on this release, which appears to be a collection of songs from recent years. I was delighted to see that "Mumbling" was the second song and it has since been receiving heavy rotation on my deck. It is hard to explain what is so "right" about this song, whether it is the affected vocals (sung in a toff's accent), the guitar breaks, or the overall effect of talking in the background, I just do not know. All I can say is that years after hearing it I still knew the words and melody. The other songs show Tim to have something in common with Pendragon, although the style is far less keyboard oriented. "Free The Chicken In Your Soul" is just plain stupid, although I love it dearly as accompanied by acoustic guitar, instead of lyrics Tim treats us to his impression of farmyard animals. If he has enough nerve to perform this on stage, then the man deserves a prize. Overall this eight-track CD is enough to whet the appetite of those curious to know what has become of Tim since the demise of his band Burnessence who supported many luminaries in the Eighties such as IQ, Pendragon and Pallas. *#46, Dec 1997*

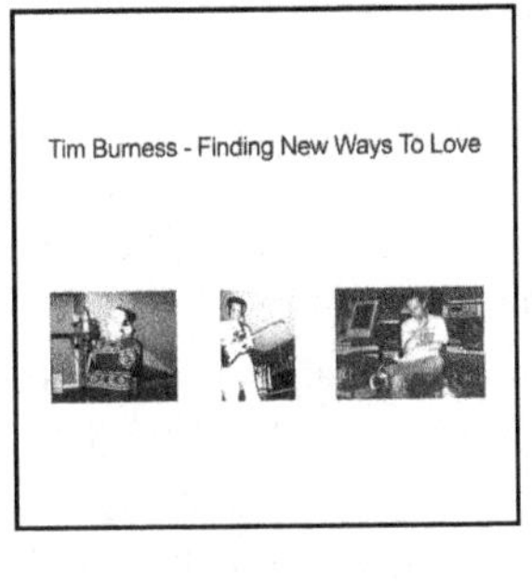

TIM BURNESS
FINDING NEW WAYS TO LOVE

Tim released his latest album last year but it has only just come to my attention. I have reviewed his work in the past and old-time progheads will probably remember his band Burnessence with which he released two albums in the Eighties. Here Tim provides all guitars and vocals plus e-bow etc., and he has been joined again by Fudge Smith (Pendragon), Keith Hastings, Monty Oxy Moron, Martin Franklin and Chris Cordrey. The result is an album that is very much based around songs – that these songs may not always be viewed as being 'progressive' is beside the point as although this will obviously appeal to fans of Peter Gabriel and possibly Steve Hackett, this is more about sitting back and let the majesty flow through. Some are fairly minimalist in their musical approach while others are more complicated, but there is a sense of joy throughout this work that is difficult to explain. It is light hearted and asking the listener to just get into the vibe of what is being performed and try not to worry too much about pigeonholing what is going on. Tim himself describes the album as "a mix of contemporary melodic pop songs, progressive rock and ambient, experimental instrumentals" and that sums it up quite well. Very solid, and very enjoyable. *#84, July 2005*

MARYEN CAIRNS
THE PICTURES WITHIN

On my CD player at present is the beautiful debut album from Maryen Cairns. This is an album that will appeal to a great number of you, whether you just love good songs with intelligent lyrics, or you adore pure clear vocals in the style of Kate Bush or possibly Maddy Prior. Maryen is a twenty-five-year-old Australian, originally from Scotland, who is now living and working in London. She was encouraged musically by her parents from a young age and is now a multi-instrumentalist, concentrating mostly on guitar and keyboards. She formed her first band, The Difference, when she was only seventeen. After a few years working with The Difference in Sydney, Maryen moved to London where it was felt that her music would be better appreciated and this proved to be the case and they gained critical acclaim after only a few gigs. However, the attention so early in the life of the band caused internal problems and eventually it became clear that Maryen would have to work as a solo artist. In 1989 she began doing solo acoustic shows around London, and by 1990 had discovered the use of computers and played live as a duo with one to fuse computerised instruments with acoustic ones. She also began working with Chris Kimsey, and the year culminated in a Friday night support at The Astoria. During 1991 she played gigs in many formats, experimenting with different musical combinations, eventually settling on violin, two keyboard players, guitar, bass, drums and herself on acoustic guitar and piano. She gained more prominence when she provided backing vocals on Fish's 'Internal Exile' album, as well as on the single "Something In The Air". She made a guest appearance with Fish at the Hammersmith Odeon last November, and in March this year she again supported him at the Odeon as well as providing backing vocals for his own show.

'The Pictures Within' was recorded during 1991, and has already been released in the USA through Progressive International, and is just about to see the light of day over here. It is an extremely melodic album which sometimes uses the barest of instrumentation so that the ear is always drawn to Maryen's beautiful four-octave voice. The music really is a backdrop curtain, but at the same time it is perfect in that is adds to the whole without distracting you away from the voice. All twelve songs on this forty-six-minute album are written by Maryen, and the lyrics are of the highest order. Subjects covered range from Aids, child abuse and arranged marriages to seal culling and wife beating. All the subjects are dealt with caringly and with a real compassion and understanding. Serious subjects are dealt with seriously, yet at the same time this modern protest singer entertains at the highest level. My personal favourite is probably "Shona", where Maryen is accompanied by acoustic guitars as she sings about a young girl searching for love, but in vain, feeling that the only way to gain love is by sleeping with them. Maryen tells Shona that she should believe in herself and love would come naturally without searching for it. It is one of the lighter songs, which contrasts well with the fuller sound used on "Too Young To Die" which is about Aids. This latter has Maryen singing backing vocals to her own voice on the chorus, which has such a commercial hook that if it was released as a single (and could somehow get airplay) then surely it would be a huge hit. One review I have seen of 'The Pictures Within' felt that there should be more light-hearted songs to provide a better balance, but I do not agree as I wouldn't change the album in anyway. The melodies, the lyrics, the (to my hearing) classically-trained perfectly-pitched vocals all combine to provide a musical experience not to be missed. If you only buy one female singer-songwriter album this year, then it should be this one.
#15, Oct 1992

CAIRO
CONFLICT AND DREAMS

I had heard plenty about Cairo prior to receiving this album, but not much of the band themselves. They are signed to Magna Carta in the States and not all of their releases make it over here in the shape of Roadrunner, but I am glad to report that their second album will be released on Feb 23rd. Why am I pleased? Because it's bloody excellent, that's why! All five guys are brilliant musicians, and while the press release praises keyboard player Mark Robertson in particular, I think it is just the way that they all seem so right together that makes this music so soaringly brilliant. This is prog crossed with AOR, albeit with a slightly harder edge, and it is at times breathtakingly in its complexity. Yes, it can be argued that at times it is commercial, but who cares? Unlike Spock's Beard, who can be accused of prog for prog's sake at times, all of this seems to make sense. It is overtly American, yet still appealing and wide-ranging. Will you manage to see this in the shops? No. Will you see it raved over by the likes of Kerrang!? No (although the fact that they are American will of course be in their favour). However, this is an album that any lover of melodic rock will like on first hearing and develop into a serious love affair after only the second or third time through. Yes, I like this a lot, and if you give it half a chance then so will you. *#47, Feb 1998*

CALIFORNIA GUITAR TRIO
CG3 + 2

Needless to say, these guys are not actually from California at all, and in fact only one of them is American! They first met at one of Robert Fripp's guitar seminars in 1987 and then toured as part of Fripp's League Of Crafty Guitarists until in 1990 they decided to form their own group. 1991 saw them all living in Los Angeles and they had taken the above name. They soon signed with Fripp's Discipline Global Mobile label and toured extensively, often with King Crimson. This album finds them now signed to Inside Out, and was recorded with Tony Levin on stick, bass and King Crimson drummer Pat Mastelotto. This album is a long way removed from any guitar histrionics album that I have come across, and in many ways is closer to The Guitar Orchestra, who I reviewed some years ago. It displays a mastery of many differing styles of music from staccato and quick, to pieces such as "Swampy Space" which sounds just as the name implies. One interesting number is their cover version of Yes' "Heart Of The Sunrise" which manages to sound respectfully close to the original yet at the same time quite different. This is an album that will only appeal to a small number as it does require concentrated listening to get the most out of it, but by moving onto Inside Out, CGT should find themselves reaching a wider audience. For those who want to hear music played by extremely accomplished musicians.
#70, Oct 2002

CALIFORNIA GUITAR TRIO
THE FIRST DECADE

Not surprising, given the title of the CD, this is a compilation album culled from the first five studio albums of CGT. Also not surprising is that there are three of them, all playing acoustic guitar: that only one of them is even American (and he does not come from California) does not seem to matter too much. Bert Lams, Hiedyo Moriya and Paul Richards met in 1987 when attending one of Robert Fripp's guitar seminars, and toured as part of his League Of Crafty Guitarists

before forming their own band in 1990. Although they are sometimes joined by other musicians (most notably Tony Levin and Pat Mastelotto), it is as a pure trio that their music is best heard. Having seen them recently I was astonished, as were the rest of the audience, at just how well these guys can play. This album goes some way to showing that as it is incredible what three guitars can sound like in the hands of masters. The music varies between folky through to classical and music that is extremely technical. It is an album best dipped in and out of as it is not hard for attention to wander, just because there is only so much music of this type that one can take in at once. It does take a lot of concentration to get the most of, and it does not work as background music either so the listener has to be prepared to spend some time on this, but there is no doubt that these guys can play.
#78, Apr 2004

CALIFORNIA GUITAR TRIO
WHITEWATER

There is something very special about an acoustic guitar when it is played by an expert, so to get three people who do nothing else it is guaranteed that the album is going to be interesting. The album has been produced by Tony Levin and as a friend and long-time collaborator he knows just how to get the best out of them. It starts with "The Marsh", a dreamy reflective piece of music named after the area where Robert Fripp's 96-year-old gardener lives in Wiltshire (I kid you not). This song is also available as a live quick time video at the end of the CD. Having played together for many years these guys have an intuitive feel of what is right for the music and they manage to produce modern music that is timeless yet will find appeal not only within the rock spectrum but also by those who just love the sound of an acoustic guitar played in whatever style. They manage to keep this as music, not a jaw-dropping 'how do they do that' experience and the album is the better for it. It may not be to everybody's tastes but I have found that although it can be played in the foreground this is wonderful music to be playing as a backdrop.
#81, Dec 2004

LAURENT CALOMNE
MONSTRES ET CHIMÈRES

Laurent Calomne is a Belgian music teacher (clarinet, percussion and saxophone) who also specialises in music theory and is a composer of electronic music. This is his debut album, released late last year on the Musea imprint Dreaming. The result is something that is at times, although not always, far removed from what one would normally expect from this style of music. While there are obvious nods to Vangelis and Tangerine Dream, this is often far more classical in outlook (perhaps this is 'job' coming through) and at times inhabits a similar sort of space to Richard Wileman (Karda Estra) although Richard uses more 'real' instruments in his work.

This is pleasant music, never overly exciting or dramatic, but listenable nonetheless. This is something either to drift away to or to play gently in the background when doing something else and on these levels works quite well. Not essential, but not to be easily discarded either. *#87, Apr 2006*

ROBERT CALVERT
REVENGE

Robert Calvert will always be associated with Hawkwind, although he did also record two well-received solo albums in the Seventies ('Captain Lockheed & The Starfighters' and 'Lucky Leif & The Longships'). Hawkwind keyboard player Simon House, who played him some backing tracks that he had recorded, introduced Robert to cellist Pete Pavli. Robert went away and came back a few days later with melodies and lyrics and recorded them in an afternoon. The tapes were then forgotten about for some ten years, and it was only after Robert's death that they were released as a limited edition. They were never finished, there are only four songs, and they were intended only as demos. Only the supreme Hawkwind or Calvert fan will be interested, so if you are not one of these then leave well alone. *#60, Oct 2000*

CARPATHIA PROJECT
CARPATHIA

Zsolt Daczi (A well-known musician in Hungary according to the blurb) and Tamas Angyan have formed this band with some of their friends. It is another instrumental album, with the lead again being a violin. It is not as 'produced' as the album by Marius Kahan, and has quite a fresh feel. This is probably assisted by the other instruments involved, which include a flute. This is particularly true on "Friends" when the flute and violin are in a duel, sometimes accompanied by the acoustic guitar, or sometimes with it as a backdrop. It is very effective indeed. Zsolt is also not afraid to drop in power chords when they are needed, to provide a more metallic air to the proceedings. In fact, they describe their music as "Rock, jazz, Latin, ethno and a little bit of metal…". This is a very good album indeed and one that is definitely worth seeking out. *#56, Jan 2000*

THE CARPET KNIGHTS
LOST AND SO STRANGE IS MY MIND

The Carpet Knights are a five-piece band from Malmö, who have been together since 1998 and this is their debut release. The album title itself gives away that this is music from a different era, something that is compounded and reinforced by the production which also sounds as if it is from the best part of forty years ago. This is psychedelic prog with an exceptionally heavy (when it suits them) bass line that is more distorted than Chris Squire. They also use a flute, but only sparingly so that it is always a welcome surprise as the band obviously do not want to be known as the next Tull as they have other things on their mind. There are a few Floydian touches here and there and overall it definitely feels as if this is a 'lost' album as opposed to one that has only recently been recorded. Well worth investigating if this is the sort of music you enjoy. *#85, Nov 2005*

CARPTREE
SUPERHERO

Carptree are a new progressive rock band to me, but 'Superhero' is their second album. They are unusual in that this is a two-man line-up with extra guest musicians. Niclas Flinck (vocals) and Carl Westholm (keyboards) got together in 1997, having known each other for some twenty years, and released their debut two years ago. This is quite an unusual album to try and describe as they are a keyboard-oriented band that have taken on elements from many different acts yet have managed to create a sound that is very much their own.

Imagine Peter Gabriel-era Genesis getting involved with Pink Floyd and then you may have some idea of what this is like, but only some. It is very much a songs-based album, with the longest being only six and a half minutes long, and it has a great deal going for it. It is extremely accessible and while I have seen reviews on their web site calling them a neo-prog outfit they are in fact quite different to the bands in that scene. Of modern bands I think that the closest I can think of is Jadis, but without the guitar. This is an immensely enjoyable album that can be listened to closely or also works extremely well in the background.
#74, Jun 2003

CARPTREE
MAN MADE MACHINE

Carptree are a Swedish duo comprising Niclas Flinck on lead vocals and Carl Westholm supplying piano, synthesizer, vocoder, and Theremin. They are joined by various unnamed guest musicians to provide the sound of a full band, and this is a band that definitely sounds very full indeed.

They go from beautifully delicate passages (such as on opener "Titans Clash Aggressively To Keep An Even Score" – what a great proggy title) through almost lounge core on "Sunshine Water" to areas that are far more dramatic and powerful. At times they remind me of Floyd but that is not really a fair comparison as Niclas's vocals are far more melodic and warm. Easily their best work to date 'Man Made Machine' is an essential discovery for all progheads. *#85, Nov 2005*

CASHMERE
CASH – ROMANTIC BAND

There is just so much music coming out of Poland at the present, and CashMERE is another act to follow. This is a three-song demo CD, and the band has just gone into the studio to record their debut album, which they hope to have available at the beginning of next year. Tylda Ciolkosz is the leader of the band, providing both vocals (in English) as well as some strong dynamic violins. Even with only three songs to listen to this time around it is possible to see that these guys have a breadth of talent and sounds. "Songs For Narcissus" starts with a call and response from the violin and guitar before settling into the vocals. When it comes down to describing the style of music these guys do not seem to mind what you call it. On their web site they state "A one-girl violin ensemble, acoustic and electric guitars, suave rhythm section and a voice that can tell as many good tales as bad jokes, Cash is a band like no other. You can call it what you like. Call it folk or call it prog, porn-groove or lala-rock. Call it pop, we will not mind. Gosh, you can even call it jazz, if you do not know any better. Compare it, contrast it, believe it or distrust it. But whatever your verdict and your reaction, Cash will go its own way and do whatever it pleases." These three tracks show a lot of promise and I for one will be looking forward to the debut album with interest as this is music with intelligence that does not fit into any of the normal boxes.

#85, Nov 2005

CASHMERE
CASH-ROMANTIC MUSIC MACHINE

In #85 I said just how much I was impressed with the three-track CD that I had been sent from Poland. Now I have had the opportunity to listen to the debut album and all I can say is that the praise that I heaped on them back then is just not enough. The three songs from 'Cash-Romantic Band' are here, along with another eight, and the extra length has really allowed the band to expand and show that they can blend folk with jazz in a way that manages to be challenging and inviting all at the same time.

Some of the lyrics are in English and some in Polish but that just adds to the mystique and the joy of what is taking place in front of your very ears. Violin and vocally led by Tylda Ciolkosz this is a band that is refusing to be put into any pigeonhole and instead appear to be taking a delight in touching as many musical bases as possible. What strikes one most is the inventiveness of what they are performing and the feeling that this is a band that really does come to life onstage – I can 'see' them playing and bouncing ideas off each other while at all times having huge smiles on their faces. This is progressive music in its very truest sense, producing something that is very unlike what is around yet at the same time bringing in recognisable influences such as Fairport or Hatfield. This is just superb and definitely needs to be heard far more widely than just in Poland.

#88, Jun 2006

CASINO
CASINO

It seems somehow fitting that the last album recorded by Geoff Mann has been regarded by many as his finest work since the heady days of Twelfth Night. It was suggested to Clive Nolan by SI that it may well be interesting for him to record an album with Geoff, and after a few phone calls and a meeting it was duly decided that an album would indeed be recorded, hopefully with a Twelfth Night "feel" to it. To that end Clive brought in Brian Devoil (drums), Jon Jeary (bass, Threshold), Mike Stobbie (keyboards, Pallas), Sylvain Gouvernaire (guitar, Arrakeen) and Paul Flynn (drums). Of course, the Thin Icemen themselves (Clive, keyboards and Karl, guitar) were also very much in attendance. Lyrically the album was a concept based, surprisingly enough, on a casino. Geoff provided all the words, and Clive provided the music, which was written the week after he returned from touring with Pendragon. I've decided that Clive must have a time condenser that I would dearly love to own, and also has the ability to segment his ideas so that no two musical projects sound the same. Working to a tight deadline, as always, Brian, Paul and Jon managed to lay down all the drums and bass part in seven days. On the eighth day they rested. Well, sort of. The hard disk on the computer went down and it took a day at Atari to get it sorted out. It contained all the keyboard and arrangement information, so they were rather relieved when the problem was rectified. Geoff arrived and laid down all the vocals in just three days. All it took now was some sterling keyboards and driving guitar. Only thirty-one days after recording commenced, 'Casino' was finished: six tracks of excellence.

It is strange indeed to play this album back to back with 'Second Chants' or 'Ring of Roses', as it sounds nothing like either. Indeed, the album sounds very much like what I would imagined Twelfth Night to sound like if they were around today, except for the fact that although Jon Jeary is a five-string bassist there are not many in the world who can hold a candle to Clive Mitten when he got going. What we have then are six songs, "Prey", "Crap Game", "Drunk", "Crying Onto Baize", "Stranger" and "Beyond That Door". It is an album that is totally accessible, full of great lyrics combined with great melodies. I mean, any person into good melodic or prog rock could not fail to fall in love with this album. I did. For me the best song is "Stranger", which has a keyboard solo that segues into some wonderful harmonica. It is a song that has to be cranked right up - it has that driving beat that means it is just impossible to sit still to. 'Casino' has proved to be very popular, and there were plans for a follow-up album and possibly a tour later this year. Obviously that can no longer take place. What we are left with is an album by a line-up that can never be repeated. Geoff and Clive worked together in a way that produced an hour of sheer magic. For any lover of Twelfth Night, or just good melodic prog rock then here is an album that really shouldn't be missed. In #16 I said that 'Ring of Roses' and 'More Than Meets The Eye" were my albums of the year, but I knew then that I hadn't heard all the ones I should have. 'Casino' rightfully claims its place with them at the very top of the tree.

#17, Mar 1993

CAST
LANDING IN A SERIOUS MIND

CAST
SOUNDS OF IMAGINATION

CAST
THIRD CALL

CAST
FOUR ACES

No, these are not the Brit pop Scousers, but rather a Mexican progressive outfit.

'Landing' is from '94, 'Sounds' is a split CD from '85 and '94, 'Third' is another split CD, this time from '89 and '94 while 'Four' is from '95.

I hadn't heard of them prior to being given these albums and all attempts to contact them have failed miserably, although I do believe that they are on the internet if you have access. Cast have obviously been paying very close attention to early Genesis, and play a very symphonic version of that. Vocals are extremely good and melodic, while the guitar definitely plays second fiddle (as it were) to the multi-faceted keyboards. I have to say that they stand up extremely well when compared with bands from other countries. I never imagined Mexico to be a hotbed of prog, but it may well be.

With all of the lyrics in English these albums are extremely accessible. While not as dynamic as many, and at times quite laid back, these albums all have layers of depth that are just waiting to be discovered. I enjoyed these four CDs very much, and am sure that many prog fans will feel the same way.
#41, Apr 1997

CAST
BEYOND REALITY

Since #41 I have heard from Mexican proggers Cast, who have now sent me their new album 'Beyond Reality'. As well as the four albums I reviewed last time they have also released a live album called 'A View Of Cast' and another studio album called 'Endless Signs'. They formed in 1978 and are finding it strange that they have taken so long for them to gain international recognition as they feel that their music hasn't changed much during that time. An example of this can be found on the new album as one of the sections of "The North" is called "All The Way From Nowhere" and appears here as it was originally conceived back in 1983. As with the other Cast albums I have seen, the presentation is superb (fantastic cover art for this one), with all of the lyrics plus some extra information.

Again this is multi-layered prog of the highest order with keyboards playing a pivotal role. The lyrics are all in English, and as I said last time I find it hard to imagine that this band is from Mexico, not an area that I would have thought of as having a thriving prog scene. As well as the four songs that form the album, there is also included "Another Night" which Cast performed for the Mellow Records' Camel tribute album 'Harbor Of Joy'. If you like your prog well-structured with superb keyboards and good interplay with a rooting in traditional Genesis, then Cast are definitely worth discovering.
#42, July 1997

CASTANARC
JOURNEY TO THE EAST
Castanarc began life in Doncaster in 1983, when Mark Holiday (vocals), and David Powell (keyboards) were joined by Paul Ineson (guitar), Neil Duty (guitar, bass) and Dave Kirkland (drums). They soon signed to Peninsula Records and recorded this their debut album in 1984. However, sales figures were never released and royalties not paid, and the band broke up.

Holiday and Powell were overheard jamming in local bars by a wealthy entrepreneur who paid for them to return to the studio where they were joined by Vincenzo Lammi (drums), Rich Burns (guitar), Rob Clarke (bass) and Steve Beighton (sax, keyboards). A 12" single was played on Radio One, then in 1989 they signed to RCA and 'Rude Politics' was released. A session was recorded and broadcast on Radio One, which was then repeated in 1990, while their current plans are to release a new album this Summer and also to re-record 'Rude Politics'. It has taken an American label to uncover this lost gem, and very enjoyable it is too. There is more than a hint of Camel about this band, although at times it is also reminiscent of Pendragon.

The band rarely rocks, but rather use clever interplay between guitar and keyboards to provide a swirling backdrop for Mark Holiday's clear vocals. It is these vocals that are at the forefront of the mix, and what the ear is guided towards. The album is not very long, only thirty-eight minutes of eight songs, but anyone interested in melodic or progressive rock in the style of Pendragon and Camel should really check this out. "Rhyme" is one of the shortest songs around, at only 2:41, but the use of acoustic guitar and piano combine with softly sung vocals to make it a beautiful track worth purchasing the album for on its own.
#23, May 1994

WELL, WHAT DID YOU EXPECT?

CASUAL AFFAIR
WELL, WHAT DID YOU EXPECT?

February 1992 saw the demise of one of the more popular progressive bands around, Casual Affair. Their history can be tracked all the way back to March 1984 when vocalist Mark Colton (ex- Fair Exchange, Goliath and Famous Last Words) met guitarist Mike Mishra after placing an ad in a local record shop. They started writing together and the first two songs were "The Game" and "Auf Wiedersehen". In June 1984 Mark Eckersley (ex-Red, Goliath) joined on drums and Neil Mathars (ex-Kudos) came in on bass. With Mark and Neil both playing keyboards live, this line-up gigged as Liar (for just one gig) before changing the name to Dirty Trix (which lasted about a year) and recorded a demo. By May 1985 both Mike and Mark Eckersley had left the band, so Mark Law joined on drums with Graeme Wilde on guitar, together with Barry Nuthall on keyboards, and September that year saw them using the name Casual Affair for the first time. Mark Laws left in June 1986 (later playing in Jadis) and was replaced by Carl Sampson.

In January 1987 a two-track cassette single featuring "Learning To Fly" and "Monday Mournings" was recorded, but it was June 1988 that was the real turning point for the band. Graeme decided to leave, and when wondering how to replace him, the conversation turned to founding guitarist Mike Mishra. Mark got in contact, and the definitive Casual line-up was now in place. Mike and Mark had always written well together, and the band continued to progress. The first single was recorded in January 1989, with the songs being "Reflections" and "Perfect Timing". The band continued to garner more support, and it was now being supported by press and radio airplay, but yet again pressures took their toll and Carl left. He was quickly replaced by Jason Clark, and it was finally time for the band to do some serious recording and the result was the tape, 'Well, What Did You Expect?'.

First song is the powerful "Learning To Fly", which often opened the live set, and is an upbeat rock song showing their policy of writing accessible rock, with keyboards being used more as an accompaniment than as a main instrument, which is often the case with prog bands. Mark's vocals are very much to the fore, and the lyrics are very easy to distinguish on first listen

Also featured are two of the Casuals most memorable songs, the soaring "Whisper In The Wind" and the poignant "Auf Wiedersehen". "Whisper" starts off gently, but picks up when the verse starts, and provided many a crowd singalong at their gigs. "Auf Wiedersehen" starts off atmospherically as Mark contemplates suicide, and features some beautiful guitar from Mike. Gradually Mark's voice takes on a harder aspect as the reality of the situation becomes apparent and Mike puts in some wonderfully restrained notes as the song builds to its close. "Between The Lines" is wonderful power pop, to say it's commercial is an understatement, and is a fun song. It may be a little surprising to find a cover on an album of only eight songs in length, but the Casuals version of "Spirit of Radio" is well worth hearing. "Too Late To Cry" was the highlight as well as the last song of the live set. A song of many parts it shows

Mark's vocal strengths, as there is real venom there.

The album was well-received by fans and media alike, and is still selling. February 1991 saw the last line-up change as Jason left (now in Walking On Ice) to be replaced by Andy Bunker. Mark and Mike continued writing new material that found its way into the live set, but gradually they became more disillusioned with the setup and decided to break the band. Casual Affair are dead, long live Freewill! Current line-up is Mark, Mike, Steve Tuckwell (bass, ex-Jackal), Louis Parish (drums, ex-Traitors Gate) and Jon Evans (keyboards, ex-Kick). Although the set is currently comprised mostly of Casuals number, they have been totally rearranged and improved with a far heavier rock element. The band plan on spending time writing and rehearsing, but they can be seen supporting Galahad at The Standard on May 22nd.
#12, May 1992

MARC CATLEY & GEOFF MANN
FINE DIFFERENCE

MARC CATLEY & GEOFF MANN
THE OFF THE END OF THE PIER SHOW

Marc Catley recorded his first album, 'This Is The Birth of Classical Acoustic Rock', in January 1986 with guitarist Paul Donnelly. A review of this album appeared in NCM magazine on the same page as a review of Geoff's 'I May Sing Grace'. Marc then contacted Geoff, who lived in nearby Salford, and they met up and became friends. Geoff produced Marc's next EP, 'The Peel Tower Hop', which included shorter songs, and Marc then often supported Geoff's rock band The Bond. The result of their friendship was the release in 1988 of 'In Difference'. This tape consisted of five songs by Geoff that he considered to be too acoustic for his current band, and four songs by Marc that he had re-written, going for a more progressive sound. This release by Plankton finds this album available on CD in its entirety, but it has been expanded to include four songs from Geoff's long-deleted 'Chants Would Be A Fine Thing' (the forerunner of his very excellent 'Second Chants', the last solo album he recorded before his death), and three tracks from Marc's 'The Peel Tower Hop' and one from his 'This Is The Birth...'. All in all, this is of real interest to prog completists and lovers of acoustic music. But is it any good? For the most part the songs alternate vocals between Marc and Geoff (they rarely harmonise together), and the CD starts with Marc's extremely powerful "We Are One". The riffing acoustic guitar of this song contrasts greatly with the multi-layered vocals of Geoff in the next, "One Of The Green Things". It is certainly very reminiscent of the sort of material he delivered on 'Second Chants'. Contrast is the order of the day as Marc's "Keep On" is again far more gentle, with his vocals taking a far softer approach. Geoff provides the hard edge to Marc's softness, and I found the album fascinating. Not only do the vocals show the different approaches of the two artists, but the music definitely reflects it as well. Marc has a subtle approach, with lots of

acoustic guitar, while Geoff seems more at home with contrast and experimentation. As a whole this album definitely works, and while Geoff is far the more well-known of the two (certainly in prog circles), Marc's songs are certainly not mere fillers. 'The Off The End Of The Pier Show' was recorded over a two-year period, and is a totally instrumental album. There is a wonderful short story written by Geoff about the two of them attempting to get a gig on a pier, and then playing on a pontoon instead. All totally fictitious of course, but written with a wonderful humour that brings a smile to the lips. If you count "The River" as three separate songs, there are eight songs on the album with four by Geoff, three by Marc, and one joint effort: what I did find strange is that they only play together on two of them. For the most part they are either joined by Clive Davenport on guitar, synth or drum machine or they are playing totally solo (although flautist Jill Towers and keyboard player Steve Ridley make fleeting appearances). There is a great depth to the album, particularly with the many layering of guitars. In fact, there are many differing styles, and it is possible to discern influences ranging from Mike Oldfield and Tangerine Dream to Pink Floyd and beyond. Geoff's guitar playing has proved itself to be a real revelation to me, especially on part two of "The River" (entitled "White Water"), but a special mention must be made here of the song that opens side two of the tape. I mean, only Geoff Mann could write a song called "Terence The Termite Stares Down His Underpants In Growing Amusement"! As on the earlier album, Marc provides most of the subtlety and Geoff the harder edge. For an instrumental album it has a surprising amount of differing styles, yet it all manages to work well together.
#21, Jan 1994

CATWEAZLE
ARS MORIENDI

Catweazle are the brainchild of Michael Thorne (vocals, keyboards), who has been involved with different Swedish symphonic rock bands since 1980. The group was formed in 1987 with Patrick Enwall (vocals, bass), Peter Rendus (guitars) and Roger Johansson (drums). In 1990 Michael moved to Dalarna and it was there that he met Ulf S. Danielsson and a few years later the two friends formed Ad Perpetuam Memoriam, "The CD label dedicated to timeless sounds". Somehow Michael also found time to play keyboards for the band that later became Anekdoten. Right, so now we are in 1996, and Catweazle have finally released their debut album but what is it like? Very melodic, symphonic, progressive, interesting and bloody enjoyable probably answers it well. Unlike many of the releases on the APM label, 'Ars Moriendi' is very much a Nineties release and the guys have taken loads of different influences and melded and moulded them into a totally new being. As I listened to the first song my initial musical reference was Jadis, although a little harsher, then it changed to IQ and by the time I had worked through Pink Floyd, Genesis, early Seventies prog and middle Eighties Yes I decided just to enjoy this wonderful album. I have no hesitation whatsoever in saying that this is by far the best and certainly most immediate album to come out of the APM label. And is an album that no progressive, melodic, symphonic fan can afford to be without.
#36, June 1996

CEREBUS EFFECT
ACTS OF DECEPTION

This is the second studio album from Baltimore-based quartet Cerebus Effect. They are virtually totally instrumental, although keyboard player Dan Britton does provide some 'vocals' on some songs. These are kept deliberately low in the mix and are almost spoken and the effect is that they add to the music as another instrument as opposed to being a clear vocal line (and the reviewer who said that these were death metal vocals needs to listen to some of the stuff I hear!). Technically these guys are really tight, playing a complex form of prog that is both dark, and reliant on the listener enjoying weird time signatures and music moving in many directions at once. This really is progressive music in its truest sense as they are breaking down boundaries but managing to stay within a rock based area instead of moving over too far into jazz. Patrick Gaffney is a strong drummer, who needs to play like an octopus to keep this all going, while Mike Galway has a wonderful skill on his fretless bass that allows him to put little fills or lead lines that add to the overall sound. Dan is often fairly restrained in what he is doing, and probably adds the most jazz-like features, while guitarist Joseph Walker is a real find with Allan Holdsworth style intentions. This is not music that is easily accessible, and is something that does need to be worked at, as initially the first thing you hear is the skill of the players involved and not the music they are creating but the more I played this the more I liked it.

#86, Feb 2006

CENTROZOON
NEVER TRUST THE WAY YOU ARE

This album was released last year in Germany, and is now being made available through Burning Shed in the UK. Although Centrozoon have been recording for a while, this is the first time that they have been joined on a full-length album by no-man vocalist Tim Bowness. Combining with Markus Reiter and Bernhard Wöstheinrich the result is an album that while mostly electronic, contains enough touch guitar and bass to give it shape. Tim's vocals are breathy and emotional which removes the clinical aspect that can so often be prevalent in electronic albums, and instead of something that is sterile instead is something warm and interesting although still maintaining a bleak and almost threatening edge. Pat Mastelotto from King Crimson is mentioned on the cover, but his contribution was just to mix one of the songs. This is a trio effort with all of them involved in the composing of the music while Tim took on responsibility for the lyrics. This is not a style of music that I often listen to, but I have found that this is a compelling piece of work that I have been returning to time and again. If you want to hear electronic music that is definitely out of the ordinary, and a long way removed from what I would expect from the genre, then this album is definitely worth seeking out.

#83, Mar 2005

CHAIN
RECONSTRUCT

CHAIN
CHAIN.EXE

Chain was originally formed in 1994 by keyboard player Stephan Kernbach, with drummer Thorsten Hannig and bassist Christian Becker. The latter two were only fifteen years old, but already had an interest in prog rock and metal. Henning Pauly joined on guitar but after much rehearsal all that was left was one tape recorded during a session as they never found a suitable singer and so they broke up. Eight years later Henning found the tape, put it on and found out just how much he enjoyed listening to it and decided that the time was right for Chain to be reborn and for the music to be given a new lease of life. Singer Matt Cash was the final piece, and a year later 'Reconstruct' was ready. To say that Henning is a fan of Douglas Adams is a bit like saying Bobby Moore quite enjoyed the odd game of football, and there are quite a few lyrics that some will recognise in this concept album. It is not as hard and heavy as one might expect, although there are plenty of very guitar dominated passages, but is an album which contains a great deal of light and shade. It is accessible yet complex, melodic and full of hooks yet always striving forwards, the result being an album that all prog fans who enjoy their guitar will greatly enjoy.

Of the actual band, only drummer Eddie Marvin was the new boy on the second album, but this is far removed from the debut not only musically but in the amount of guests making their presence felt whether it be with instruments or on vocals. The important thing is not to be over-awed by what is going on, and rather just enjoy the music. There are some who would set the CD player to go to track eleven and listen to Michael Sadler sing on a very different version of his own classic "Hot To Cold". I mean, who else could sing it as well as he can, but the dynamics of the song have been changed quite a lot and Saga have never riffed it quite as Henning does in the chorus. But before you get to this song there are plenty of other great numbers, but the very best is the one that is left to last. This album arrived on my birthday, and on that day I was 42 years old (God – I was reasonably young when I took this job on…). I spent the day overseeing the plumber and painting the study.

While decorating I was listening to this album and when I got to this song I was taken not only by the ethereal beauty and delicacy of the pianowork and incredible vocals by Victoria Trevithick but also by the subject matter. Even if you have not been paying attention to the vocals the bridge of a banjo gently plucking "Journey of the Sorcerer" gives it away and the music thereafter builds to a climax. It is one of the finest songs I have heard for a long time, and has to be one of the most complete and fitting tributes ever given in song. Dedicated to Douglas Noel Adams, I have to confess that it felt strange to be listening to this for the first time on the very day that I turned 42.

Both of these albums are well worth hearing, but 'Chain.exe' is compulsory for those who like their prog to be modern and interesting while still being accessible.
#84, July 2005

DENNIS CHAMBERS....
BOSTON T PARTY

Actually this is not a solo album by drummer Dennis Chambers (Steely Dan, Santana, Brecker Brothers etc.), but is credited to all four musicians: the others are bassist Jeff Berlin, David Fiuczynski (fretted, fretless and ¼ tone guitar) and keyboard player T Lavitz. The result is music that has some progressive undertones, but in reality is fusion of the highest order.

All of these guys have the ability to take the lead when they desire or to provide support to the others and the album just manages to stay melodic enough to maintain interest. The one problem is that all of the guys are so skilled that at times there is the feeling that they are going to go off into the realms of showing how technically capable they are instead of sticking to the music. But overall they just manage to keep on the right side, and this is an album that those into jazz-fusion will most definitely enjoy. Whether it is essential is debatable, but it is pleasant and the digipak packaging is well presented.
#87, Apr 2006

CHANDELIER
FACING GRAVITY

I have been meaning to catch up with German proggers Chandelier for quite some time, ever since hearing "Itai" on the 'SI Compilation Disc Too' set.

In fact, "Itai" is on this album which came out in 1992 – there have been line-up changes and problems since then but the new album should be out anytime now. Not including "Itai" (which is more experimental and oriental, but also coming across with a heavy dose of Galahad), a totally different song to the rest of the album, Chandelier are a band that are very mellow at times but do have their moments such as in "All My Ways" where there is very good guitar.

They almost cross over into the AOR field, and certainly come across as a prog band in the Saga mould. Of course, that could all have changed now, and the band may seem totally different. 'Facing Gravity' is worth hearing if you get the opportunity, while not an essential purchase, but I am looking forward to hearing the new album.
#38, Nov 1996

CHAOS CODE
PROPAGANDA

This is the third album from Chaos Code, and chaos is probably a good way of describing the music that they are playing. Each song is very different to the others, so while one may have a staccato power pop attack with guitar solos over the top, another may come across as if Alex Harvey had never left us! In between there are gentle numbers, the use of brass instruments and a feeling that the band are not really sure if they should be pursuing rock, prog, jazz, or anything else that might take their fancy and in many ways that is the problem with the album in that it confuses the ear (well mine at any rate) so that one is not sure what to expect. Now, I hate putting labels on bands as much as the next person but with the music here being quite diverse it may well be that the proghead will like one or two and not others, the rocker the same, and again with the jazz freak. I am really not sure about this album, and while it is definitely not something to be disregarded out of hand as there are some very interesting moments here, I am just not sure who this is being aimed at. The music itself on a song-by-song basis is very accessible; it is just that there are so many styles at play. Patrick Gaffney is also the drummer in Cerebus Effect. *#87, Apr 2006*

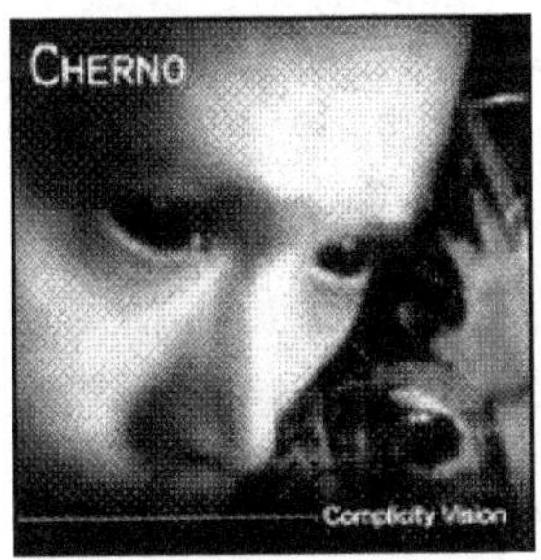

CHERNO
COMPLICITY VISION

This is the fourth album from the duo of Sugawara Shin (alto sax, wind synth, programming) and Kishimoto Junichi (guitar, guitar synth, programming) plus guest drummer Onuma Shiro who performs on two of the nine songs. This is strange stuff indeed. A lot of the music sent to me by Hiroshi Masuda is jazz based, but this appears to be jazz played on sax etc. mixed with RIO mixed with metal style guitar. At times it is almost as if the two musicians are not even playing the same piece of music but somehow it all seems to come together. I am just not sure how or why. This is complex and complicated music that is challenging to say the very least and there will be very few indeed who want to go through listening to this, but there are going to be some others who feel that this is wonderful stuff indeed. *#87, Apr 2006*

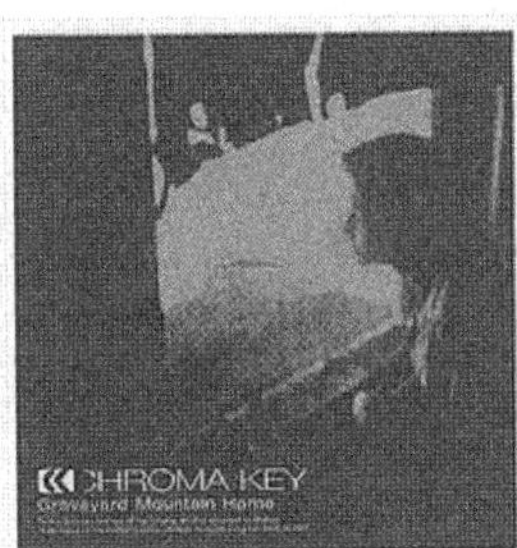

CHROMA KEY
GRAVEYARD MOUNTAIN HOME

This is the third Chroma Key album from ex-Dream Theater keyboard player Kevin Moore. Having recently recorded a soundtrack album he found that he missed the structure of working in that format so found an old film that he could work with to help inspire him. He found it in 'Age 13' which is a 1955 film about a boy wanting to bring his mother back to life by staring at the radio she used to listen to. He played the film at half-speed, and states that although the

music is not directly related to what was happening on the screen, there is a link in the atmospheres being generated. The result is an album that is quite unnerving at times. This is not pleasant easy to listen to stuff, as he has taken influences from bands like Pink Floyd and maybe even Björk and made it far darker, much more threatening. Sure there are some lighter moments, but I found that this is something that definitely needs to be listened to and is strangely compelling, but I am not sure if I could say that I really enjoyed it. I did feel myself being drawn back to it repeatedly, so there must be something in it, albeit on a deeper level. You may not enjoy this too much but it certainly is intriguing.
#82, Jan 2005

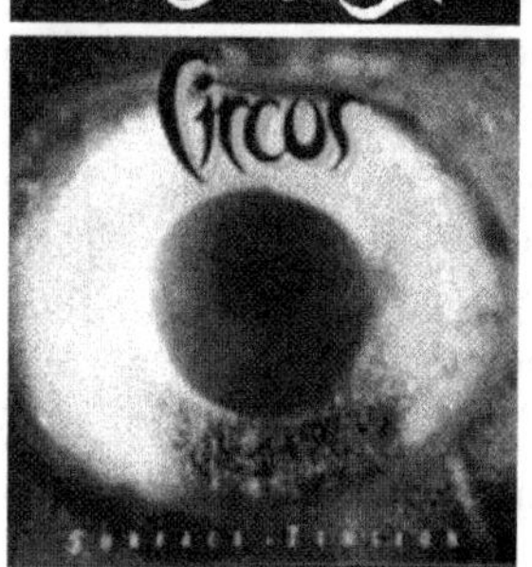

CIRCUS
FLASHBACK

CIRCUS
SURFACE TENSION

It is indeed unusual for a prog band in the UK to release two albums yet bypass virtually all of the fanzines dealing with the subject, but this may well be because instead of being influenced by Genesis, these guys are coming from a totally different area altogether. Circus have much more in common with VDGG or King Crimson, and because of this their albums take very definite listening to, and it took me a while to get into their music. Formed five years ago, the main songwriter is guitarist, violinist and sometimes keyboard player Patrick Case, who cites his influences as Love, Suede, Waterboys, the Fall and Jon Gabarek. Looking down the list given by the other band members, influences range from Nick Drake, Rick Wakeman, Monochrome Set, Led Zeppelin, to 10 CC and beyond. It should be of little surprise that the songs switch from one style to another, yet they are all linked by the rich melodic voice of Dave Brayley, who was compared by 'Progression' fanzine as having more than a passing resemblance with a young Peter Hammill.

'Flashback' is very short, in the sense that fifteen songs are crammed into a mere forty-five minutes. 'Surface Tension' also contains fifteen songs, but that album is longer at just over an hour. The debut starts with a musical interpretation of "Flanders Fields", which serves as a good indication of the rest of the album, with the emphasis on melody and depth rather than commercial hooks. Indeed, it is unlikely that after playing the CD that you will go around humming any of the tunes, at least not after first listen. The music is not intended for that, but instead harkens back to the early Seventies, yet also takes influences from the punk era that was supposed to kill off prog forever. Melodic and gentle, "Flanders Fields" leads into "Viewer", which for the most part has a lot more energy, being led by the rhythm section, and David singing without a seeming need for breath. This song remains my favourite on the album, as it is such a fun number to listen to. From the breathless energy, there is a gentle short keyboard interlude, which leads into "I'm Waiting" which starts off with a very Eastern style. This does not last too long and changes into another soaring goody.

'Surface Tension' builds on the power and promise of the debut, and manages to progress in the truest sense as Circus develop the musical themes portrayed therein. As in the debut, there is continuity within the songs, yet at the same time there are many different styles which means that the listener has lots to look forward to. It opens with "Relove" which has a wonderful Sixties feel, yet at the same time it is very modern in its approach. Again, it has an almost jaunty style that makes it a joy to listen to. Next up is "Sanctuary", which is so restrained and controlled that it can only be described as classic Fairport Convention: the violin soars, the acoustic guitar is restrained, the bass only makes a fleeting appearance, and the drums are nowhere to be seen. The real highlight of the songs is Dave's wonderful melodic vocals. From the beauty and tranquility of that we are transported away on the wings of "Interview", which manages to combine elements of the Sixties, ELP, VDGG, Genesis and many others all in one rushing dynamic song. I must confess that when I first listened to the albums I was not very impressed, but having now played them a few times I realize that the fault lay not with the music but rather with my ears. The albums are definite winners, especially to those who appreciate good melodic music, yet find the new set of prog bands too "samey" for their tastes. Circus are for any lover of Sixties or Seventies music: I have recently heard from Patrick Case, who has sent me a tape of yet more songs (that makes 35 recorded in just over a year!) and I must say that there seems to be no end of the amount of great songs they are coming out with. Circus are a band to look out for.
#21, Jan 1994

CIRCUS
BRISTOL STREET
I enjoyed the first two albums by Bristol based outfit Circus, 'Flashback' and 'Surface Tension', yet I can't get a handle on this one. This is far more than an album by a band, as they have collaborated with an array of remixers who have put their own stamp on the proceedings. The result, to my ears, is confusion as the band want to go in the new direction yet at the same time still manage to provide us with some gems that show what might have been. Many reviewers, myself included, likened their earlier work to VDGG, but now the listener is faced with dance tracks that manage to smother the ability of the band, as the remixer takes over. Still, "Bristol Street" itself is so good that it stands out like proverbial sore thumb. The lyrics are taken from "As I Walked Out One Evening" by WH Auden, and the mostly acoustic backing works well. This is an album that will take a lot of listening to, but I fear that Circus may well find themselves ostracizing themselves from their regular audience without managing to find a new one. There is too much dance-oriented material for the casual listener, yet it is not dance enough for lovers of that genre.
#32, Dec 1995

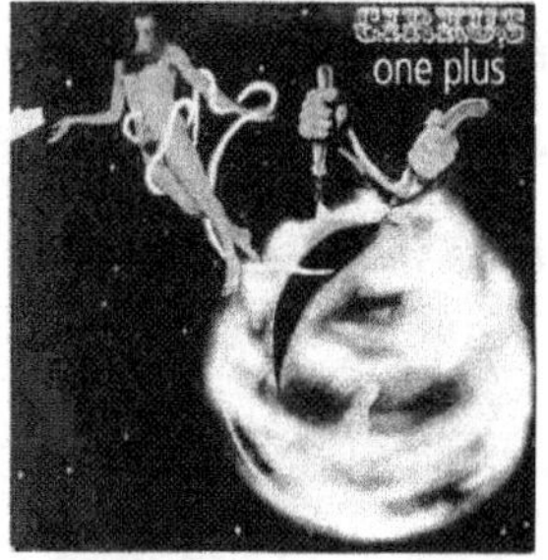

CIRKUS
ONE PLUS

CIRKUS
TWO: THE GLOBAL CUT

Cirkus were a popular North Eastern band in the early Seventies and their album, which was released in 1973, was a great success locally and has since become very much a collector's item. 'One' has now been re-released on CD, along with the three tracks that appeared on the "Melissa" EP from 1976, and two demos from 1971. Musically there is no mistaking where this music hails from, as it has all the classic stylings of early Seventies progressive rock. However, the almost pop feel (especially on songs such as "April 1973") and the use of many differing genres, puts them a cut above much of the rest. A musical reference might be Uriah Heep, but with a far broader base, and this may have been helped along by producer Ron Richards who had also worked with The Hollies. It is of little surprise that the original vinyl copies fetch so much money, or that it was reviewed so well by Sounds when it was originally reissued in 1986. This is an album that should be in everyone's collection. Cirkus finally split in the Eighties, but the name was revived by keyboard player Derek Miller in 1994 to highlight the vocal talents of Ian Weatherburn, with the only other musician featured being Paul Baker on guitar. The music produced from these sessions is very different from the earlier Cirkus, as there is a heavier emphasis on keyboards, and although the music has a wide approach it does not have the same "must purchase" appeal. Still, there are some wonderful moments here such as the delicate ballad "While I Sleep" where Ian shines. It would have been better to use a 'live' drummer but this small matter should be rectified for the next album, 'Pantomyme', as original songwriter and drummer Stu McDade is again working with Derek and it will also feature contributions from all previous band members. That is an album worth waiting for, but for now the Cirkus is back in town and you can't afford to miss it. *#33, Feb 1996*

CIRKUS
III - PANTOMYME

Following on from the success of the reissued 'Cirkus One' (originally released in 1974) and the follow-up 'Cirkus 2: The Global Cut' (only twenty years later), the guys have moved a bit more quickly this time to release this, their third album. It is probably the best to date, mixing and melding styles but always with wonderfully fluid and melodic vocals. Keyboard player Derek Miller was inspired to start Cirkus up again when he heard the vocals of Ian Weatherburn and it is easy to see why. Whether it is on the wonderfully commercial rock opener "Live For The Moment" (which I defy anyone not to enjoy) or the far more delicate "Letter To Simone", Ian is at home and in his element. This is music that belongs in the Seventies and today. I

would have liked to see lyrics in the booklet, which is basic, but the album more than makes up for it. Progressive and regressive, this is also bloody enjoyable.
#48, Apr 1998

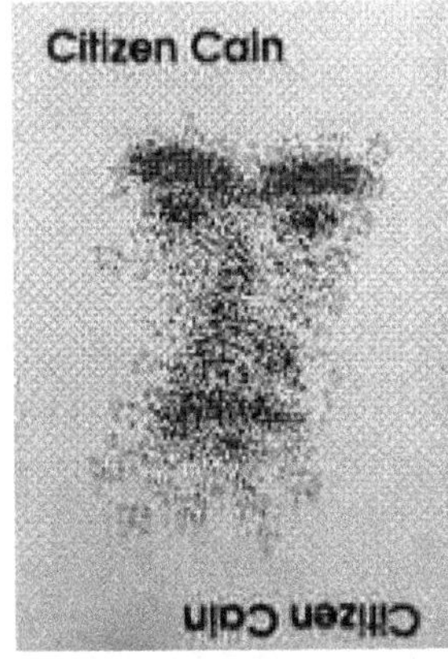

CITIZEN CAIN
DEMO

Citizen Cain were originally formed in 1984, and were based in London, consisting of George Scott (bass and vocals), Tim Taylor (guitar, keyboards) and Gordon Feenie (drums, flute, keyboards). Their support grew and they gigged with many name bands, as well as contributing a track to the 'Fire In Harmony' album and supporting The Enid for several gigs in 1988. Unfortunately, that same year a car crash left George unable to play bass due to hand injuries, and the band split up soon afterwards. On returning to his home city of Edinburgh, George met up with old friend Frank Kennedy (guitars), who along with Stewart Bell (keyboards) and David Elam (bass) had already been experimenting with their own progressive rock for some time. George (now calling himself Cyrus) expressed a wish to join on vocals and flute, and the line-up was completed with Chris Colvin (drums). This new Citizen Cain then played their first gig at The Venue in Edinburgh, on 12th September 1991.

They have just released their first demo and it is easy to see why The Organ is raving over them so much. With feet very firmly in the Seventies Genesis camp these four songs show how this type of rock can be played (now is only someone could tell Genesis...). Cyrus sounds like a mix between Peter Gabriel and Phil Collins and the music also reflects a mix of all that was best about Genesis. It may seem that Citizen Cain are a copyist band, but nothing could be further from the truth. Sure, their influences are there for all to see, but the music is wonderful soaring prog and has every right to be judged on its own merits. All four songs ("Stab In The Back", "Liquid Kings", "Nightlights" and "The Gathering") are musically complex and beautiful. Indeed, this demo has all the makings of a classic album, and at thirty-five minutes long is only just short of album length. If you like this style of music, then this is a tape that you cannot afford to be without. Citizen Cain are going to be huge, if there is any justice in the world. *#13, May 1992*

CITIZEN CAIN
SERPENTS IN CAMOUFLAGE

For those of you who have been around a while, you may remember my review of Citizen Cain's excellent demo tape back in #13. I, along with just about everybody who heard the tape, was extremely impressed and forecast great times ahead for the Scottish proggers, and at long last here is the CD. Three of the six songs appeared on the tape, but here they are in re-recorded form. I had played the CD a few times when I started to hear disturbing news about the band. I managed to get hold of David Elam (bass), only to have the sad news confirmed that due to disagreements with Cyrus (vocals), David along with Frank Kennedy (guitar) and Chris Colvin (drums) have left the band. This leaves Cyrus with Stewart Bell (keyboards) as the only two members of Citizen Cain who played on the CD. Apparently, they have recruited a drummer and have a new guitarist in the shape of Alistair MacGregor, but no bassist yet. It will be interesting to see if this is the end of the band, as David used to run all the admin side of things, and of course he and Frank were heavily involved with composition. I had been hearing things about the band for quite a while, and if this is the end of the road then it is a great shame, as here is an album that they can be rightly proud of and it could have heralded greater things to come.

'Serpents In Camouflage' kicks off with "Stab In The Back", which was my favourite song on the demo. Immediately your head is transported back into the Seventies, while your feet are kept firmly in the Nineties, and it is not as painful as you might think. Cyrus sounds like a mix between Peter Gabriel and Phil Collins, and the music is very heavily influenced by classic Genesis, although with a harder edge. The music started off very menacingly, with some grumbling bass from David: the keyboards join to lighten the mood, but it takes Cyrus to lift proceedings, although the menace never goes away. This is prog at its very best. The band gels and combines to produce music of the very highest order. Can they have broken up? "Liquid Kings" was thought by many to be their best song, and here it is as more than eleven minutes in length. At times, this could be from 'Foxtrot' or 'Nursery Cryme'. The epic has many different parts but they combine to add to the majesty of the whole, instead of detracting away from it. There are instrumental passages led by the keyboards, or delicate vocals, or powerful soaring rock. You want pomp and majesty? Here it is, in spades. So, there are six songs on this hour-long CD. When reviewing the tape, Graham Younger in Blindsight #3 said "This is so damn good. It's like someone has just put a prog grenade in my mouth and pulled the pin". If the tape was a grenade, then the CD must be a tactical nuclear warhead. I would urge anyone, everyone, who likes Genesis (when they were a proper band) to get this album, you will not be disappointed. It is a real pity for Citizen Cain that they will always be compared with Genesis, but that is the way of the world. All in all, this is a masterpiece. Citizen Cain in this form may have gone forever, but they have left something behind they can be rightfully proud of. STOP PRESS: The new line-up is Cyrus, Stewart, Alistair MacGregor (guitar), Nick Arkless (drums) and Andy Gilmour (bass). *#18, May 1993*

CITIZEN CAIN
GHOST DANCE

'Ghost Dance' is a collection of songs that were recorded by the original Citizen Cain between 1984 and 1987. At the time, they were a three-piece comprising George Scott (bass, vocals), Tim Taylor (guitar, keyboards) and Gordon Feenie (drums, flute, keyboards). They played at The Marquee, supported many major bands, and had a track on the famous 'Fire In Harmony' prog compilation. In 1988 George suffered a car crash that left him with hand injuries, and was no longer able to play bass. Citizen Cain consequently split up and George returned to Edinburgh where he met up with an old friend, Frank Kennedy. After a while the new Citizen Cain were born that went onto release the excellent demo and even better CD 'Serpents In Camouflage'. So, is this a viable release or is it just tidying up the loose ends? Well, there are eight tracks on here, and they are all brilliant! It is possible to discern the heavy Genesis influences, but that is probably due to a large part to George's voice.

There is a hard jazz-rock influence, and the combination of these factors mean that this version of Citizen Cain managed to produce music of the very highest quality. Favourite? Impossible, they are all so good. For any lover of Seventies Genesis taken and expanded then this must be the tape for you. In fact, the only glaring fault is that this is a tape and not a CD. Still, I understand that the new Citizen Cain would much rather be promoting their own recordings. To that end I was very pleased recently to receive a tape containing parts of three tracks from the next album, which will be called 'Somewhere But Yesterday'. The songs are "Johnny had Another Face", "Junk and Doughnuts" and the title track (the other two songs on the album will be "The Eggling" and "Strange Barbarians").

This is just rough demos, before the songs were finished, and therefore are literally only bits and pieces, not the finished article but they manage to show a definite move in style for Citizen Cain, much more into the progressive arena. Of course, it should not be forgotten that Cyrus (as George now calls himself) on vocals and Stewart on keyboards are the only ones that remain from the CD. I found myself thinking a lot about classic Tull, from the 'Thick As A Brick' era, combined with definite Genesis influences and some sounds more typical of Marillion. I have always enjoyed Citizen Cain's material, and from what I have heard the new songs show them getting even stronger.
#20, Oct 1993

CITIZEN CAIN
SOMEWHERE BUT YESTERDAY

Since their debut CD 'Serpents In Camouflage' was released in 1992, Citizen Cain have undergone some dramatic changes in personnel but vocalist Cyrus is still there, as is keyboard player Stewart Bell, and they have been joined by Nick Arkless (drums), Andy Gilmour (bass) and Alistair MacGregor (guitar). For anyone who hasn't heard of Citizen Cain then the year is probably 1974 and the band is Genesis. Now, that statement is probably unfair to both bands, but there is more than a touch of truth in it as well. Citizen Cain mix Genesis styles with others (most notably 'Thick As A Brick' era Tull) and then have them sung by Cyrus, the original Peter Gabriel sound-alike. Having upset a lot of people (including probably the band), what about the music on show? I am a great lover of this band, and anyone who has heard their debut CD or tapes will absolutely love this. Sure, it is regressive as opposed to progressive but who the hell cares? This album clocks in at over 67 minutes in length but there are only five songs! There are small pieces in-between the others, as a sort of break (shades of 'Aqualung'?). It kicks off with "Johnny Had Another Face" and is so powerful that it just sweeps you along on a wave of soaring guitars and keyboards. This is what progressive rock is all about, heavy and melodic, more than just bash and crash yet not sanitised out of existence. Highlight of the album must be the title track, which manages to provide interest for nearly twenty-six minutes ("Supper's Ready" anyone?). There is some stunning interplay between Stewart and Alistair, and the music twists and changes, getting ever more complex and complicated with Cyrus rising about it all. This is quite simply, a stunning album. Yes, it sounds very much at times like another band did twenty years ago, but there is far more to it than that. Genesis fans will love this, but it will also appeal to anyone into complicated music (and excellent lyrics). A classic. *#26, Dec 1994*

CITIZEN CAIN
PLAYING DEAD

It has been way too long since I last heard a new Citizen Cain album, and I see that this one was actually released at the end of last year. Does that mean that there is another one on the horizon? Not sure, as the web site hasn't been updated for a few months, but the site is live and it is possible to order the album through it. I also note that the X's have been dropped, so the band is again Citizen Cain and Cyrus is, again, Cyrus. The line-up has also been fluid, something that the band have suffered with over the years, but Cyrus is now not only providing vocals but also bass, as he used to years ago, and for this album Stewart Bell has not only provided keyboards but also drums, again as he used to years ago. They have now been completed by guitarist Phil Allen. It took nearly three years to record, and much of the momentum gained from their earlier superb albums such as 'Serpents In Camouflage' has been lost, and the new album has been released on their own label whereas the reissues of their SI albums had been on Cyclops. So is this enough to be able to get them noticed again? Hopefully the answer to that will be a resounding "yes", as yet again Cyrus and Stewart have produced an album that will have critics and progheads alike wanting to play it repeatedly. Citizen Cain will always find themselves compared to old-school Genesis because of Cyrus's vocal style, and the fact that he can sound uncannily like Gabriel when he wishes to. But, and it is a big "but", this is not an album of a Genesis copyist but rather an album that takes that musical ideal and moves with it. Genesis may have become something of a parody of their former selves but CC have shown that it is possible to develop that musical style into something that is still worthy of the label 'prog'. I love the Python excerpt in "Inner Silence"! The underground scene is not nearly as active as when they first came onto the scene, or even the second time, but now they are back for the third with a complex complicated album that any proghead will surely enjoy. It's time for progheads to rediscover the joys of Citizen Cain. *#76, Oct 2003*

CITRINITI
BETWEEN THE MUSIC AND LATITUDE

This is the debut album by Cintriniti; a band put together by drummer Danilo and his bassist brother Domenico with guitarist Fabrizio Leo. That the Cintriniti brothers can play should just be taken as read; I get the impression that Fabrizio is on board just to provide the extra tonal colour that they need to make the music interesting, otherwise this could be drum and bass all the way through! Mike Varney is exec

producer on this instrumental album, but unusually this is a trio where the guitar is probably the least in your face of all the instruments. This digipak release is something else with outstanding performances throughout. They know how to lay it down a bit more gently when they require, and they have brought in a couple of extra guests, but the joy here is listening to someone making a bass guitar sound like a lead instrument backed up by a drummer who is as adept as he is. Fabrizio is also playing some very fine licks indeed but this mix of fusion and prog is firmly in the hands of the brothers. The result is an album that is probably more of interest to the musician and those interested in playing ability than those who want to listen to some music without their jaw permanently wide open, but it is a good listen all the same.
#88, Jun 2006

CLEOPATRA'S NEEDLE
DEMO

Cleopatra's Needle is the brainchild of bassist Cliff Orsi and was formed in 1991 when he teamed up with guitarist Colin Wilson and vocalist, lyricist Chris Smith. Chris is the driving force between Whistler's Mother, with whom Cliff had been involved with in the Eighties. The line-up is completed by Miles Evemy (also of WM) and Mark Dolman. By 1992, when they were booked into Thin Ice to record 'Hunt The Snark', things were not working out and Miles, Mark and Colin all left. Replacements arrived in the form of Julian Hunt and Louis David (both of Grey Lady Down) and Tony Grinham (Threshold, Whistler's Mother). The material was developed by Cliff, Julian and Chris but external problems caused a delay in recording and by 1994 Louis and Tony had left, the line-up then changing to include David White (Moria Falls) and Brendan Loy. This demo showcases four songs that will appear on 'Through The Round Window', which will be recorded early next year. Cliff points out that they are only rough demos, with lots of fleshing out to be done, but already they augur well for the future. I like Chris's clear vocal style and he sounds as much at home here as he does on the more folky WM material. Julian Hunt shines on these songs, and to my ears he is more polished than he is with GLD! There is a strong mix of folk and prog, with clear vocals and strong lyrics and I am sure that Cleopatra's Needle will be an important addition to the UK prog scene. *#37, Oct 1996*

CLIFFHANGER
COLD STEEL

This is the debut album by Dutch band Cliffhanger, and what a debut it is too. Many of the prog bands around seem to fixate on Marillion, IQ or Genesis, and try desperately hard to either sound like them or to crank up the guitars and sound like Dream Theater. However, this new band (only formed in 1993) has neatly avoided these pitfalls and has come up with a sound of their own. This could well be because they are only a four-piece, and the music is based around the keyboards, but they are not laid back Jadis copyists but rather a band that takes ELP as a

starting point and heads off from there. There are definite similarities with some of the styles, aided by the fact that Moogs are in evidence, but Cliffhanger are very much a Nineties act, not 70's regressionists. From first to last this is a genuinely enjoyable, and genuinely progressive, album. Because they are not copying others it means that they have a sound unlike many, and the heavy use of keyboards in an attacking as opposed to passive role will have many prog fans rubbing their hands with glee as only a few bands manage to carry this off well. The instrumental passages show that here is a band confident in their own ability and they do not feel that they should pander to commercialism. If you like good conventional prog in the vein of ELP or VDGG then you will surely love this.
#32, Dec 1995

CLIMATE OF EARTH
CLIMATE OF EARTH
Climate Of Earth is two keyboard players from Tokyo, and apparently the band has been working since 1994 but I think that this is their debut release. Recorded in 2004 they bring other sounds into the music as well as just keyboards so that it has quite an earthy feel. I notice that all the five songs on this rather short album (just 25 minutes) are credited as coming from different parts of the world but with a website that is all Greek to me (well, Japanese anyway) I have no way of knowing what these mean. I do not know if some of the sounds are from that area, or if that is what they are trying to evoke with their music. More electronic than progressive, they do at least return to themes although sometimes this can be too much and "Sand Dance" is very repetitive. This is okay, but it could never be any more than that. *#86, Feb 2006*

CLOUDSCAPE
CRIMSON SKIES
Cloudscape evolved from Doctor Weird, who appeared at the Sweden Rock Festival in 2000. They released their debut album as Cloudscape last year and have already been back into the studio to record the follow up. They describe their music as melodic, semi-progressive, symphonic heavy metal and that is probably an accurate description. This does touch a lot of bases and so should find favour in many circles. The songs are punchy with good hooks, but there is a lot going on and the keyboard lines which run behind the main rock thrust are quite complex. The vocals are very good indeed and there are lots of layered harmonies, and the result is an album that rocks yet at the same time is very melodic as well. This is not normal AOR, and is too light and melodic to fit within the normal confines of prog metal but there are bits of both that combine to make an album that is accessible yet complicated, hard hitting but also very melodic indeed. This is a little gem of a CD that is certainly worth hearing – Mike Anderson has a strong powerful voice and if you are into this style of music you will want this.
#88, Jun 2006

THE COENOBITE
MY HABIT

Coen Vrouwenvelder is a graduate chemist and biomedical student who is currently working towards his PhD in medical sciences. As well as this, he is also The Coenobite which started off as a one-man project in 1988. Coen wanted to create atmospheric music, alternating between tension and relaxation, mixing rock and classic influences. He had previously taught classical and electric guitar for eight years, and used a myriad of techniques and influences to create his ideal. His first release was the 1990 cassette 'Turn The Page', and although it was well received there was a view that the vocals needed improvement. Still, encouraged by the response Coen spent a lot of time practicing various instruments and getting used to MIDI technology. Then in 1992 he went back into the studio and recorded 'My Habit', which has just now been released on CD. This is an instrumental album, with virtually everything being played or MIDI-ed by Coen. There are only four tracks, but one of these is over fourteen minutes in length while "The Aquarius Man" clocks in at just under half an hour. Coen sent me the reasoning behind every song, and it would have been nice to see this reproduced on the CD insert as it makes fascinating reading. This album is very much a 'grower', and demands careful listening. I play all CDs initially in the car when going to and from work, and it was only when playing it at home that I fully appreciated it. "Atmosphere" is very much the key word, as 'My Habit' lives up to Coen's original thoughts. My favourite is the closer "A-Band-On-Music" which contains a guest guitarist, and he and Coen develop interplay between electric and classical guitars. This is an album for those who just want to sit and relax to some wonderful sounds.

#18, May 1993

DR. COENOBITE
CASTLES IN THE AIR

Since the release of his debut album, Coen Vrouwenvelder appears to have gained his doctorate, so The Coenobite has become Dr. Coenobite. This is not the only place where there has been a change as this CD marks a huge step forward in both musical and production terms. Coen has again been joined by Joost Cornelisson on rock guitar but has also added a female vocalist in the form of Nynke Kooistra. The result is an album not too dissimilar to the Strangers On A Train project as classical forms are mixed with rock music and Nynke appears to have been listening to Tracy Hitchings as she breathes her way through the emotive vocals. Like SOAT, it has been put together with great care and is intensely listenable. The rock guitar supplied by Joost is never over stated and provides the perfect foil for Coen who supplies some wonderful keyboards (most notably some stunning piano) as well as guitars etc. To my ears the album works extremely well: it will appeal to fans of both classical and progressive rock music as it moves and mingles the two musical forms.

#25, Oct 1994

COLLAGE
MOONSHINE

I first heard of this Polish band a few years ago when Artur Chachlowski of Art Rock in Krakow started raving about them to me. He sent me some of their material and I was suitably impressed: they have now signed to SI and have a new CD out, with English lyrics. It has one of the most dramatic openings of any album I have heard recently, with keyboard chords that grab the attention. They are very much a rock band, and have a strong vocalist in Robert Amirian: the keyboards and guitar vie for dominance, while the rhythm section is more than willing just to provide a strong framework for it all. It goes from one superbly strong track to another without a pause for breath, 67 minutes 8 seconds of brilliance. They have had top twenty hits in Poland and with this CD I am sure that they will breakthrough to a much wider Western audience. There is no doubting their musical expertise, and the songs are just wonderful. I hope that someone will see fit to pay for them to get over here and play some gigs because that would be an experience not to miss. A prog album that should be in everyone's CD player: I defy you not to fall in love with it on first listen. *26, Dec 1994*

COLLAGE
CHANGES

This compilation is currently only available in Poland, but as their last album (the excellent 'Moonshine') was released by SI Music, this may well change. A history of the band is provided, along with full details about the line-up and details of the recording for each song. These go all the way back to their first recording session in 1985, and it must be said that from a development point of view the songs contained here are interesting, especially as there are version of songs which later appeared on 'Basnie' and 'Moonshine'. However, the quality of the songs does vary a tremendous amount, so although this may well sell in Poland (where there is a large following), I cannot see it doing much elsewhere. Buy their last album and look forward with eager anticipation to the next, but leave this well alone unless you are a completist.
#31, Oct 1995

COLLAGE
SAFE

The line-up hasn't altered since 1994's brilliant 'Moonshine', but musically Collage appear to be a very changed band indeed. Gone is the power and drama, and instead in comes a far greater reliance on keyboards and vocals which means that the Western audience that flocked to them in droves after the last album may now leave just as quickly. There are still the strong songs and good vocals, yet now there is much more use of acoustic guitar than previously and this is a lighter affair. So far this album has only been released in Poland and Japan, and it may well be that it will only be available from these countries as it has not been picked up by SI Music. Like the collection CD 'Changes' I would hesitate to say that it is worth all the extra effort and cost to obtain this, but I have found that the more I played it, it really grew on me and the closing "I Will Be There" is a little gem.

Possibly this is only for the diehards, but I am sure that we have not heard the last from these Polish proggers.
#33, Feb 1996

COLORSTAR
VIA LA MUSICA
It is not often that I feel at a total loss for words but I have no idea how I am going to describe this album for you. At times, it is world music, at others obviously eastern European, while others progressive, or is it pop? There are samples, music coming in at strange angles, bits that do not make sense, but then again do, perfectly. I attempted to listen to this initially while doing something else, but the something else failed miserably as I found my attention taken more and more by the music as I tried to work out what was going on. In the end, I decided that I did not have a clue but was going to enjoy it anyway.
#65, Dec 2001

COLORSTAR
KOMFORT
This was the third album from Hungarian band Colorstar (who apparently took their name from the brand of TV available under communism, which often exploded!) and was released in 2004. It is now available through Periferic although I think that it was probably released locally as an independent. Apparently, the band were originally very influenced by Ozric Tentacles but that is not immediately clear on this album which has moved far more into the pop arena with a lot of keyboards being used.

With all the lyrics in English there are times when this just manages to stay on the right side of electro and is something that is interesting and enjoyable. However, there are times where they move far more into the dance arena and while I can see that this would be popular in the clubs, it probably is not something that I would listen to a great deal myself. The songs where the guitars are to the fore are much more interesting to me but overall this is not a bad effort – just not my style
#88, Jun 2006

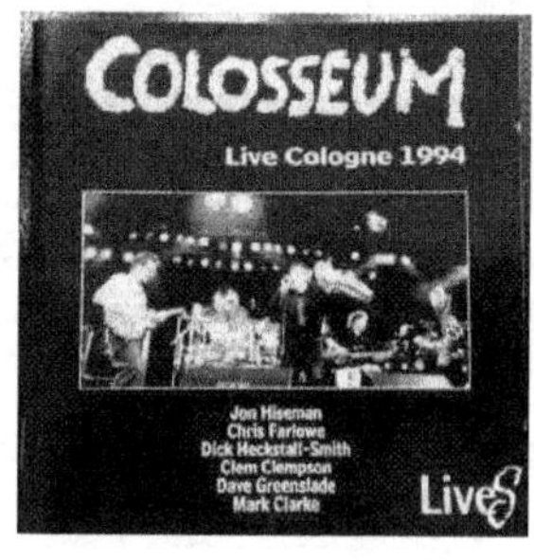

COLOSSEUM
LIVE COLOGNE 1994

I have previously raved about the superb Angel Air DVD of this concert, and this CD features six songs from their 1994 reunion tour. Considering the band were only in existence for three years they had enormous impact on the progressive and jazz rock scenes, and to hear them again some twenty-two years after they broke up is quite something (even more remarkable is that they are soon to release a new studio album and are touring again!). The band came from many backgrounds, but brought into the rock arena a strong love and understanding for both the blues and jazz. Jon Hiseman has long been rated as one of the best jazz drummers around; while there can be few sax players in the world that can stay the pace with Dick Heckstall-Smith. Add to that the guitar skills of Clem Clempson and keyboard playing of Dave Greenslade, with the vocals of Chris Farlowe (surely one of our most under-rated singers) and bassist Mark Clarke and here was the 1971 line-up back in full flow. Not a band made for singles or the radio, this is a band that strived on improvisation and building on each other, and so many years later that is still very evident in their performance. Yes, there are loads of solos and long instrumental passages, but the music just sounds right – created by people with tremendous skill and mastery of their craft but at the same time not being overindulgent (well, not too much). They know when the time is right to bring the rest of the band back in. A tremendous gig by a band on top form – Hiseman says that the years apart have meant that they now play better than ever, he could well be right.

#76, Oct 2003

COLT
FROM THE FRIDGE

This is another from the Polish label Wydawnictwo 21, and on the rear of the tray card it says 'Hardrock trip into the progressive 70's'. As is normal I played this for the first time in the car, and I certainly concur with that statement. So, it was with some surprise that I noticed in the booklet that this was recorded in February 2001 (between the 19th and 24th to be precise). Everything about this album cries out late Sixties/early Seventies, from the cover to the production, and of course not forgetting the songs in between. With the one cover on the album being an Atomic Rooster number ("I Want Your Love So Bad") it shows where these guys are coming from. Colt sound as if the last thirty years have passed them by, both in style and the instruments they use (there is some wonderfully classic organ), and they sound as if they have taken Rooster as a base and then gone out as far as Uriah Heep and picked up a few other bits and pieces as they have gone along. The last four-section song is over thirteen minutes long, and they have mixed classic prog with classic hard rock for an album that should have been released thirty years ago, not recently. With English lyrics, they have recorded something that is very listenable if you like the period.

#84, July 2005

COLTSFOOT
A WINTER HARVEST

It has taken seven years from initial idea to getting this CD completed, during which time the three members of the band found themselves in the same room only three times.

Hard to believe? Not really, when one of those involved is Rog Patterson. Rog provides guitars and bass (when he hasn't been all around the world as tour manager for acts such as Therapy?, Rage Against The Machine and Skyscraper or touring in his own right), while Geoff proudly provides keyboards and Stuart Martin provided the vocals and the constant nagging to get anything done at all. This is an album to be listened to and enjoyed at the end of the day, in a darkened room, with a few friends just sharing a quiet drink or four and mellowing out. 'A Winter Harvest' is based on the natural cycle of decay, rebirth and renewal, and as they say "Nothing ever really ends, as anyone who's heard an early Yes album will be aware..."

There is a greater use of keyboards than I would have imagined, but it is all done so terribly well and is an album of moods that relies on good musicianship rather than volume or energy to maintain interest. There are some folk influences here and there (especially on "Coracles") and overall the album is a delight. Favourite track is the twelve-string attack from Mr Patterson that is "The Runner" (where thanks to technology he also provides fretless bass)
#33, Feb 1996

CONCERTO MOON
RAIN FOREST

When I started listening to this album, I had the impression that it was by a Scandinavian outfit as it is very much in the Royal Hunt vein and many of the best European bands seem to be coming from that neck of the woods. Imagine then my surprise when on reading the biography I saw that these guys are Japanese! I think that this is the first album to gain a major release outside of their own country, but Limb Music in Germany are going to be re-releasing their other two albums to coincide with this one.

These are five guys who know what they are doing, and play intricate complex technical prog metal. They have recently been touring with Stratovarius and that must have been a gig worth seeing as in some ways they are quite similar.

All the lyrics are in English, and the music is very accessible indeed with superb musicianship. A very confident release and one that anybody who remotely enjoys melodic metal or prog metal will do well to search out.
#58, May 2000

CONQUEROR
STORIE FUORI DAL TEMPO

This is the second album from Sicilian prog act Conqueror, following on from their 2003 debut, 'Istinto', which is also available through Ma.Ra.Cash Records in Italy. I was surprised to see that Conqueror have been around for more than ten years, as this is the first time that I have come across them. Musically they have a lot in common with the early Seventies scene, mixing jazz in with some dreamy prog. The band use both flute and sax, but that is not where the similarity ends with Tull as there are some Tull-like keyboard and piano passages. In Simona Rigano they have a delicate singer who is at the same level as the instrumentation, never over the top but adding another element. This is the soft reflective prog of a bygone age, something that is powerful because of the lack of force, capturing elements of Genesis, Tull and possibly Camel but with their own distinctive edge. This is a wonderful album to play and drift away to, and I found that the Italian lyrics added to the experience as it meant that instead of concentrating on the words I could just let them pass me by. I have enjoyed this album and look forward to hearing more from both the band and the label if the quality of the rest is as good as this. *#85, Nov 2005*

CONSPIRACY
THE UNKNOWN

Conspiracy is the project of Chris Squire and Billy Sherwood, with the addition of drummer Jay Schellen. Chris provides bass and vocals and Billy guitar and vocals, and somewhat not surprising the result is an album that sounds suspiciously like Yes in many places, although without so many keyboards. It is only on listening to this that it becomes clear as to just how important Chris's vocals are to Yes, as while the music is interesting melodic rock it is the vocals that drive this album home. It is not possible to play this without comparing it to Eighties Yes, although the music itself is quite different, it is just that all the time the sound seems quite familiar. Is it an album that is worth purchasing on its' own merit? Having been a Yes fan for more years than I would care to remember I would probably want to hear this album just to see what it was about, and I am not sure how I would approach this if I was not so interested in knowing what the offshoot sounded like. But, this is an album that does keep the listener involved throughout. It is a bit laid back in places although the result is an album that does sound more like a band than a project. Melodic rock with just a hint of progressive tendencies which never falls into the trap of typical AOR, it will probably appeal more still to fans of Yes than of the genre. *#78, Apr 2004*

COURT
AND YOU'LL FOLLOW…

Court were obviously paying attention when they were listening to early Genesis and Tull as this album mixes together quite a few recognisable influences. Add to that some medieval ideas along with some good musicianship then this should be a great album. Scratch great and make that reasonable. There is nothing wrong with this, and at times it gets

quite lively and interesting but for the most part, although not quite prog by numbers, it does beg the question why bother? Maybe if it hadn't been quite so self-indulgent and serious, and maybe if the electric guitar had cut loose a bit more often, then possibly I could view it more kindly. Still, there is no use relying on maybe's. It may be a grower but I have only had the opportunity to play it twice, and on that basis, will probably not be doing so again.
#31, Oct 1995

THE COVENANT
SPECTRES AT THE FEAST (ADVANCE TAPE)
The Covenant have been together for about three years, and comprise Stephen Thomas Hall (keyboards, vocals), Steven Perkins (guitar), Ged Hambly (bass) and Nick Lister (drums). 'Spectres At The Feast' is going to be their debut CD, and is due out in a few months. Apparently, I am the first person outside of the band to hear this, and all I can say is that I am looking forward to having the finished article in my hands. Pomp/prog is the order of the day, with powerful rock songs., if they can cut it live, and I see no reason why they can't, then they must be superb. Expect a full review of the CD in the next issue: I know it's going to be a stunner.
#22, Mar 1994

THE COVENANT
SPECTRES AT THE FEAST
Well, back in #22 I mentioned the tape that I had been sent by those Macclesfield mayhem merchants The Covenant. At long last I have the CD in my grubby paws, and even though it arrived at the eleventh hour I just had to cobble together a review to get into #24, instead of waiting until the next one. The guys obviously have a huge sense of humour as they are all dressed up in medieval clothing, and have suitable descriptions along with the photos, such as "Sir Stephen Thomas Hall, the infirm, yet dashing young Duke of Marlboro and G 'n' T". Even before I had got as far as putting the CD on I was already impressed. I mean, so many of these bands take themselves so damn seriously. If a band are confident enough to take the piss out of themselves then they must be something special. Opener "Flowers In The Desert" is a song that has quality stamped all over it. Tom has a great voice, one that is full of emotion and depth, no thin reedy high pitched vocals here. Harmonies are provided by David Bower and this use of harmonies is a world away from Jadis as they convey emotion and power. In fact, this song is all about restrained power as it is almost balladic yet there is the strong feeling that there is a rock band being held back on a tight leash. Normally a rock band feels that the opener must be right there in your face, but not here. They start to open up with "Don't Come Running" and the pomp/prog feel that came across on the tape is definitely here in spades. They seem to combine elements of Galahad and Magnum to great effect, often within the same song. Tom does not sound like Bob Catley, but Steve Perkins seems to be influenced by Tony Clarkin. I have only had the album a few days but it is already a firm favourite. Best track is probably the title cut, which tells the story of life on the road with a real sense of humour running through it "so cue the music, cue the lights and trousers that are way too tight" or "the

hunt for the hairspray fags and beer, hysteria as time draw near". Great lyrics, powerful guitars with keyboards running melodies over the top and a spot-on rhythm section. Wonderful. The Covenant have yet to make a name for themselves among the prog world, and if they were in London then everyone would be talking about them. As it is they have a geographical mountain to climb, with Cheshire not exactly being the prog centre of the universe. This album could do it for them and personally I can't wait to see them live, as Tom not only provides sterling vocals but is the keyboard player as well. "Here entombed beneath the surface of your disk lie the immortal remains of the mighty Covenant, preserved for future generations". Dig it up, put it on, play it loud.
#24, Jul 1994

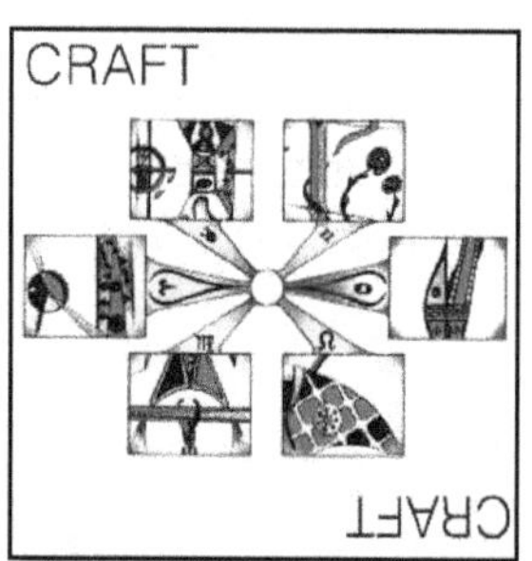

CRAFT
CRAFT

This is a reissue of the sole album by Craft, who comprised William Gilmour (keyboards), Grant McKay Gilmour (drums) and Martin Russell (bass, keyboards): all the guitar sounds were played on bass using a custom pedal board. William and Martin were both ex-members of The Enid, and obviously, this has played a large part in the sound of Craft. An instrumental album, it has taken the sound of The Enid but added a larger rock element, and it is strange to think that the crunchy guitar chords are being played on bass. Again, it is under forty minutes in length and contains only eight songs, two of which are bonus numbers so the original album must have been quite short indeed. The original songs are all based on different signs of the zodiac and is going to appeal to those who like their instrumental music to be meaty and not New Age, and to those who like the orchestral side. Obviously, it is a must for Enid fans, who are probably totally unaware of its existence or availability. The moods and styles swing and change, but there is always a sense of purpose and reason as the music builds and builds to climactic conclusions. There is even a Scottish element in songs such as "Leo", with good interplay between 'guitar' and keyboards. A very enjoyable album.
#23, May 1994

CREDO
FIELD OF VISION

Well, at long last it is here. I seem to have been waiting for this CD forever. Those of you with long memories may remember me reviewing Casual Affair at The Red Lion, Brentford, many, many moons ago. That was the first time I met up with vocalist Mark Colton, and we seemed to hit it off straightaway. It was not long after this that he told me of the break-up of the band and the formation of a new outfit, Freewill. Freewill were an extremely heavy band who managed to alienate prog fans by playing rock, yet at the same time not being appreciated by the metalhead as they retained their proggy roots. Success was not as good as it should have been and they split up. Oh yes, I was assisting them with gigs as well as writing their newsletter. However, for some time Mark hadn't been altogether happy with the way the band were "progressing" and had become vocalist with another band, Ad Hoc. A four-track demo was recorded and some gigs played (with a name change to Chequered Past) and after the demise of Freewill the band became Credo and were soon snapped up by Cyclops. Earlier this year I agreed to become their manager after seeing them play in Winchester, but it soon became apparent that I was not able to spend the time they deserved due to other commitments, and had to stand down. Credo are an extremely tight outfit, and musically very strong, which is probably because they are OLD! Well, bassist Jim 'Mudrock' Murdoch and guitarist Tim Birrell have been playing with each other for more than twenty years (most notably in HR outfit Armageddon). They have honed their skills on the live circuit and have brought influences from so many spheres that they defy categorisation. Are they prog? Does the label matter? Here is a rock band that puts accessibility and damn good tunes at the forefront. Mik (Stovold, keyboards) and Mark are both lyricists of the highest order and so it is that the songs have real meaning. I was a little concerned that the power of the live performance may not have been transferred to the CD, and a big part of their act is the sheer presence of Mark, who must be one of the best frontmen around. Live, every song is explained, each has a story. This was all missing here, so would it manage to convey just how good they are?

I shouldn't have worried. "Rules of Engagement" kicks things off very nicely indeed. Mik does not fit the normal keyboard player norm, as he only has a little one and concentrates on providing deft touches here and there as opposed to walls of sound. Paul Clarke and Jim keep everything nailed down, and Mark and Tim manage to stay restrained during the verse until it is time for the lead break and the venom to rise. The song is about the way that relationships can change after marriage and the consequences "And if you get caught out on a sortie into the red light of no man's land, a firing squad of lawyers will shoot you out of hand". "Good Boy" was, until very recently, the set opener. Hell, this is rocky enough to get everyone up and bopping. Commercial? Possibly, although somehow I can't see Mark having the opportunity to spit his vitriol on TOTP. Like so many of their songs, it is the sudden change in tempo or musical direction that provides the emphasis. "Don't Look Back" is a ballad about the passing of time, and asking about what happened to the person we used to be, how it affects us all. Again it is the musical change that makes this song, as just when it gets all a bit sugary and sentimental the song takes on new life "the weekend comes, I visit my folks, the only entertainment's when my grandma chokes". "Alicia" starts off slowly but gradually picks up tempo. It is a beautiful song with some wonderfully restrained guitarwork from Tim. Again, the guitar break signifies the total change in emphasis as the song suddenly gets a much harder edge.

"Power To The Nth Degree" is a cheerful little song about how we are ruining the planet we live on because all we are interested in is money. These are Mik's best lyrics, as visual images abound in one frightening form after another. "There's power to the Nth degree, computerised hysterectomy, your way of life rips the womb from Mother Earth". It starts off just a simple bass and drum line, but all the way through both instrumentation and vocals combine with the words to give a real edge to the horror they are describing. As the song picks up speed Mark sings faster and faster, but it is the solo that demonstrates real speed as Tim attempts to melt the frets in a blur. "Phantom" is another that is bass-driven, and picks up menace as it progresses. Tim's flashing fingers combine with Mark's poignant vocals to create a powerful visual image. "Sweet Scarlet Whisper" was one of the first songs performed by the band, and is full of beauty and majesty. "Party" is the new set opener, and is in a similar ass kicking mood to "Good Boy": the scene is that a party is held but the host only invites girls he has slept with, thinking that it will give him a real ego trip. However, the dream becomes a nightmare as the guests realise what they all have in common. A driving rock number. That only leaves room for "A Kindness", the gentle ditty about a serial strangler, and is the song that was chosen for the Cyclops sampler. Mark takes on the persona of a twisted individual and the music twists and climaxes with an extended solo, and Tim's guitar rises and soars like an angel.

Phew! It is possible that I am just a little biased. However, in my favour I can only say that I have been playing this to anyone who will listen and they all rate it highly. Paul, Tim, Mik, Mark and Jim have produced an album they can be proud of. Credo * Believe. I know I do
#25, Oct 1994

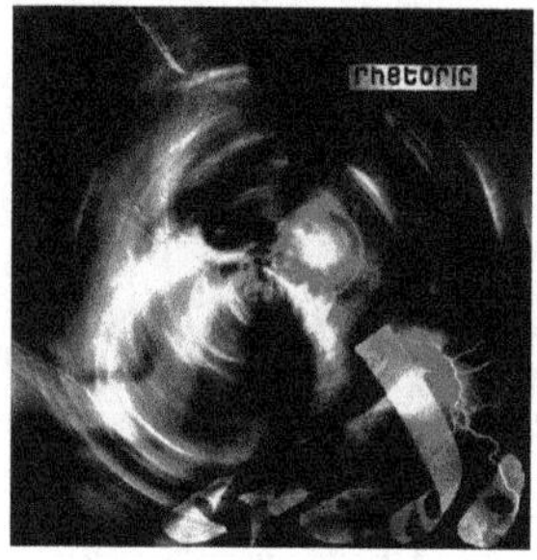

CREDO
RHETORIC

Just to let you all know the score between me and this band, at one time in their career I was getting gigs for them and assisting them with promotion etc. I was there the night when the contract with Cyclops Records was signed for 'Field Of Vision', and this album has followed only eleven years later. Singer Mark Colton and I first got in touch with each other when he was with Casual Affair: when that band broke up I then wrote the newsletter for his next band Freewill, and when he joined Chequered Past (later renamed Credo) I started following them around as well. When I got married only two people knew in advance as they were the witnesses, and one of these was Mark. Many years later I was asked by Mark and his wife Elaine to be godfather to their younger son, and I even traipsed out one night to see Mark front a folk-rock band called Phyre!

So, there you have it. Eleven years is a long time for any band to produce their second album, during which time more than a few things have happened. Musically they brought in Shadowland (and currently Landmarq) keyboard wiz Mike Varty which changed their sound as it meant that Tim Birrell finally had someone to play against (poor old Mik Stovold was never in the same league), while drummer Paul Clarke announced one night after a blinding gig that he was also off and he was replaced by Martin Meads from the aforementioned folk group! The line-up is completed of course by the one and only Jim Murdoch who as well as playing bass also assists Mike with the backing vocals. And then there is Mark, who got married, had two children, and was at one point only thirty minutes from dying. Luckily there were some very clever consultants around that managed to keep him in this world, but there were many who thought that this album would never be completed. Even now he is still having to attend hospital and is a long way from being fully fit, but he is back singing and very much full of enthusiasm for the band.

The album which I first heard clips from back when Mark was still single has finally made it out. It seems years since I was in the studio listening to Martin lay down the drum tracks with Karl Groom et al, but it was. There can probably be as few waiting so eagerly for the finished product as I, and it was not until the CD finally arrived that I believed that it was real. Looking at the track listing I recognised many from those heady days playing in Staines and other toilets, but putting it on the player I know that it never sounded like this! This is polished neo-prog that we never hear these days, songs with a meaning, with a singer who can turn on the vitriol when he needs and somehow is also singing better than ever – given what Mark was going through during this process the result is nothing short of incredible as they have produced an album that is going to rate as one of the best of the year, whatever the genre. But you're biased I hear you cry, and maybe I am, but hopefully those who know me would realise that if I felt that this was under par then I would say so. It just is not possible to fault this in any way – Mike is an incredible keyboard player as anyone who has seen him will agree: there are not many who have been chosen by Clive Nolan to fill his own shoes, while Tim Birrell managed to shrug off an approach from Fish who wanted him for his own band and who is, I firmly believe, one of the best guitarists around, and is Credo's secret weapon as no-one outside of those who follow the band know who he is! Martin and Jim have a real understanding, nailing the rhythm to the floor either slowly or flying with a passion, and then there is Mark. Mark is more of a frontman than just a singer, as he throws himself into every performance with passion, but here he has proved what a bloody good vocalist he is as well.

Nine songs, with two of them over eleven minutes in length, but the one that I feel should be singled out appears half way through the album and is just under eight minutes long. I was there at The Compasses the night that "The Letter" had its first public airing, the night when the person that it was directed at fled to the toilets in tears. Back then it was full of passion and incredible guitar, but somehow it has now become so much more. If ever a song builds to a climax then this is it, with Mike much more to the fore – giving the song balance, while Jim also changes his bass approach during the song which gives it further depth. There is a polish and togetherness which was not there before, with the vocals flowing and providing the background for Mark to vent his passion, his anger. I could rave about these songs – the wonderful intro to "The Game" or the closing masterpiece that is "Seems Like Yesterday", but all the numbers have benefited from a new approach and cleaner, sharper, but also very layered, arrangements.

There are various quotes within the well-designed booklet, one of which is "Nostalgia is not what it used to be" and while in some ways I look back to those days when Credo were playing anywhere and everywhere, even driving up the M1 to Mansfield, but I know that the band I prefer are the one who have finally released their second album, an album that is going to surprise and delight a great many people. 'Rhetoric' is a delight, an album of great songs by

a band who have been through a lot to get this far – so now is the time to support them by going out and buying it. It does not get any better than this.
#85, Nov 2005

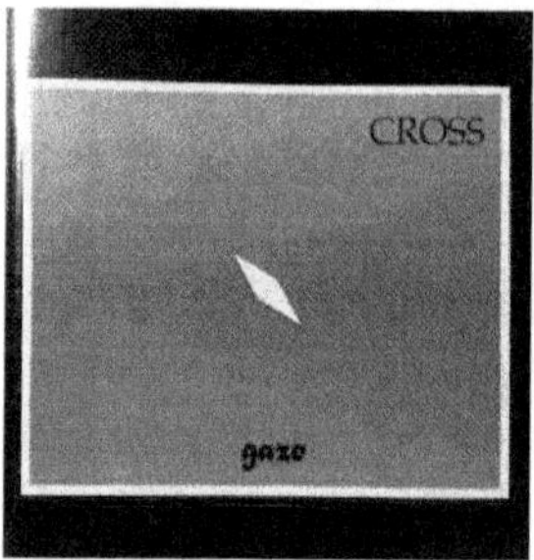

CROSS
GAZE

I can tell you very little about this Scandinavian prog band except that this is their fourth album (the others having already been deleted) and the first one to be made available in the UK. There is nothing new about what they are doing musically, they have been playing close attention to IQ as well as taking note of bands such as Genesis and Kansas (although there is not a violin in sight), but it is a fun album nonetheless. All the lyrics are in English and it is an incredibly accessible piece of work. "Introverted Mirrors" shows the extremely technical side of the band, as the introduction blasts in best IQ fashion, then mellows, then blasts again. The bassist is doing some interesting work here. Although the name Cross is not well known in the UK at present, this album could well change that. Of course the term 'progressive' is at its most inaccurate when describing the music of Cross, but if you are into this genre of music then 'Gaze' is an album you will almost certainly enjoy.
#37, Oct 1996

CROSS
DREAM REALITY

Cross's last album, 'Gaze', was so well received that a decision was made to put together a compilation of songs from their first three albums which were only previously released in Sweden and were no longer available. However, instead of just picking some songs and doing nothing with them, Hansi Cross took his band back into the studio and re-recorded some while he also remixed and re-mastered some others. In the booklet he lists personnel, instrumentation played, and a little bit of history about the songs: us anoraks like to see this, even if we have never heard the originals. Some of the music is quite symphonic in nature while at others I found myself thinking of Genesis crossed with 10CC (I can't help the way that my mind works, honest). The length of the songs varies considerably as well, with one lasting under a minute while another lasts for nearly fourteen! Also, Cross is at times a band while at it others it is just Hansi accompanied by one or two others. He is no mean musician, as can be seen on "The Fake", where he and drummer Hadders play jazz rock for fifty-nine seconds, in which time there are some very speedy guitar runs. Overall this is not the greatest album in the world, but it is solid and enjoyable and worth casting an ear to.
#47, Feb 1998

CROSS
VISIONARY FOOLS

I remember reviewing an album by Cross which was released on Cyclops some time ago, but I know that they had released other albums even then. They have now set up their own label and their latest album is its' first release, but with no bio I can further very little else. Cross are based around lead singer, guitarist (plus extra keyboards and mandolin) Hansi Cross, although the others do get some input on some of the songs. This is soaring prog, with large elements of Eighties Genesis and Pendragon, and at some points, it is almost Camel-esque. While there are many intricate passages, the focus is much more on songs with a purpose instead of meandering aimlessly. While the vocals are important, the main elements are the interplay between the guitar and keyboards along with some very strong, almost tribal, rhythms. This is an album that I have enjoyed playing immensely.
#59, July 2000

CROSS
SECRETS

The most recent album from Swedish proggers Cross is easily the best of theirs that I have heard to date. Intricate and sometimes quite menacing (check out opener "Bleeding In Silence") with good musical interplay, all fans of modern prog will enjoy this album. A few guests add some extra touches (such as cello), but for the most part this trio rock on quite nicely with no outside help. Hansi Cross provides guitars, synths and vocals while Lollo Andersson is on bass and Taurus and Tomas Hjort is on drums. It is a very accessible album, one that can be listened to and enjoyed immediately. I nearly did not hear the 'hidden' piece of music as the first time I played the album I turned it off when the last song ended. The next time I was too far away from the player, and after a while I heard some keyboard chords and wondered where it was coming from… I did not see much point of this unless it was to see if reviewers were listening to the album all the way through!! They move through one style to another very comfortably and while this may not be ground-breaking progressive music, it is very nice all the same and I for one enjoyed it.
#60, Oct 2000

CROSS
PLAYGROUNDS

There were four years between the release of the previous Cross album, 'Secrets', and 'Playgrounds' and this was eventually released last year. The line-up was Hansi Cross (guitars, keyboards, lead vocals, harmony vocals, and percussion), Lollo Andersson (bass) and Tomas Hjort (drums, harmony vocals). There were also various guest musicians used during the process who all added their individual

talents to the overall sound (such as the beautifully restrained sax by Linus Kåse on "A New Beginning"). Hansi has developed the sound of Cross over the years so that although there are sections that one might say has been influenced by Yes, Genesis, IQ or Jadis this is a band that is developing very much its' own sound and must be seen as an important band in their own right. This is one of those prog albums that is very accessible first time it is played, with lots going on but the more that it is played the more the layers become apparent. The guitar is an important instrument, but in the style of Steve Hackett as opposed to crunching riffs. Harmony vocals and well-structured songs make this a joy to listen to, and any fan of intricate prog will enjoy this. Only two longer numbers, but the album flows very well and this is a wonderfully laid-back album full of atmosphere and ambience.
#83, Mar 2005

DAVID CROSS
CLOSER THAN SKIN

David Cross was of course violinist during one of the best-loved periods of King Crimson's long existence, and here he is with ten new songs co-written with bassist Mick Paul and ex-King Crimson lyricist Richard Palmer-James. So is this a King Crimson album by another name? No, definitely not. Is it something worth listening to? Different answer altogether. This is a hard rock album first and foremost, with concentrated riffs, and often more going on in the bass line than in the guitar – often playing in harmony with David's electric violin. Arch Stanton has a powerful voice that is not too high and combined with the instrumentation of the band makes this a rock album unlike many others. Those looking for a progressive or neo-progressive work will be fairly disappointed, although David does sample part of "LTIA2" and "Awful Love" is not as pressurised as some of the rest of the album, but this is a rock album with extra instrumentation. While some people will want to get this album just because of the KC link, they may well be pleasantly surprised as this is an album that is certainly enjoyable in its own right, no matter what the history of David is.
#85, Nov 2005

CROSS 'N' CRAZY
WET

Cross 'n' Crazy are another German outfit happy to tread on the line that tries to divide prog rock from 'normal' rock and the result is a very melodic album (although not as heavy as label mates Ivanhoe) that should appeal to many into the prog scene. They manage to avoid sounding like Americans, although the vocals are good, by having more of an edge to the guitar and therefore to the whole proceedings. Songs like "Vertigo", the longest at over eight minutes, display Galahad-style touches and time changes while maintaining a heavier guitar presence. They do not feel the need to provide epics, with four songs clocking in at just four minutes, quite a

rarity in prog these days as the move is to longer and longer songs. The material is good, and the musicianship high, and if you enjoy your prog with a larger element of guitar (although not nearly as heavy as Dream Theater or Threshold) then this could well be for you.
#32, Dec 1995

CRYPTIC VISION
LIVE AT ROSFEST 2005

Cryptic Vision's third ever live gig was at the Rites Of Spring Festival, in front of an audience who probably had never even heard of the band before, let alone own their debut album 'Moments Of Clarity'. The only thing to do then was to take the place by storm and start off as they meant to go on with plenty of hard rock guitars mixing in with the swirling keyboards. The band had been playing for more than five minutes before the vocals started, and what vocals! Again, may as well aim to impress and four part harmonies with more than a hint of Yes does it for me every time. Lead singer Todd Plant may be better known in AOR circles due to fronting Eyewitness and Millenium but it can't be long before he is known by the progheads as well. All of the material is written by drummer Rick Duncan who is content just to do his stuff and let all the others provide the harmonies while he concentrates on driving the band along. They may not be a prog metal band, but they sure know how to rock – there is not anything wimpy or laid back about these guys. It really is difficult to comprehend that this is only their third gig as they come across very polished and happy in this environment. The album is a delight from start to end and I am already looking forward to the album they are currently working on. If it was not enough to perform their own material they also put together a very enjoyable medley of material from Spock's Beard, Yes, Kansas, Dream Theater, Genesis and ELP – not bad for guys who have not played together a great deal. This is well worth investigating.
#87, Apr 2006

CRYPTIC VISION
IN A WORLD

So, Florida based progressive rock quintet Cryptic Vision are back with their second studio album, and while in the past they have been likened at times to Spock's Beard and Kansas (among others), they have now taken that to the next stage by asking Alan Morse and David Ragsdale to guest on the new work. If these guys are not careful they are going to find themselves being held in as much acclaim as those two bands, although this will also appeal to progheads of every style, whether it is the keyboard driven Saga, the symphonic harmonies of Yes or just lovers of good music. This is prog that while looking backwards is also very much looking forward and is very much of the moment. Whatever you could possibly wish for in prog music you will find it here. Whether it is stomping solid bass lines, complex complicated

rhythms that come together to make musical sense, great soaring vocals, tunes to stick in the skull, it is all here. For some reason I do not think that these guys have been getting as much publicity this side of the pond as they richly deserve – let's hope that they play some dates over here soon to rectify that. This is progressive rock of the very highest quality, and one that all progheads definitely need to investigate.
#89, Sep 2006

CRYSTAL MAZE
WAITING IN THE SPIDER'S WEB

This German outfit's debut album was released in the late Eighties, and shows a good mix of styles, depending on which song you are listening to. Sometimes they are dreamy and laid back like Camel, while at others there is more venom and bite, and they sound more like classic Yes. The vocals work well, and although there are plenty of harmonies there is still a rougher edge at times that takes away the sugar sweetness. The same is true of the guitarwork, just when you feel that they are being sanitised out of existence they come storming back to centre stage with a vengeance such as on "Floating Ice". It is in the harder passages, such as the introduction to "Menhunter", that Crystal Maze really shine. That is not to say that they do not play the reflective material well, rather that here is a rock band struggling to get out. There is a lot to like about this album, but if they had concentrated on the heavier material then I feel that it would have been even better.
#31, Oct 1995

CRYSTAL PHOENIX
THE LEGEND….

'The Legend Of The Two Stonedragons' follows on some fourteen years since the debut. At that time the band was just one person, Myriam Sagenwells Sagliembeni (who on this recording provides vocals, guitars, bass and harp). A band was formed to play some gigs but they had disbanded by 1992. In 1993 Black Widow put out the album, their first ever release. In 2000 Myriam formed a new band, and she has now been joined by Tina Vadalà (vocals, cymbals), Raymond Sgrò (piano, keyboards, bass guitar, flute, recorders) and Robert Mazza (drums). But this is now a band and Myriam shares song-writing duties with Raymond. The album is divided into two, the past and the future, and contains a complex story that ranges from fantasy to science fiction. Luckily the background and all of the lyrics are provided. Musically this is quite a dreamy album, with the emphasis on delicacy instead of bombast: the vocals are extremely important with a high vocal line often being used as an instrument. The impression is of a time gone by, and the label calls this 'Epic Folk Prog'. It is almost as if Legend had joined forces with Steeleye Span, so that even when the band try to break free they can only do so within certain constraints. Overall an interesting album, but I am not sure how often I will be returning to it. *#74, Jun 2003*

VEDRES CSABA
BREATHED PRAYER
The sub-title of this album is 'The Editors' Choice'. Label boss Gergely Böszörményi chose what he felt were the best pieces from Vedres' canon, to which another ten short unreleased pieces were added. The result is an album which contains thirty songs, with the piano very much the instrument of choice. Some of the songs are instrumentals, others songs with Vedres singing in Hungarian, with very little in the way of extra musicians. He has a delicate touch with the piano, much more restrained than the more bombastic Keith Emerson although he does have some similarities with the gentler more laid back Rick Wakeman. This is music that any pianist will enjoy, much of it is in the classical form but he can add some flourishes of jazz when he wants to. It is an album that seems to have a deep sadness within it, and it is quite melancholic at times. This is particularly true of track nine (much better than another horrible exercise in inserting symbols) where a violin displays a particularly sad voice. An album that is full of restrained passion and a dark beauty, which will be of great interest to lovers of classical and piano music.
#78, Apr 2004

CURIOUS WORKS
WHERE FABLES DIE
Artur gave this to me when he stayed here last, and I know nothing about this band except that they are an American five-piece fronted by a female vocalist, Marissa Von Bargen. On top of that, this album is very short, being less than thirty minutes in length. Overall it is pleasant, but really nothing much more than that. Marissa's vocals are fairly good, but certainly not outstanding, and the same can be said for the six songs on show.

Not prog by numbers, but nothing here that stands out enough to latch onto. The music shows leaning towards Grey Lady Down, but I cannot say that I am surprised that I had not heard of the band before and unless they show rapid improvement I doubt I will hear of them again.
#34, Apr 1996

CURVED AIR
ALIVE 1990
As may be guessed from the title, this was a reunion album from 1990. It was sixteen years since they had played together, but this CD captures Sonja Kristina, Darryl Way, Francis Monkman and Florian Pilkington-Miksa in full flight. Original bassist Rob Martin even makes a guest appearance on "Vivaldi". This is definitely a case of give the crowd what they want, with the songs coming from the first three Curved Air albums. They close with "Back Street Luv", and it is almost a shame that this is the song that most people know them for, as I have always felt

that "Melinda (More Or Less)" is the highlight, although the ten-minute long "Vivaldi" is also a classic. If you are a fan, then this is an album that you cannot live without. They had a sound all of their own, and while it does sound dated, it is still an album that I enjoyed hearing.
#60, Oct 2000

CYAN
FOR KING AND COUNTRY

The story of Cyan is a strange one, to say the least. They recorded a demo in the Eighties, sent it to various bands and fanzines, and then promptly sank without trace. Nick Barrett of Pendragon had been sent one of these demos, and he eventually passed it onto a French music lover who was so impressed he wrote to the contact address. Robert Reed, the ex-keyboard player, was amazed to find someone interested in a group that had finished four years earlier: he decided to do something with the material, and set about re-recording the songs, playing all the instruments and providing the vocals. This daunting task was completed with the cassette release of 'For King and Country – Reworks 1991'. I am assuming that this CD contains all the material on the earlier tape (which I have not heard) as all attempts to contact Robert have failed miserably. So, on this CD Robert plays various guitars and keyboards, and programmed the drums. What the end product is, to all intents and purposes, is very much a 'group' album yet recorded by only one musician. I must confess that I have never heard a solo multi-instrumentalist album like this before, as instead of self-indulgent meanderings that can so easily arise, here is someone totally confident in his ability to do full justice to some wonderful music. The opening track is the epic "The Sorcerer", and immediately one forgets that this is just one musician, and instead concentrates on the song. Over eleven minutes in length, it really brightens up with some great guitar passages mirrored by the keyboards. There are also ballads and instrumentals, but it is the rockier passages that captured my attention, reminiscent at times of IQ or Pendragon: all things considered this is one helluva achievement. It will be interesting to see if Robert will put together a band to take this music on the road as it is really should be heard in a live environment. The weakest part in my mind is that of the vocals, as although Robert can sing well I feel the music could do with a stronger vocalist. Still, it is more than well worth discovering. STOP PRESS: I have now heard from Robert, who has joined Ezra as keyboard player. It will be interesting to hear them live as they intend to play material from this album as well as their established set.
#18, May 1993

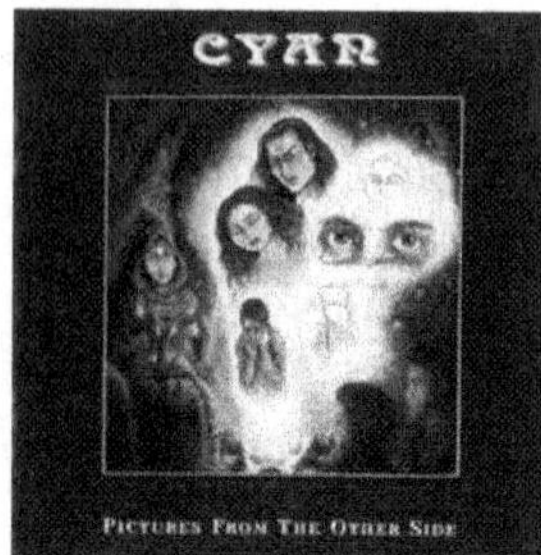

CYAN
PICTURES FROM THE OTHER SIDE

One of the most amazing CDs to come out of the prog scene over the last few years was Cyan's 'King and Country', and when I say "Amazing" I really do mean that, because Cyan are a one-man band with Robert Reed providing all of the parts yet managing to sound like a commercial prog rock outfit in full flow. It was then with some anticipation that I put the new CD on the player, having noticed that for this album Robert has engaged the vocal talents of Nigel Voyle. I was a little surprised as Robert is a fine vocalist in his own right, but here he is playing second fiddle, but I soon realised why he had done that as Nigel is superb. He used to be vocalist in Just Good Friends, who were signed to Polydor and played the Reading Festival in 1983, while more recently he was one of those who lucked out to Steve Hogarth in the Marillion audition stakes. You may as well start as you mean to go on, and 'Pictures From The Other Side' commences with the extremely hard hitting "The Guardian", which is twelve minutes in length. I feel Robert has been listening to some Kansas in his spare time, as some of the piano breaks could have come straight from that band, but the guitarwork is far more than that as the pomp rises majestically. Robert has definitely moved on with this album, and it will appeal to anyone who likes good commercial rock.

Hell, I am sure that many of you may wonder why on earth people reviewing use neat little pigeonholes or labels to put bands into, I review a lot "prog", simply because that is what gets sent to me. Sure, it is very easy to say that this is progressive rock music, but this covers such a multitude of sins that really it does not mean anything. There are bands around that are clones of others, but for the most part each of the bands in the underground scene have very much their own identity and could be huge. Do you like Genesis, Marillion, Tull, Journey, Magnum or any of the other hundreds of good commercial acts around that could be labelled, prog, pomp or AOR? Well, there are bands in the UK that could take these on and play better songs and give better live performances that you could ever imagine. You will not read about them in the mainstream rock press, and in this country, Cyan will be lucky to sell a thousand copies of this album. Most of that will be through mail order outfits as even Pinnacle reps cannot be bothered to sell into record shops even though labels such as Cyclops and Now & Then have arranged distribution. A review of an album has turned into a diatribe against the music industry in the UK. I really feel for these guys as I love this album, and I know that many of you would as well, but will you go out and buy it through a mail order company? Probably not. If you could go into a record shop and see it for sale, then you could ask for a few tracks to be played and see that I am saying about this and all the other CDs I review is correct. There is damned good music out there, if only you could hear it. These bands literally exist hand to mouth, but where is the future going to lead us? Looks at the charts: the few records that are any good stand head and shoulders above the crud, but it is rare for these to do well. What the hell is the rubbish that is normally No.1 doing there? Yet it will be religiously played by the radio and is featured on numerous TV programmes. Maybe no-one likes this sort of music anymore, but that can't be right, surely? How many copies of their last album did Genesis or Marillion sell? Marillion were the last prog band to really make it big in the UK, but that was ten years ago so what is going to happen to the UK scene? Bands like Cyan, with their class albums and songs will just cease to exist. Record companies do not make albums just for the fun of it, there has to be a return. Luckily for many of the bands, at least the European scene is a little more switched on than the UK. Enough. I could write and ramble forever. I feel drained, as if I am pursuing a one-man crusade for the cause of good music. Take it from me, this Cyan album has a lot to offer and deserves better than I have written about it. But will you buy it?
#25, Oct 1994

CYAN
REMASTERED

Way back in time, the artwork for Cyan's 'King and Country' CD featured on the front cover of an issue of Feedback. Inside I told the story of the keyboard player of a defunct band taking it upon him to re-record a demo and release the album through SI. Not only did Rob Reed play all the instruments, he also provided all the vocals. For the next album, 'Pictures', he was joined by Nigel Voyle (vocals), and a few guests (including Andy Edwards from Ezra). Rob played keyboards with Ezra for a while, before co-founding The Fyreworks with Danny Chang (which also features Andy). Because Cyan was a solo project as opposed to a band, live gigging was limited, and after the demise of SI of course the CDs were no longer available either. This has now been rectified, as though another record company had suggested releasing both CDs again, possibly with extra material, Rob has decided instead to release 'Remastered' through Festival Records (to whom The Fyreworks are also signed). The first four songs are taken from 'King and Country' (with one being remixed) and the next five from 'Pictures' (again with one being remixed). Although Rob has a good voice, it is the second half that is the more enjoyable of the two, not only is there a better singer but also by now Rob had gained quite a bit of confidence and was able to explore his sound. Although in this country Cyan possibly did not make the impact they should have, this is probably due to the lack of gigs and certainly not down to the quality of the material. This is high-class prog that soars and swoops, at times Floydian while at others dynamic and driving. If you like class UK prog, then now is the time to discover again the joys of Cyan.

#44, Sept 1997

ISTVÁN CZIGLÁN
SEVEN GATES OF ALHAMBRA

This is a posthumous solo album by Istvan Cziglan, who used to be guitarist with Solaris, one of Hungary's premier progressive rock bands. I have to say that this is a wonderful looking release, being a foldout digipak in a slipcase. It is just a shame that all the words are in Hungarian, as I get the impression that a lot of care has been taken over this. Apparently, the guys from Solaris tidy up some of the uncompleted ideas, but otherwise the music has been left untouched, as they did not want to make this just another Solaris album. It opens with "Personal Gravity", which at more than seventeen minutes in length is easily the longest song on the album, although the title song does also creep in at over ten. It is mostly an instrumental album, with voice being used more as an instrument than being the main focal point. There is also quite a lot of different styles with keyboards much more to the fore than one would expect on an album from a guitarist. Although there are touches of folk, there was not much to point to this being an album from Eastern Europe. Overall, a very interesting album, with some good musical ideas, and one that can be listened to many times, finding more on each hearing.

#56, Jan 2000

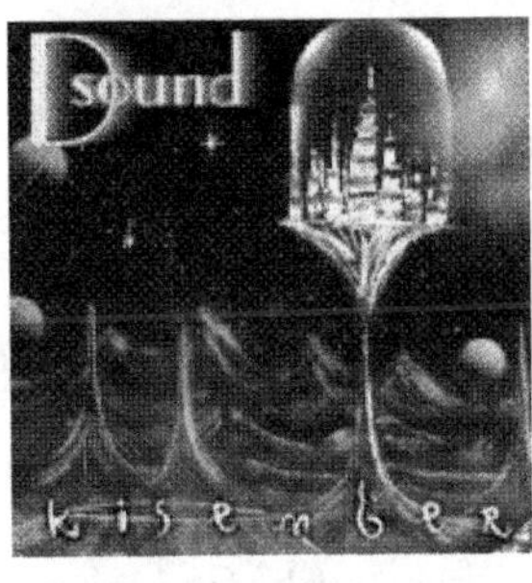

D SOUND
KISEMBER

Zsolt Dezső Murguly formed D Sound in 1992, but by 1994 they had broken up due to the old onion 'musical differences'. Over the next eight years he kept writing material and over the last three years has been recording more than one hundred minutes' worth of music with different musicians. It is this that has formed the basis of the album, although he has played most of the music himself as well as providing the vocals. The lyrics are in Hungarian, but in truth that is not of great importance as they appear more for effect, with most of the album being instrumental. This is an album that has been heavily influenced by Pink Floyd, with touches of Ozrics here and there. It can be light and exciting, but often is dark and haunting. It is divided into four separate movements, and I kept thinking that at times this is what music would sound like if Pink Floyd were being led by Gordon Giltrap at a Hawkwind convention. It is spacey, effective, and very enjoyable.
#70, Oct 2002

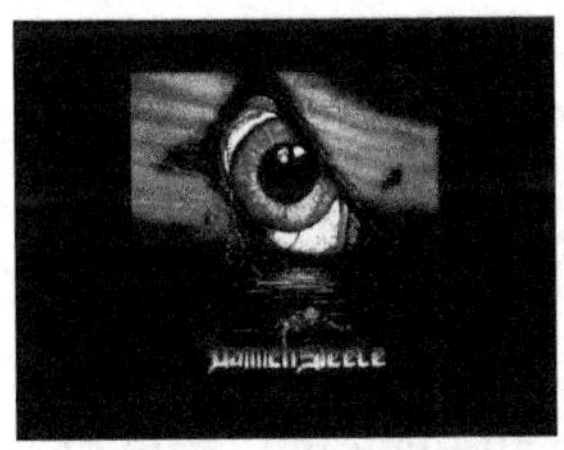

DAMIEN STEELE
DAMIEN STEELE

Damien Steele were quite well-known in Erie, PA, but like many other bands recorded a few demos and then disbanded. Guitarist Mike Learn took up a career in art, and anyone who has Megadeth's 'The System Has Failed' might recognise the name. Steve Matusik did stay in the business and played with Chris Rodler, and it was Chris who convinced Steve to let him send out some of the demos to find out what the reaction would be. It was so positive that Chris started getting orders for a CD that did not exist, until now. These nine songs have all been cleaned up and remastered from the original demos, and listening to these now we can hear a band that was clearly influenced by the likes of Rush, Queensrÿche and Fates Warning. This is technical rock music, no room for keyboards, which is intricate and heavy at the same time.

Then on top of that are the vocals of Mark Hopkins who has a voice not too dissimilar in some ways to Geoff Tate (the line-up was completed by bassist and vocalist Paul Staub and drummer Ben Tomlin): Mark can really hit the high notes that provide the perfect counterpoint to what is going on beneath. Overall this is an interesting album that metalheads will get quite a lot out of. The music is often fairly intricate and although there are plenty of riffs this is no way a straightforward heavy metal album. It does sound a little dated, if the band were performing now I am sure that they would be heavier, as that would suit the overall approach even better, but this contains some strong moments and is definitely a worthwhile release from PMM.
#87, Apr 2006

DAIMONJI
IMPROG

The title of the album is taken from combining two words, 'improvisation' and 'prog'. It is at this point that some people will leave this review, shaking their head sadly, while others may be a little more intrigued. Yes, this is a fully improvised album, divided into four 'songs', where this Japanese trio certainly kick up a storm: this album has much more in common with jazz than it does with prog, and the freeform style that they portray will certainly find more fans with the former than with the latter. There is no doubt that they are all extremely proficient musicians, but does that in this case make for interesting music? It is certainly more challenging than it is enjoyable, and is hard work. Does the listener get much out of it apart from a headache from the amount of concentration that is required? Probably not.

#78, Apr 2004

MARTIN DARVILL AND FRIENDS
THE GREATEST SHOW ON EARTH

Well, I can't think of the last time we had a 'prog superstars' album, but that has now been resolved by the release of the new album by Martin Darvill and friends. Martin is guitarist (plus some keyboards) in Moon, who are fronted by Moon Gould (ex-Landmarq) and also have in their line-up Ian Salmon (Shadowland, Janison Edge etc.). The album tells the story of a journeyman and his voyage across time and space seeking out humanity and hope for all mankind (how did you guess that this was a prog album?). Produced by Karl Groom and Martin Orford, mixed by Rob Aubrey, you would have thought that this had enough prog credentials, but not so. There are numerous guests on this album (and there are full details about who played on what tracks) including Kenny Jones, John Wetton, Al Stewart, Noel Redding, Don Airey, Nick Barrett, David Kilminster, Arena (Clive Nolan, Mick Pointer, John Mitchell, Paul Wrightson, John Jowitt), Martin Orford, Karl Groom, Brendan Loy, Wild Willy Barrett plus others! Being a cynic, I honestly thought that the album would be awful, but somehow Karl and Martin have managed to keep it sounding as a cohesive whole instead of a mish mash of bit parts. The songs are good, and the playing is unsurprisingly good throughout. I have always been a fan of Moon (who at one time was thought to be landing the Judas Priest role) and although he does not sing the whole album certainly does not sound out of place against the more well-known vocalists. This album will get the respect it undoubtedly deserves, but if you can get past the list of names on the cover and put it in the player you may well be pleasantly surprised. The booklet is very good, crammed with photos, lyrics and details of the story behind the recording of the album. If you thought that this sort of album died out over twenty years ago then luckily you are wrong. Worth investigating.

#54, July 1999

DARWIN'S RADIO
PICTURES

I have only recently come across Darwin's Radio, which was formed after the break-up of Grey Lady Down, a band that I reviewed many times and saw in concert more than once (including at The Marquee with Jump I seem to recall). Mark Westworth and Sean Spear from GLD joined forces with Declan Burke (The Spirit of Rush) in the summer of 2002 and a few months later the line-up was completed by Dave Pankhurst (Unlimbo). Less than a year on and they were in the studio recording this three track EP with Robert John Godfrey, so fans of The Enid will probably want to investigate this for that reason if for no others.

They are currently recording their debut album, but until that is available this will have to suffice – and as it is only £4 from their web site it is definitely worth investing in. This is strong neo-prog, with the rhythm section really tight and good interaction between guitarist Declan (who also provides vocals) and keyboard player Mark. The songs are well structured, and extremely punchy although they are all over five minutes long and two are over seven. In some ways reminiscent of IQ, they are probably a little rockier and the harmony vocals shows that here is a band that can cross over into melodic rock when they need to. I look forward to the album but until then this is a fine introduction.
#83, Mar 2005

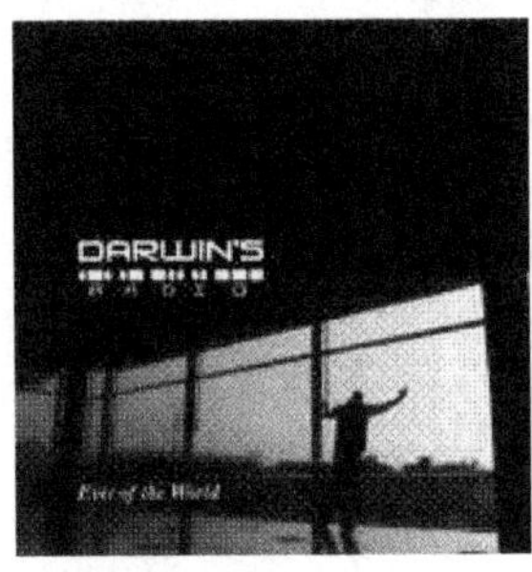

DARWIN'S RADIO
EYES OF THE WORLD

So, the debut album is finally with us – far too long since their debut three-track EP (of which only one number makes it to the album). I was speaking to Mark Colton about the arrival of this and he told me that as far as he was concerned they were the best band that Credo have had as a support act – one that he would happily go and see himself: not bad praise at all. I already knew that I was onto a winner and the more I played this album the more I knew I was right. This is good old-fashioned neo-prog with loads of influences and styles.

They move from Pendragon into IQ and then Genesis and then mix the whole thing up in a solid dose of classic rock along with some great vocal harmonies and far too soon the album has finished and it is time to put it on again. When I hear albums like this I know that the progressive underground in the UK is still pushing forward and has yet to suffer the death that the major press seems to think took place more than a quarter of a century ago. This is fun, this is accessible, it is guitar-led prog music with time changes and complexity mixed with melody and is a damn good time for any proghead.
#88, Jun 2006

DARXTAR
DAYBREAK

As far as I am aware, this album is unavailable in the UK, which is a crying shame. Artur thought that I may be interested in this CD from Swedish band darXtar, and he is definitely right. The artwork gives a space rock feel to proceedings, and this is continued with the music. DarXtar are musically a mix between Poisoned Electrick Head and Hawkwind, and definitely know what they are about. It took a while for this CD to actually reach the player, and I am glad that it did so because it would have been a real pain to have to put it to one side while I listened to others, knowing just how good it was. There are six tracks on here, and from "Eternal War" to the fifteen minute plus "Into The Unknown" they are all superb. Hopefully I will get in touch with the band before the next issue, but if you are intrigued by this solid slab of space rock then get in touch with the label.

#29, Jun 1995

DARXTAR
STARLOG 1990 - 1994

This is a cassette only release by Swedish space proggers darXtar, which attempts to capture highlights and rarities, so as well as tracks from their three albums there are also two songs which are only available on compilations as well as three songs that were recorded in concert in 1994. Now, I loved their last album (the only one I've heard) and am pleased to say that the new one should be out by the time you get this, but as a stop gap this tape is very good indeed. Actually, the only fault is that darXtar have decided to only make 100 of these available, and needless to say they have just about all gone. Still, if you are quick (and lucky) you may still be able to get this collection of otherwise unavailable (all the other CDs will not be repressed when stocks are cleared) material.

#32, Dec 1995

DARXTAR
SJU

Since I was sent 'Daybreak', I have kept an eye on what is going on with darXtar as their psychedelic space rock, firmly grounded in bands such as Hawkwind, has been of great interest. The Swedish music scene seems very vibrant at present, but what is great is that darXtar sound quite unlike any other of the bands that I am in touch with. The opener, "Obstakel", is a short instrumental that gets you into the mood of the album, setting the tone for what you are about to receive. So, after that you are just ready for "7", over sixteen minutes of melodic psychedelic rock that is at times moody and at others almost threatening. DarXtar show that they

command many differing styles, as "This Alien Nation" is a far more in your face rocker, although never straying too far from their space rock ideals. DarXtar are not Hawkwind copyists, rather that they have taken them as a major influence and then moved away from them, and it is of little surprise that they played with Nik Turner last year. With 'Sju' darXtar have again proved that they are masters of their craft and this is an album that all space rockers should dig out.
#35, June 1996

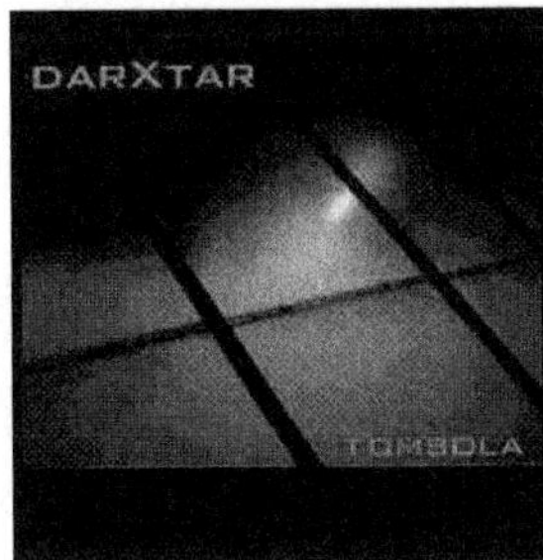

DARXTAR
TOMBOLA
It has been a long time since I have heard from darXtar, the last being when I reviewed 'Sju' back in #35 (1996) and it is some surprise to discover that this is the first full-length album since then. I have always viewed them very favourably and thought that within the realms of space rock there were few bands that could touch them. That viewpoint has been reinforced with the release of 'Tombola' that was completed as long ago as 1998 but has taken until last year to see the light of day. Apparently, they are now starting on their next project, which they are determined will not take as long to be released. DarXtar are still very influenced by Hawkwind (and have recorded with Nik Turner in the past) and songs such as "Compromised Space" contain passages that are so close to their sound that a Hawkfan would say that they were previously unheard recordings by them. But there are also strong elements of Floyd and even at times The Beatles, which make this the strongest release of theirs to date. They admit that this has been overdubbed many times and is certainly multi-layered with the band using many different instruments to create a sound that is both unique and highly recognisable. Although it is an album that may only appeal to a few it is a space rock album of some considerable strength and one that I have enjoyed playing immensely. I urge all fans of the genre to check this out immediately, if not sooner *#71, Dec 2002*

DARXTAR
WE CAME TOO LATE
I was up in the roof sorting through my cassettes when I came across some by darXtar, so when I came back down I checked on the internet to see if they were still active as I hadn't heard from them for many years. Not only are they still active, but they had just issued a new album, the first for four years! I then got in touch with both the band and the German label, Nasoni, and the result is that I am now listening to the newest darXtar release. Also, like Italian label Black Widow, they seem to release all albums both on vinyl and on CD and here the CD contains twelve songs, and the album ten. It was recorded in their own studio, and the time that was taken comes through. At times, it is still the space rock that I would expect, at times it is quite psychedelic, and at other very heavy or it can be awash with these styles at once. The vocals

are better than I remember, with good harmonies, and this is a very powerful album indeed. Some of the guitar breaks and solos are almost brutal, but it is layered together so well that it all fits dramatically. I know that it has been some years since I last heard from the band, but they have stepped up to another level and this is an album that all space rock and psych freaks should grab with both hands. Highly recommended.
#86, Feb 2006

ALAN DAVEY
CAPTURED ROTATION
At the time, Alan Davey was Hawkwind's longest serving member, after Dave Brock, having been bassist with the band for more than sixteen years, and he has now branched out with a solo album. Ron Tree guests on vocals for three songs, but for the rest of the time Alan is on his own, providing all guitars, synths and even a vocal. Still, for the most part this is an instrumental album and it does not suffer for that. It is not surprising that parts of this album sound as if they have come straight out of the Hawkwind songbook, given that he has been responsible for writing or co-writing much of the band's material over the last eleven years. This is particularly true of opener "The Call" which is classic Hawkwind, with riffing guitars and keyboards swirling and coming in and out all over the place. The instrumentals are also spaced out and tripping, with lots going on all the time. It is quite a heavy album, very intense, and one that belongs in any Hawkfan's collection. If you ever felt that Hawkwind were the band for you then this is an essential purchase.
#37, Oct 1996

SIMON DAVIES
REQUIEM
What we have here is something that I have not come across before, namely a requiem written basically for electric guitars. Simon wanted to mix rock music with the drama of classical forms and decided to use as his vehicle a requiem mass. Apart from the opening track, which is an adaption of Bach's "Kyrie Eleison" from his B Minor Mass, all the music was written and performed by Simon. As well as providing electric guitars (and some of the harmonies required seven lead guitar lines) he also added acoustic guitars, keyboards and drums. This is very much a work of love and it is amazing to my ears just what has been achieved. There is no doubt that Simon is an amazing musician, and he scored the first four songs (there are six overall) so that the piece can be performed in the traditional sense with either a choir or an orchestra. What is plain throughout the tape is that as whole the requiem works perfectly which is down not only to the considerable guitar skills but also the songs. For anyone who loves rock guitar, albeit in a very strange setting, enjoys classical

music or a touch of Sky should get this tape. It is a real bargain and should be treated as such and grabbed while the opportunity is there. Simon has now started work on a new project which apparently is much more of a rock showcase album from blues to prog to metal, which should make interesting listening.
#21, Jan 1994

SIMES DAVIES
JUPITER COLLISION

This is the follow-up to 'Requiem', which was reviewed in an earlier Feedback. Back then he mixed classical and rock music in an extremely successful fashion while 'Jupiter Collision' sees him more in the mainstream with some hard-riffing guitar. Again, this is an instrumental album, but the five tracks more than grab the attention without the need for vocals. Four of the five are rock based, and my favourite of these must be "We Have Lift-Off" which is a real belter: any fan of rock guitars will fall in love with this one. To provide a gentle respite, the third song is "Cascadence" which is a beautiful classical piano piece with extra keyboards – apparently, this will eventually form part of Simes' Piano Concerto No. 1. This tape will certainly appeal to all those who love Simes' earlier work as well as lovers of instrumental music, as here it is played at the highest level.
#25, Oct 1994

DAWNLIGHTS
THE FOURTH DIMENSION

This is basically a solo project by Phillipe Dutrieu, although he has a guest guitarist, and is predominantly keyboard based (yep, no 'live' drums). This is mostly electronic pop although there are times when he does sort of venture into progressive. The vocals are not the best I have heard and it might have been better if he had kept this as an instrumental album. I have not come across Philippe before, but apparently he led a progressive pop trio in the Eighties called Fusion, and has only just returned to the musical fold. There is nothing unpleasant about this, and it is certainly more interesting that some of the keyboard based material that I get sent, but overall this can never be anything more than background music. If that is what you want then this may be one to seek out if New Age etc. is your sort of thing, but I would rather that my music had a bit more get up and go, whereas this has got up and already gone.
#85, Nov 2005

DAY SHIFT
IMAGINARY MENAGERIE

Only formed in 2004, these guys are already in the throes of recording their second album, hot on the heels of this their debut, which came out last year. They call themselves a psychedelic space rock band, apart from the fact that they are missing out that they also contain prog influences (is space rock a subset of prog, or are both independent subsets of rock? – discuss). But these guys are far more than just a Hawkwind clones – yes, they do include some keyboard sounds that are similar, as are some of the riff styles, but they are very different indeed. They have more in common with Porcupine Tree, and I am amazed that the debut is self-produced as the sound is very strong indeed – and any band that admits to using a Theremin must be okay! Five numbers, at just over 42 minutes long, with the last ("The Unwashed Platypus") being the longest at just over twelve minutes – this is an album that space rockers are going to love. Bob Leek's vocals are more clear and distinct than is often the case with the genre which means that he quite easily cuts through the mass of noise being created by Nick Beers (guitar), Jason Tilbrook (bass) and Archie (drums) – Bob plays the keyboards himself as well as being lead singer, but any thoughts of these guys being Coldplay should be quickly dispelled. A very enjoyable album indeed and I look forward to the next one with great interest – and do you know what is good news as well? These guys are British, are touring, and need your support.

#86, Feb 2006

DAY SHIFT
OF WHISPERS

They may describe their music as psychedelic space rock, but in it reality it is much more than that. What we have here is an album of ten songs, real songs with verses and catchy choruses, which are soaked in progressive stylings – whatever sub-genre that may be. It is an immediate piece of work that falls into the brain as soon as it is placed on the player with the songs staying in the noggin long after it has been turned off.

The guys keep it tight without being formulaic, and bring in influences as diverse as Funeral For A Friend and Hawkwind while obviously being impacted by neo-prog; the shorter numbers of IQ and Galahad in particular. It is not as overbearing as some of the prog bands around, and certainly does not belong in the symphonic genre, but the feeling is there. These guys have been out gigging recently and surely based on this they will not have to play support for much longer as this is a goody and they're British so get out there and support them!

#89, Sep 2006

DEAD SOUL TRIBE
A MURDER OF CROWS

Progressive metal can be a very powerful musical force, as demonstrated by Dead Soul Tribe on this their second album. This has seen the band rein in the keyboards so that they are not as dominant as before and crank up the guitars so that the metal part of the prog metal tag is the one that people hear. The ideas are very much still there, with musical twists aplenty, but the sheer crunch of this album is more brutal than many within this genre. The guitars are now even further to the fore than our own mighty Threshold, and it certainly gives the album a different perspective. There is a real intensity about this album, so much so that at times it becomes like a great weight, which does take away from the enjoyment of it. After a while it gets that it is almost a chore to listen to, which is not how music should be at all. This is not a CD to be played for a bit of light relief in the background, it is music that demands commitment. Because of that it is an album that needs to be selected from, as opposed to played in its' entirety. When dipped into there are some great songs and performances but as for listening to the whole thing repeatedly then that is another matter altogether.

#76, Oct 2003

DEAD SOUL TRIBE
THE JANUARY TREE

Devon Graves is back with his third album under the Dead Soul Tribe moniker. Joined by Adel Moustafa (drums – Devon provides everything else), he has again produced an album that is full of differing styles – music that can be crunching along one minute as a full-on rock onslaught and then a gentle acoustic number the next. The switch between these passages is such that it all seems to make sense, that the music is flowing continually instead of just being chopped and changed. It appears to have evolved to the state that it is in, instead of separate pieces being put together to make a whole. This is music that switches and changes, it is full of atmosphere and power, while there is also a strange bleakness within it. Following on from the last album ('A Murder Of Crows') this album also has a meaning behind the title which Devon explains, as "A tree in winter is a mirror image of today's world. A leaf is only a leaf but it is a small wonder that a tree lives with the help of his leaves. It is just the small things which decide over life and death and the level in between". Powering and thoughtful, this is progressive rock with the emphasis as firmly on the word 'rock' as it is on the word 'progressive'. It may be too heavy for some, and others may not feel that it is progressive and that is true in the respect in that it sounds nothing like the neo-prog bands but this is music that is determined to break new ground, and hopefully capture some listeners on the way.

#81, Dec 2004

DEAD SOUL TRIBE
THE DEAD WORLD

Devon Graves (previously known as Buddy Lacky when he was with Psychotic Waltz) is back with his fastest recorded album, taking less than a month, and here his band of merry men have again followed his lead and have produced something that is essentially dark. Although some numbers such as "Some Sane Advice" are a bit more light-hearted, and even contains some acoustic guitar, this is an album that is heavy in atmosphere and very heavy in the guitar stakes. Devon started the writing process for this album after Dead Soul Tribe had toured with label mates Threshold, and he said that he felt that audiences enjoyed both bands, even though they are light years apart when it comes to sound and style. Threshold come very much from the prog camp, but very rocked up into their own form of prog metal while Devon approaches music from a rock angle, then throws in some strange time signatures and rhythms to get the sounds he wants, along with the atmosphere that pervades all that he does. This may not be to everyone's taste, and is intense and intriguing at the same time. *#86, Feb 2006*

DEATH ORGAN
9 TO 5

APM have yet again pulled a gem out of the hat with one of the most arresting albums I have heard recently. What we have here is a very unusual mix of Vincent Crane, Jon Lord and Keith Emerson style intense keyboards in an ELP setup (no guitar) with two vocalists. These two guys have very differing styles with one singing in good old fashioned heavy metal while the other favours death. This combination of growling and demonic screaming with real melody works very well. It is the sheer heaviness of the outfit that is amazing, as it is comparable to classic Sabbath for its' weightiness while not utilising any guitars! Opener "Hate" mixes "Speed King" style workouts with Atomic Rooster and death: these songs must be heard to be believed. Anyone who feels that progressive rock is regressive, without any new ideas and nothing to offer the metalhead should listen to this. It is an album of draining intensity that dares the listener to turn it up just that little bit more.
#29, Jun 1995

DEATH ORGAN
UNIVERSAL STRIPSEARCH

I was very impressed with the first Death Organ album, and am even more so with the follow-up. They are a five-man line-up, but two of these are lead vocalists, playing no instrument. Add to the fact that of the other three (playing bass, drums and organ) another two are singers should make this a very unusual sound, but it does not. What it does do very much is bring back memories of the great Hammond players of our time, namely Keith Emerson, Ken Hensley and Jon Lord. Of these the band probably owe the greatest debt to Uriah Heep, although of course the

Box/Hensley interplay is missing because there are not any guitars. There is just no room in the sound with the heavy organ swamping everything in sight. The rest of the guys sing and play as if their lives depend on it just to be heard. The two lead singers also have a very different approach, with one being a traditional rock singer while one favours the death mould and they are fantastic!

This is just so heavy and intense, yet there are lighter moments as well. The cover version of "Tom Sawyer" must be heard to be believed. I must admit that I hadn't noticed that it was on there and when the classic words "A modern day warrior" kicked off the song you could have knocked me over with a feather as the last person I would have thought of these guys covering would have been Rush! There is no doubt in my mind that this is the best release (and thinking of it, the only one for a long time) to be released on the Swedish Ad Perpetuam Memoriam label. You probably will not hear a better album out of Scandinavia this year, and you certainly will not hear another like this.
#50, Aug 1998

DEGREE ABSOLUTE
DEGREE ABSOLUTE

This album has apparently been completed for a few years, but has only just been released. Although it is a band, in many ways this can be seen to be the work of multi-instrumentalist Aaron Bell who provides vocals, guitar and keyboards as well as all the songs and produces the album as well. When he had recorded the original demos, he felt that he needed to get other musicians on board and Dave Lindemann (bass) and Doug Beary (drums) complete the line-up. Although Araon produced the album he then brought in Neil Kernon to mix and the result is a sound that is very heavy as well as being sympathetic to what the band are trying to achieve musically.

And what is that?

Well the answer is slightly more complicated than just a simple nod to a genre or band. Mostly they are prog metal with hints of Fates Warning, but at times they are far more atmospheric. Listen to the instrumental "Distance" and you may just understand. From power and complexity on songs like "Exist" here we start with gentle keyboards, bongos, and a wonderful fretless bass line which makes one think that this is a different band altogether! All the music here is delicate with a feeling of jazz and enlightenment, not one would normally expect from a metal band! This is an interesting album with a great deal going for it. The shifts in style and three instrumentals do give the band more depth, and balances the record as a whole. The music is complex but never unapproachable and is a damn fine listen.
#87, Apr 2006

DEIMOS
NEVER BE AWAKEN

According to their label's web site this debut by Russian band Deimos is Death Doom Progressive Metal. One thing is sure, and that is that this is unusual to say the least. There are parts of this album which are 'straightforward' death metal with full on guitars and growls, but it can also be very gothic, and there are the female lead vocals to consider, as well as all the melodic stuff that is going on. There are some keyboards but this is primarily a guitar band, and one that is led by Leonid Gezalyan who knows what he wants and it certainly is not anything normal. Those who want their death metal to be straightforward and uncomplicated are going to have to look elsewhere while prog metal fans may also find it hard to get on with. It is not difficult to believe that Russia is quite removed from us musically, as this is so different to everything else. It is not an album that could be used to shift dandruff yet must be played at such a volume that many progheads would just back away. It is to be admired for the approach, but this should only be sought out by the musically adventurous although I did enjoy playing it. *#84, July 2005*

DELTA CYPHEI PROJECT
VIRTUAL WORLD

This is Delta Cyphei Project's second album, and is a fine example of keyboard dominated bombastic prog. Although there are two vocalists, DCP are at their best when they are running at breakneck speed through the instrumental passages. That is not to say that the other musicians are superfluous to the keyboards of Wolf Khavlan, but rather that he is the driving force. Some of the songs, such as "Neptune", have an American style to them while there are vocals; this soon disappears when it is purely instrumental. Jewgeny Wasinger also proves himself to be a fine guitarist, with not only some jazz-like meanderings, but also some fine forceful interplay with Wolf. "Forgotten Signs" probably shows this band in their best light, as they sound like Saga as they pound through this keyboard led song, which also features some rocking guitar. If you enjoy prog of this style, which is melodic and enjoyable on all levels and has some great guitar and keyboard interplay, then this album is worth pursuing.
#32, Dec 1995

DELUC
WHEN TWO WORLDS MEET

Fred is back with another album, and what a fine album it is. There is a band around him, but the idea is just to provide a framework so that Fred can craft spells with his classical guitar. It can be quite dreamy and contemplative at times, but at others, it is invigorating and exciting. He sometimes plays against or with a sax, but at other times he takes the melody all on his own. It is much more than just a relaxing album to listen to, it has a groove and soul that while at many times has a jazz beat to it but always maintains the interest. It is much more modern and listenable than the work even of Gordon Giltrap, who is another acoustic guitarist that I greatly admire. It is modern, yet at the same time going back to an earlier age, when music did not always have to be in your face but could be reflective and almost passive. This is going to be a regular to the Sunday relax desk, that I can see already, and although this will not be easy to get hold of in the UK you should persevere. *#62, May 2001*

DER SPYRA
HEADPHONE CONCERT

This concert took place in August 2002 and must have been quite a strange affair to witness, as all the audience were wearing headphones (provided by Sennheiser). From that I think that I can presume that this did not take place in a vast amphitheatre, but something far more personal. With two keyboard players, but with violin and flute also making their presence felt, this is electronic music that has a little more heart and soul than normal. The guitarist is also no fool and the result is a musical passage that must be heard to be fully understood. There are some Floydian touches, especially on the guitar, but also feelings of Eloy and quite definitely Tangerine Dream also come through. Due to the style of music and the way that it was being performed there is not a lot of vitality, apart again from some of the guitar, and the feeling is that this could have been massively overdubbed in the studio instead of being a performance at a live event. Overall this is interesting and enjoyable but not essential. *#84, July 2005*

DEYSS
AT KING

Deyss are a real rarity among rock bands, in that they are Swiss. This album is a reissue of their debut, which appeared back in 1987 when the line-up was Giovanni De-Vita (guitar), Patrick Dubois (bass), Paul Reber (guitar synth, bass pedals) and Guistino Salvati (keyboards). The more observant among you may notice that there is no singer or drummer, these being provided by "guests". Seeing as how Patrick Fragnere's clear vocals are an integral part of the sound I cannot understand why he is not fully credited, but I am sure that there must be good reason.

The album is only thirty minutes long, and starts with a sword fight, which leads in turn into a synthesised voice saying that the meetings of the Lords Of Ages would be the start of our universe and that there was only room for one, and that was Deyss (pronounced "Dice"). So, what about the rest of the album? Well, I thoroughly enjoyed it as the songs are extremely well-crafted and with great hooks. In fact, anyone who remotely likes good melodic rock will instantly fall in love with it. I have seen them described as the "Swiss Marillion", and although I can see where that comes from, I wouldn't necessarily agree with it. True, there are

definite elements there, but also very strong are aspects of Genesis or even Yes. In other words, they have taken the best of many bands and created their own sound. One would expect this to be very heavy as there is not only a guitar but a guitar synth, but the sound is restrained, relying more on keyboards in a Genesis fashion. I loved this album the first time I heard it, and it has grown on me even more with each play. Instantly accessible, it is a real joy.
#17, Mar 1993

DFA
WORK IN PROGRESS LIVE
DFA were formed in Verona in 1991, and released their debut album in 1997. 1999 saw their second album, this time on one of the most important Italian prog labels, Mellow, and this secured them an invitation to play at NEARfest in 2000. That show was recorded and has now been made available by American label MoonJune. Opening track "Escher" lays down the rules, namely that there are not any! That this four-piece know their way around their respective instruments is never in doubt, and while there is a large element of jazz it is much more in the fusion area as they mix together sounds and styles.

They bring together Ozrics and Hawkwind, but are as happy to also bring in influences as diverse as Gentle Giant and ELP. But even after the first song I was not ready for the next, "Caleidoscopio", which is far more gentle and reflective while there are vocals. It certainly changes style throughout, from almost Georgian to intricate interplay.

Vocals are used sparingly, but there is so much going on during the instrumentals that they are not missed at all. The crowd are deathly silent during the peaceful moments but they certainly react when each song finishes. Only six songs, but with a length ranging from six minutes to fifteen it gives DFA the opportunity to branch out. I have been sent a few MoonJune albums this issue and have been told by Leonardo that there will be many more in 2002. If they are all this standard, then that will be something to look forward to indeed.
#65, Dec 2001

DGM
CHANGE DIRECTION
'Change Direction' is the first full-length album from Italians DGM, and with the lyrics in English is far more accessible than many of their counterparts. This is driven hard rock, which will probably be appreciated by those into plain good rock as it is by the progheads who may find this a little too fast and powerful for their liking. Does it matter that this is being distributed by a prog label when the music is as good as this? Maybe it is time to cast away all the labels and just

grab hold of people and say BUY THIS - IT IS BRILLIANT! Unfortunately, the world does not behave like that, but if we work on the principle that at the end of the day there are only two labels that matter, namely good music and bad music, then this falls into the former category. If you like rock where the guitars belt along, yet at the same time there is a strong sense of melody with great vocals and tunes, then this is surely an album for you.
#47, Feb 1998

DIALOG
CRY OF THE HAWK
I think this is probably the first Russian band I have ever reviewed, and unsurprisingly they do not sound like many of the prog clones that are around. They are a six-man band, utilising both twin guitars and twin keyboards, and the result is an extremely powerful sound as they are a rock band first and a prog band second. The rock seems to be of an American style, with riffs threatening, but never breaking free a la Threshold. The vocals are superb, with great strength and vigour, and the production is spot on. The result is that 'Cry of the Hawk' manages to win over the listener, although the Russian language is a little strange on the ear. Thankfully an English translation is provided in the booklet so at least it is possible to see what they are singing about even if it can't be understood. There are twelve songs on here, and it shows great belief in themselves that they opt to open with the extremely powerful instrumental "Not A Strange Guy". My favourite is probably the belting "Phantom", which contains some great guitar runs, while "Sailing Eastwards" is an up-tempo pop rock number that wouldn't be out of place in Western charts. If you think that music from behind the old iron curtain is behind the times, then do yourself a favour and get this piece of Russian mastery.
#32, Dec 1995

DIFFERENT TRAINS
ON THE RIGHT TRACK
I have listened to many CDs over the last few years, so to get one that sounds quite unlike anything else around is unusual to say the least. I have also often said that some CDs grow on you, but probably none more so than this one. After the first listen I was not sure what to think, but after I have played it ten or twenty times I knew that here is one of the major releases of the year. Different Trains are built around the leadership and songwriting talents of Damon Shulman. Does the name seem familiar? It should, as his father Philip and uncles Ray and Derek were founder members of Simon Dupree and the Big Sound, and consequently Gentle Giant: obviously, Damon was introduced to music at a serious level very early in life. The other members of the band are Michael Payne (drums, used to be with Damon in The Working Stiffs), Alan Woods (bass) and John Rozzell (keyboards). This, their debut, is a full-blown concept that brings together music, spoken words, and even a speech from Damon. It is obvious that all the guys

are masters of their craft, with Damon proving himself to be quite a multi-instrumentalist. Michael also provides many types of percussion as well as just drums, and with everyone singing backing vocals there is a lot to listen to.

The music is very complex on first listen, but becomes more simplistic the more it is played. Sure, there are myriad sounds and styles to take in, but as you get into Damon's mind the more it all makes sense. Obviously a very big influence is Gentle Giant, but there is more than just that, with jazz and modern classical music making more than a transient impression. Different Trains have set themselves up to be shot down in flames as this is a band that many music critics are going to savage for no other reason that they are 'different'. On top of that they have the nerve to release a concept album of all things, and as a debut as well! If only people listen to this wonderful CD, they will discover a new world. It is not any good just playing it and possibly hating it, as it must be loved and nurtured and the result will be more than worth it. My personal favourite is "In My House" which shows all the best sides of the band with some great harmony vocals. I am afraid I doubt that Different Trains will ever make serious inroads into the popular field, but those who are prepared to search them out will find their musical outlook all the richer for it. *#23, May 1994*

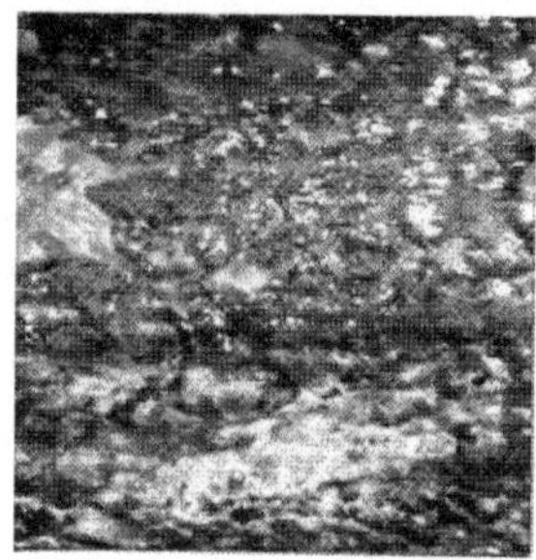

DIFFICIL EQUILIBRIO
FLOOD

This is the fifth album from this Spanish instrumental trio, and appears to be a catching up of pieces that have been recorded over the years as the notes for each song show that they are from a long period. According to the press release the band play "a powerful instrumental progressive rock influences by King Crimson, Van Der Graaf Generator, Peter Hammill and even Magma". But, what it does not say is that these are improvised pieces that have as much in common with free form jazz as it does with the above. Consequently, the result can be quite painful (okay, very painful) to listen to at times. This is music that is striving to break down limits of what is aurally acceptable and while there is no doubt that the guys can play there is the question at times of whether they are playing in the same key, let alone the same tune. I think that the only way to fully appreciate this music is by watching them play, or to see another art form in conjunction with it, but on its own at home in a stereo it does not work at all. *#89, Sep 2006*

DIGITAL RUIN
DWELLING IN THE OUT

The second album from American progressive metal band Digital Ruin is interesting, and certainly warrants playing a few times, but I found that it did not quite capture me as I thought it would. There are some interesting parts of songs, with the guitars and vocals coming together just right, but there are plenty of times when somehow it does not quite gel. With Savatage and Queensrÿche being obvious influences one would imagine that this would be a stormer of an album but it is not.

Probably this is not an album to be dismissed as quickly as I have, but I just found it difficult to maintain the interest: maybe another time. *#57, Mar 2000*

DILEMMA
IMBROCCATA

Dilemma are a new Dutch band, although drummer Frank van Essen has been heard on the last two Iona albums playing his second instrument, the violin. 'Imbroccata' (a fencing term meaning counter attack) has great depth and strength in a way missing from many of the albums by continental prog outfits. They are not trying to follow the AOR route favoured by many, and have their own sound and ideas. It is the small touches and nuances that can make or break an album, and there are plenty on here that are working to good effect. In the middle of "Rock Blossom" (a good example of a song with many twists and turns) they put in some Japanese lyrics which is mirrored in a musical way. This leads into the more rocking "Duck", which is more powerful just because it is in total contrast to what has gone before. You must feel empathy with vocalist Butler as he sings that his mum "thinks James Last is quite loud enough". All in all, an album of great merit with some very strong positive points. The only thing I'm not too sure about is that Butler's voice does appear to be a little lacking in some places, but that is probably being a little picky. The music shifts and changes so often that it is probably only going to be of interest to the hardened progger, but for me is it is great to hear a prog album from overseas that can be called that.
#28, Apr 1995

DISCIPLINE
UNFOLDED LIKE STAIRCASE

Discipline have a few musical strings to their bow as while they have a standard line-up with guitars (Jon Preston Bouda), bass (Matthew Kennedy) and drums (Paul Dzendzel), they also have frontman Matthew Parmenter. Not only does he write all the songs, he provides vocals, keyboards, violin and alto sax. This gives them the edge in adding different touches and nuances to the overall sound. Matthew has a good strong voice, and apparently is an amazing frontman (although whether we will ever get the chance to witness that on this side of the pond is another matter), and has an ear for the complex. There are only four different songs on here, although these are sometimes subdivided it is only possible to access five on the CD. Talking to Malcolm Parker of GFT he told me that this was one of the few American bands that have been exciting him recently and based on this album I can see why. The band can move effortlessly from one musical style to another and I found the more I played this the more difficult it was to pick out a favourite. I thought that it would be opener "Canto IV", but then I

started to move more in favour of "Crutches". There again, tracks such as "Chock Full O' Guts" with much more guitar and a real menacing threat are worth hearing. Overall this is an album that refuses to conform to most people's ideas of what prog should be about, with heavy rock elements without ever falling into hard rock territory. If only this could get a more widespread release over here I know it would do well in Europe.
#53, May 1999

DISCIPLINE
LIVE - INTO THE DREAM...
There are some extremely exciting progressive rock bands coming out of the States now, and Discipline are one of those which I am convinced are about to make it big. This live album shows them at their best, with Matthew Parmenter at his most threatening. Matthew is more Gabriel than Fish, and he somehow manages to provide all the keyboards as well as being the focal point. The line-up is completed by Joe Preston Bouda (guitar), Matthew Kennedy (bass) and Paul Dzendzel (drums) and while they sound nothing like the classic Genesis line-up, it is with them that they musically appear to have the most in common. So instead of going to see ReGenesis, or buy albums by bands that are either shadows of their former selves or by bands who wish that they had been around twenty years before, get this album which is by one of the exciting talents that are around making music for today. While I am a hardened fan of Spock's Beard as you all know by now, Discipline are a different facet of the same musical area, much more 'progressive' and full of passion and depth. If you want Prog that is dangerous and exciting, harkening back to the past but very much looking to the future then this is the album for you.
#57, Mar 2000

DJAMRA
TRANSPLANTATION
This is an instrumental album by a band with a somewhat unusual line-up (drums, bass, alto sax, trumpet). With a group like that there is only one place to go, and that is jazz. That they do so with so much finesse and style is a credit. The drums fairly drive the music along but they are for the most part the under-stated part of the group, and while the bass plays behind the melody there are sections where it takes the lead. Of course, it is the two brass instruments that can be seen to be taking the band on their musical journey but there are times when they themselves are quiet so that the others can be heard, with the bass taking a much more important focus with some different styles of playing. This is not music for the faint-hearted conservative, as this is trying to push boundaries so that they are often avant-garde as well as bringing in some more standard progressive tones. It will not be to everyone's tastes but this is a record that I have enjoyed playing a great deal and will be again. *#78, Apr 2004*

DJAMRA
14 FACES VOL. 1
This appears to be the first four of fourteen tracks that were recorded at Fandango in May last year. Djamra are a four-piece comprising drums, bass, trumpet and sax. The word of the day is jazz, and these guys can certainly play. This is uncompromising material, with all four willing to take the lead when required, although it is usually left to the brass musicians playing as one to define the mood. The real problem with this album is the quality of the recording. Although it is not as poor as a bootleg it does leave a lot to be desired so some of the undoubted force of this music is lost. But if you enjoy jazz that is at the limits then this is for you – the musicianship and interaction is incredible.
#79, May 2004

DJAMRA
KAMIHITOE
The title of the album references the difference between genius and madness, 'Kami' means paper and 'Hitoe' means a very little difference, so it is the thickness of a sheet of paper. This is the third album from this instrumental quintet (guitar, bass, keyboards, sax, drums) and there are times when all five of them are on the same wavelength and others when they are all pushing forward to front to try and wrest control of the songs from others. But, and this is a huge but, there is always a great deal of control so even if the sax is going off like crazy during the title song he is straight back in with the others at exactly the right moment. There is the feeling that the music is very carefully constructed with an agreement for one or the other to go mad for a set number of bars but that they must be able to drop right back into the theme at the right moment. Although this is very much jazz based the guitar is far more from the rock area, much more metallic, but this does not come across as lightweight fusion. If you like inventive progressive jazz, then this is one of the most interesting releases from Poseidon. *#89, Sep 2006*

JULIUS DOBOS
MOUNTAIN FLYING
Apparently, Julius is well-known in Hungary for his compositions, and this recording with the North Hungarian Symphony Orchestra plus extra musicians, the Budapest Monteverdi Choir and Marta Sebastyen (the latter was on 'The English Patient' soundtrack), is a revised version of his first collection of demos, which were all performed on a synthesiser. I do not listen to nearly as much classical music as I should, so in all honesty find that I can't review it properly. I know I like it, with the melodies and interplay between synths and traditional orchestra working well, and finding that it is very easy to listen to (as opposed to easy-listening).
#57, Mar 2000

RUDI DOBSON
AUDREY HEPBURN

This album is truly a work of love and devotion, and is based on Ian Woodward's biography "Audrey Hepburn – Fairy Lady of the Screen", and the CD is accompanied by a 36-page booklet with text by Woodward and numerous photographs. There are new arrangements of "Moon River", "Charade", "Breakfast At Tiffany's" and a "Fair Lady" medley. Apart from these, all the music was written by Rudi Dobson, using Audrey Hepburn as his inspiration. Rudi provides the keyboards, but has drawn on many friends to provide a full band feel, these include Tony Fernandez, David Paton and Tim Cansfield among others. Clive Waite provides vocals on "Moon River", with all the rest of the material being instrumental. As a package this is quite an achievement. For the most part the music is reminiscent of Wakeman, who Rudi cites as a main influence, and it works well. The gentle opener belies the fact that are some good keyboard driven rock songs on this CD, such as "A Fight For Time", while "Moon River" sounds as if it should have been sung by George Michael, arranged with him in mind. I enjoyed the music, and the detail of the booklet is quite amazing. If you are interested in Audrey Hepburn or just want to share in one man's obsession, then this could be for you.
#24, Jul 1994

TIM DONAHUE
MADMEN & SINNERS

For his seventh album Tim Donahue decided that it was time to take his music to the next level and started writing an album of progressive metal hoping that he would be able to find a singer to do it justice. A mutual friend introduced him to James LaBrie (Dream Theater), who was intrigued and brought with him drummer Mike Mangini (Extreme, Steve Vai). This is the line-up that recorded the album, with Tim providing guitar, bass and synth as well as engineering and producing it. It certainly is a long way from Tim's work with Kelly Hansen. Initially I found that I was being reminded of Threshold, but that is an unfair comparison to both bands. Here Tim moves the music all over the place, so that is possible at times to get lost in so many different sounds and ideas. At one place during the opener the band is going like the clappers, there are sirens wailing and a spoken overdub all at the same time. The feeling is one that there is madness, but that it is very much under control. Contrasting that is church organ, acoustic guitars and even Gregorian chanting! There is no doubting the quality of James' vocals and here he enjoys the opportunity to pit his voice against a different style of music to that with which he has made his name. Interesting, musically different with various tangents being explored, then dropped, this is not an album that can be played in the background but should be listened to properly to get the most from it.
#79, May 2004

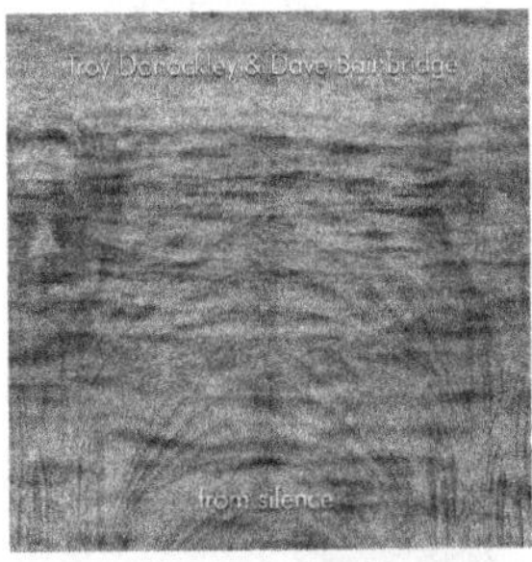

TROY DONOCKLEY & DAVE BAINBRIDGE
FROM SILENCE

TROY DONOCKLEY & DAVE BAINBRIDGE
WHEN WORLDS COLLIDE

When Joanne Hogg went on maternity leave in 2003, Troy and Dave started to experiment and improvise in a way not possible within Iona. They were working on tracks for their first album when Rob Ayling asked if they were interested in playing in Lincoln Cathedral. The music would be recorded for an album (and a DVD), but there would be no audience. They were excited with the idea of performing in such a space, and decided what instruments they would be using but wanted to take their inspiration from their surroundings. The combination of traditional instruments such as low whistles and uileann pipes from Troy with keyboards and electric guitar from Dave combined with the feelings of their surrounding results in music that is compelling and beautiful at the same time. The guys have been playing together for a long time and know what each is capable of and the ideas are taken from each other, gradually changing and flowing. This is not fast paced "see how quick I can play" music, but something that is beautiful and inspired. It is music to relax to, simply wonderful. 'When Worlds Collide' combines five studio tracks with five taken from two concerts. In some ways, this is more folk based than the other album, with some songs finding both Dave and Troy on acoustic guitars, bouzoukis etc. and there is a less of bringing together of two different styles.

It is also less atmospheric than the other album and there are actual songs here with Troy providing the vocals. Some of the numbers are even trad. arr, with "Banish Misfortune" being one picked up by Richard Thompson while "The Blacksmith" is one from John Renbourn. Again, this is an album that contains some wonderful moments, but when playing it after listening to 'From Silence' I found that I was disappointed as I come across this style of music fairly frequently but the debut is something that is wonderful and haunting, beautiful and compelling. I am sure that I would be giving this far higher praise if I had just heard this and not the other but while this is worth hearing the other is an essential purchase.
#87, Apr 2006

DONNAMATRIX
CYBERSPHERE

I am still struggling to get a handle on this one. It is undoubtedly prog, but it is the type that gives you the impression that the band are in the studio jamming, totally stoned. Some musical phrases are repeated to give the band some backbone to rest the music against, with the feeling that it is all very spaced out.

The result is that you end up feeling that to appreciate what is going

on it is necessary to be a participant or at least to be there while it is taking place. It is mostly instrumental, with one piece "Prelude To A Camera" starting then fading out rather quickly, as if it just did not make it any further. Overall this is an 'interesting' album, but possibly one that needs to be played a great many times to reap the benefit.
#52, Feb 1999

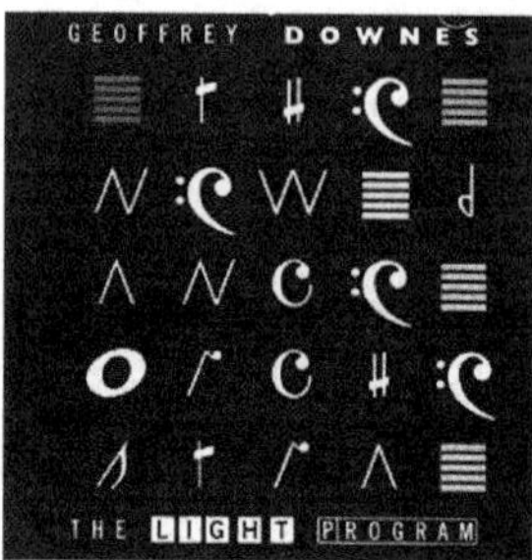

GEOFFREY DOWNES
THE LIGHT PROGRAM

This was the first album released by Geoff Downes under The New Dance Orchestra banner, and according to the CD "it performs an alternative form of music designed to bring tone and colour to the stereo sound spectrum, and at the same time retaining a deep musical foundation, upon which are built a series of images to stimulate the listener in his or her own personal domain." This is purely a keyboard instrumental album, and on the level at which it is aimed I think it works very well. However, although it is enjoyable and technically very clever, there is still the impression that there is something missing. Geoff may have replaced Rick in Yes (for the surprisingly good 'Drama'), but to my ears this album shows that when it comes to solo works Geoff still has a lot to learn. The thirty-three pieces' form five distinct movements utilising different moods and style, but overall I feel that only those into electronic music, as opposed to out and out rock keyboards, will appreciate this. *#34, Apr 1996*

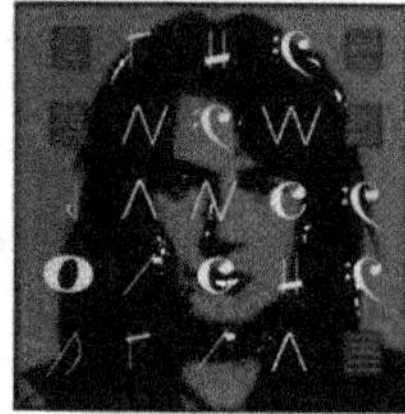

GEOFFREY DOWNES
VOX HUMANA

This is an interesting album by the Asia/Yes/Buggles keyboard player Geoff Downes, and the second to be released under the New Dance Orchestra banner. The idea behind that was to use the human voice as a technological instrument against a variety of sonic backdrops, and to that end Geoff has utilised a different singer for each song. It opens with Max Bacon on "Tears", which suits both his voice and Geoff's style perfectly. It is the sort of opening track that makes one feel glad that one bothered listening to the CD, an out and out classic that leads into a gentle "Video Killed The Radio Star". This is a way more laid back, piano and instrumental version of the song that shot Geoff to fame and the singer on this ballad is none other than Glenn Hughes! This new arrangement works extremely well and makes one wonder if it this is how it was originally conceived. Another Buggles number comes up later when "Plastic Age" gets a new treatment as well, this time far more up-tempo, with vocals by John Payne. "Concerto" is a classical interlude with some gorgeous acoustic guitar; Steve Overland makes an appearance on the soaring "Moon Under The Water" while Yes' "White Car" also gets a makeover. All in all, this is a fascinating album that is very enjoyable indeed.
#33, Feb 1996

GEOFFREY DOWNES
THE WORLD SERVICE

I can still remember the excitement I had when I first heard the debut Asia album, or the fun of "Video Killed The Radio Star", or the sheer enjoyment of taking the piss out of a mate of mine who was a huge Yes fan when we heard that Buggles were joining Yes (although 'Drama' was actually a good album). What has all of this to do with this review? Well, Geoff Downes was the keyboard player in all of them and now here he is with his newest album, his first solo project in over five years. Thirty 'songs', and the only positive thing to say about this album is that it may just about be okay background music, but nothing more than that. *#58, May 2000*

GEOFFREY DOWNES
THE BRIDGE

This is a somewhat unusual release, as the main point of focus is a twenty-two-minute-long instrumental, "The Bridge". This has not previously been made available but was recorded back in 2003. It was then premiered at a gig on 26th April 2003, along with a medley of Buggles, Yes and Asia numbers and these live versions were then made available to the Asia Fan Club. Now they have all been put together on this new release from Blueprint that has a limited pressing of 1000 copies so I would have thought that this would sell out quickly. The live recordings are binaural which means that they fade in and out to try and capture a sensurround effect which I found quite annoying when playing on normal speakers but it does say that to get the best from this effect then it should be listened to on headphones. Certainly, listening to a keyboard only version of "Tempus Fugit", even with Geoffrey triggering virtual instruments it shows how much the rest of the band are needed to make this work. Of course, he does not have this problem on "The Bridge" itself, which contains many different sections and allows Geoffrey to spread out more than he normally can within Asia, which has never been geared towards this sort of music. At times, dreamy, it does not contain the passion and fury of much of Wakeman or Emerson's work, but is still interesting for all that as it develops and changes. This is for diehard fans only, but those that are will certainly find the album interesting. *#87, Apr 2006*

DRAHK VON TRIP
HEART AND CONSEQUENCE

Apparently, this Malmö based sextet has been together since the late Seventies, but their music must have seemed somewhat dated even then! Recorded live in the studio over two days last March, this captures a band that are mixing together some prog with out and out psyche and thanks to the female vocals do come across rather similar at time to Jefferson Airplane, although the keyboards and Hackett style guitar do manage to give the music quite a different take. All the lyrics are in English, and it is the combination of Susan's clear vocals with some of the strange things that are going on behind her voice that makes this so interesting. She has good clear vocals, and knows her range and she is often left carrying the melody while the band are seemingly working on a different arrangement altogether.

Fans of space rock will also get something from this, although Hawkwind these guys are not! They can lift it up and rock it out when they need to but for the most part they keep that side in check and the result is something that does not belong to this time and place, and is one that does take quite a lot of playing to get full benefit from but those who persevere will feel that this was time well spent.
#86, Feb 2006

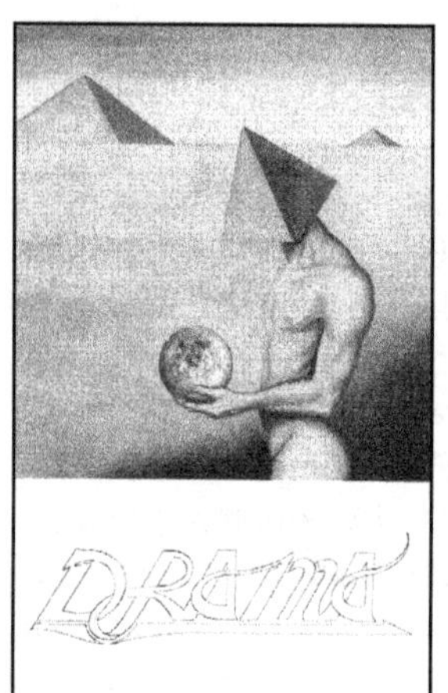

DRAMA
STRANGE EXPRESSION
Drama were founded in 1991, in Erie Pennsylvania. Their philosophy is "stretching the boundaries of the typical live act while striving for something different". Initially they were a three-piece comprising Kevin Hultberg (vocals, bass, Chapman Stick), Chris Rodler (guitars, keyboards) and Brett Rodler (drums) and it was this line-up that recorded the very professional tape now in the player. My initial reaction on hearing this is that here was band very influenced by Rush, and although I do still think that, there are a myriad of other influences as well. There is a very high standard of musical proficiency, but what the ear is drawn to is the real melody within the songs. "Handed Down" may have Rush stamped all over it, but is that such a bad thing? It is refreshing to hear a prog/technical band that do not take Genesis as the starting point. Commercial? Certainly, here is a band that knows how to deliver quality product. Kevin's voice is extremely melodic and enjoyable, and it makes a pleasant change to hear controlled singing that is not too highly-pitched. There is a lot of variety between the eight songs on this tape. I enjoyed it immensely and it is a real shame that it is not for sale over here. Since the tape was released Gary Madras has joined on keyboards so that the band can spread their wings in the live environment. If you like good melodic rock, extremely well played and with great songs to boot, then you should discover the music of Drama.
#19, Aug 1993

DRAMA
STIGMATA OF CHANGE
This is not an album by the American band that later turned into Leger De Main, but rather the third album by the French band of the same name. They have a new singer for this release, and all lyrics are in English. This is a concept album, but unusually for a prog band they are singing about unrequited love – not a subject normally associated with the genre. There is a symphonic feel to this album,

without ever being overly bombastic.

A combination of well thought out song structures with delicate instrumental passages means that this is a very accessible album and one that even my eight-year-old daughter has been enjoying immensely. I hadn't come across this band before, but the mid-Genesis feel to some of their songs combined with Floyd means that this is one that will gain the interest of many, and well deserved it is too.
#85, Nov 2005

DREADNAUGHT
MUSICA EN FLAGRANTE
Words cannot possibly do justice to this album. I defy anyone to write a bad review about this, just because it is so far away from the normal confines of what one would consider musical melodies and songwriting that you either get this or you do not. If you do not get this then you will hate it with a passion and there is no point even writing about it – if you do get it you will probably just stay very confused and wonder what on earth is going on, followed by the realisation that somehow you have to convey in words what this music sounds like! This is their fourth studio album, and since this came out last year they have a live album released as well, but this is all that I have heard so far from the band. The line-up is Bob Lord (bass, keyboards etc.), Justin Walton (keyboards, guitars, sax) and Tim Haney (drums) plus the occasional guest – four songs are also solo pieces by Bob. How can you describe music that literally defies definition? Anything I write cannot do justice to this. Prog? Jazz? Modern Classical? Anarchic? These things, none of these things, maybe less, and certainly more. Is it constructed or is it free form – deliberate or accidental? The only thing I am convinced about in all honesty is that if you picked 100 people at random and played this album to them 99 of them would be out of the room in less than a minute – the remaining one would probably be sat there with their mouth open trying to take it all in and understand what is going on. If you want to go with the flow and are happier staying closer to the mainstream, then avoid at all costs. Me? I think that this one of the most original albums I have ever heard, and there are times that I know I will be returning to it again, and trying to understand just what is going on. These guys are on a different plane to me, and to probably the rest of the planet, but is that such a bad thing?
#85, Nov 2005

DREAM ARIA
IN THE WAKE
There are times when the only way to describe an album is by hearing it, words just do not do it justice and that is the case with the new album by Dream Aria. The name itself gives away some of the clues as to the music itself, but this is quite unlike anything that I have been listening to. The music has been written by keyboard player Don

Stagg, and along with Josef Pilasanovic and drummer Gary Gray he has created the stage which is being graced by Ann Burstyn.

Both of Ann's parents were musicians in Winnipeg Symphony Orchestra so she was very much brought up around music. Her voice is obviously classically trained, and from a young age she enjoyed singing both in rock bands and in operas and here she can do both at the same time! Mind you, it should be said that for a prog rock act there is not too much rock (although "Blue Lady" is a cracker), more of a voyage of experience and discovery as the music moves through countless different styles and contents.

Within these Ann uses all her talents so that she can be singing 'straight' one second and the next she is just reaching up the scale going higher and higher until her voice disappears into the stratosphere. I do not think that Don has heard of 4/4 time, but he does know what he wants and sometimes that can be prog or it can be far more mystical and difficult to define. This is truly progressive, bringing together musical styles from areas normally deemed to be either rock or classical, as well as east and west. Ann has an incredible voice and this album is truly very different to everything else around.
#84, July 2005

DREAM MACHINE
TRILOGIA

Given the line-up of musicians who recorded this album it is logical as to the type of music they play. The guys are Gabriele - bass guitar (ex-Thunderdogs), Champignon - flutes, duduk, nay etc. (ex-Ozric Tentacles), Alex - guitar (ex-Damidge), Seaweed - synthesisers (ex-Ozric Tentacles, Thunderdogs & Damidge), Julian – keyboards, Maurizio – drums. This is an instrumental band that has a lot of history behind the individual members, and it is obvious that Ozrics are a key player in their musical past. The music was all recorded live on 15th July last year, with Champignon and Seaweed then adding some overdubs. Some of the music is dreamy as one would expect but often this is music is far more dramatic and rock oriented than one might imagine with two keyboard players.

The rhythm section is particularly strong, and this allows Alex to either take the lead or to provide backing as required. Champignon often takes on the role of front man, something that he has been doing for eighteen years with Ozrics, but here he often is playing against and with music that is more direct than much in his past. I was not surprised to find that this was an album that I have enjoyed playing time and again, and am sure that any fans of this style of music and of Ozrics are going to find this an essential purchase. Seaweed has since left to concentrate on studio projects and he has been replaced by Joie. This is very much an ongoing outfit and I for one am looking forward to hearing a lot more from them.
#87, Apr 2006

THE DREAMING

SHADOW DAYS

'Shadow Days' is the third album from this Buffalo New York – based band, which features Ann Janish-Schieder (vocals, piano, synth), Leah Pinnavaia (vocals, clarinet, keyboards), Daniel Haskin (acoustic and electric guitar, e-bow, synth) and Pat O'Connell (drums). At the time of this 2004 album they also had Ray Lorigo on guitar and bass but although he played on all three albums he does not appear to still be with the band who expect their fourth album to be available later this year. I am not sure of the original influences of these guys, although they have opened for The Strawbs on more than one occasion, but they do come across as an American more sanitised version of Mostly Autumn, along with singers such as Anna Ryder and Talis Kimberley. The music is strongly based around the vocals of Ann and Leah and is extremely enjoyable and accessible on first hearing. Although they do use electric guitars this is often a fairly acoustic album, with wonderful arrangements that mean that while the music is flowing and is at times very complex it is always the vehicle for the vocals, always being designed to augment and add to the vocals and never detract from them in any way. There is a strong understanding and use of dynamics, which adds to the light and shade so that even though there may be a riffing electric guitar at the beginning of "Piglet and the Black Fox" it soon gives way to something that is far more delicate. Overall this is a very enjoyable album indeed and one that folkies will probably get as much out of as progheads, while those into good music are in for a treat.

#88, Jun 2006

DRIFTING SUN

DRIFTING SUN

Brennus is a label that I had not heard of before but is a sub-division of Musea. Unlike the parent label Brennus are concentrating on heavy prog, and Drifting Sun sit happily within that area. DS were put together by Frenchman Pat Sanders (keyboards): Manu Sibona (bass) is also French, while Rafe Pomeroy (vocals) is American, Rob Thompson (guitar) is South African and drummer John Lyngwood is the sole Brit. A cosmopolitan band not only in format but also in the styles they employ.

Drifting Sun with be labelled progressive by many, and is as good a description as any, but they are not 'definitively' prog. They have brought elements of hard rock, 70's rock (with a feeling towards Wishbone Ash), choral and acoustic styles, along with their own brand of AOR. The result is a very diverse and interesting album that grows more and more. Songs such as "Jamie Was a Vampire" are extremely catchy, and the music and words meld together. In fact, if there is such a musical genre, the song could be described as light-gothic! Conversely, the next one starts with overlaid keyboards and piano with some acoustic guitar. At times this is Marillion-esque, but the strength is that they manage to conjure up fleeting images of influences but at the same sound nothing like them.

The album was mixed by guitarmeister Karl Groom who also plays on the instrumental "Call It Love." One of my favourites is the album closer "Dancer" which combines speed with beauty and elegance. Drifting Sun are a band new to me but I am sure that this is not the last that the UK prog scene will hear of them. A definite goody.
#39, Jan 1997

DRIFTING SUN
ON THE REBOUND

It seems ages since I last heard from Drifting Sun, but they are back with a new album; not on the Brennus label this time but a self-release. It is a very well-produced album for all that, and shows a more thoughtful side to the band. Chris Martin has a very soulful voice and Pat Sanders's delicate keyboards and John Spearman's guitarwork provides for a restful release. This is not to say that this boring, far from it, but rather that this is not progressive music that is in your face, but is more on the reflective side.

The vocals are probably the most important part of the music, with Chris very high up in the mix, being used as a musical instrument in its' own right. I enjoyed playing this and I am sure that many others who do not normally listen to 'progressive' music will find much in here to enjoy.
#53, May 1999

SERGEY DUDIN
GUITAR BALLADS

This is Sergey's third album, originally released in 2002 and now been given a new lease of life by Mals. This is very pleasant, but it is never going to be much more than that. This is a reflective guitar workout with progressive undertones, so that he comes across more as Andy Latimer, Roine Stolt or David Gilmour as opposed to Yngwie Malmsteen.

There is certainly a deftness of touch and the result is something that is very accessible indeed and is fine for playing in the background – but there is a certain lack of dynamics which means that although it is pleasant it just is not exciting. Some of the runs are quite aggressive but they get lost in the mix and possibly if he was playing live then this would be much more furious and therefore a bit more fun.
#88, Jun 2006

SERGEY DUDIN
ETERNAL CALL

After reviewing Sergey's third album in the last issue, I am now listening to his debut that came out in 2000. This is much more of a song based album, heavily influenced by Pink Floyd but again with hard guitar lines over the top of it all. All the information in the booklet is in Russian, as are the lyrics, so it is not possible to know what he is singing about, but that does not seem to be too much of an issue here. This is a very approachable album, with the vocals being quite forceful at times with more passion than one would expect from either Dave or Roger, and the guitar lines have been influenced far more by hard rock than by Mr Gilmour. This mix works very well indeed and the resulting album is one that will appeal to progheads, as the fusion of hard rock solos with Floyd is very pleasing on the ear indeed. *#89, Sep 2006*

DULCIMER
ROB'S GARDEN

In 1970 progressive folk duo Dulcimer launched the Nepentha label with their debut 'And I Turned As I Had A Boy', returning in 1980 with 'A Land Fit For Heroes', and then in 1993 released 'When A Child…' on President. Only two years later they are back with another gem, and my wife, who occasionally suffers me listening to CDs in the car, told me on hearing this that I had better give it a good review. High praise indeed. Dulcimer are David Evans and Peter Hodge, who are both masters of all manners of acoustic instruments and share the vocals, sometimes individually but more often in harmony. Reminiscent at times of Simon & Garfunkel or even Harry Chapin, these are songwriters and lyricists of the very highest order. The only word to describe this album is "beautiful", as it is such a joy to listen to. Probably the best song is "Indiana Jones" where an old man looks back over his life and thinks of all that he has done. He concludes that he has never been Indiana Jones, rather that he has just been an ordinary man and for that he is glad. An outstanding album that will be enjoyed by all who love good music. *#32, Dec 1995*

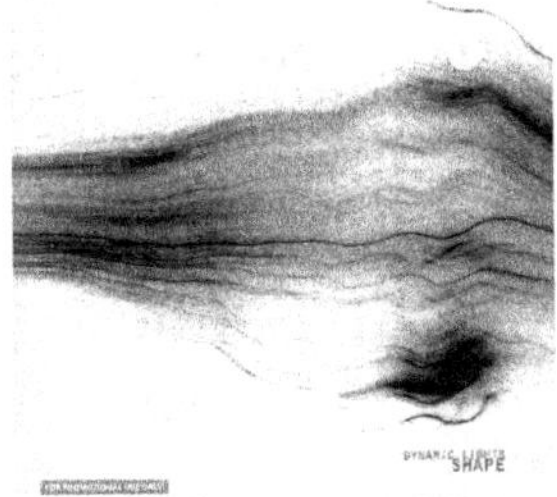

DYNAMIC LIGHTS
SHAPE

Formed in 1997 this is the debut album from this Italian quintet, and although they have been playing gigs with the likes of Pain Of Salvation they are not that heavy, although they are working in that area between melodic rock and prog metal. The opening song "In The Hands Of A Siren" is the second longest on the album, and contains a guest female vocalist in Jamina Jansson who adds something as she duets with Metteo Infante. But there are times during this number and others where the band almost appear to be marking time, waiting too long for the next phase

which means that instead of being dramatic as they had hoped instead it can have the opposite effect. There is a lot of piano on the album, but again the overall effect is somewhat diluted as there are times when the music is not constructed as well as it might be. Some judicious editing might have made an enjoyable album containing some good ideas into a great one, but it hasn't happened yet.
#84, July 2005

DYONISOS
DYONISOS

This is not a band, but instead is the work of Dan Cowan, an American multi-instrumentalist who for some reason is signed to the Russian Mals label. I know very little about Dan, although I do believe that he has released some other albums as well, but this is a 2006 release and there is no title so is being portrayed possibly as a debut? Whatever the reason, this is an album that fans of classic Floyd are going to be seeking out. This mixture of instrumentals and songs show that here is a musician who not only has Dave Gilmour's guitar sound off to a tee but also has an innate understanding of the music and emotions behind 'Wish You Were Here' era Pink Floyd. It is a great album, with passages that let the listener blissfully drift away. From the sound, I would say that the drums are programmed instead of being 'real', but they are tastefully done and are not too intrusive on the album. The more I played this the more I felt that here is an artist that the prog scene are just waiting to discover – all power to Mals for picking up on this and releasing it. Here is an album that need to be picked up upon, even if it does mean some work in sourcing it.
#89, Sep 2006

EARTHSTONE
SEED

The idea for Earthstone came out of the demise of Ranata Spirit as when that band split, bass player Chris Phillips decided that he would continue to record music in the same vein, but this time playing all the instruments himself. However, while writing music for this project he joined Silas as guitarist and met Chris Bond who was acting as sound engineer, as well as providing additional keyboards and lyrics. After Silas disbanded, Chris Bond recorded some keyboard music under the name Stealing The Fire, and recorded Gods Acre and The Ire (reviewed in an earlier Feedback), which featured Chris Phillips. It was out of this that Earthstone emerged with Chris Phillips providing guitar, bass, keyboards, drums, vocals and programming and Chris Bond programming and keyboards while sharing the songwriting. The band see themselves as technical pagans, being enthusiasts for high technology but without losing touch with the forces of nature. They say that they are influenced primarily by nature and by their fascination with the unknown and the forgotten. Their musical influences, as well as the lyrical ones, appear to be quite different to many other prog bands around as the music has a very hard edge to it, although at the same time it is quite keyboard oriented. However, instead of swirling meandering chords the keyboards are used in a much more direct fashion, such as in the music of Poisoned Electrick Head. Good use of melody means that here is an album that will appeal both to the progger and to those interested in melodic hard rock. One element that is a little distracting is the use of sequenced drums, but Chris Phillips tells me that on the new album (which they have already begun to record) they will be using a conventional drum kit as well as a Simmonds SD9 electronic kit. They can MIDI this to drum modules and play various types of percussion as well. All in all, 'Seed' is an excellent album that I am sure will be enjoyed by many. They are putting together a full band for touring and are also working on an hour-long video. Earthstone are very much a band to look out for and if you like prog with a hard edge that has its own identity and are not Marillion or Genesis clones then this could be for you. *#25, Oct 1994*

EARTHLING SOCIETY

ALBION

Those who follow Julian Cope through his website may already be aware of this album, as it was his record of the month last August, although at that time it had not been made fully available in the UK and was instead released on the Chilean Mylodon label. It should be much easier to source from Germany, and is available both on CD and on vinyl. All formats have only been made available as limited editions, which is somewhat surprising as this is a very interesting album indeed. Apparently, the trio were inspired to produce music that was influenced by their heroes Funkadelic, Ash Ra Tempel, Can, Amon Düül II and Hawkwind and there are times when it works very well indeed. The one problem is that the vocals, when they are being sung as opposed to being spoken or being used as another instrument just are not working for me. They just do not seem to fit in with the rest of the sound and although they are quite Hawkwind-ish in style, to my ears they jar which is a shame as the rest of the album is very powerful indeed. There is great guitar from Fred Laird both holding it down and putting together some wonderful lead lines (he also provides the space keyboards) while David Fyall and Jon Blacow hold down the rhythm. These are a British underground band, hailing from Fleetwood, and remember that Julian Cope, who is seen by many to be a musical guru, loves this album a lot so it could be just me.

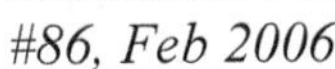
#86, Feb 2006

EAST WIND POT

EAST WIND POT

This is the debut full-length album from East Wind Pot (they have previously released a limited-edition CD-R), a Japanese instrumental quartet who are mixing together prog and jazz in a quite interesting way. There is no guitar here, with the melodies normally being carried by Yuko Tsuchiya on keyboards and Daisuke Yamasaki on woodwind, although the wonderfully named "An Argument With Illya Kuryakin

Whom I Loved In My Childhood" features a gentle duet between Yuko on piano and fretless bassist Yoshiyuki Sakurai (the line-up is completed by drummer Eiichi Tsuchiya). That track is probably my favourite on the album (and not only for the name either), as this is music that contains a real beauty, with restrained musicianship as each look to the other both for support and for inspiration until it is time for the rest of the guys to come in and the music moves to a new level. Overall this is a well-constructed album, and certainly one of the best that I have heard from Poseidon with well thought out ideas and the impression that they all know what they want to achieve with each other instead of just playing furiously until they run out of tape. Well worth hearing. *#88, Jun 2006*

EAT STATIC
THE ALIEN EP'S

EAT STATIC
DECADANCE

I have never listened to Eat Static, but have long been a fan of Ozric's, so thought that it was time that I gave them a try. The first album captures rare singles etc. (including their first ever 12"), while the second contains unreleased and live cuts from their first ten years (89-99).

I must admit that even a hardened old metalhead such as myself found that there is something in this that is far superior to the norm. I was happy bopping away when Nicola came in, demanded to know who I was playing, then took the CDs away for further investigation! Apparently, she is going to take them to school to play to her mates in the sixth form – high praise indeed.

This duo also performs the music live, not miming to DAT's – must be some show. Dance music that is worth casting a lug to.
#64, Oct 2001

ECCENTRIC ORBIT
ATTACK OF THE MARTIANS

This band were always going to sound a bit different to the rest, given that all the music has been written by bassist Bill Noland (a man who could give Chris Squire a lesson in what a deep and heavy bass can sound like), and the line-up is a little unusual in that not only do they have a keyboard player but are also joined by someone playing wind-controlled synths through a MIDI.

Add a drummer to the mix and that is the band, playing music that is going to strike a chord

with anyone into ELP and Gentle Giant. That the chord is often played on Hammond Organs or Moogs is only going to endear them further. I was not sure what to expect from this album as it starts with slowly played held-down keyboards but I needn't have worried as after a minute and a half of "Star Power" the drums and bass come in and at two minutes Bill takes the music by the scruff and kicks in with a dirty bass which then allows the keyboards to come in over the top. It works incredibly well, and this was not the only time that I was surprised with this album as there are loads of things going on and there is a definite space theme to the song titles, which carries through to the music. Unusually for an independent release this is a digipak (I love the simple cover), and is worth investigating.
#84, July 2005

ECHOLYN
AS THE WORLD
When a band is signed by a major (Sony) and is then told to go and away and tour for a while (and get paid), then you realise that there may well be something special going on. Malcolm has managed to get the UK rights to this (hence the release on Cyclops and although it has only been out a few weeks and is yet to be reviewed anywhere, sheer word of mouth has already led to it being his biggest seller). So, what is making 'As The World' such a hit? Is it the quite brilliant musicianship from the five guys, the interplay between them, the mix of many styles into a potpourri of prog and AOR, the wonderful harmony vocals or the great songs? Oh, by the way, I think it is superb (in case you hadn't noticed). There are a lot of songs on here (sixteen), and each of them show the sheer class that is putting Echolyn well above many of their contemporaries. A few years ago, everybody in the prog scene was talking about Enchant, now the focus has moved onto Echolyn. There is just not a weak point on the album, they change moods and styles so fluidly that just when you feel that you are into a groove it's all change, and it's all being done so terribly well. The album oozes class and quality. The harmony vocals must be heard to be believed, and they are combined with the instruments in a way that beggar's belief. This is music of the very highest calibre and must be viewed as such by even the harshest of critics: it has hints of Kansas, but Echolyn are clearly defining their own sound. This is a superb band, and a brilliant album.
#30, Aug 1995

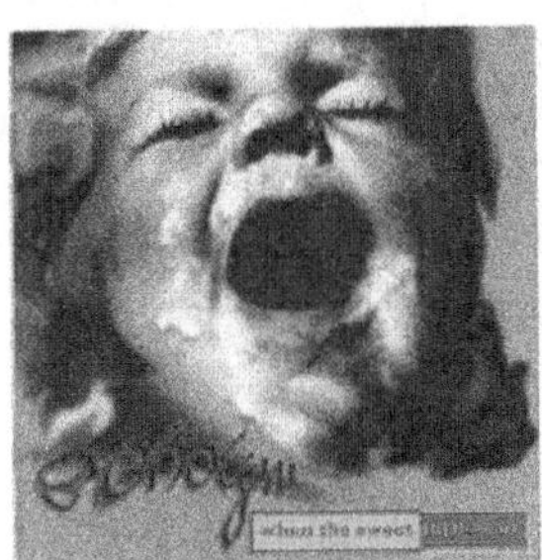

ECHOLYN
WHEN THE SWEET TURNS SOUR
This album is a collection of unreleased songs, plus two live cuts taken from their last show on September 3rd 1995. In fact, reading the booklet it almost seems as if Echolyn have broken up. I sincerely hope that is not the case because 'As The World' is a storming album that should be in every prog lover's collection. Anyway, I am not here to review that album but this one, 'When The Sweet Turns Sour'. These may for the most part be unfinished songs, as far as Echolyn are concerned, but by most bands' standards they are superb. Their mix of Kansas

and Genesis with rock comes to the fore, along with those wonderful harmony vocals. You may have guessed that there is a cover on this album, the old Genesis number, "When The Sour Turns To Sweet", which they recorded for a Genesis tribute album, but Sony put the block on it and they were not allowed to take part. Over recent years there seem to be quite a few new prog bands coming out of the States and Echolyn can rightly claim to the one of the best of the crop. If you like your prog with an American slant then you should be listening to Echolyn, and this album is as good a place to start as any.
#36, Aug 1996

EDEN BURNING
BRINK

'Brink' is the fourth album by Cheltenham based outfit Eden Burning, who have been going for five years now. They first came to my attention when they recorded a song for the Geoff Mann tribute album 'Mannerisms', but this is the first time that I have heard a complete set of their material, Acoustic guitars play a large part of proceedings (although electric guitars do get used for strong effect), along with woodwind, but the major star is the melodious voice of Paul Northrup. These wonderful vocals, combined with well thought out songs means that this album is not only immediately accessible but bloody enjoyable to boot. "Wrap It Up" has "hit" written all over it, as the hooks and vocals take it into a territory that Damon Albarn would be proud of. Eden Burning are a Christian band, and demonstrate their faith in "With A Kiss", but the lyrics have been written so carefully that even the most profound atheist could listen to this and enjoy it. With the songs and melodies on 'Brink', Eden Burning could well just be on the "brink" of being very big indeed.
#36, Aug 1996

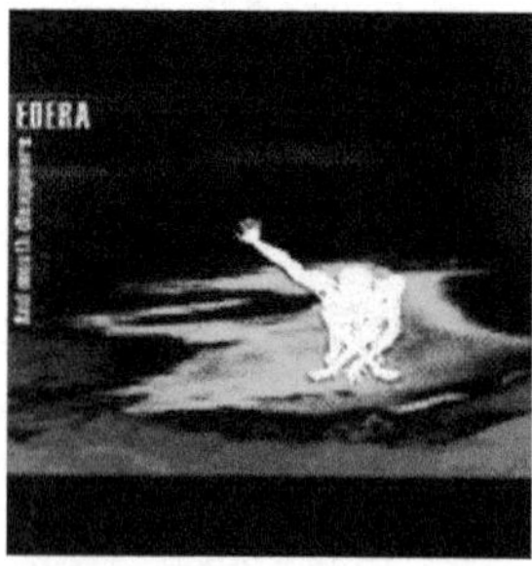

EDERA
AND MOUTH DISAPPEARS

Edera have been together since 1994, and although they have released some demos (and a compilation of these) this is the first full-length album, and it is a concept work as well. Although there are two guitarists within the seven-man line-up, the band do not hit the riffs as hard or as often as they might but instead this is all about song structure and arrangements. Singer Valerio Valentini has a lot to do in this album as it is a very wordy story, but luckily he is up to the task and although this does mean more of a back seat for the guitars and keyboards than might otherwise be the case, it still works very well indeed. There is an interesting mix to their music so while they are solidly in the neo-prog sector with obvious nods to classic Marillion and even IQ there are also times when the guitars and piano work well together and bring back memories of Savatage and Winter. There is good strong sound and the songs stand up as they tell the story, and this is an album that I have enjoyed playing a great deal.
#87, Apr 2006

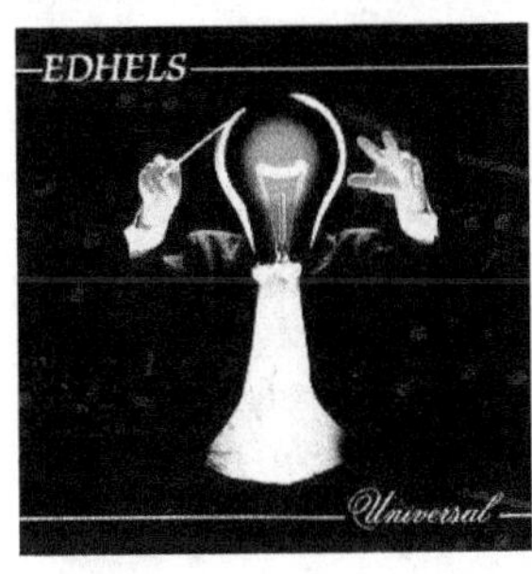

EDHELS
UNIVERSAL

Edhels are more well-known for their instrumental albums whereas this contains vocals throughout, and I think that this is a reissue of an album from 1998 although there are no details within. Most of the songs here were recorded live which demonstrates that all the guys involved are certainly no slouches when it comes to musical expertise but in many ways, this is a very difficult album to listen to. Part of that is down to the vocals where Jean-Marc Bastianelli just does not have the range or style to make his singing work. Also, musically the guys are going all over the place and while I would say that they have been influenced by 'Discipline' era King Crimson there are also elements of VDGG and early Genesis but instead of blending in together there is the feeling of deliberate disharmony and anti-melody. This makes the album uninviting to all but the most hardened proghead and even they will be wondering what all the fuss is about. It feels like an experiment that has gone wrong and Edhels would do better to place more focus and attention on the music and forget the vocals altogether.
#88, Jun 2006

EGDON HEATH
HIM, THE SNAKE AND I

This is Dutch band Egdon Heath's third album, although it is the first time I have heard their music (apart from appearances on compilations). Their last album, 'The Killing Silence', was widely acclaimed, although since that release vocalist Jens van der Stempel has left the band (and resurfaced with Brassé, whose album I reviewed in an earlier Feedback).

Having replaced him with Maurice Kalbeek the band then took two years to write and record the follow-up. With two keyboard players, it could be expected that the band would be top heavy in that area, but the rest of the band are very much in evidence and tracks such as "Gringo" really rock, with plenty of guitar. This track shows the many strengths of Egdon Heath, with some very powerful vocals and guitarwork, yet at the same time there is enough width and breadth for an interesting use of keyboards. The following track, "On A Bench", is very short, being less than two minutes long, yet shows that good songs can be this length. It just involves vocals and piano, but is well worth a listen. Overall I found the album very enjoyable.

There is some great musicianship, and the album is a real 'grower'. They have made a real find in their new vocalist, who has a similar power and range to Damian Wilson; not a bad thing in my book. The songs are not as immediate as they could be, but they are worth persevering with, and are well worth the effort.
#21, Jan 1994

ELDRITCH
SEEDS OF RAGE

I do not know anything about this band, except that they are a five-piece hailing from Europe. The album was recorded in late '94 but has only just become available within the UK, and shows another band that has been paying attention to Threshold and Dream Theater as they pummel those guitars and use the keyboards as a lightening element.

However, I'm not sure what they would be like live as they only have one guitarist who here has been suitably overdubbed to provide a wall of sound. All lyrics are in English, and this is an album that will appeal to those into technical rock as their Queensrÿche influences also shine through. The music moves and twists as they crunch through the ten numbers on show, with "Under The Ground" working best with some wonderful fretwork combined with powerful double bass drumming. They are not afraid to switch between different time signatures, and the songs are always there right in your face (and ears). Happily, on the progressive/technical rock border, this is an act with much to offer. They blast through numbers like "Chains" as if there is no tomorrow, and then slow it down before blasting off again. Terence Holler has a powerful voice, which he needs to be heard in the maelstrom. One for those who like good tunes and variety.
#33, Feb 1996

ELDRITCH
EL NINO

It is a while since I last came across Eldritch; I reviewed their debut 'Seeds of Rage' in #33, but never heard the follow-up 'Headquake' which was released early last year.

Anyway, onto the new one, and although they are on the same label and are also viewed as a progressive metal band Eldritch are a different kettle of fish to Vanden Plas. Whereas VP are basically a progressive rock band that have gone heavier, Eldritch are a metal band that arguably are using a few progressive elements. The result is an album that most prog fans will find far too intense and heavy to understand, while the headbangers will love it. That is not to say that there are not softer points to the album (such as the beginning of "To Be Or Not To Be (God)", but rather that this is a metal band crunching out the riffs and challenging the dandruff.

A lot of the music has a quick tempo and the fingers of guitarist Eugene Simone and keyboard player Oleg Smirnoff fly as they duel with each other. With good songs and strong vocals and musicianship this will be a pleasant addition to any metallic collection but proggers need to be wary.
#51, Jan 1999

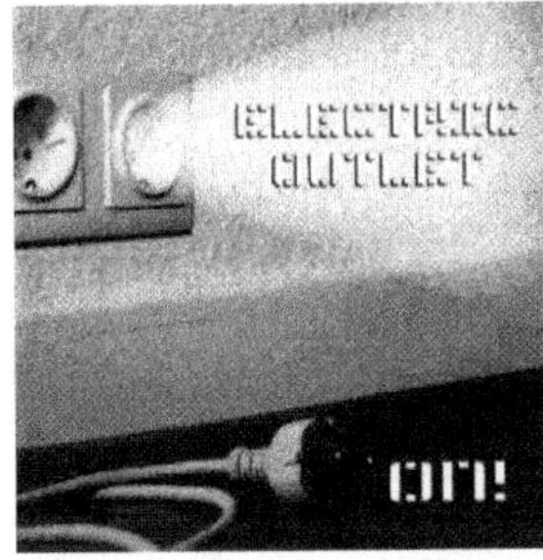

ELECTRIC OUTLET
ON!

According to the press release "Electric Outlet are a killer rock fusion instrumental power foursome that showcase formidable technical expertise but in a framework, that is easily digestible for even the most hardened instrumental snob!" That is quite a succinct way of putting it! The line-up is Marcus Deml (guitar), Tom Aeschbacher (keyboards), Ralf Gustke (drums) and Frank Itt (bass) and they are out to prove that instrumental fusion can be fun and that it is not necessary to stand still when playing or listening to music like this but that it is fine to have a smile on your face and a groove in your soul and just to get into the flow. Here is a band that are taking some of the pretentiousness out of jazz influenced rock and instead are producing music that is light and accessible while also maintaining the complexity and complicated time signatures that one would expect from this style of music. This is music for the Summer, music to play when the sun is shining and the skies are blue. It is instantly accessible, something that all can get into and with any of the three melody instruments taking the lead or interacting with each other, repeating themes and melodies, it is just pure fun. A goody.*#89, Sep 2006*

ELEGANT SIMPLICITY
NATURAL INSTINCT

ELEGANT SIMPLICITY
SAMPLER TAPE

Elegant Simplicity is the work of Steven McCabe, a multi-instrumentalist who decided to go solo in 1993. He released three tapes that year, another three in 1994, but only 'Natural Instinct' in 1995, which was due to a couple of reasons. Firstly, he released a sampler tape of his work, which was very well received and ran to three print runs, and secondly he spent a lot of time looking for a vocalist, which was resolved when he started working with fellow multi-instrumentalist Ken Senior (Evolution).

Ken is featured on six of the seven songs that appear on Steven's newest venture, a CD titled 'The Nature of Change' which will be out on Proximity later this month (the other song is a forty-three minute long instrumental). I am not sure if Steven is primarily a keyboard player or a guitarist, as he is more than happy to combine both to make songs of an exciting and dynamic nature. They are indeed very much songs and not mindless meanderings or technical twaddle, and do not fall into the trap of self-indulgence but instead keep the listener involved throughout. For more details about the availability of the tapes, and whether he has any more of the FREE sampler, contact him directly.
#33, Feb 1996

ELEGANT SIMPLICITY
THE NATURE OF CHANGE

Multi-instrumentalist Steven McCabe has now released his first album with vocals, care of fellow multi-instrumentalist Ken Senior (who records under the name Evolution). Obviously, the use of lyrics has given Steven's work an extra dimension, and Ken's gentle vocals fit perfectly with what is going on.

One of Steven's great strengths is that he is able to play both keyboards and guitar to a very high standard which gives a strong 'group' feel to the proceedings, Six of the seven songs have vocals, the best of which (although there is not a weak one) is "20th Century Breakdown" which talks about the way that countries starve to death while we do not appear to care: "I really thought that we had progressed, reached the nexus of our success. We're nothing. We're nothing but apes with cars, breeding our lives away to excess".

Final track is the forty-three-minute-long instrumental "The Nature of Change" and Steven shows that rock guitar does have a place in prog, as does guitar and keyboard interplay. Light and shade, mood and time changes, this is a glorious piece of music, and the CD is the best Elegant Simplicity product to date.
#34, Apr 1996

ELEGANT SIMPLICITY
REVERSAL OF TIME

Following on from last year's 'The Nature of Change', multi-instrumentalist Steven McCabe has again joined forces with Ken Senior (and other musicians if the sleeve is to be believed) and produced a new album. Unlike the last, there is no forty-minute instrumental, as this is far more of a songs-based album. That is not to say that there are not instrumentals as well, just that they are far shorter and are within the album as a whole whereas last time the album was very much divided in two.

Ken's singing appears to have improved to my ears, possibly mellowing a bit, and it now seems that he and Steven are going to keep working on each other's projects, following on as this does from Evolution's 'The First Signs of Life'. Not only does Ken's singing appear to have taken on a new life, but also Steven's guitarwork is moving into higher levels.

Yet again the two have combined to produce a very high quality prog album. Yes, it is laid back for a lot of the time in a Camelesque sort of way, but that is not always a bad thing. The presentation of the album is also improved, making this one that many prog fan will be searching out.
#42, July 1997

ELEGANT SIMPLICITY
THE STORY OF OUR LIVES

ELEGANT SIMPLICITY
PALINDROME

ELEGANT SIMPLICITY
ARCHITECT OF LIGHT

I was searching through the web looking for music related to Ken Senior one night when I came across the excellent web site of Elegant Simplicity. I had forgotten that Ken sang for Steven McCabe, and realised that I had also lost touch with Steve himself. I made contact again and discovered that the reason Steve had not been in touch over recent years was that his computer had died and he had lost many of his contact addresses.

To rectify the situation Steve sent me his last three albums so that I could hear what he had been up to in recent times. Steve is prolific, and since 1993 has released fourteen full-length albums, four promo tapes, and two sampler tapes. But just because he has a large amount of output it does not mean that there is any reduction in quality, he is just an artist with a lot of ideas.

It appears that the last album I heard was 'Reversal Of Time' which I reviewed in #42 (1997). Between that one and 'The Story Of Our Lives' (2000) there were two more that I have not heard so it was interesting to be able to sit down and see what changes there had been during that time.

Elegant Simplicity started life as a one-man band, with Steve providing instrumental albums where he not only performed and produced the music, but also all the sleeve design and artwork. This is the case with this album as it is an instrumental, which is one piece of music just under forty-eight minutes long (subdivided into twelve so sections can be easily accessed). The whole thing was recorded and produced in about two weeks, which is quite an undertaking for music that is as layered and complex as this.

The music is laid back as opposed to dynamic, and there is a great deal going on with keyboards and guitars interacting in a mellow Camel, Floyd style. It could be construed then that this is background music but that is not the case. It is uplifting music that made me keep thinking of the sea, music that I could drift on and wanted to hear to the end.

'Palindrome' was the next album, in 2001, and saw Steven yet again back in partnership with Ken Senior. Ken is a multi-instrumentalist in his own right (releasing material as Evolution) and has more recently been gainfully employed as bassist in Parallel Or 90

Degrees. Within Elegant Simplicity he finds work as vocalist only, while Steven yet again provides all the music, songs, production, artwork etc. This is an album where the dynamism has been turned up a lot, and while half of the songs are instrumental, even these have a power that was missing from the previous album.

Throughout the album the guitars are much more to the fore, and the scene is set with the powerful opening title cut which shows that instrumental prog music has a right to be included within the term 'rock'. It builds and grows, with subtle changes of style and mannerisms, so that the listener is always moving with the flow not knowing what each layer is going to reveal.

Ken understood what is required and his vocal style fits in with the music extremely well, no matter what demands are being made. "Let It Be Me" starts with riffing guitar prior to a great keyboard lead where Steve proves just how quick his fingers can move, yet then takes a total change in direction before the vocals kick in. This is a great song, whatever the genre, and although at ten minutes is probably slightly too long for commercial radio it is a song that anyone can get into straight away.

And so, it is now up to date with 'Architect Of Light', which was released earlier this year. It is dedicated to "whatever it was that saved my life on February 4th 2002" – this is something that I can relate to as tomorrow is the fourth anniversary of my motorbike accident, and Steve's dedication is concerning a car accident he suffered on that date. There are a few albums I have reviewed in this issue that appear to be what the artist has been building to for a period, and that is the case with this one.

It is ten years since Steve started releasing cassettes, and on this album, he not only has Ken providing vocals but also now has a drummer in Christopher Knight. There are a couple of guest musicians on the album providing diverse elements on some tracks, and Steve himself also provides some stunning flute along with his other instruments. With three of the five songs over sixteen minutes long, this is an album that is bringing together a multitude of styles that are at the same time different yet belonging.

It is an album of complexity, yet also simplicity, bringing Floydian styles in with Camel and mixing them up with a solid dose of new prog that it is very much music that is relevant for today. Again, it is mostly instrumental, but Ken very much plays his part.

So, an update then on what has been happening in the ES camp. All the albums are extremely good, although it is 'Architect Of Light' that gets the votes for being the best (and is available for only £10!). The web site is one of the best prog sites I have seen and well worth a visit. Let's hope that it is not five years until the next time Steve and I are in contact with each other!
#69, Aug 2002

ELEGANT SIMPLICITY
PURITY AND DESPAIR

Moments Of Clarity

ELEGANT SIMPLICITY
MOMENTS OF CLARITY

Following on from #69 where I reviewed the three most recent Elegant Simplicity albums I now have had the opportunity to hear the two albums before that. 'Purity and Despair' was released in 1998 and was the follow-up to 'Reversal Of Time' which I reviewed in 1997. This album is solely instrumental, and Steven McCabe has again employed some extra musicians, this time in Peter Douglas (guitars) and Gilbert Ross (basses). Of course, Steven then manages to bring the kitchen sink to the ensemble, giving it a very full sound indeed (one small niggle, a 'live' drummer would have given it a better sound). What is immediately apparent is the way that the music moves and flows, sometimes returning to a previous theme or moving on in a new direction. The music can be led through 'modern' style keyboards or a Mellotron, or acoustic guitar or electric, but it always keeps the interest and could never be considered boring or background. Instrumental albums need to be something a bit special to keep the listener involved, and this is laid back yet at the time passionate and brings together melodies in a way that works. Camel are again a main influence and I would urge fans of that band to search this out. 'Moments Of Clarity' was released in 1999. Steven again changed the line-up, deciding to play all the music himself but bringing in Ken Senior to provide vocals on five of the seven tracks. The vocals seem quite upfront, with little in the way of reverb and it is as if they have been put this way to bring 'honesty' to the piece. It may seem a strange thing to say, but that really is the best way that I can describe it. This is not an album to play when you are feeling depressed, as while the music is often quiet and dreamy the lyrics are telling some harrowing and indeed insightful tales, which gives us the clarity of the title. I am not sure if it is intended as a concept album but certainly it can be taken as such. It is an album about loss and despair, even about having to sit by the side of a loved one and agree to have the life support machine turned off and watch the light go out as they die. While there are some Camel-esque moments, this album is much more influenced by Floyd and even though it has a depressing subject matter I found that this is an album that I enjoyed immensely. Two more Elegant Simplicity albums reviewed, which means that I have reviewed all of Steven's output. So, which one would I point to as his best release? Favourite would still be the newest album 'Architect Of Light', but 'Moments Of Clarity' is an album that deals well with a tough subject matter. *#70, Oct 2002*

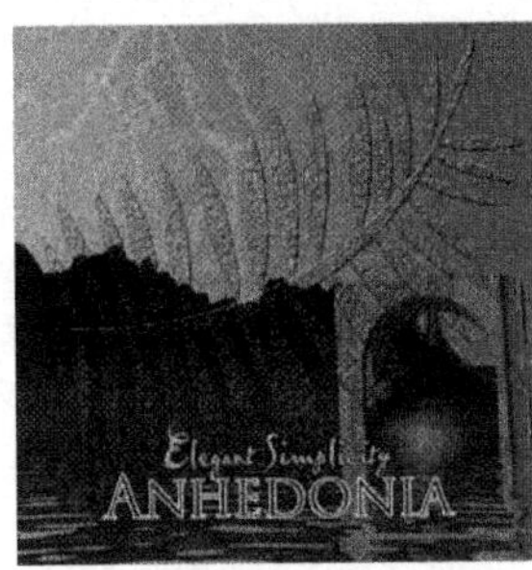

ELEGANT SIMPLICITY
ANHEDONIA

I always seem to be running behind Steve McCabe, doomed never to catch up. Here I am writing about his sixteenth album only to find out on his site that he has just released his seventeenth! Oh, well, maybe one day. This album is quite different to the previous 'Architect Of Light' as here all the music is played by Steven apart from drums by Christopher Knight. The use of 'live' drums always makes an impact, at least in my experience, and it is always for the better. Steven has been likened to bands like Camel in the past but this time although he maintained the fluidity, this is a very different prospect altogether. Yet again this is an album that certainly feels as if it is by a band, and not what is basically a one-man project. It did take me a while to get into this album as the first time it washed right over me and I was not sure if I liked it or not, and probably felt more inclined to the latter than the former. But as always perseverance pays off and I found that there is a lot to take in. Instrumental it may be, and sometimes it is elegantly simplistic, but at others it is complex without being over the top. It never drifts down as far as New Age and veers away from being too heavily keyboard based but manages to maintain a nice level between the keyboards and guitars with the flute etc. being a nice touch. Of the seven tracks, I think that "Anhedonia VI: Lost" is my favourite, with some wonderful passages that should be thought of as modern classical music as opposed to 'simple' prog rock. Yet again another gem worth discovering. *#84, July 2005*

ELEGANT SIMPLICITY
STUDIES IN HEARTBREAK

At long last I am back up to date with Steven McCabe and his seventeenth album under the Elegant Simplicity banner. He is joined by Christopher Knight on all manner of drums and percussion (including marimba and vibraphone), but the rest of the instrumentation is provided by Steven himself. Having played this album a few times now, I can honestly say that I think that this is his most complete work to date. The music flows and changes direction, rarely happy to stay in one place for too long, but there is still continuity throughout the album. There is something for every prog fan on here, and it even starts with an acoustic guitar duet, but this is much more than 'just' progressive rock. Steven has explored the idea of modern classical music before, but never to the extent that he does on this album and in some ways, it is a bit reminiscent of Karda Estra in that respect, although of course without the vocals. It will appeal particularly to fans of Floyd with some luscious guitar lines, but it is the use of all the instruments that makes this stand out. It might be just the use of an acoustic here, or a sample there, but it is the way that it has all been combined that to me makes this such an enjoyable album to listen to. The double-tracked guitars may only be together for a few bars before giving way to some Hammond style keyboards, but that is all that it needs. The more I play this the more I like it, and if you want an album to fall deeply inside then this is the one for you.
#85, Nov 2005

ELEGANT SIMPLICITY
NOWHERE LEFT TO TURN

Steven McCabe is back with his eighteenth full-length album, and again Christopher Knight has joined him on drums while Steven provides all the other instruments. The album contains just four songs, but two of these are more than seventeen minutes long while the other two are no slouches either. The longest song is the title cut which is over twenty minutes in length and contains some vocals, here provided by Stephen Lyons. What is immediately apparent that Steven has decided to produce an album that while maintaining the Camel, Floyd traits that we have come to love, has also decided that it is also time to produce music with a harder edge to it. This will never of course be a hard rock album but there is more concentration on riffs and chords from his guitar as opposed to just sinuous complex guitar lines. These are there as well of course, but here he has allowed his heavier influences to come through. This is prog music that is going to appeal to a wide number of listeners, and while he never gets into prog metal territory this slightly heavier approach is going to gain him new fans. If you have never come across Steven previously then you need to do so. His website is one of the best prog sites around and there is plenty of music there to listen to, to get a flavour of what this guy is all about. If you have never listened to Elegant Simplicity, then you owe it to your ears to do so. *#89, Sep 2006*

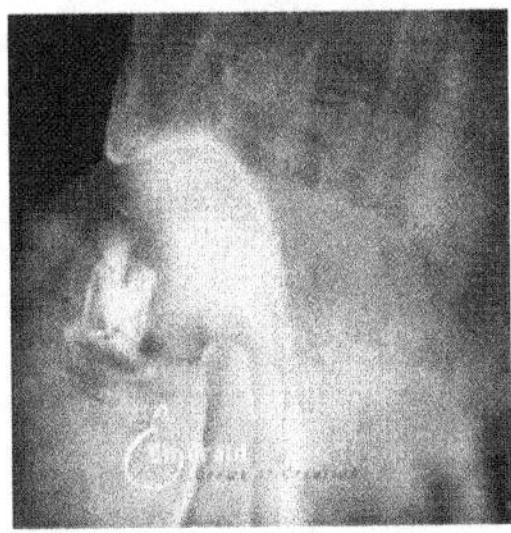

EMERALD
CROWN OF CREATION

This album was released in 2004 but has only just come to my attention. It is the debut album from five guys who are all students of the Rock Academy in Tilburg, so it is probably of little surprise that they seem to know what they are doing with their instruments. What makes this a joy to listen to are the songs and the way that they have been arranged. This is not complex prog for the devotee, but songs that have been influenced by the softer side of the genre such as Alan Parsons Project and Camel and then brought in a serious dose of AOR. While opener "The Reverse Side Of Mosquito's Battle" is a fairly up-tempo number, this is followed by "Losing You" which is far more piano-based to begin with before the guitar solo kicks in and the band start to move it up a peg or two. I also found that the more I listened to this the more I also became reminded of bands like The Byrds with their vocal harmonies. The result is an album that it is just impossible not to listen to with a smile on the face as it is so much fun. The more I played it the more I smiled, and the first time I played the first song I had a grin! This is a delight that does not tax the brain cells, and I only hope that they will be releasing another album soon! *#87, Apr 2006*

EMERSON, LAKE & PALMER
BLACK MOON

EMERSON, LAKE & PALMER
LIVE AT THE ROYAL ALBERT HALL

So, fourteen years after the disappointment that was 'Love Beach', six years after Emerson Lake & Powell, four years after 3, one of the most important and influential prog bands of all time got their act back together and released 'Black Moon'. It showed something of a return to form with the opening title track showing that during the intervening years they had lost nothing of their power. A top band has returned to form, and is proud to release an album that bears comparison with their heyday in the Seventies Of course, this meant a dramatic return to the concert halls and as would be expected a show recorded for posterity. Only a single CD, which means that it is not truly representative, but hey, it starts with "Karn Evil 9 (1st Impression, Part 2)" and any album that

starts with the immortal words "Welcome back my friends to the show that never ends" can only be good. From there it is straight into the "Tarkus" medley that illustrates more than anything else not only their musical skills but also how they have never been afraid to mix musical forms. Vocals, who needs them when it is as good as this?

Of course, Greg Lake has a melodic style perfectly suited to this music (far better than Robert Berry who was his replacement in 3, and far better than John Wetton who Greg replaced for a period in Asia). This is not just a trip down memory lane with various songs being taken from the new album, which stands up well against the classics. But for me, "Still... You Turn Me On" is a highlight, as is the finale that starts life as "Fanfare For The Common Man" then works through "America" before finishing with "Blue Rondo A La Turk". A stonking live album, although it must be said that it is not as good as the triple album 'Welcome Back My Friends To The Show That Never Ends, Ladies and Gentlemen, Emerson Lake & Palmer'. But what is?
#42, July 1997

EMERSON, LAKE & PALMER
LIVE IN POLAND
Recorded in Katowice on 22nd June 1997, this was ELP's first ever concert in Poland. I have been informed that this was a limited-edition release in that country, and as far as I am aware has not been released over here. That is a great pity as this stands up as a wonderful resume of their work to date. Starting off with "Welcome Back", taken from "Karn Evil 9", this leads rather surprisingly into "Touch & Go". Surprisingly? "Touch & Go" was not actually recorded by ELP, but rather on the only album by Emerson Lake & Powell. Greg Lake shows his prowess on acoustic guitar during "From The Beginning" while "Knife Edge" is as threatening as ever. Keith Emerson of course has his solo piano slot just to prove that he can show off at least as well as Wakeman any day. For the ELP lover this album is just a delight with also "Take A Pebble" and "Lucky Man" making welcome appearances, but it is to tracks nine and ten, both more than seventeen minutes in length, that most fans will turn to. The first of these is a segue of "Tarkus" and "Pictures At An Exhibition" and it is almost as if the last twenty-five years had never happened. Punk was supposed to kill off all the dinosaurs, but these are still going strong. The CD finished with "Fanfare For The Common Man" leading into "Rondo, and all too soon the seventy-minute album is at an end. Wonderful performances of a great set mean that this is an album that any ELP fan cannot do without.
#49, May 1998

KEITH EMERSON & THE NICE
VIVACITAS
Who would have thought that The Nice would be playing together again in the 21st Century? Certainly, not me, and although I came to The Nice through ELP, it was a band that I had been interested in for a long time. When I was given the opportunity of seeing them in concert I grabbed it with both hands, and had a great time. This triple CD set is taken from the concert that was recorded in 2002 in

Glasgow. The first CD is The Nice, with Dave Kilminster, and he certainly fits in well with the old blokes! Keith Emerson played the concert with his normal abandon, and I seem to remember that both Lee Jackson and Brian Davison played with huge grins on their faces. The Nice were one of the most important bands in the progressive rock vanguard, bringing more than a hint of classical music into proceedings which gave rock an air of respectability, while at the same time managing to upset everyone by setting fire to the Stars & Stripes during a performance of "America". No fire this time, but "America" (combined with "Rondo") is the opening number – proving as if it were needed that they do not need vocals to make an impact. Of course, there are 'proper' songs as well, and special mention should be made of "Cry Of Eugene" which all these years on is still a powerful song.

The second CD finds Keith alone, as he performs "A Blade Of Grass" and "A Cajun Alley" then a new line-up takes centre stage. Dave is back on guitar, but Pete Riley on drums and Phil Williams on bass now join them. To cheers from the crowd, Keith announces that they are going to play "Tarkus", all twenty-one minutes of it! It has been adapted from the ELP version so that it is an instrumental, with Dave playing Greg's vocal lines on the guitar. To hear this was one of the highlights of the concert for me, and on CD it comes across with great power. A raucous "Hoe Down" (which Aaron Copland could never have conceived of) completes this section of the concert. There is just time for the old boys to come back on and all six (yes, two drum kits) blast their way through "Fanfare". There is just enough time for "Honky Tonk Blues" and it is all over. Well, nearly. The third CD contains an interview with Keith, Brian and Lee talking about the glory days. One of the joys of this album is that it is possible to hear the bum notes, the fluffs, as this is a band on stage that are having a ball. There is no need to go back and adjust all the errors as that takes out the soul of the performance. If you had been there on that night this is what you would have heard, and what a fantastic time you would have had.
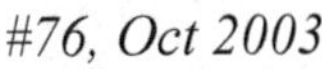
#76, Oct 2003

E MOTIVE

E MOTIVE

This is an intriguing album in many ways, and just from looking at the back of the CD there is the idea that possibly these guys do not take it all too seriously. The band comprises Jay Tausig (vocals, acoustic guitar, flute, didgeridoo, pomposity), Frank McGlynn (keyboards, backing vocals, and "more problems than that"), Erik Feder (drums, percussion, backing vocals, haggler), Pas (fretted, fretless six-string basses and occasionally proper intonation) and Antonio Mattera (guitar, bass tech, smiles). We are also informed that the length of the disc is 408,200 milliseconds and that "at no time were livestock or any other animals harmed during the making of this disc". So, with all the bull out of the way what is the music like? It is very good indeed, symphonic prog with a big sound while there are also elements of jazz. Jay has a very powerful voice and during songs such as "For Me" it is almost like listening to the sound deployed by Pink Floyd on "Comfortably Numb", but with more of a rock element and more in your face. Then to finish that number there is a quick burst of keyboard driven power that

would not have sounded out of place on an album by The Nice. There are small improvised pieces that give a break from the intensity of the album and considering this is a debut then this promises a bright future. At times, quite dark and foreboding ("Big Daddy In The Big House") and at others light and accessible I am sure that this is a band that we are going to hear more from.
#54, July 1999

EMPTY TREMOR
THE ALIEN INSIDE

This is Empty Tremor's third album, but the first for the Italian outfit for some five years. They have suffered from losing lead singers but with Oliver Hartmann now on board they have resolved that issue. The result is nothing short of a masterpiece, one of the finest albums I have yet heard on the Frontiers label. Frontiers are normally thought of as a melodic rock label, but in 'The Alien Inside' they have released an album with feet firmly planted in the prog world. It may be too much to call it prog metal, but this album is far rockier than most progheads would normally consider. Hey, but I take that as a plus! Twin guitarists as happy to riff as to play widdly-widdly and music that is complex, who could wish for more? On top of this complex and highly constructed music soars the powerful vocals of Oliver, this does seem to be a match made in heaven. There are times when they come across as IQ, and while they do not often go as full on as Threshold or Dream Theater it is obvious where their inspirations and aspirations lie. Opening with the longest song at nearly ten minutes, the title cut shows the way the band feel about their music. There is a long introduction which allows the listener to be gradually brought into the music as the climax builds, then the guitars and keyboards intertwine before letting the vocals add their voice to proceedings. This is music that will be appreciated by those into hard rock, prog metal and prog rock. Refreshing and joyous this will be one of the albums of the year from Italy. *#78, Apr 2004*

ALAN EMSLIE
DARK MATTER

Alan has an unusual background for a progressive rock musician in that he was for many years working in orchestras on timpani, percussion, ethnic percussion and drum kit. It was only in 2000 that he decided that he wanted to take his own music further and this is his fourth album since then. He is joined in this project by guitarist John Irvine, but Alan provides the other instrumentation and vocals. They are also a live act, with all the keyboards etc. being sequenced, and they obviously have a strong understanding as the album was recorded in just four days, but one wouldn't guess that from the quality of the music. The title cut gives away that this is going to be a heavier album, and opener "Misanthropic Myopic Man" is what Prodigy would sound like if it were not full of beats. It is aggressive, hard hitting, and overall great fun with wonderful hook in the chorus. The album is very different to the rest that is around now, and

the drums are quite high in the mix, but this is progressive music that has a real edge and in some ways, a simplicity that drags the listener in. At times, it is sparse; this has not been over-layered as it is meant to be reproduced onstage but in many ways, that is one of the joys and when John crunches in this becomes music with real balls. Overall this is interesting, if a little unsettling at times.
#87, Apr 2006

ENCHANT
A BLUEPRINT OF THE WORLD

I first heard about this CD when Graham Younger of Blindsight told me about it. Then Artur Chachlowski from Art Rock (in Poland) asked me about it, and finally Stu Nicholson (Galahad) was talking to me about it. When an album creates that much of a stir it should be something special and when I was sent a copy by Mark Ashton I could not wait to get it in the player. Enchant were formed in 1989 in San Francisco by Douglas A. Ott (guitar), Michael Geimer (keyboards) and Paul Craddick (drums): the line-up was completed with the addition of Ted Leonard on vocals and Edward Platt on bass towards the end of 1992. This album was originally recorded in their home city, but was completed in Liverpool under the watchful eyes and ears of Steve Rothery, who had long been a fan. It opens with "The Thirst", which is nice and gentle. Well, at least it is until the guitar break and then you get the distinct impression that there is a rock band here waiting to break out. The vocals give the song a Kansas, Rush feel, which is not a bad thing in my book. Lots of different moods and changes within a song that always rocks in AOR mode, yet is still proggy at the same time. There is some outstanding guitar on this song that is a harbinger of things to come. It was the case of "follow that!", but I needn't have worried as "Catharsis" provided a totally different feel, being far more of a ballad, yet at the same time there is a lot of guitarwork going on in the background that gives the song a very powerful edge. By the time that "Oasis" heralded its entry with some powerful fretwork and drumming I was a total Enchant fan. The song slowed down to allow Ted to provide yet more good vocals. Each of the nine songs (one of which, "Mae Dae", is an instrumental) is well crafted and guaranteed to satisfy the hunger of any American prog rock, AOR lover. The closing track, "Enchanted", has loads of different styles and is just wonderful. Now I know why this CD is being talked about by everybody: it's a stunner. *#22, Mar 1994*

ENCHANT
JUGGLING 9 OR DROPPING 10

Is it eight years since I first heard this band? Time flies, and during that period American act Enchant have released more albums and have found time to tour Europe. This new album is certainly going to gain them many more friends yet again they have put their own slant on progressive rock, and have brought out an album that is packed full of high melody tunes. They are much more into rock than many of their British counterparts, having more in common with bands like

Saga, Kansas or even Rush. Ted Leonard is a great vocalist and it helps in putting the band ahead of many of their rivals.

While none of the songs are inordinately long (all less than eight minutes), relief is provided by the last song on the album, "Know That". This lasts only one minute twenty-seven seconds, and features Ted singing a ballad accompanied by Doug Ott on acoustic guitar. It just shows the confidence of the band in being able to close an album like that. As I did with their debut 'A Blueprint Of The World' all those years ago I again heartily recommend Enchant to the discerning prog rocker.
#61, Feb 2001

ENCHANT
BLINK OF AN EYE
I can still remember how impressed I was when I heard the debut Enchant album, 'A Blueprint For The World' but that was many years ago now and as I had also been suitably impressed by their last album 'Juggling 9 Or Dropping 10' I was intrigued to see what their sixth studio album would bring. The band is built around the song-writing and guitar playing of Doug Ott and the wonderful vocals of Ted Leonard. Put them together with bassist Ed Platt and new drummer Sean Flanegan and the result is Spock's Beard meeting Kansas and an album that is superb.

It is very American, but as they are then that should be okay, and this is a highly-crafted rock album that has almost as many influences in the AOR field as it does in the prog scene. It is not prog metal in the same vein as Threshold, more a prog rock act with the emphasis on rock. There are plenty of hooks and melodies, along with strong soaring vocals that are very reminiscent of Steve Walsh (no bad thing) or Steve Perry. It is an album that all prog fans that enjoy melodic music to listen to and enjoy (as opposed to some of the cutting-edge stuff that is like having teeth pulled) should discover immediately if not sooner.
#69, Aug 2002

ENCHANT
TUG OF WAR
Enchant are back with their seventh album, and yet again show that when it comes to prog rock with the heavy use of guitar they are one of the best around. When I saw them support Spock's Beard at the Astoria I was extremely impressed, and having followed their career with interest since reviewing their debut album some eleven years ago I was pleased to be able to listen to the new album. This is prog rock that also has a foot firmly in the melodic rock camp, with guitarist Doug Ott providing the foundation for the band while Ted Leonard has much more in common with rock frontmen than most prog singers. The result is an album that is packed full

of melodies and hooks, yet also has room for time changes and dramatic shifts in musical direction. It opens with “Sinking Sand”, a song that contains just what every melodic rock fans wants in great harmonies, strong tunes and arrangements and enough space and drama for all. This standard is carried all the way through the album which closes with the longest number, “Comatose”. This starts off gently enough with just Ted and piano but ever so slowly and gradually the tension builds, and the rest of the band come in. The passion keeps building and there is the feeling of a full-on band just straining to be released. One of the joys of Enchant is that they are so easy to listen to and enjoy, even on first hearing. Yet another strong album to add to their canon.
#78, Apr 2004

ENCHANT
LIVE AT LAST
After seven studio albums, the Oakland band decided that it was time to finally release a live album, and what better place to record it than in their home town? Apparently, this is also available as a DVD, which I have yet to see, but the double CD alone is worth picking up. Enchant are very much a guitar-led progressive rock band, with Doug Ott very much in control, but the rest of the guys form the musical platform he needs while singer Ted Leonard shows why he is often compared with luminaries such as Steve Walsh with great control and range. While Enchant are not a prog metal band in the same sense as our own Threshold for example, they are much more rock based than many of their contemporaries. Prog-melodic rock anyone? I felt when I saw them in concert supporting Spock’s Beard that they were much heavier in concert and this comes through in this show. Listening to songs such as “At Death’s Door” there are huge chunks where the band are blasting out, while at others it is far more melodic and controlled. They can be riffing ahead or there might be interplay between the keyboards and guitar while one may then dominate the other, or a single slapped note on the bass can provide the emphasis. All in the same number! Twenty-three songs, all very different (including some acoustic interpretations) make this in some ways the perfect introduction to one of America’s most consistent progressive rock bands over the last decade.
#82, Jan 2005

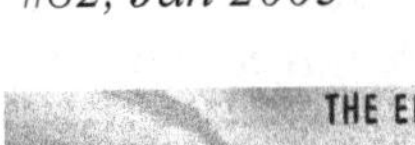

THE ENID
TRIPPING THE LIGHT FANTASTIC
After six years of silence, The Enid are back. Joining Robert John Godfrey (keyboards) is Nick May on guitars, with two drummers and a bassist on two tracks. I am not sure of the actual line-up, but it has changed since I saw them after they reformed when Nick was on bass and Neil Shepherd was on guitar. For some strange reason the cover is a version of the cover for ‘Something Wicked This Way Comes’, but the CD contained within is far more than a cheaper version of what has been before. It is great to have The Enid back as Robert John Godfrey is one of the

most under-rated keyboard players around. Straight from the off he creates sounds and moods that are instantly recognisable as The Enid, more than ably abetted by Nick who has slotted right in the groove (some great guitarwork on the opener "Ultraviolet Cat"). Again, it is mostly an instrumental album with soaring synths and guitars, as well as the harder edge when the moment is right. It is an album that will appeal to the hard school Enid lover yet at the same time I am sure that it will attract new followers who missed them the first time around. Personal favourite is probably the menacing "Dark Hydraulic", but to my ears there is not a bad song on the album. Mantilla have re-released all The Enid's previous albums on CD, so if you like this then there is no excuse not to go out and get the rest!
#26, Dec 1994

THE ENID
TEARS OF THE SUN

The Enid has been around for over twenty-five years, and this is an attempt to put all their best songs onto a single CD. The fact that it fails is due far less to any problems created by HTD but more to the fact that they have released so much great music. Compilations are always a problem in the sense that the only person who may be truly happy with the result is the compiler himself, and I and a good many other Enid fans would argue that to have a "Greatest Hits of The Enid" without "Fand" is nothing short of an outrage. But, if you are going to have a song lasting more than twenty minutes then it does restrict you as to what else you can do with the rest of the time. It has been put together with the assistance and blessing of Robert John Godfrey, and if you are looking for an introduction to The Enid then this is probably a good place to start. If you are already a fan, then note that there is a new song included.
#54, July 1999

ROGER ENO
FRAGILE

When I first put this album in the player I did not know quite what to expect, as it is Roger's first album for four years and is described as "a series of haunting and spacious computer-manipulated piano pieces". I certainly did not expect an album that would stay on my CD player for a week, refusing all attempts to be removed from it. This is one of the most minimalist albums I have ever heard, full of space and delicacy, but there is something hauntingly beautiful about it that defies all my attempts to try and convey this majesty just in words. It is an album to be listened to intently in a quiet room, as in this piece more than any other I have heard, the gaps between the notes are as important as the notes themselves and play a major role. It is just an incredible album and while many people will probably just dismiss this as some basic meanderings on a piano I would urge all of you who want to discover an awesome piece of work. When I play this I feel more calm and relaxed, as if the world has become a more tranquil place, and all that matters are the notes that form with modern classical. A wonderful album. *#86, Feb 2006*

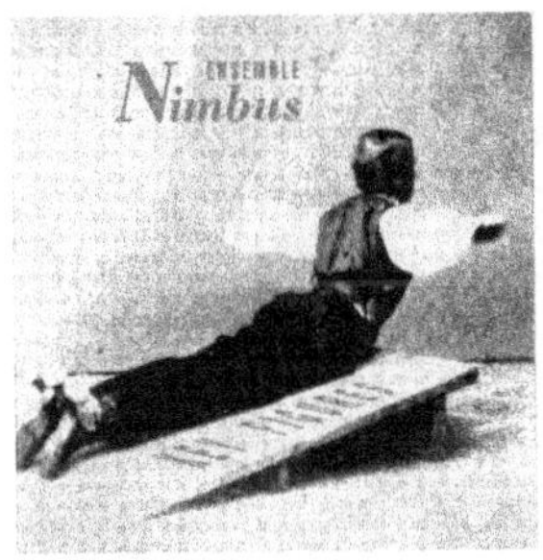

ENSEMBLE NIMBUS
KEY FIGURES

Ensemble Nimbus are a five-piece Swedish band signed to the new Swedish progressive label Ad Perpetuam Memoriam. One of the band members, Hass Bruniusson, used to be in Zamla Mammaz Mannan and apparently, they are similar. The label describes the music as "Art Rock", with influences such as Henry Cow, Albert Marcoueur, Univers Zero etc. To my ears it is a strange combination of avant-garde jazz and prog. Most of the songs are instrumentals and while there is no doubt that they are all very fine musicians, I am afraid that most of this CD just washed right over me and if I hadn't been reviewing it I probably wouldn't have finished played it. As I far as I am aware, this is only available on mail order from Sweden. *#23, May 1994*

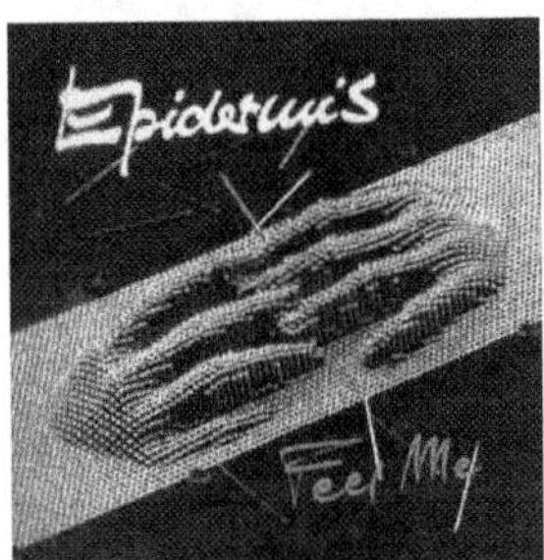

EPIDERMIS
FEEL ME

This is an unusual looking CD in the sense that it comes in a 7" 20-page book. However, the information contained within is not much more than would be expected in a good booklet. Still, it gives a different impression to many. Epidermis appears to be a four-piece based around Rolf Lonz who writes the material, although many other musicians act as guests. This is light-hearted prog with very much a jazz feel to the proceedings. The use of many extra instruments (particularly woodwind and percussion) means that Epidermis develop a sound quite unlike many of those in the prog field, and some may say that it is too out of centre to be called prog as it is currently defined (please do not ask me for a definition) and art rock or jazz could be seen as being a bit closer to home. The twenty-two-minute long "A Speck A Dream" shows these tendencies off best. The lyrics are in German and overall I think that it will have a very limited appeal within the UK market.
#32, Dec 1995

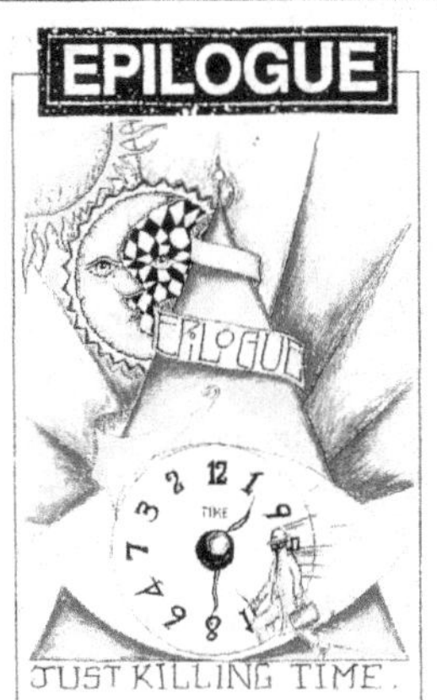

EPILOGUE
JUST KILLING TIME

Epilogue were formed in the summer of 1990 by Gareth Evans (guitar), Chris Frost (keyboards) and Scott Evans (bass) as something to do while still studying at Stoke on Trent Sixth Form College. After a few months Shaun Lowe asked them if they would like to use his home studio after hearing a rehearsal tape. They then spent the next two years writing and rehearsing, but still did not play a gig. The search for a drummer and singer ended in September 1992 when Shaun offered his services. He had by now set up Prism Studios and worked with both Grace and Framework. Within six days of Shaun joining they played their first gig, supporting Framework in Nottingham. They decided to record this eight-track demo at Prism, and kept on gigging in the area, gradually building a following. They played their first large gig in rather bizarre circumstances on December 22nd when all the members went to see Grace, duly paying their entrance fee. However, the support act that night was supposed to be Citizen Cain, who blew the gig at extremely short notice. Seeing Epilogue in the audience, Grace promptly asked them to perform, which they did, although they had to use Grace's instruments to do so (which included Dave's five-string bass, a strange instrument for the unwary). The demo was released on February 27th when they again supported Grace at The Wheatsheaf. It took me a couple of listens to decide that I like the tape. Shaun is a fine vocalist and overall the tape displays a maturity far beyond the band member's tender years. They have the confidence and ability to perform varying styles of songs, from ballads to rockier numbers and are not afraid to let the keyboards take the sole musical role at times.

Sometimes young bands are afraid to stop playing, but good music relies as much as on what is missing as one what is played. My favourite is "Matthew", which has a wonderfully commercial rock hook in the chorus, a great song. Chris Frost is involved with the 'A Flower?' fanzine and did a seriously heavy hatchet job on Casual Affair's 'Well, What Did You Expect?'. It would have been very easy for me to get revenge by burying 'Killing Time', but the quality of the music just does not allow me to that. If you want to hear a prog band at the beginning of their career that could well have a great future ahead of them then you need this. Mark Price of Grace tells me that Epilogue are making big waves in the Midlands: it will not be long before that spreads further afield.
#18, May 1993

EPILOGUE
HIDE

I remember hearing Epilogue's demo tape 'Just Killing Time' quite a while ago now. It took me quite a long time to get into it and the same is probably true of the debut CD. Three of the tracks on that tape reappear here, along with seven others. Epilogue seem to inhabit a region of prog that is overtly "poppy" and commercial, which also appears to have the strange effect of nullifying the guitars.

That is not to say that the CD does not have its high points, just that for a lot of the time it comes over as rather bland. When they do get going a bit more, as on "Living A Lie" then they manage to convey an impression of just what they are capable of. "Matthew" is also good, being a radio friendly song that in a proper world could be a hit single. I like Shaun's voice, and he is a good producer to boot (working with Framework and Grace as well), but maybe someone from outside the band should be brought in next time to give them a kick up the backside and stop them from sanitising everything. Not a bad album, maybe it hasn't grown on me enough yet to say that it is superb. There again, maybe it never will.
#26, Dec 1994

RÓBERTO ERDÉSZ
MEETING POINT

This album has been released on Solaris, which appears to be part of the StereoPeriferic label, and this album is subtitled 'Hungarian World Music', which is exactly what it is. While the music is mostly piano or keyboard driven, there are lots of different elements and style. Vocals are used as an instrument, so there are no lyrics. There is interplay between different instruments, but what gives this album its' joy is that there is a freedom of expression, and lots of different ideas coming through. The music may have a folky poppy feel, but then turn into Gregorian chant. It is not rock music, but is still music from the soul, that can lift the spirit. It is not an album that I will be returning to a great deal but there are going to be times when this will be just the perfect thing to play on a warm Summer's evening. Sixteen musicians combined to make this CD, and they work together extremely well.

#63, Jul 2001

ER MALAK
DEMO

Artur recently sent me four tracks by Bulgarian band Er Malak. I know relatively little about them, except that they are a four-piece who have released two Bulgarian language cassettes in their own country and are now looking to expand into Western Europe, and have realised that to do this they need to be recording in English. These four songs are a taster of their music in the hope that someone will be able to provide them with the finances to be able to record more English language versions of their own material.

Hopefully this will indeed be the case as I loved the songs on this tape. The vocals are far harsher than is normal with this type of music, and at the same time the guitars are far heavier and sustained in attack. Er Malak are a band that are mixing prog with HR and therefore should appeal to a wider audience than most. If they can find someone to provide them with the necessary money to be able to record an English language CD, then I can see them doing extremely well.

#29, Jun 1995

MICHAEL ERNST
EXCALIBUR

Although this album has been credited to Michael Ernst, the sleeve does state that it is with two other people, namely Alan Parsons and Chris Thompson. That is enough to get many people more interested in this album than they would have been otherwise, is this an Alan Parsons project album by another name? Well yes, and no. Michael has wanted to create a rock epic based on the story of Excalibur, and he has involved

Chris Thompson who has co-written virtually every song on the album and certainly the impression for the first half of the album is that this is one that could belong in that famous canon. The music is the right level of rock and orchestration, with vocals taking a primary role and in Chris they have one of the most recognisable voices around. The problem is the experimentation that happens with the last songs on the album: this does not work and distracts from what has been an enjoyable listen up until then – the pop and fashion does not sit well with the rest of the album. But this is an album that will certainly be of interest to fans of Alan Parsons, even though it is not as good as the real thing.
#78, Apr 2004

ESKATON
4 VISIONS
Eskaton were a French band that recorded this, their debut album, in 1979, but for some reason it was only made available on cassette, and then only in America, so their first general release was the follow-up 'Ardeur' in 1980. Swedish label Ad Perpetuam Memoriam has now made it fully available for the first time. The music being produced here is quite unusual. Firstly, it was an eight-person line-up, with two singers in Paule Kleynnaert and Amara Tahir, and the vocals were sung in a classical style, pure and clear, giving it a very different feel to most other bands. Beneath the soaring vocals there is a lot going on with three different keyboard players, as well as bass, guitar and drums. However, strangely enough this is not a keyboard led band but rather a group bringing together many different influences including noticeably Magma and Zeuhl. The most important single instrument is probably the bass which pins the overall sound, and is an album that takes a lot of work to get the most out of it but is ultimately rewarding. APM plan to bring out Eskaton's other recordings later this year and I look forward to that with interest. *#33, Feb 1996*

EVENFALL
CUMBERSOME
It is a while since I have heard an album like this one that mixes together so many threads of extreme and death metal, and combine it with progressive rock in such a distinctive manner. Since they released 'Still In The Grey Dying' in 1999 the band has been in a state of flux and it is only recently that guitarist Ivan D'Alia has managed to get the line-up right. New vocalist Roberta Staccuneddu is quite a find and her vocals singing clear and angelically above the chaos is a major factor in this album being as good as it is. But, she is not the only singer, and Ansgar provides the brash, dark and harsh element with traditional coarse growling. Added to the mix is the complex music that can be gentle and sweet with piano one second or crashing bombastic heavy metal the next. Sometimes Ansgar does his best sore throat singing while the music is gentle, while Roberta sweetly sings as the speakers self-destruct, yet often switch roles. There are times when sequencers set the style, and the riffs are timed to coincide with

the electronic beat, and the result is an album that at times sounds surprisingly mainstream while being for the most part quite experimental. This is an album that is truly progressive in many ways, although many progheads will probably find this music too heavy and extreme. But given this album and yet another Genesis or IQ imitator I know which I will go for.
#67, Apr 2002

EVENT
SCRATCHING AT THE SURFACE
This is the third album from Boston-based outfit Event, and in many ways, is quite a hard thing to try and describe. They obviously come from a prog background but are mixing and moulding it with loads of other styles and tricks, some of which are down to the production and the way that they treat the vocals. Looking at the bands they have played with does not give that much of a clue as while some of them are label-mates, they are quite diverse (Porcupine Tree, Tony Levin, Planet X, Spock's Beard, Dokken etc.). The band that for some reason I kept thinking of was Faith No More but these guys sound nothing like that; it is just the attitude and the way of throwing it all in the pot. All the guys are great musicians, of course, but Dave Deluco is a star. The label compares his style with Gary Cherrone, but to me his register is slightly lower although there is no doubting that the guy can sing, and the band play to that strength. The music is designed to keep the vocals at the forefront, no matter what chaos or weird stuff is going on in the background. In many ways this is one of the more commercial of Inside Out's releases yet at the same time it is also totally out of left field so it does take quite a lot of listening to. The rewards are great as it is an album of great depth, but unless you put in the time you will not get the benefit. Strange, but good. *#73, Apr 2003*

EVERGREY
IN SEARCH OF TRUTH
This is the third album by the Swedish prog metallers, and is probably their best to date. Sounding very American on this concept album, the music fairly drives on. The guitars crunch through some extremely quick harmony leads, and if they turned them up a little more and dropped the keyboards this would be a hard rock band of some force. However, the keyboards add some extra touches of class to proceedings, which allow the guitars to play not only against each other but also against another melody line. The initial reaction was that they are similar in many ways to our own Threshold, but they are probably more diverse, with more light and at some times much more dark. More prog metal than a band like Stratovarius they would undoubtedly appeal to fans of them as well. If you are interested in well-crafted melodic rock with more than a hint of prog then give this a try.
#64, Oct 2001

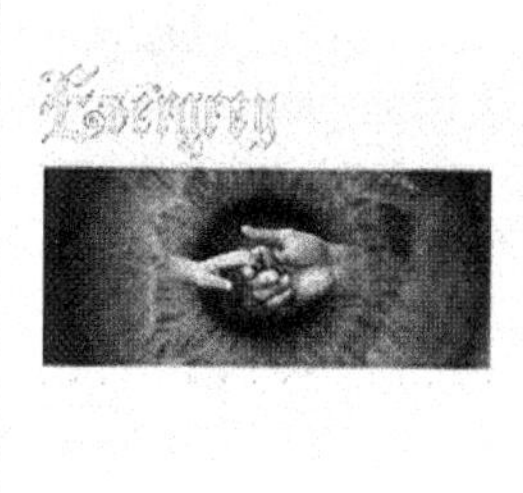

EVERGREY
THE INNER CIRCLE
Evergrey are one of those bands who do their level best to defy comparisons with others. They are more to the metal end of the prog metal genre than their contemporaries, and the result is a type of music that is extremely loud and heavy while maintaining the melody and invention of the genre. When they decide that they are going to crank it up and belt it out there are few bands that stay the pace – listen to sections of some of their songs and without the keyboards it could almost be Machine Head.

This is a concept album, and to get across the themes, singer Tom S. Englund uses different vocal styles, differentiating the characters. It is an extremely intense album, one that has to be played loud and proud: this is not a subject matter or music that can be pushed into the background. The concept is about religion and what fanatics can do with it and the t-shirts for the tour are apparently going to say "I am my own God, God walking". There is something here for every rock fan, whatever your particular genre, as long as you like your music heavy.

There is room for contrasts, light and shade, but the power of the album is always there in your face. This has to be one of the best albums from Sweden, ever.
#79, May 2004

EVERGREY
A NIGHT TO REMEMBER
Recorded in their hometown of Gothenburg last year, this double CD shows why Evergrey are regarded as one of the top European prog metal/melodic rock bands around. The band is kicking, and the crowd are just lapping it up. Production is extremely strong, much better than a normal 'live' album, but I do think the drums are a little too high in the mix.

Whether you want the band to be riffing, or playing complicated music or ballads, it is all on here within the twenty songs. There is an apology for speaking English between the songs (all lyrics are in English of course) but when this explained that it is because it is being recorded the crowd go mental. There is a good use of female vocals to provide extra depth but it may be surprising to some at just how heavy these guys can be – but from my experience those in the prog metal field do seem to put the latter before the former when playing in concert. It is incredibly intense and at times there is a wall of sound coming out of the speakers, with the keyboards just managing to change the level of attack. This is not something that could ever be played in the background, as it is needs to be played extremely loudly to get the best out of it. There is also going to be a DVD available of this concert in the summer but until then this album will more than suffice.
#83, Mar 2005

EVERON
PARADOXES

Everon are a German band I hadn't heard of until this CD came through my letterbox. I was impressed even before I put it on as the band bio is in full colour (extremely unusual), and the artwork for the album is beautiful. The line-up is Oliver Philipps (vocals, keyboards and lead guitar), Christian Moos (drums), Ralf Jansen (guitar) and Schymy (bass). The album was produced by E Roc, who used to be in Grobschnitt and has built a reputation as one of Germany's top rock producers. First song is "Face The World", and I was immediately drawn into the wonderful world of Everon. The music is extremely melodic and in a similar vein to a heavy Saga or Rush. I do not see how on earth they can produce this live because harmony vocals play a large part, as do the keyboards: maybe they use keyboard pedals a la Geddy Lee. Each song contains majesty and beauty, and also quite a high level of commerciality. I do not know how big their following is in Germany, but I can imagine Everon going down a storm in America. They have been together for five years, and it shows in the depth and quality of their material: there is a very high level of professionalism, and if this band can get the break they so richly deserve they could be very big indeed. If you like your rock commercial with great songs and musicianship in the style of Saga or Rush, then this is the band for you.

#18, May 1993

EVERON
FLOOD

If there is one thing I really hate doing, it is reviewing the same album twice. Unfortunately, I have just managed to wipe my review of this CD out of the memory, so it looks like I have no choice. Still, any excuse to put this on again when I should be listening to something else is a bonus. When German pomp/prog belters Everon released their debut 'Paradoxes' a few years ago, I went into heaven. It was just superb, and still finds its way onto the player now so you can imagine how much I was looking forward to the new one, and I am glad to be able to report that I was not disappointed. Actually, 'Flood' is even better than the debut, something I would not have thought possible. Vocalist, keyboard player, guitarist, songwriter Oliver Philipps is still very much in control, but the rest of the guys are no just bit-part players. Everon is a band, not a one-man ego trip. They have developed their sound into a very heavy sophisticated version of Saga, with wonderful songs to boot. Right from the opener "Under Skies of Blue", which starts with gentle piano and synth then develops into an over the top rocker with soaring guitars, keyboards and vocals with dynamic powerful drumming, you know that you are going to be privileged to hear something very special indeed. This is an album to capture the imagination with its power and strengths. Producer E Roc has yet again done an amazing job, capturing the delicacy and bombast that makes this such a joy to listen to. All in all, Everon have produced as masterpiece which wouldn't be out of place in any rock lover's collection, whether they like prog or not.

#28, Apr 1995

EVOLUTION
FUTURE

EVOLUTION
PART OF THE MACHINE

EVOLUTION
NATURE'S REVENGE

My brain does not believe what my ears are telling it. Namely that here is another prog band that are not only musically superb and prolific (three demoes in front of me), but are also unsigned. Now, it is easy for my brain to understand all of that, the more difficult part is realising that Evolution is actually the pseudonym of Ken Senior who provided not only the songs and engineering etc., but vocals, guitar, keyboards and drum programming. I mean, what the hell? On top of that, not only does he produce an excellent product, but lots of it! Ken has been around as a musician for some years, but his first break was getting the song "Shock Of The New" played on Radio 1 in 1987. After that he wanted to produce a full-length demo, but 'Future' did not see the light of day until 1992. The songs are heavily influenced by issues such as technology and the way that it effects people. Another theme that runs through Ken's songs is the way that people use and abuse others. The second demo, 'Part Of The Machine' includes the concept of children being manipulated by huge companies to become part of the computer console where, soon, all their senses will be cut off from the outside world and reality will become something different to them. The third demo, 'Nature's Revenge', should now be out, but here I have a rough mix of Side One. The title track concerns itself with the fact that no matter how much the human race tries to wreck our world, in the long term nature will put it right. Nature may or may not have humanity in its' own long-term plans. So, as you can see, Ken's lyrics have a little more to them than just boy meets girl. In musical terms prog is very much the order of the day, with lots of keyboards, intricate guitar solos, and a real love of what is being achieved. Ken has woven loads of different influences together, and it is possible to recognise Genesis (some of the guitar work is reminiscent of Hackett), or Twelfth Night and Galahad (although the songs are more involved). There is a lot of work going on here, and it certainly does not sound like a one-man outfit. The music is definitely Seventies based as opposed to Nineties, but there's nothing wrong with that. True, the recordings could be a bit better (due to financial constraints they were completed on a four-track), but the songs really shine through. Ken is in the throes of putting together a band so that they can go out and do some gigs, and he has been joined by Robert Hirons (drums) and Mike Stringer (bass) but is still on the outlook for a keyboard player. If you find today's music transient and shallow, then you will not be disappointed with the music of Evolution. There is real depth, feeling, and wonderful guitar lines. Ken is hoping to get more music out on CD in the future, but at the moment the demoes are available only

from him. All of the fanzines seem to be saying that this guy is brilliant, and who am I to disagree?
#19, Aug 1993

EVOLUTION
ACTIVITY
Evolution are still a one-man band when it comes to getting into the studio, and here again Ken Senior proves that it is possible to produce high quality music with only basic equipment. He plays keyboards, guitar, bass, drums programming and of course provides vocals to boot. It never ceases to amaze that one man can have so much obvious talent, yet does not have a record contract to show for it. There is some stunning guitarwork on here, particularly on "The Nightwatch", and although the keyboards can be a touch over-intrusive at times (along with the computerised drumming), all in all Ken has yet again produced the goods. If you want some high quality prog that takes its influences from many sources, most notably Seventies Genesis, then get in touch.

#25, Oct 1994

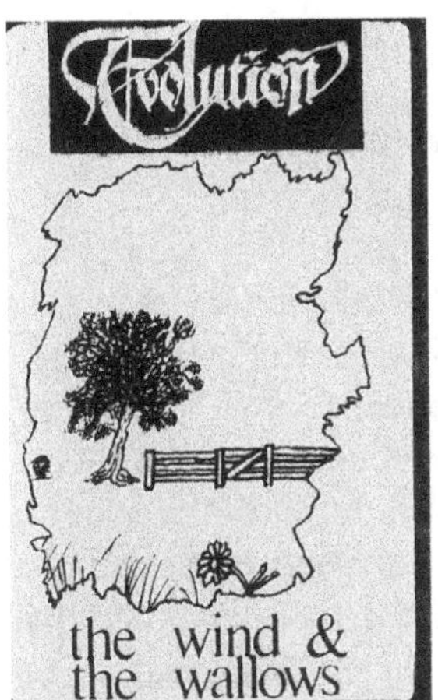

EVOLUTION
THE WIND AND THE WALLOWS
Evolution is still a one-man outfit, namely Ken Senior who provides vocals, guitar, bass, keyboards and drum machine. This is his fifth demo tape and yet again Ken shows that not only is he a great musician, he can write some damn good tunes. "Dominator" is an instrumental where he mixes sounds such as Genesis and Jadis together so well that you can't hear the join. 'The Wind and the Wallows' is another success for Ken, and surely it can only be a matter of time before he gets signed up for a CD release. He is still looking for a keyboard player to enable him to make Evolution a gigging outfit, so if you know someone please get in touch.
#28, Apr 1995

EVOLUTION
THE FIRST SIGNS OF LIFE
Ken Senior, a wonderfully jolly and enthusing Yorkshireman, has been promoting the cause of the multi-instrumentalist for some time now and at long last he has been able to get himself a deal after issuing numerous cassettes, and here he is with his first CD. He has enlisted the services of Steven McCabe, whose album Ken provided vocals for, as co-engineer and co-producer but yet again "other

musicians are mysteriously non-apparent on this album!" Unlike most multi-instrumentalists, Ken also has vocal abilities, but of the eleven songs, five are still instrumental. In some ways this is a shame, not because they are not interesting and enjoyable, but rather because he has so much to say in his lyrics. My favourite is probably "Mousetrap" which compares the way that an employee can get on in business to a mouse in a cage, similar in some ways to Tull's "One Brown Mouse". Ken is at home on keyboards as he is on guitar, and the only area which could be improved upon is the use of live drums, but that is down to my ever-growing hatred of drum machines in general. Overall this is an enjoyable album, fairly mellow and relaxed in places, which well may find favour among those interested in the softer side of prog.
#39, Jan 1997

EXHIBIT A
A DIFFERENT DIMENSION

Exhibit A were formed in 1984 when the remnants of Essex proggers Mithra (Steve Watts, bass, Nick Hampson, guitar and Barrie Cannon, drums and chief writer) joined with the infamous Foss brothers Dave (vocals) and Neil (keyboards). The line-up was slow in producing original material and because of this gigs were few and far between. It was fairly obvious that something had to change, and the result was that Barrie left and was quickly replaced by Tony Robertson. Tony had previously played in soul bands, and the songwriting moved from 'epics' to something of a more commercial nature in the It Bites, Genesis, Rush mode. Demo tapes got some airplay on BBC Radio Essex, and gigs around Essex followed, but they have only managed a few gigs outside of their home county, supporting Jadis and Landmarq. Their first album, 'A Different Dimension', is a good representation of their work between 1989 and 1991, and is a very professional looking package (full colour inlay etc.) and I was impressed even before I played it. At Neil's own admission, the album is commercial, being a mix of melodic rockers and prog. It Bites are very much in evidence, but so are Big Big Train (although Exhibit A are more commercial). There are some real winners on here, such as "No Compromise" which has a guest female co-vocalist (stand up and take a bow, Jane Winberg) or "Never The Same". For a debut tape by an 'unknown' band I was quietly pleased and surprised. The album does not take much work to listen to, and is totally enjoyable. The band are all good musicians, work well together, and Dave has a great voice then on top of that they have some great tunes. Exhibit A are due to be mixing and mastering the new album (which will be available on both CD and tape) during October for a November release. Neil has sent me a rough mix of the final song, "Learning The Hard Way" and it shows the band moving away from the overtly commercial material of the debut with a higher emphasis on keyboards. If this is truly indicative of the rest of the songs, then they could be onto a real winner here. Exhibit A are a band we could be hearing a lot more of.
#20, Oct 1993

EXHIBIT A
OUT THERE

Following on from my review of Exhibit A in #20, I am glad to be able to say that at long last the CD is out. Working on from the tape album and demos, there is still in evidence a very heavy It Bites and Big Big Train influence, but I was surprised to find that opener "Within These Walls" is actually very close to the sound produced by Angel (bearing in mind that no-one sounds quite like Frank Dimino). The opener is probably the strongest song of the set, with good melody and hooks, combined with good clear and strong vocals. "On The Edge" takes us firmly into It Bites territory, the guitar taking a back seat on this song as it relies on the bass to drive it along and the keyboards providing extra melody to bounce off. "Against The Flow" starts off as a rocker but it is a song of many sides. The more I play the album, the more my thoughts have turned towards Mr So & So, a band that I know many of you have time for after the free flexi last year: they are similar in many ways. The only negative part about the whole album is the track "Scared To live", a song that is virtually a duet with guest vocalist Lisa Moss taking the part of the girl who is literally scared to live. Unfortunately, her voice is not strong enough and my teeth grate whenever I hear it which is quite sad, as it really detracts from the overall effect of the CD. Some of the songs, like "Pseudo City", really belt along and even though "Scared To Live" does detract, I still have no hesitation in recommending this to you.

#23, May 1994

EXISTENCE
SMALL PEOPLE, SHORT STORY, LITTLE CRIME

It has taken a long time for any band to come up with packaging to rival Tull's 'Thick As A Brick', but Canadian band Existence have managed it with this their second album. Inside the slip sleeve is a booklet that is fifty-eight pages long (although it has to be said that some of this bulk is due to much being printed in both English and French). What we have is a magazine, with features and even record reviews. However, unlike the Tull review in the paper that accompanied the album the Existence review was a genuine one, one that was so bad that bandleader Alan Charles had to include it somewhere. It takes a lot of guts to put together a package like this as it means that the music has to work hard to keep up with it. So the only way to start is with a multi-tracked drum solo. Hell, they are going to be killed by critics before they play a note anyway so why not the whole ten yards? The music that follows is classic English rock, and although they have added a violin, "Beauty Teen" could easily feature on a Jump album. The lyrics appear in the booklet, inside the magazine articles, printed in bold type so that it is easy for the listener to follow. What I found when I played it first time is that sometimes I was losing the lyric as I was so involved in reading the story behind it. They are planning to perform this as a rock drama, with all the characters that feature in the album. That will be some work. While bringing many styles to the fore, this is very much a progressive album that is modern yet classic, which steadfastly refuses to sound

like much of the current prog scene. This is a total entertainment experience, as the listener feels compelled to read the booklet when playing the CD. It is comforting yet at times very menacing (particularly the effective violin during "No Hero"). The band proudly announces that they completed this with no subsidy, and work like this should not go unrewarded.
#65, Dec 2001

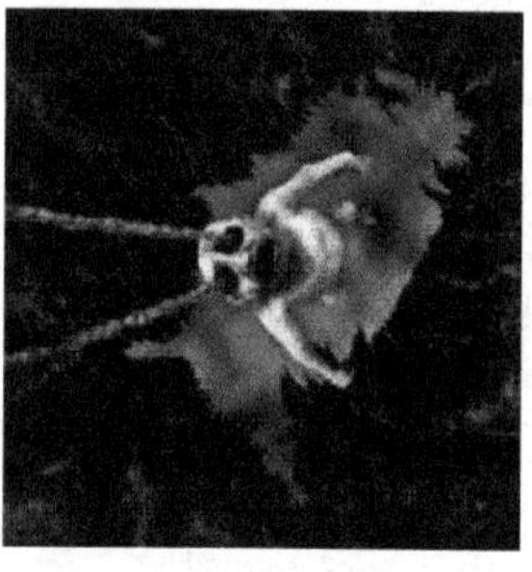

EYESTRINGS
CONSUMPTION
If I hadn't known who was involved with this album I think that I would have pointed to Discipline as an influence anyway, but given that bassist Matthew Kennedy used to be in that band and that frontman and keyboard player Ryan Parmenter is a nephew of Matthew Parmenter who was their frontman then probably this is not surprising. That is not to say that Eyestrings sound like Discpline, far from it, but there is the same fractured frenetic approach to the music that is both complex and exhilarating. You are in for a musical ride guys, and you had better keep a firm grip with both hands. This is prog music that really is, breaking through the accepted boundaries that many bands keep to and instead creates something that looks at the past for some ideas but is very much a sound both for now and for the future. This is not easy listening later period Genesis, or pleasant Floyd, but something that can lull you in with harmonies and gentleness then break your ears on something that is far more dark and dramatic. The lyrics are powerful, with "Valid For A Week" managing to conjure up similar images to "We Are Sane" with the idea that the state is all powerful and that everyone is to believe what they read and what they are told. The final few lines are particularly poignant, "Lights Out, Minds Out, You Will Not Find Out". I found that I enjoyed this album immensely the first time I played it but the more I listened to it the more I got from it and it is wonderful to just sit with this and the booklet looking at the images, reading the words, and letting the music take it's place in your mind. This is grown up prog that I very highly recommend.
#86, Feb 2006

EZRA
NEW HORIZONS
When I was at Whitchurch at Chritsmas I was given a flyer for Ezra and was intrigued. Here was a glossy four page package on a band that I had never heard. On looking at the contact address I quickly surmised why: if there is anything worse than being a prog band, it has to be being a prog band in Wales. Anyway, I had a long chat with their manager and was duly sent a tape. To say that I was surprised was something of an understatement as here was a tape that had been out since 1991, which was of the highest quality, yet I had heard nothing about them. Ezra were formed in 1990 and comprise Andy Edwards (guitar, vocals), Jaz Joseph (drums), Steve Hughes

(bass, vocals) and Dave Warner (keyboards). The tape is intended solely as a demo, so it is not being made widely available, which is a shame as I really liked it. True, it needs working on and cleaning up a little bit, but it is the production that lets this down and the format, rather than the songwriting and musical ability of the band. "First Light" opens proceedings, and the gentle birdsong soon gives way to sweeping majestic keyboards which lead into a driving prog force reminiscent of It Bites and some of the pompier bands. Good musicianship always shines out, but the vocals let it down slightly. "Hourglass" has plenty of time changes, yet at the same time remains commercial and likeable. Lastly we have "Raingods", which starts off with a healthy storm, but some stunning guitar soon takes you into prog heaven. Definitely a song of many parts, I cannot see how anyone into good melodic rock could fail to love this as the guitar takes the lead. Ezra should have a CD coming out in May, and are supporting Hawkwind in Porthcawl. There is even talk of a tour in Florida where they have apparently got themselves quite a following. I look forward to the CD with great interest, and hope that at some point I will be able to see them live. Until then, remember that if you see the name Ezra, then here is a band that means business. *#17, Mar 1993*

① JUST A GAME
② SMILED AT ME
③ FIRST LIGHT
④ SHE CRIES
⑤ TEA AT CYRILS
⑥ HOURGLASS
⑦ RAINGODS

RECORDED AT: ①②③ COACH HOUSE - BRISTOL '93
④⑤ FLAT RECORDS - REIGATE '91
⑥⑦ HTV - CARDIFF - '91

EZRA
A THOUSAND DAYS

After my review of Ezra's 'New Horizons' demo, here is the most recent. It includes two of the three songs from that, plus a re-recording of "First Light" with new keyboard player Rob Reed. Of the other four, there are two more newbies plus two that were actually recorded back in 1991 but the band have only just had the masters back. Ezra have now split with their management and are looking after themselves. The tape starts with the three new songs and it is "Just A Game" which kicks it all off, and a great starter it is too. There is bags of energy and this song is just so accessible and commercial. Andy has a distinctive voice that has really grown on me, and he's not half bad a guitarist too! Having seen Ezra in concert I know that the songs transform into out and out belters, but they are still really enjoyable in this form. Next up is "Smiled At Me" which is led by the bass. Ezra's great strength is that the songs are just bloody good, in the It Bites vein. The newer material is the strongest (I mean, fancy having a song entitled "Tea At Cyril's" and salivating at the thought of jacket potatoes!), but it is nice that the older material is also being made available.
#19, Aug 1993

EZRA
SHAPES

Sometimes I hear a demo or two from a band and I am suitably impressed, I then get to see them live and I am even more impressed. Then I hear that they have a record deal and I sit back and wait for what I know will be a killer CD. More times than not I end up being bitterly disappointed, but not here, not with Ezra! The Welsh trio have come up with a wonderful debut, aided and abetted by Robert

Reed who has guested on keyboards and helped with production (Robert may be better known to you as Cyan, whose two albums I dearly love). Right from the opening "Just A Game" you cannot fail to fall in love with the songs and the enthusiasm for the music that comes out of the speakers. These guys actually sound as if they are enjoying what they are doing, and isn't that what music is supposed to be all about? The songs and musicianship are just so strong that it is strange to think that this is just a debut and not one of many, as Ezra sound as if they have been doing this for a long time, so confident they appear. The only comment I must finish with is that "Tea At Cyril's" is on the album, and those who remember the review I wrote about their last demo may know what I am going to say next. Only a Welshman could get excited about jacket potatoes! A goody, get it. *#27, Feb 1995*

EZRA
BIG SMILEY SUN

It has been a long time since I heard from the Welsh guys, and had all but given them up for lost until I received this from Malcolm. The last I had heard of from Andy Edwards (vocals, guitars, keyboards) was when he appeared on the Fyreworks project. I see that Andy is providing keyboards on this whereas they had previously been utilising the talents of Robert Reed (aka Cyan), so I am not sure what they are doing about playing this live. I am glad that I make the point of playing CDs carefully as the first few times I played this it definitely washed right over me, but it was on the third or fourth listen that it started to click into place. Andy's vocals are fairly limited, but he is a fine guitarist and for the most part it is in the instrumental sections that the band really shine, although there are obvious exceptions to this. A case in point is "Waiting For The Day" which is a fine indie style rock number. This is definitely not an album that sees Ezra stick to what is expected of a 'prog' band, they seem instead to be taking on board lots of different styles and making them work, basically asking the listeners to accept them as a band and not be fitted into any particular category. The one number that typified this approach and is the winner for me on the album is "Blinding Line" which starts off acoustically but turns into a soft rock number with good vocals and melody. This is a lovely slow summer number that could do chart damage if picked up correctly. I am glad that I persevered with this one, as it does need time and patience. By the way, I know many bands will do anything to get a deal, but putting a picture of the label boss in the sleeve? (I saw you Malc..) *#53, May 1999*

EZRA
SONGS FROM PENNSYLVANIA

I can remember the first time I met Ezra, it was in Whitchurch village hall at one of the prog events being held there. Rob Reed was with them at the time, and back then I used to think of him as being the man behind Cyan whereas now he is in Magenta! Well, it was a long time ago because I can recall Andy Edwards having hair but looking at the photos in the booklet it is now all gone!! I am sure that I saw them gig at that time, and I can certainly remember reviewing their albums, but at long last they have now released their third CD and like Credo have moved from Cyclops to F2 Music. Like them, it has been a long wait for the next album, and again like their labelmates it has been more than worth it.

What we have here are seven songs, which are bringing together different styles of prog and rock and creating something that is very accessible and pleasing to the ear. Halfway through the first song "A Little Bit More" I found that I was singing the chorus – this should not be allowed, progressive music is not about having fun and joining in. It is all about sitting studiously and waiting to be impressed.

Haven't these guys seen the audience on 'Pictures At An Exhibition'? Obviously not. Mind you, they are Welsh aren't they, which could well explain a great deal. It might explain why a band can take influences from lots of diverse sources and blend them so that while they can be a little Floydian here, it may a touch IQ there, but the most important part at all times is that this is Ezra who are creating great little songs that are there to be enjoyed. Neo-prog? Well, yes, I suppose, but instead let's change that label to classic style rock and that may get a few more punters through the door. Nice one guys, but why leave it so long? One to investigate.
#88, Jun 2006

FAITH
LIVE BACKSTAGE

Carbon7 are a Belgian label (distributed in the UK by Proper Music), that has a wide range of musical artists, but this is the first one that has interested me enough to request the CD. With no bio, and very little idea of what to expect, I was not sure if I would be pleased or not with the band. I am very glad to say that it is definitely very much the former and not the latter.

Having played the album a lot the closest I can come to describing the music is Eighties Genesis (the longer non-pop songs) crossed with later Pink Floyd and Jadis. This is a real find as far as I am concerned, as I have not seen any reviews of it anywhere, which is nothing short of criminal. Bandleader Andy Kirk says in the booklet, "This is the outcome of a group of people's hard work, gut energy and pure commitment into achieving what they firmly believe in against many odds". This live album captures a band that certainly enjoys the live environment, and there is very positive crowd reaction.

I do not know when the album was recorded but even though it may be more difficult to find in this country, it is still more than worth the effort for all prog heads. Just one thing I do not understand is that I thought that this was a new release but it is copyright 1997?
#59, July 2000

FANCYFLUID
KING'S JOURNEY

Fancyfluid are a Turin-based rock band that came together in spring 1988 with Paolo Annone (bass, guitar), Sandro Bruni (keyboards) and Fabrizio Goria (vocals, guitar). In January 1989 they recorded their first demo, which was well received with the French fanzine Varia voting it the fifth best European demo of the year. This led directly to Musea contacting the band and their first album, 'Weak Waving' was officially released in January 1990. Excellent reviews, and well-received live work led to the recording of their second album, 'King's Journey', which was released in October. Many guest musicians helped during the making of the CD, including Rodolfo Maltese of Banco, one of the biggest Italian bands. This CD is a concept, telling the story of a king's search for the dwarf Sieg and his treasure, to help the people of the king's kingdom. All of this is explained in the very detailed story at the front of the booklet. The lyrics are all in English, and are complex and interesting, although sometimes the feeling is that they are just a little over the top ("a whistle is turning round and round like the sword of Damocles" - what does it mean?). On a musical front the "guest" musicians are employed to great effect with some powerful drumming and great flute, sax and violin work. Because these latter instruments are only used sparingly they definitely add to the overall feeling of depth when they are employed. Overall their sound is very much a mix of Seventies and Nineties, with a depth that is sadly missing from many of today's recordings. Fancyfluid are far more than just a keyboard-oriented rock band and all the better for it. True, the songs are not the type that you will go around singing and the music needs to be sat and listened to, to be fully appreciated. But these are not necessarily bad things. I enjoyed the album a great deal and it is a real shame that it has not yet got a UK release.
#18, May 1993

FANTASMAGORIA
ENERGETIC LIVE DEMO

This is a six-man instrumental band from Japan, and although this is issued as a demo it does sound like the finished article as the sound is spot on. With two guitars, violin and keyboards as well as bass and drums the band could be forgiven for going totally over the top but here is a band that are mixing prog with fusion in a very fine way indeed. There are times when they are reminiscent of Kansas, but there is much more fusion in what they are doing and while the violin is often the lead instrument the guitarists are no slouches either – it is just that they tend to stay in the background and let Miki Fujimoto take the melody. These guys know what they are doing and it does not come across as a live recording as it feels far more polished. Overall a good album and it will be interesting to see how they develop.
#86, Feb 2006

FANTASYY FACTORYY
TALES TO TELL

This is Alan Tepper's second album, where a new rhythm section and also a guest flautist have joined him. Although both have been released in Germany by Ohrwaschl, his debut 'Ode To Life' was also released in the UK on vinyl by ACME. This is an interesting album, although about twenty-five years out of date! There is just no way that an album like this should be released in 1997! When I saw the design on the outside (swirling paint) and on the inside of the fold out digipak (Indian gods) I had to check that this really was a new album and not something that had dropped through a time warp. It commences with the hard rock instrumental "Eerie Woman", which drives along at frenetic pace, then gives way to the gentle acoustic "Season Of Sorcery". It is an album of contradiction, with hard going against soft, with Alan's vocals adding a harsh almost Dylan-esque dimension. "Gypsy Woman" starts life as a flute solo, and throughout it shows that guest Rainier Opical has been paying close attention to classic Tull. Of the seven songs, "New Dawn" is the longest at just over fifteen minutes and is more Floyd inspired, and although atmospheric does have its' moments. This is quite definitely for aficionados of Seventies Prog/Psych.

#42, July 1997

FARMAKON
A WARM GLIMPSE

I started listening to this CD in the car, and thought to myself that here was yet another Death Metal band. But hang on; although the vocals were pure Death, the guitars seemed to be just a little too clean. So when the vocals and music moved into more melodic rock I was not too surprised, although I have to confess that I never expected it to move into laid-back lounge. From there the only musical path to take was straight back hard into the heavy stuff. I knew without looking at the CD that this had to have been released by Elitist as they seem to be capturing the market in this style of progressive rock. Many neo-prog fans would shudder at any attempt to describe this music in that way, but this is music that is attempting to cross boundaries (successfully), so surely this really is progressing in the correct sense of the word instead of being regressive? Farmakon recorded a three-song demo in 2001 and then posted it onto the web, and were surprised to be contacted by Lee Barrett of Elitist within a few days offering them a deal. Of course, they then had to go off and write some more songs as they only had the three! This is an album that has a lot to offer, from Death to gentle acoustic pieces, but they are played within the same song. This is an album that is adventurous and compelling, yet can also be hard to listen to just because the music shifts so abruptly. Definitely not for those who follow the mainstream, this album is a delight, and those who want music that can be extremely heavy but is definitely out of the ordinary should seek this out.

#76, Oct 2003

THE FELLOWSHIP
IN ELVEN LANDS

There are times when one hears an album and is absolutely staggered at the amount of work that must have gone into something that will never reach a wide audience and that is definitely the case with this album. Much will be made of the fact that Jon Anderson is involved and that he sings lead on some of the songs, but note the word 'some' and not 'all'. This is much more than just another album from him in the vein of 'Olias', but instead there has been a serious attempt to produce music that has not only been inspired by Tolkien but is as close as the musicians believe that they have been able to get to the music described by him in his books.

When reading the introduction in the informative booklet that is part of the digipak it appears that in some ways this is almost a study as opposed to a recording process. One can imagine those involved producing a thesis on the work they have undertaken and why they use a certain type of musical construct as opposed to another. Some of the lyrics are in English, others in Elvish, and it is obviously an incredible achievement but does it work musically? While Yes fans are probably going to be one of the purchasers of this, as well as Tolkien addicts, the main winners here are those interested in mediaeval inspired folk music.

All of the instrumentation is acoustic as they bring in krumhorns and hurdygurdys and mix them with more modern instruments such as clarinets. One song that is known is the cover of "The Battle Of Evermore", but I doubt if Jimmy and Robert ever thought that it would sound like this as the music has been taken back in time and now sounds nothing at all like the original. I do not think that this is an album that I could ever see myself playing for pleasure, although there are some interesting songs on here at times, but instead is something to be admired and the players involved heartily congratulated on an educational and almost professorial approach to music making that will certainly attract the attention of the new wave of Tolkien fans. *#87, Apr 2006*

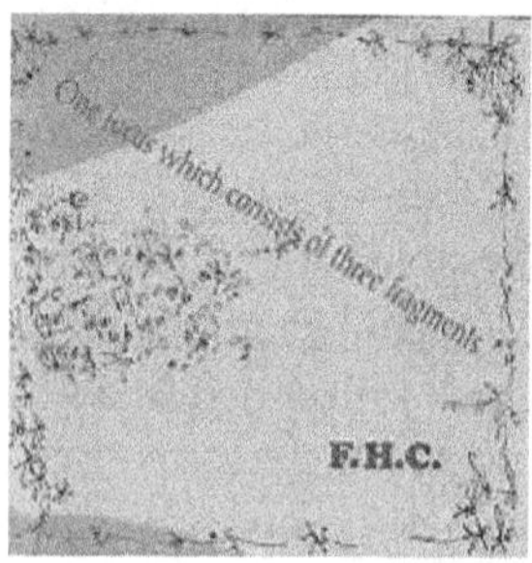

F.H.C.
ONE LOCUS WHICH….

Recorded by three different line-ups, this album is divided into the relevant sections, hence the full album title, which is 'One Locus Which Consist Of Three Fragments'.

Unfortunately, after the album title it sadly goes downhill. This is jazz, at times performed as if it was a death metal act in terms of speed, but the biggest sin is the production. I wouldn't recommend this album based on the music but the production lets even that down.

Thank you and goodnight.
#73, Apr 2003

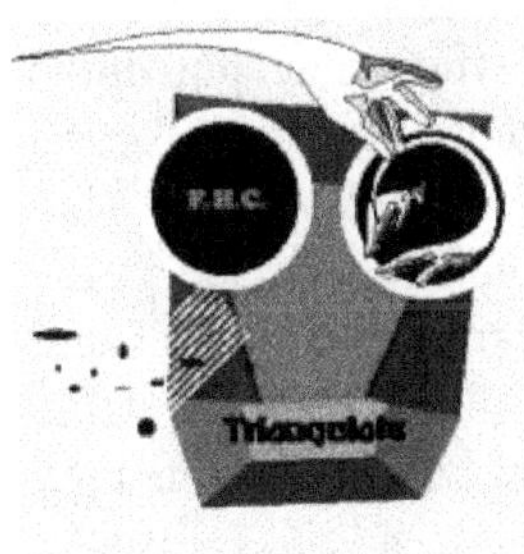

F.H.C.
TRIANGULATE

These guys made such an impression on me with their last album 'One Locus Which Consists Of Three Fragments', which I reviewed back in #73, that as soon as I saw this I groaned. I really did not like that album at all, and guess what? I'm not a fan of this one either. F.H.C. are a trio playing instrumental music on a Chapman Stick, contrabass and keyboards. There are twenty-one numbers on this album, which all seem to have been improvised, and like the last one I heard the production again is not what it could be. That they can play their instruments is never in doubt, it is just that to my Western ears they are not making any musical sense whatsoever. Maybe you have to be Japanese to fully enjoy this, but like the last album of theirs that I heard this is not one to which I will voluntarily be readily returning.
#86, Feb 2006

MIKE FIGGIS
HOTEL

This is a soundtrack, and the major problem with albums such as this is they may not make any musical sense outside the original context. That is especially true when the album contains largely of instrumental passages, instead of a collection of songs by different artists which has been aimed at airplay. There is not much that is going to find its' way onto the radio, unless that station specialises in music that is way out in left field, so in other words this is an album that is very much something to be investigated further. It starts in one of the best ways (for me) imaginable, as there is collaboration with Skin who I must admit I have not heard of since the sad demise of Skunk Anansie. There she was best known for spitting venom and (nearly) controlled anger, but here we hear the much softer and gentler side with the accompaniment very much in the background. But this is much more than just one musical style: there is a great deal going on with jazz and progressive elements combining with art rock to make an album that is always interesting and intriguing, always looking to move forwards but never being too challenging for the listener. This is very much music to be enjoyed, not endured, and I got so much out of it that I am now looking forward to seeing the film! In some ways reminiscent of Björk, others Massive Attack, it is of no surprise at all that Uncut made this Soundtrack of the Month. *#82, Jan 2005*

FINAL CONFLICT
REDRESS THE BALANCE

Final Conflict have been together in various forms since December 1985, created as the brainchild of Brian Donkin (guitars, lead vocals) and Andy Lawton (lead guitars, vocals). They recruited Mark Price (keyboards), who they had known from his work with other bands, and shared their ambition of playing a very different sort of music to the average, run of the mill rock band. They also recruited Tony

Moore on bass and keyboards, and started recording in January 1986 when they put down "Child of Innocence" and "Cornucopia". By March 1986 they had decided on a name for the band, and a theme for the cassette album release, 'Channel 8', which was released in May 1986 together with an illustrated booklet. A debut gig to launch the album took place in the band's hometown of Stoke-On-Trent, and was a great success. By February 1987 the band were working hard, with plenty of gigs, as well as writing new material, including "The Time Has Arrived". The following month they entered the UK Battle of the Bands where they finished runners-up.

By April they decided that they had enough material for another cassette album, 'The Time Has Arrived'. This featured the adventures of Steven who, when idly zapping through TV channels on his remote control, is drawn into the nightmare world of Channel 9, as the story started in the debut was continued into the follow-up. They commenced recording in the August, and in the meantime released a four-track cassette. 'The Time Has Arrived' was released in October 1987, and also received good reviews and a short tour followed. A 3-track EP was taken from the album and released under the title 'Watchers and Listeners'. In October 1988 they supported Ark at Edwards No. 8, a large venue in Birmingham and it was such a success that they were asked back to headline. In November they recorded a double A-sided single, "Across The Room" and "My England", which is actually the earliest material I have heard. A later version of "Across The Room" also features on 'Redress The Balance' and here it has all the FC hallmarks stamped all over it, with great melody, lyrics and vocals. "My England" has some standout Roger Chapman-style vocals, and great use of keyboards to create a very strong atmosphere.

During 1989 a group of friends became far more involved with the band, and finally took over the management in April 1990. This meant that Final Conflict could focus all their attention on their music, and went into Goalhouse Studios to start work on new material which would become their first CD album, 'Redress The Balance'. The eight songs were written over the course of eighteen months, with "Pangea's Child" actually being written in the studio. "The Time has Arrived" and "Across The Room" were also re-recorded for inclusion. The album was released in September 1991 on their own label, Gaia Records and since the release they have been working closely with local band Grace and also with Galahad, But, what's the album like? It's very strange for a progressive rock band to have two guitarists, and it would be very easy to fall into the trap of playing hard rock with some supporting keyboards. However, Final Conflict managed to threaten heavy guitarwork without ever delivering. This means that they have a distinctive sound removed from many of the other prog outfits around. The songs themselves are of extremely high quality, with all of them being readily accessible on first listen. There are some wonderful dual guitar runs on "The Time Has Arrived" which shows how two guitars can be used in a prog context. "Across The Room" features some very strong vocals, and although the songs themselves have a structure that lifts them out of the norm, it is probably the vocals that give the band the real class they portray. Brian is often accompanied only by keyboards as he comes to the end of a line, which shows real confidence in being able to hit and sustain notes, without an accompaniment to hide behind.

Personal favourites are the opener "Changing Fate", which totally changes style three times before the vocals bring the song driving along, and "Pangea's Child", which starts off as an acoustic number, but as the lyrics tell the story of how man ruins the environment, it takes on a much harder and menacing edge. However, I think every song is a gem, and the album as a whole is brilliant. Hopefully Final Conflict will be venturing into the London scene later this year, so keep your eyes open. 'Redress The Balance' is superb – if you like prog rock, you'll love this!
#12, Feb 1992

FINAL CONFLICT
QUEST

In #12 I said of Final Conflict's debut CD. 'Redress The Balance', "I think that every song is a gem and the album as a whole is brilliant". In #14, Dave Pointon said "For the discerning Prog fans, this album is essential listening". You can imagine, therefore, just how much I have been looking forward to their next album. The material I had heard played live boded well for the future, and talks with their management expressed great satisfaction with what was happening in the studio. So, it was with some trepidation that I put the newly-arrived CD into the player. Could they, would they, live up to expectations?

I have only managed to play the album twice (it turned up just two days ago), but I am happy to report that 'Quest' is a real driver. Even before putting it on I was extremely impressed with the artwork of the cover, which features neither name of group or album (although there is a small "FC" in one corner). Inside there is a mini-poster, on the reverse of which is a fiendishly hard prize crossword. All of the lyrics are in the booklet itself, and on studying them the awful truth is revealed… 'Quest' is a concept album. No, they did not go out with the ark (although I have difficulty in thinking of a recent one), but this one really works. The starting point of the story is that of the crossword which appeared immediately prior to the D-Day landings, containing the code words to the planned invasion. As the "hero" completes his crossword puzzle he finds that he is reminded of past events. So what is it like? My immediate impression is that the band have matured a great deal since the release of RTB. Also, there is far greater emphasis on keyboards and a real sense of unity (although the drummer has changed since the last album). Steve Lipiec also plays sax, and this is used sparingly but to great effect. The album opens with a narrator explaining the background of the album, which leads in turn to opener "The Quest" which has a long keyboard-dominated introduction. When the singing starts it is obvious that this album is very unlike the last, as it relies far less on guitar and more on structured songs and lyrics. This is heavy on atmosphere, and leads well into "Old Lady", Surprisingly this starts as a piano-based song with Brian singing gently over the top. This means that the listener is drawn more and more to the lyrics. A wonderful sustained roll around the kit by new drummer Chris Moyden finally heralds the entrance of the guitars with some crashing riffs. This in turn leads into some wonderful harmony guitarwork that Final Conflict are renowned for. They are still one of the very few prog bands with two guitarists, and it surprised me somewhat that they have taken such a back seat on this album, but the music really works so maybe it is time to act with restraint.

"Mirror Of Lies" is more like vintage FC. It starts gently with vocals from Andy, but as the song picks up momentum the harsher vocals of Brian take over. The use of wailing saxophone in the latter stages of the song works really well: there is even a guitar break which leads the song into the final stages. "A Look At Life" starts off with another keyboard introduction, but some frenetic dual guitarwork livens things up and makes way for a short guitar solo and harmony guitars continue throughout the singing. The heavier guitarwork on this song seems to have inspired a change in the album, as the guitars are still to the fore in "Waiting for A Chance". This is probably my favourite, as all the elements that make FC such a good band really gel together to make a great track.

In all, there are eight songs on this hour-long album and although they are joined together by a theme, they are individual pieces in their own right. It would have been very easy for Final Conflict to produce another 'Redress The Balance', which was widely accepted, but instead they have moved on and by releasing a concept they have set themselves up as targets for anyone who wants to make a mockery of them. It's bad enough being a prog band in most of media's eyes, without producing a concept to compound their sins. I only hope that people are willing to listen to the album with an open mind and hear some great songs and musicianship. I really enjoyed the last one, and always have it in the car, but I can honestly say this will get even more play by me. If you bought 'Redress The Balance' then you must get this, and if you did not then there is no finer place to start appreciating the great sounds of Final Conflict than right here.
#15, Oct 1992

FINISTERRE
STORYBOOK

This set was recorded at ProgDay in 1997, and was originally released on Peter Renfro's own Proglodite label. As with the DFA release this has been issued as a digipak, and that is not the only similarity as yet again this is an Italian band playing their first gig in America. Musically there are also some similarities in the way that they can both play ferocious rock that is interspersed with some gentle vocals. The major musical difference in that Finisterre also feature flautist Sergio Grazia, who provides the band with an extra melody element. The first time I played this was on a long car journey and I was taken with the clarity of the production and the way that the band can seamlessly move from one musical idea to another. There is quite a strong jazz element, and is outside of the 'normal' prog scene, which cannot be a bad thing. This is an interesting album that also contains their cover of PFM's "Altaloma" that was missing from the original release. Worth hearing.
#65, Dec 2001

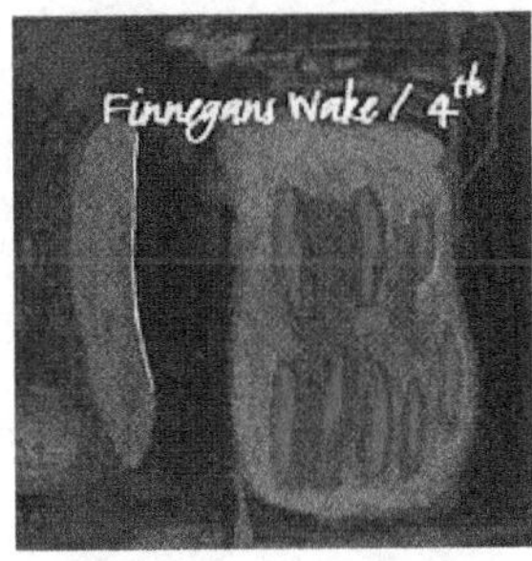

FINNEGAN'S WAKE
4TH

It is not too surprising that this is the fourth album by Henry Krutzen's project Finnegan's Wake, and is a double CD. Henry himself provides keyboards, tenor saxophone and ken (any ideas anyone?), but as well as being joined by the rest of his band there are numerous guests who provide a whole raft of extra instruments so that if he wants the bassoon to take the lead role in a section then that really is not a problem, or a violin, or trombone, or clarinet, or keyboards or, well, you get the idea. But musically what is this like? Arguably it is as far removed from rock music as one is likely to hear, but while there are plenty of jazz leanings (especially at the beginning of the twelve-minute-long "Fata Morgana"), that label does not fit either. What we have here is an album that is taking modern avant-garde classical music and melding it with other forms to create something different. This is not easy to listen to, far from it, as this is challenging but there is some sort of sense within it although the listener never has the chance to work out what is coming next. It will not appeal to the masses but was never designed to. I am not sure on this, but feel that my lack of enjoyment probably rests more with my own personal tastes as opposed to any failings on the part of those involved in this project.
#84, July 2005

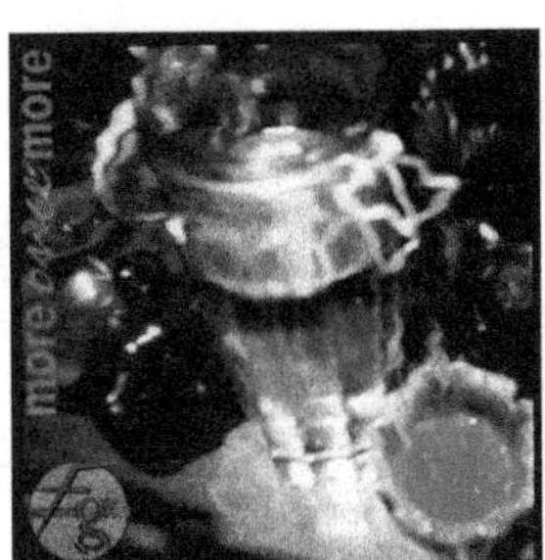

FINNEUS GAUGE
MORE ONCE MORE

I know that I am not alone in dismaying in the end of one of the most exciting bands to come out of America in the Nineties, Echolyn. However, it has meant that keyboard player and songwriter Chris Busby has been able to turn his hand to a new project, and in creating Finneus Gauge he has brought in one of those rarities, a female lead singer, although for a lot of the time her voice is just another player in the harmonies. Especially in the vocal department, Finneus Gauge are very reminiscent of Yes, although not the Yes of today, but the 'Fragile' era where they were still yet to reach the dinosaur status.

This is no way a copycat outfit, far from it, as FG has a foot in the prog camp and also in the jazz rock field and this works extremely well, particularly in the more up-tempo numbers such as the opening track "More Wants More". At times though, the music seems almost over complicated, as if the players want to show just how good they are at what they do, and this can be a distraction. There must be room for the music to live and breathe, and at times it seems that the musical creativity is being stifled because too many notes get in the way. This is an enjoyable album, but not one to which I will be returning with great regularity, and certainly not one where tunes and melodies would stay in the mind after turning it off.
#47, Feb 1998

FINNEUS GAUGE
ONE INCH OF THE NAIL

Following on from their 1997 debut 'More Once More', which was released in the UK on Cyclops (as this one may also being the future), Finneus Gauge's second album was released in America in January. Whereas the first showed some jazz influences, this is far more uncompromising as FG have a heavy menacing sound all of their own. It is highly intricate and on first hearing can almost be said to be frightening in its' intensity. This is music that is truly 'progressing' as it moves forward and tries to mix and meld different styles. The most obvious style that they have incorporated is still jazz, but not the laid back almost deferential style that can be found but rather the blistering moves to and from the melody that almost makes you wonder if the band are ever again going to find the plot. The best example of this on the album is the last song, "Holden Pretzel", where Scott McGill takes the guys on a musical exploration that allows him to indulge in breath-taking runs up and down the frets. I, along with many others, was sorry to see the implosion of Echolyn but keyboard player Christopher Buzby can be rightly proud of the band he is now in. If you like music that is a little different but very enjoyable then check this out. *#52, Feb 1999*

FIRST BAND FROM OUTER SPACE
WE'RE ONLY IN IT..

'We're Only In It For The Space Rock' is the debut full length album from Swedish outfit First Band From Outer Space, who apparently have just finished mixing their second so that should follow shortly. With a band name and album title such as these they are pretty much nailing their colours to the mast, so it is of no surprise that this sounds like Hawkwind mixed with Floyd with the more aggressive elements of Ozric Tentacles. Most of the music is well constructed and the longest track on the album, the title cut itself which is more than twenty minutes in length, also comes over well which may not have been the case given that it is an improvised instrumental! There are lots of weird sounds and keyboard touches going on behind the music in best space rock stoner session and while they might not be creating anything dramatically new, although the use of flutes is a nice touch, this is a fine example of the genre and anyone into Hawkwind style prog is going to have to get this. *#85, Nov 2005*

FIRST BAND FROM OUTER SPACE
IMPRESSIONABLE..

Following on from their debut full-length album, we now have 'Impressionable Sounds Of The Subsonic'. The band landed in Gothenburg from their home planet in 2002 and since then has been creating some very high quality space rock. To say that there are some songs, such as "Mean Spacemachine" which sound a little like classic Hawkwind is probably understating it somewhat, but the

sound is good and although not all of the songs are in English this is very accessible and pounding music. There is the sense that these are constructed songs as opposed to just jams that have been recorded on tape. When the oscillator is going and the vocals are being screamed then it is as if DikMik and Dave Brock are again on the same stage and the extremely solid basslines of course bring forward the figure of Lemmy. If you enjoy space rock then this is an essential purchase as it is a very fine example of the genre, and even if the sound is somewhat dated they do what they are doing very well indeed and if you have ever enjoyed 'Hall Of the Mountain Grill' then you owe it to your ears to hear this.
#88, Jun 2006

FISH
YIN

FISH
YANG
Here are the two new albums from Fish, comprising what he feels are his best songs from his time with Marillion and his solo career. None of the Marillion songs are the originals, but have been totally re-recorded for this release. Some have been remixed, others are here for the first time, and all in all out of the twenty-six tracks only nine are available elsewhere. It can be seen from this alone, that here is a collection unlike virtually all other 'Greatest Hits' compilations. The earliest song is "Institution Waltz", which is from 1981 but was never recorded; also, Fish decided that 'Script' could not be bettered so there are no songs from that album, although there is material from the other Marillion albums he was involved with. 'Yin' kicks off with a stonking "Incommunicado", and from here to "Internal Exile" (the last song on 'Yang'), Fish is at the very top of his form. One of the standout songs on 'Yin' has to be the re-recorded duet "Just Good Friends" with guest singer Sam Brown: the duet is full if power and emotion and works extremely well indeed. In 1993 Fish covered "Boston Tea Party", and in 1995 he has re-recorded it with SAHB so needless to say the guys provide tremendous musical backbone and Fish plays the role of Alex Harvey to perfection. 'Yang' is the one that many people will go for if they are just buying one, as not only is there "Kayleigh" and "Lavender", but also "Sugar Mice" and "Punch and Judy". Ten years after "Kayleigh" was a smash hit single, Fish still manages to make it fresh and exciting while the guitarwork of Frank Usher and Robin Boult take it away from the old Marillion sound. Fish has managed to produce a collection that portrays the very best of his songs, with some great performances. Anyone who liked the Marillion songs will not be disappointed with what Fish has done, as he has breathed new life and vigour into them. After you have bought the two CDs simply write to The Company and receive a box to keep them in, along with a booklet containing all of the lyrics and some anecdotes. If you are a fan of Fish then this is an essential purchase. If you are not, then you ought to get this and become one!
#31, Oct 1995

FISH
KRAKOW

This is a double CD of Fish's gig in Krakow on October 24th, 1995. He has been releasing a lot of gigs through his own label, but this has actually been released by Metal Mind and is only available in Eastern Europe (although I do believe that you can also get it through his fan club). It has a well-presented booklet, with Fish's views on Poland, plus some photos. But, it is the music that counts, and this is split roughly equally between solo and Marillion material, with just one cover, the wonderful "Boston Tea Party" where Fish does his best Alex Harvey impression. If you are a Fish completist then obviously this is a CD that you cannot do without. It does present Fish at his best, with the band playing well, so is worth searching out. Unfortunately, due to the way that it has been issued it could well work out expensive so you will have to decide how much you need this when other gigs are available through Dick Bros.
#39, Jan 1997

FISH
SUNSETS AND EMPIRE

A chance meeting in Southern France led to Fish being introduced to Steve Wilson of Porcupine Tree and No-man. From that they started to collaborate, and the end result was that Steve co-wrote seven songs with Fish, contributed large amounts of musicianship and also produced the album. Additional musicians were added to Fish's own band as Steve and Fish attempted to use a cinematic approach, creating a broad and diverse sound full of depth and passion. Andy Mackintosh was brought in to produce the vocals, while Calum Malcolm (Blue Nile, Prefab Sprout) was used to mix the album as he also had experience in classic musical production. Finally, Bob Ludwig mastered the album at his studio in Portland, Maine.

This is Fish's fifth album since leaving Marillion in 1987 and to my ears is his finest ever achievement, and I include 'Script For A Jester's Tear' in that statement. Considering who was involved, it is of little surprise that the production is of the very highest quality, but it is the songs that really matter. Musically and lyrically Fish is at his strongest, whether he is singing to/about his daughter Tara, or Sarajevo, there is power and passion that has never really been captured before.

The only fault with this album is that it is so good, so damned near perfect, that the next one cannot possibly be better. Melodic, progressive, call it what you will, I will call it excellent and one of the best albums of any type of music that you will hear this year, make that this decade.
#41, Apr 1997

FISH
FORTUNES OF WAR

This live acoustic set is taken from 1994, when Fish toured with a stripped down set playing places he had not been to before. The idea for the tour came from personal appearances being made to promote the 'Suits' album: they went so well that a tour with basically a non-electric band seemed like a good idea. Most of the songs on here were recorded June 29th 1994 at The Mean Fiddler and the crowd certainly sound as if they were enjoying it. If you like Fish, then this is an album that you will surely love. "Warm Wet Circles" is particular works extremely well: the use of two acoustic guitars for the whole of the first verse, and virtually nothing else, gives the song an edge that was missing from the version that made it to the album in the first place. The guitar solo is played on an electric, and the acoustic backing gives it far more emphasis and dynamism, as with "Love Song" on Tesla's superb 'Five Man Acoustical Jam'. This is not a Marillion covers album, with only three (yes, including "Kayleigh") of the thirteen songs being from his old band, but even they are treated differently and they benefit from that. There is a space between the songs, and Fish not straining to be heard above the amplification makes this an album to definitely enjoy and play time and again.

#50, Aug 1998

FISH
RAINGODS WITH ZIPPOS

This is a truly superb album, even better than 'Sunsets on Empire' which I raved about so much, and deserves a track by track breakdown which is something I tend not to do very often. "Tumbledown" is the first of two songs on the album co-written with old keyboard player and buddy Mickey Simmonds. It starts life as gentle piano piece, but the long introduction gives way to a more driving piece of music, which becomes an out and out rocker. A great way to start an album. "Mission Statement" is another rocker, upbeat and with a real groove, it is hard to believe that it was written with a Nashville veteran (Paul Thorn) and an Eighties pop star (Rick Astley). This is one of the three songs written on the writing retreat at Miles Copeland's castle last May. "Incomplete" is scheduled to be the first single from the album and is a duet with co-writer Elizabeth Antwi. This is another from the castle sessions and shows a far more delicate side of Fish, with gentle acoustic guitar and sweeping keyboards as they sing about love lost. "Tilted Cross" is the last of the castle tracks, as Fish sings delicately about the landmines in Bosnia, a country he has visited both lyrically and on tour before. It has an almost country feel about it, as Fish again has gentle female harmonies to work against. The delicate use of violin adds an emotive edge to proceedings. "Faith Healer". At long last, here it is, the definitive cover version. Fish provides an insight into how Alex would approach this number in the Nineties if he were still here. I played this, then brought out both a live and studio version from the great man himself to compare against, and Fish really has done Alex proud. Great guitar, total menace from Fish, and a driving fiddle makes this a rocker as powerful as anything Fish has ever done. “Rites of Passage” is the other track co-written with Mickey, but this is a far more emotive impassioned affair, full of melancholy. “Plague of Ghosts” can in many ways be seen as Fish’ most impressive work to date, certainly since “Misplaced Childhood”. Over twenty minutes long, subdivided into six separate pieces, this is Fish at his most complex and mysterious. It moves through so many different musical styles that it is virtually impossible to see where one style ends and another begins. It is music made to be played again and again, with the listener finding more each time. It can be listened to on one level, or studied and enjoyed on a totally different place. I never thought that Fish would be able to reach again the heady heights that he set himself with the last album, but ‘Raingods With Zippos’ sets new standards to which many will aspire but few will attain. *#53, May 1999*

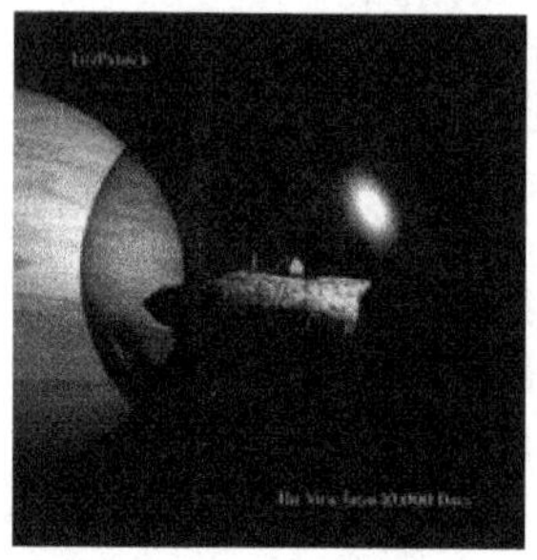

FITZPATRICK
THE VIEW FROM 10,000 DAYS

I think the best way to start this review is with a quote from the CDBaby site, where it says “Basically, FitzPatrick is what you’d get if Genesis, Toto, and Fleetwood Mac met at a T. S. Eliot convention. Or is it Phil Collins, Pink Floyd, and Dire Straits at a C. S. Lewis convention? The masses can’t decide.” In the email that I had from Michael FitzPatrick it stated “FitzPatrick: Where Genesis, Fleetwood Mac, and C.S. Lewis meet” and he says that the music is more pop/ rock with progressive leanings as opposed to ‘just’ progressive. Of course that opens up the whole can of snakes as to what does the term ‘progressive rock’ actually mean and I am not going to go into that here. FitzPatrick the band are the brothers FitzPatrick, Michael and Shaun, with some guest musicians. There is no list of who played what and when, and the ‘booklet’ itself is just a single sheet but the listener is guided to the website where there are lyrics, more information on the stunning cover artwork etc. A few years ago I would have said that there was not much happening in terms of Christian music, but that is definitely not the case anymore. Study the lyrics and you will see that this is very much music with a message, something that is trying to do far more than just entertain. But even if one is not a Christian this album is just so easy and enjoyable to listen to that the casual listener will get a great deal out of it. As can probably be guessed from the bands listed earlier this is a very melodic album, and while it probably wouldn’t be viewed as being progressive in the traditional sense (if that is not a contradiction in itself) it is probably the proghead who will get the most out of this. Well-structured songs which have been well performed and sung, this is a very interesting album indeed. *#85, Nov 2005*

DAVID FIUCZYNSKI
JAZZPUNK

This has to be one of the most unusual and outrageous albums that I have ever heard. David is a master of the guitar, and combined with his love of free jazz then the results can be musically different to say the least. Although he has been recording since 1994 this is his first solo album, which was initially recorded for a jazz label that then refused to release it as they found it ‘shocking’. It was only in an out

of court settlement that Fuze managed to get the recording back, and he has now released it on his own label. I can understand why a jazz label would have had kittens over this. I grew up listening to jazz and I have not heard anything quite like this. There are areas that conform to normal jazz ideas, but these are rare. David goes off at tangents, getting sounds from his guitar I did not think possible. His use of fretless guitar as well as fretted adds to his own unique sound. If you enjoy Steve Vai or Joe Satriani then be aware that there is another phenomenal guitarist around, but be warned, although this is an album of 'standards' you will have never heard any of them played like this before (he has turned "Third Stone From The Sun" into a new song completely). This is a challenging album, but it is worth the effort.
#60, Oct 2000

FLAMBOROUGH HEAD
UNSPOKEN WHISPER
Flamborough Head are not British, although they do sound it with a moniker like that, but have captured some of the best sounds of British prog around. At times they are similar to IQ, at others Jadis or Steve Hackett, but probably they come across best as a new version of Landmarq. I am sure that a lot of this is down to vocalist Siebe-Rein who has a dynamic and vocal style similar to Damian Wilson. Although Siebe-Rein provides keyboards, along with Edo, this album also has its fair share of guitar. It is a very symphonic album, plenty of light and shade, and a real grower. However, even from the beginning of the first song, "Schoolyard Fantasy", the listener is in no doubt that here is a real find. Only two songs stretch out to over ten minutes, but for those who enjoy the softer (for the most part) side of prog, while not wimping out, will find an album that is a joy to listen to. *#49, May 1998*

FLAMBOROUGH HEAD
ONE FOR THE CROW
This is the third album by the Dutch prog outfit, but their first with vocalist Margriet Boomsma (who also contributes recorders and flutes). This is album of great depth and contains influences and styles that grow on the listener the more it is played. Margriet has a voice in the style of Tracy Hitchings, with good range and power and harmonises well with guitarist Eddie Mulder. While the cop out is to say that Flamborough Head are a progressive rock band, it is much harder to decide on all of the musical strands that the band are bringing together. The obvious ones are Pendragon and Pink Floyd, but there is also 'Wind & Wuthering' era Genesis, and even Gryphon to consider. It is an album of delicacy with plenty of space for the music to move, and is never intrusive but far more laid back. In many ways it is the perfect dreamy summer album, with the long instrumental passages showing not only the musical talents of the band but also how they react to each other. The direction can shift quite suddenly at times, but somehow it always manages to make sense. There is a real feel of the Seventies and this is heightened by the use of delicate instrumental pieces, often just acoustic guitar and piano,

which lead onto the longer songs. The electric guitar is rarely riffed but used instead to provide melodic leads, sometimes in harmony with the keyboards or providing a supporting role. A very enjoyable album indeed.
#69, Aug 2002

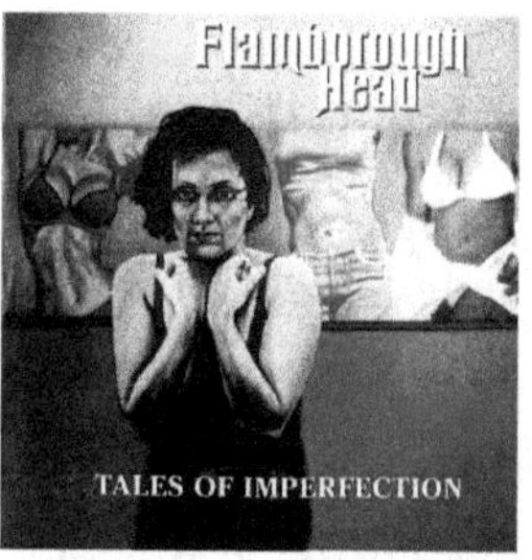

FLAMBOROUGH HEAD
TALES OF IMPERFECTION

It has never been much of a secret, but Cyclops boss Malcolm Parker is not very fond of female lead singers. I have had many chats with him over the years about a new album that I have enjoyed but he is not keen on, primarily due to that. So when he has a band on his label that does include a female lead singer then one must realise that he thinks a great deal of them, and in their fourth album Flamborough Head have definitely delivered the goods. This is classy melodic prog at its' best, with plenty of longer songs for progheads to get their teeth into. Margriet Boomsma has a great voice, but she never totally dominates the proceedings, as in many cases these guys seem to be almost an instrumental act with the vocals coming in when needed, but not taking over what is going on. She also adds flute and recorders which gives the music an extra edge, but it is the whole make up of this band that makes it so good. There are times when the keyboards are in full flow, with just a few guitar touches here and there, or it can be the other way around. There is the feeling throughout that this is very polished, very finessed, but there is just a tiny edge to what is going on so that it never drops just into background music. The result is something that progheads will definitely enjoy as there is plenty of movement within the music and plenty of twists and turns and some dynamic changes without ever getting too heavy or over the top. For those who want their prog to be thoughtful and pleasant without being too rocky and in your face.
#86, Feb 2006

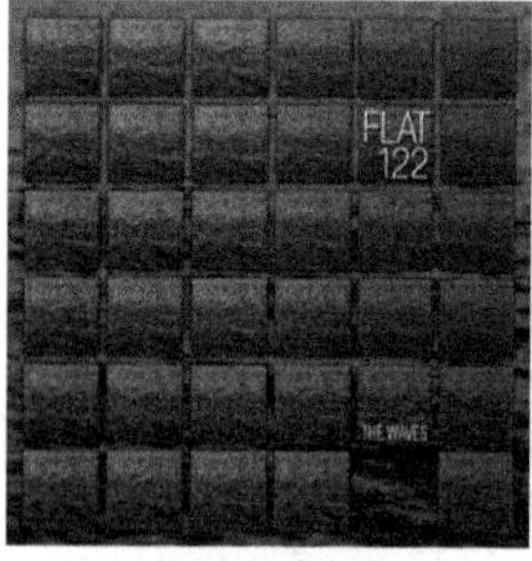

FLAT 122
THE WAVES

This Tokyo trio was formed in 2002 by Takao Kawasaki (keyboards), with Satoshi Hirata (guitar) and Kiyotaka Tanabe (drums). As one can see there is no bass with the line-up, which means that the band have a very clean and high end sound. There are three short tracks with a guest female singer, but this is mainly about the interplay between the three guys. It has to be said that there are times when it does drift into background music, but when they get it right as they do on "Neo Classic Dance" then it is a joy. Here Takao uses different light and airy keyboard sounds while Satoshi is well controlled at the top of the neck and Kiyotaka keeps it nailed down. There are two lengthy pieces, and the band are certainly not afraid to spread their wings and try different styles, but although there are some nods to prog here and there this is much more like fusion except not quite so jazzy. Overall an interesting album, and if it had all

pulled together the same way it would have been incredible, but even as it stands it is still worth hearing.
#86, Feb 2006

FLIGHT 09
HUMAN NATURE

Flight 09 started as long ago as 1983, and is the oldest and possibly best known progressive band in Uzbekistan. Their first two international releases, "Rifflection" and "Forbidden Lullabies" were released through the American Neurosis label and this is their third, on the Russian Mals label. This is very solid neo-prog, with all lyrics in English, with the sound of the band very much built around the guitar and singing of Igor Savitch (who also plays keyboards within the three-man line-up, which may explain why they are a smaller part of the overall band). This is punchy music, but the band are also prepared to slow it down and play acoustically to create a more sombre and relaxed mood when they want to. The result is an album that contains a lot of depth and variety with "One Night Without You" being a wonderful IQ style belter. If this was a British band I am sure that we would be hearing a great deal more about them, and are well worth discovering.
#88, Jun 2006

THE FLOWER KINGS
BACK IN THE WORLD OF ADVENTURES

Last year Roine Stolt released one of the most impressive albums you could ever wish to hear, 'The Flower King', and here is the follow-up. Although Roine has used many of the same musicians the project now has a band name, but he still provides vocals, guitar and keyboards. All the elements that made 'The Flower King' so special have been faithfully used again and the result is yet another classic that needs to be in every melodic rock lover's collection. Although there are many musical hooks on which to hang a comparison, probably the closest is with Jadis. The long drawn out guitar notes which extend into solos, totally dominating the rest of the band, as well as the pleasant but relatively small amount of vocals, are trademarks of Gary Chandler as well as Roine, but here all comparisons end. While Jadis rely on dreamy worlds to get their musical point across, Roine is fronting what is very much a rock band, which means rock guitar solos and riffs that rely as much on volume as they do on subtlety. Opener "Wheel of Adventures" sets out the stall as during it's thirteen minute plus length the band display their tightness and musical prowess, while Roine is very much in charge. The vocals act to highlight the instrumental passages that are the main focal point of the piece. The time and mood changes abound, but they all seem to make perfect sense and there is not a hint of self-indulgence. If any of you are lucky enough to hear some of 'The Flower King' then you will be pleased to know that 'Back In The World Of Adventures' is also in the same "must purchase" category.
#32, Dec 1995

THE FLOWER KINGS
RETROPOLIS

Roine Stolt is producing great albums at a pace that puts most other progressive bands firmly in the shade. Two years after 'The Flower King', one of the best albums ever to come out of Scandinavia, and following on from last year's 'Back In The World Of Adventures' (which saw Roine become a band), we now have 'Retropolis'. The line-up is basically the same, although the music has moved on. Never content with relying solely on beautiful guitarwork this album sees keyboards play a greater role. Roine will not let the music sit in one area, but likes to mingle and move, bringing just a hint of jazz, or classical. At times it is possible to hear late Seventies Genesis at work, or Yes, but the overall result is that of Roine Stolt. He has a very melodic and magical voice, but it is one that he tends to use sparingly, rather letting the instruments take control and within a beat the music can move from being dreamy and gentle to guitar-driven rock a la Steve Vai. He is in total control at all times and the result is yet again another brilliant album from the Flower Kong. An essential purchase.
#35, June 1996

THE FLOWER KINGS
FLOWER POWER

When Roine Stolt released his solo album 'The Flower King' some years ago it caused a great stir in progressive circles: the ex-Kaipa guitarist had produced an album of real majesty and wonder. He has continued to pursue this path with his band, with the latest offering being 'Flower Power: A Journey to the Hidden Corners of your Mind' which has a running time of more than 140 minutes! Most of the first CD is taken up with "Garden of Dreams", a suite of eighteen pieces, which last an hour. An unusual way to start an album, as most people opt for the shorter songs approach as a way to get into the music, but niceties such as convention do not matter too much to Roine. But, no-one ought to think that this is Roine and a collection of hired guns as Tomas Bodin (keyboards), Hasse Froberg (vocals), Jaime Salazar (drums) all either write or co-write numbers. It only leaves Roine's brother Michael (bass) and Hass Bruniusson (percussion) as the non-writers. The music?

The only way to really describe this is as symphonic; as there is a real orchestral feel too much of what they do, although "Mr Hope Goes To Wall Street" (track six of the suite) starts life as a real keyboard fest with dazzling runs. It is the voices and the majesty that also lull you in, as some of the tracks have a dreamy quality that relies on the majesty and warmth of the voice. This is music of the highest quality and if you like progressive/symphonic rock then you owe it to yourself to discover them today.
#53, May 1999

THE FLOWER KINGS
ALIVE ON PLANET EARTH

Although Roine Stolt first came to prominence in Kaipa in the 70's, it is since his solo album 'The Flower King' and the formation of this band that he has become popular outside of his native Sweden. This double live CD, with the first being from the North American tour in 1998, and the second from the Japan tour of 1999, shows just why The Flower Kings are so highly regarded. Unusually for a prog band they have two guitarists, and with four of the five providing vocals there are also harmonies to go around. In some ways they are quite 'traditional' in their sound, and the one cover "The Lamb Lies Down On Broadway" does not sound at all out of place (although it has been given a Flower Kings treatment which includes an electrifying guitar solo). Six of the songs are in excess of ten minutes long, with two over fifteen, but the music is never boring or overly self-indulgent. Sometimes the keyboards are just gentle piano combining with delicate guitar, while at other times the music is quite bombastic. My personal favourite is the title cut of the solo album, which is still a regular visitor to my deck. Here Roine starts gently, meandering up and down the frets as the band slowly comes to life. It is laid back and glorious, soaring keyboards combine with blistering guitar runs, as the gentle verse gradually leads into the singalong chorus. A superb album - essential for the proghead.
#57, Mar 2000

THE FLOWER KINGS
SPACE REVOLVER

Roine Stolt has pulled in his wings with this album somewhat, just a single CD this time with only one song over twenty minutes in length, and even that is divided into two so that it opens and closes the album. Why, the whole album is under 75 minutes long! (Just). I made the mistake of initially playing this after listening to the new Spock's Beard album about ten times in a row, and feeling that I needed something different. I heard this then through ears that were not quite ready for it, and I could not help but dislike it. The only thing to do was to give it a break and go back to it, and I am glad that I did.

There is now a new bassist in Flower Kings, Jonas Reingold, who has brought a much jazzier feel to proceedings. Add to that the inventive sax playing of Ulf Wallander (which is used sparingly but to great effect), then the music does seem to have shifted in feel. While losing none of the power, this has allowed Roine to spread the wings of the band. It is distinctively still Flower Kings, but there is more passion and more emotion. Roine has always tried to progress his music and like his counterpart Neal Morse he has created a band that has very much his own sound, something of a rarity in today's progressive scene. A good addition to their catalogue.
#60, Oct 2000

THE FLOWER KINGS
THE RAINMAKER

This is a band that has managed to move on yet not change their sound very much since their inception in 1993. I still regularly play Roine Stolt's solo album 'The Flower King', and the sound of the band that he put together around that still keep that vision shining through. There are not many bands that are immediately recognisable, and Roine manages to keep his work in this band fairly distant from his work in the prog supergroup Transatlantic. Well what can you expect from the new album? Great musicianship, of course, songs that are as short as 70 seconds ("Red Alert") or as long as fourteen minutes ("Road To Sanctuary"). There are slow numbers, quick ones, some that are slow and some that are quick, but for the most part they all contain those elements and many more. Their use of layered vocals almost comes across as The Moody Blues at times, and the whole result is a prog album that is a joy to listen to that does not take too much concentration. Call it prog, call it melodic rock, call it good.
#64, Oct 2001

THE FLOWER KINGS
UNFOLD THE FUTURE

Given that Spock's Beard have just released a double CD in 'Snow', it is really not a surprise to see that Neal's Transatlantic bandmate has also come up with a double album lasting over two hours. I have recently been playing Roine Stolt's tremendous solo album again and it was interesting to be able to compare the two. In many ways it is a shame that I did as although this is a huge undertaking, encompassing many differing musical styles, I kept wishing that Roine had kept a bit closer to the musical template he had originally set out for himself. What do I mean? This is in many ways a very progressive album, in that it is deliberately taking musical strands of various types and weaving them together. My personal complaint is that these are sometimes taken to extremes so that the music is too much one way or another. The opening number, "The Truth Will Set You Free", is a great number and at thirty minutes somehow still does not sound too long. What it does sound like is as if it belongs on 'Close To The Edge' and sounds at times so close to classic Yes that I wondered if The Flower Kings had gone for a break and Jon and the boys had played some of it for them. It is great music but it does not really sound like the band themselves. Add to that, some songs are so jazz that they are totally removed from prog. It can be argued that this is not a bad thing, but I am not a great lover of jazz although I do play some from time to time, so if I wanted a jazz album I would have bought one and some of these songs are so self-indulgent that one wonders who the audience is. But, when they get it spot on, then there are few that can touch them. The result is an album that in many ways is a disappointment, yet does contain moments of brilliance, so perhaps a severe editing would have been the right thing to do. Masterpiece or overblown, that opinion has to be your own.
#70, Oct 2002

THE FLOWER KINGS

ADAM & EVE

I was not the only one to be extremely disappointed with the last Flower Kings CD, as although they have some excellent ideas and are superb musicians, there was the feeling that the effect would have been much better if there had been someone to cut the CD from a double to a single. So it was with a little trepidation that I put this in the player. I certainly did not expect to be playing the most consistent album since Roine's own 'The Flower King' album which started this all off. The first song, "Love Supreme", is twenty minutes long, but stays interesting throughout. It is packed full of Yes references, but is much more than just a copied style as The Flower Kings' make it very much their own. Shorter songs intersperse the longer ones, and even though there is another song that is over eighteen minutes in length there is never a feeling that they have outstayed their welcome. "Vampires View" at nine minutes is a delight, a gothic dark number with sinister overtones that certainly never feels as if it comes from Scandinavia as it the sort of eclectic number that surely could only be English. If you have investigated this band before but have been put off by the sense of self interest and 'aren't we clever', then rest assured that this is an outstanding return to form with strong songs and musicianship throughout. A must for all progheads.

#80, Jul 2004

THE FLOWER KINGS

PARADOX HOTEL

It may be two years since their last album, but Roine did release 'Wall Street Voodoo' last year, so I think that one has to forgive him. Again we are confronted with a double CD and as soon as I saw it I was feeling a little uneasy, as although the band do provide excellent value for money there is sometimes the feeling that a little judicious editing may help their cause. Guess what, that is probably the same again this time although it is definitely not nearly as pronounced as previously. Most of the album was recorded basically live in the studio in one week and Roine has handed over some of the songwriting responsibilities, although it does have to be noted that out of the 19 songs on the album he did write 10, and co-wrote another six but that's good for him! One knows that musically these guys are going to be covering a lot of bases, from Yes to Zappa pausing only for tea with King Crimson en route combined with many other styles on the way. There is actually a section within "Monsters & Men" that reminds me a lot of some guy called Roine Stolt and his album 'The Flower King'. They have definitely gone back to their roots while at the same time moving the music forward and this is going to please a lot of progheads. Although there are times when they do appear to be playing for their own enjoyment (hence the need for an external editor), overall this is a very enjoyable work.

#88, Jun 2006

FLUXURY
PERISHABLE GOODS

The thing that one notices more than anything else when listening to Dutch band Fluxury for the first time is the power and depth of the arrangements. There appear to be numerous layers, which must have taken a long time to create, yet there is also a simplicity which is beguiling and entrancing. Singer Marjolein van Tongeren has a wonderful tone to her voice, warm and passionate with great control and a strong range, but behind her vocals the band are in total control – either playing delicately and gently or bringing all of their strengths to bear. This is a solid gold prog album but although one can say that there are elements of Gentle Giant, BJH or Genesis, they really have very much their own sound. It is interesting to compare them to our own Magenta as while both have female singers and similar musical line-ups that is all that links them as this music is far more gentle – not exactly laid back but more of 'come to here to listen to what we are doing' as opposed to throwing it hard in the face. It would be interesting to see how they play live as either they must have a second keyboard player on board or Jan Kuipers is going to have to grow two more arms as piano is as important to their overall sound as synths, but they can still punch it out when they want to, as on "I Will Be There". All of the lyrics are in English, and there is even one 'epic' with the title cut coming in at just over ten minutes long. Overall an excellent prog album with a lot going for it.

#86, Feb 2006

FOCUS
8

Yes, you read the name of the band correctly; this is indeed the Focus of "Hocus Pocus" fame. Apparently three guys decided to form a tribute band as a surprise for Thijs Van Leer and he enjoyed what he had heard so much that he decided to join them, and then said that they ought to be called Focus. The result is a new album that shows that even without the likes of Jan Akkerman they can still kick up a storm. It is a long time since I have heard any Focus and this album is the sort that makes the listener wants to go out and grab the back catalogue as soon as possible. It is the opener "Rock & Rio" that sets the stage as the band blast and funk along, with Thijs providing yodels over the top as only he can. It is fun, it grooves and has a life of its own and the band let rip when they can with guitarist Jan Dumée showing that he is quite a find. It is a mostly instrumental album, with the band on fine form, definitely hearkening back to the good old days. It is of little surprise that Thijs has high regard for his bandmates, saying, "They inspire me to explore new horizons and unknown tonalities". Whether they are rocking along or providing a more reflective air this is a very good album indeed. Just do not play the 'bonus cut' as that is banal and shouldn't have been included as it just grates.

#71, Dec 2002

FONYA

PERFECT COSMOLOGICAL PRINCIPLE

Fonya is just one man, Chris Fournier, and like label-mate Jeremy is a multi-instrumentalist although this is where the similarity ends, as Fonya has a much harder sound, although never really leaving the realms of keyboard domination. Reminiscent at times of Camel, the overall sound is rockier as there is genuine interplay between the guitars and keyboards: it definitely sounds like a band at work, not just one man. There is a very symphonic feel to the proceedings, and at times almost a wall of sound with an instrument such as bass patched against it to great effect. All of the songs are original; apart from "Delerium's Gate" where Fonya takes part of the live version of "The Gates of Delerium" which appeared on 'Yesshows'. Of course there are no lyrics in the booklet, so instead we are treated to some of the stories behind the songs such as the "Flight of the Rigel Orion" being about the space ship of the same name which was caught in the pull of the black hole Artena in the 26th Century. If you enjoy good symphonic music, then you will love this.

#50, Aug 1998

FOR ABSENT FRIENDS

RUNNING IN CIRCLES

FAF were formed in 1987 in Holland, and having released various demo tapes, a single and a mini-CD, 'Illusions', they signed to SI and released 'Both Worlds' in 1991. Still with the same line-up they have now just released their latest album, 'Running In Circles'. I hadn't heard any of their earlier CDs, only tracks that had appeared on SI compilations, so I was interested to hear just what this best-selling Dutch band were like. A.T. has a good clear voice, and it is immediately apparent that like their Dutch counterparts Wheels of Steel and Timelock, their version of prog has its feet firmly in the American AOR camp.

Some of the songs, like "A New Day", are very commercial and definitely worth listening to. However, I wish the guitar had been higher in the mix as at times it is almost sanitised out of existence. I am sure that it is the American influence that is affecting this, but it is a great shame as I am sure that Edwin Rose should be far more prominent. There are some very good points though, especially with "The Fight", which is a very strong ballad. A.T. sings of love lost, accompanied only by piano, which works very well.

After a suitable silence, there is an instrumental, "The Bald, The Fat & The Ugly", which manages to add to the previous song by its difference. Another song that works well is "Running Scared", but I may be feeling this as it is the only song on the CD I already knew, as it is on the 'SI Too' compilation. Overall this is an enjoyable album, but not a great one.

#22, Mar 1994

FOREST STREAM
TEARS OF MORTAL SOLITUDE

Forest Stream was originally formed as long ago as 1995, but this is the debut album from the Russians who have signed a four-album deal with Elitist. Among other problems, which have included equipment being stolen and rehearsal rooms destroyed, it hasn't helped that Sonm The Darkest (drums) has relocated to Holland where he is studying for his Doctorate in Physics (who says rock musicians have to be dumb?); the line-up is completed by Ungel (guitar) and Silent Anth (bass). The label is promoting this as "Symphonic, blackened doom of the highest possible quality". It may be doom Jim, but certainly not as we know it. This is extremely powerful atmospheric music that Elitist appear to be capturing the market in. It is evocative and harsh, yet also dream-like and entrancing. The band themselves say that they are trying to play the most sorrowful music in existence, and there is a depth of despair within this that is hard to explain. The emotion is never underplayed, and while the music itself is not always ramming itself into the listener's ears the feeling is always intense. The vocals are harsh and definitely inspired by Norwegian metal, but if it was sung in a different manner then I may be discussing this as an impressive prog album. So, progressive doom anyone? This is the first album in a planned trilogy, the concept being "All the sorrow, all the majesty and all the hate" with this understandably representing the sorrow. For the more adventurous rock fan, but if you want rock music that refuses to conform and is also extremely complex and emotive with many different strands then this is worth hearing.
#72, Feb 2003

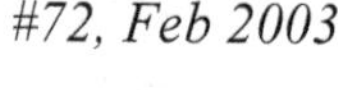

FORGOTTEN SUNS
SNOOZE

In Europe there appear to be some countries that are hotbeds for progressive rock, but others, which are fairly quiet. Portugal is certainly one of the latter, as I can't remember the last time I heard an album from there but I am currently listening to the new double CD from Forgotten Suns, which is their second album, following on from 'Fiction Edge I'. Since the release of the debut the quintet has formed their own label, built their own studio and have even recorded a video so they have certainly been busy. This is a concept album, with a story about someone who has dreams that he cannot fulfil, and then ends up working in an office job that he hates. Instead of putting up with this he decides instead to stay in bed and sleep and of course works out the meaning of his own life in the process. Unfortunately, the lyrics are not in the booklet, but instead have been included as part of the multimedia content on disc two. The booklet is the one thing that lets this release down as the music itself is of the highest order, and the vocals are strong and in English. "Dreaming Of Reality" kicks off the album, with an alarm clock giving way to an angered scream, which is then followed by an instrumental passage. This is based on the interplay between guitars and keyboards and shows that they have been paying careful attention to their Eighties prog as it mixes Marillion and IQ together and

throws in some Twelfth Night for good measure and perhaps a dash of Jadis. But what makes this album so interesting is the way that the band moves and switches, often within the same song. "Senses" could have come from Saga, and there are other areas that are much more like Dream Theater. But when you are listening to the album it is all about all of these different styles mingling and working together that make it such a treat. If this is an example of what the Portuguese progressive rock scene is like at the moment, then it is in very good health indeed.
#83, Mar 2005

JACK FOSTER III
EVOLUTION OF JAZZRAPTOR
It is always useful to read press releases, especially when the CD in question is by an unknown artist. I hadn't heard of Jack Foster, but when I saw the names of Trent Gardner and Robert Berry then I put the CD into the player and started to take notice. Trent produced this debut album, and is of course most well-known for Magellan. The album was recorded at Robert Berry's (3) studio and like Trent he could not stop himself from getting involved in most of the tracks in some way or another. This is an album that while it will appeal to many prog fans will also probably put quite a few of them off, because it actually progresses. Jack feels that music shouldn't be pigeonholed and decides to cover many bases from jazz and blues right through to more normally recognised forms of prog through to some hard rock. Of course, with Trent involved there is always the room for a trombone or two. He has a voice that is perfectly suited to blues, fairly low but with loads of emotion a la Coverdale, and this gives his songs a distinct sound. There is plenty of space, as Jack lets the songs breathe. A particular favourite is "Feel It When I Sting" where he moves through different musical styles in a way that shows that he is home in all of them. There is only one real epic, "Nirvana In The Notes", which at 14 minutes long has everything going for it, including an extremely delicate piano introduction. This was originally independently released in the States until it was picked up by Musea, and I am sure that this is not the last we have heard of Mr Foster III.
#79, May 2004

FRÁGIL
SORPRESA DEL TIEMPO
Frágil have been one of Peru's most important progressive rock bands for over twenty-five years, and to show that they are not at all pretentious this live album was recorded in 1999 with a 26-piece philharmonic orchestra. The booklet and all of the songs are in Spanish, so I can't tell you a great deal about what is going on, but I do know that the band are a five piece with Andrés Dulude on vocals and acoustic guitar (and he seems to wear quite strange make-up), César Bustamante on bass, Luis Valderrama on guitar, Octavio Castillo (keyboards, flute) and

Jorge Durand (drums). I have been racking my brains and can't think of any other South American prog bands that I have heard, the closest I can get to is Cast from Mexico, but I do know that when prog bands tour over there they get a rave reception. This is one of those annoying live albums that does fade in and out a bit (I know that it is rarely an actual concert, but I like to imagine that it is) yet the music does manage to make up for it. The crowd are obviously huge fans and on "Mundo Raro" it takes a while for Andrés to start singing just because all of the crowd are doing it for him. This is not exciting or ground breaking prog, but rather music that takes lots of influences (at one time the guitar sounded exactly the same as Gary Chandler's) such as Camel, Tull, Genesis and mixes it with a Spanish feel and local sounds to make music that is enjoyable and listenable without being hard work. The orchestra are used mostly as an extra keyboard player although it can take on a more driving edge when the brass is more to the fore. Overall while not essential it is a very pleasant album.
#70, Oct 2002

FRAMAURO
ETERMEDIA
This is another band that I heard about from Artur, a Polish act. I have heard some very good Polish prog bands in the past, most notably Collage and Quidam, but I have to honestly say that Framauro is not one of them. When they turn up the guitar and rock it a bit more then there is promise, but for the most part this is forgettable music and certainly not worth going through all the effort of trying to get it from Poland! Even allowing for the fact that they sing in Polish and not English, this is not a band I think we will hear of again. *#51, Jan 1999*

FRAMESHIFT
UNWEAVING THE RAINBOW

FRAMESHIFT
AN ABSENCE OF EMPATHY
When Henning Pauly first developed Framework, the project had three distinct goals which were 1) to record James LaBrie in new and exciting musical settings and environments, 2) bring together elements of prog rock with film scores and modern production 3) use the work of Richard Dawkins as a basis for a concept work. Henning Pauly is one of those musicians who seems to be able to play anything that he wants to, but he knows not to use programmed drums when a sweating person will do, so employs his brother Eddie Marvin as the only other musician. Henning wanted to let James really shine, and sing styles that he liked listening to, so there are some solid a cappella sections which have been inspired by Spock's Beard or Queen while at the same time there is plenty of the hard

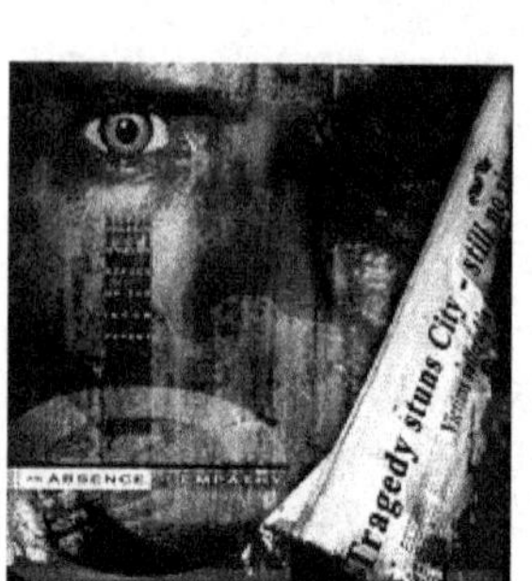

stuff also kicking around. This is a rock album first and foremost, with the guitars very much an important part of the picture but the vocals are key to the overall sound and James is at the front laying down the law. James LaBrie has many fans from his work with some outfit called Dream Theater, but here he is able to show that he has other sides to his vocals and whether it is with a power ballad, vocal harmonies, or blasting out at full power he is always in control. This is an album that I heartily recommend but what would the follow-up be like?

There are times when I look at album artwork, and think that there is no way that the music can live up to the expectations – in this case I am extremely glad to be proved wrong. This concept album is about violence, and I am sure that it is no coincidence that the cover is reminiscent (at least to me) of 'Seven'. Musically it starts with a radio being tuned (we hear a snippet of "Hotel California"), before dying away. This is replaced by some blistering runs that any shredder would be proud of: it is strange to think that all of the music on the album is played by Henning, apart from drums which are again provided by his brother Eddie Marvin. That just leaves one element, the vocals. For the first Frameshift album these were provided by James LaBrie but for this album Henning wanted someone who could also provide a more theatrical take on the music. Who better than a rock vocalist who has also performed on Broadway? Step forward none other than Sebastian Bach. "Human Grain" is one of the most powerful prog metal, melodic rock, technical rock numbers I have ever heard with the music dramatically shifting and changing while never losing the intensity, and Sebastian showing why he was at one time one of the highest rated rock singers around (I will never forget watching him running from one side of a stage to another while singing "Youth Gone Wild", what amazing breath control). This album is so intense that it may actually scare off some prog metal fans, and has to be one of the heaviest albums released that could be thought of as 'prog', but that is what it is and any proghead who also enjoys losing the dandruff will find that this just a delight from start to finish. It has to be played in its' entirety, this is not something to be dipped in and out of, and it definitely has to be played extremely loudly.

This is most definitely going to be one of my albums of the year – dramatic, powerful, rocking and proggy, who could want more? *#84, July 2005*

FRAMEWORK
NINTH IN AN OCEAN OF TIME

FRAMEWORK
PICTURE GLASS THEATRE

FRAMEWORK
A SLICE OF LIFE

In October 1990 Final Conflict were recording the excellent CD 'Redress The Balance', when drummer Arny Wheatley and keyboard player Mark Price left the band. By January 1991 they realised that they were missing out on the prog scene, and a new group was envisaged. Bassist Rob E. Harvey was the first recruit, and by

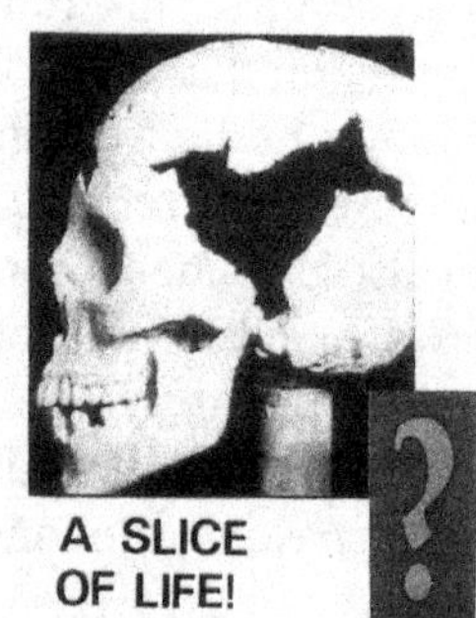

February guitarist Rob Bailey was also in the fold. Steve Jones joined as vocalist in March, and Framework was complete. After much rehearsing Framework played their first gig in June, with an hour long set of original material. Totally confident in their ability, the end of July saw them in the studio working on material for their first album. A decision was made to release some of on the songs on a mini-album, and 'Ninth In An Ocean of Time' saw the light of day in October. Available only on cassette, with a run of just 400, the album is no longer available, which would be absolutely criminal if not for the fact that four of the five songs ("Sojourn", "Toys In The Attic", "State Of Mind" and "Silent Eyes") also appear on the full-length album 'Picture Glass Theatre'. The fifth track, "Snow Trumpet", is a great powerful instrumental which only suffers from being too short! The band continued gigging and recording, but it became apparent that Steve was suffering from health problems, and a decision was taken that he would leave the band and take over as manager. The digitally recorded 'Picture Glass Theatre' saw the light of day in January this year, and at an hour in length it is a considerable achievement., especially bearing in mind that the band had only been together for ten months.

It kicks off with the great opener "Sojourn", which features some soaring vocals and keyboards. "Toys In The Attic" is far rockier, but at the same time contains some sterling piano work. Steve's vocals are distinctive, yet may not be to everyone's tastes. The songs certainly vary in style, and within each one there are often many different sections. "State Of Mind" is a prime example of this, which is a wonderfully rocky (dare I say commercial) number which contains a great switch from guitar to keyboards for the chorus. "Silent Eyes" really show Mark's use of atmospheric keyboards to wonderful effect, and yet again the song transforms and ends up as a keyboard driven rocker with some great guitar. "Cold Comfort" is more of a standard rocker with keyboards used only as an accompaniment. As always, it would be easy to list all the songs, but having played the album five or six times now, it has really grown on me and would be of interest to any prog rock fan. A week after the album was released, Framework kicked off the 'Glass Tour '92' with new singer Steve Hammersley, who is a real find for the band, in the style of Geoff Mann.

The band appear to have gone from strength to strength with the new vocalist, and a decision was made to record one of the gigs on the tour for release as a live album. Consequently, their February headlining gig at The Wheatsheaf, Stoke, was recorded and the album 'A Slice of Life' saw the light of day. Featuring twelve songs, seven of which originally appeared on 'Picture Glass Theatre', it really is an impressive album. The songs have been improved by being in a live environment, and the new vocals have worked wonders. The band are heralded onstage by the Old Spice music, and kick off with "Cold Comfort". Right from the off it is obvious that here is a very tight outfit, with great songs. It is hard to believe that the band still hadn't been together for a year, let alone with a vocalist that had been with them for less than a month! "Blindeye" is one of the songs not on the album, and I hope it is on the next as it is

an extremely powerful rocker with the band gelling and rocking the house down. Numbers like "Breaking the Child" really benefit from the new vocals, but the best song has to be the phenomenal "State Of Mind". More heavy rock than prog rock, it just has to be heard to be believed. Arny drives the band along with extremely powerful drumming and Steve puts his heart and soul into the vocals as the lads really rock out. Apparently Framework decided that the masters were not of sufficient quality to justify a CD release (they sound fine to me), so 'A Slice Of Life' is only available on cassette. One thing to note is that they have decided on a run of only 500 so get yours now! It is a tremendous work, and will appeal to all those who like their prog beefed up with great guitars. Framework are currently working on their next CD, titled 'Confidential Whispers'. I mean, they've been together nearly fourteen months now and have only released a mini-album, full-length CD and a live album haven't they!
#13, May 1992

FREE LOVE
OFFICIAL BOOTLEG VOL. 1
Recorded at Sapporo on 1st October last year, this captures Free Love with two instrumentals and two vocal tracks. They might have been better just sticking to the instrumentals, as while Hiroaki Shibata can play guitar okay, he can't sing. This is a quartet that are very much based on musical styles of the late Sixties and early Seventies, and have obviously been listening to Heep, Purple and ELP but just have not managed to quite get it all together yet. The sound does not help much, and I get the feeling that you really had to be there to appreciate it, but with some rich Hammond Organ style sounds and some great drumming this sounds as if it could be fun if it were captured correctly and Hiroaki stopped singing.
#88, Jun 2006

FREEWILL
ONE
Those mellow boys from London town, Freewill, have recently been working hard in the studio and have just come out with their debut masterpiece, 'One'. It is strange to think that this is the first time that Mark and Mike have been in the studio together since they recorded Casual Affair's 'Well, What Did You Expect?' back in 1989. The four-track tape was finally put on sale at Whitchurch last Saturday, as the band had only finished recording it the previous Sunday. The cassette inlay is a B&W photocopy, and there is a separate lyric sheet. I realise that as I write their excellent (well, I would say that) newsletter 'Whispers' then you would all expect me to rave about this. True, I think it is absolutely brilliant, but I wouldn't hesitate in telling you if I thought it was rubbish. This is not prog, Freewill have definitely moved away from that, rather it is out and out melodic hard rock by a band firing on all cylinders. Roy Keyworth (Galahad) told me how he much admired Mike's guitar playing,

and there is ample evidence here that he is a terrific and under-rated player. On top of that there is one of the heaviest rhythm sections around (various methods have been discussed on how to turn Louis, the drummer, down a bit, but all have failed) and rising above all is Mark giving the best vocal performance of his career. 'One' starts with "From The Cradle To The Grave", which is actually an old Casual number they never recorded. It starts off as fairly gentle, gradually building momentum as Steve's bass drives the song along. The production is excellent, and Louis' restrained (for him) playing really gives the feel of a rock band ready to blast out at any moment. Mike brings it all back down, slowing proceedings just so that they can all speed it up again and make it that bit heavier. Next we are treated to "Sometimes I Cry" which is a typical Freewill song with loads of changes in tempo and style, darkness and shade, and Mark singing about broken love. A short drum interlude leads into the bass solo (which is a real killer live, unlike most bass solos). "Skin Trade" is Freewill's newest and heaviest song, and here it is in all its glory. Mark spits venom into the mike and hits the high notes with ease, all the others combining behind Mike's riff to produce a song of epic proportions: something to cure your dandruff.

The guitar break means that it is really is heads down and go for it time and drives along at frantic pace, and Louis pounds the double bass drums as if there is no tomorrow. After all that has gone before, it seems only fitting that the tape ends with the slower, more balladic, "Picking Up The Pieces": definitely a song of emotion and melody, it allows the listener to relax before turning the tape over and playing it all again. 'One' has been approached in a totally professional manner, with a printed cassette (unlike a lot of bands who only print labels, if they bother) and also the four songs have been put on both sides so that there is not the bother of having to rewind it. On a personal level, I am extremely proud to be associated with guys who can produce music and magic of this high quality. If you like good melodic hard rock (without a keyboard in sight) then get 'One'.
#16, Dec 1992

SALLY FRENCH
THE OTHER SIDE

Sally has quite a voice, of that there is no doubt. She soars high, sounding at times like Kate Bush, Maryen Cairns or even Maddy Prior. However, there is far more to good music than just having a voice: good songs, now there's a starting point. Sadly, these seem to be lacking. The songs are self-penned and seem designed for Sally to show off her singing prowess rather than creating good music. The choral style favoured by Sally may have its fans, but I'm afraid that I am not really one of them. She could well have a future ahead of her, but first she needs to go back to the drawing board and make some decisions about what she is trying to achieve. With the help of someone like Clive Nolan the next album could be a lot better. It could not be much worse.
#25, Oct 1994

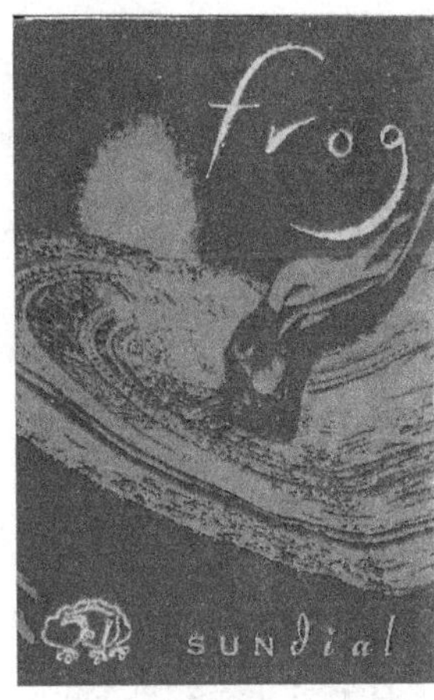

FROG
SUNDIAL
Apart from Ian (guitar), the entire band knew each other from schooldays. Wiff (keyboards) was classically taught on the piano, Wilge took up the bass as a hobby about three years ago, Martin discovered drums, so Dave said he would sing if they formed a band. This took place in early summer 1991, and it soon became apparent that they had some great ideas and songs but they needed a guitarist to carry them off.

They knew Ian from a local club, and that he could play guitar, so they gave him a recording of a few jam sessions and he agreed to join: Frog was born. The first demo tape, 'Insanity Fair', was recorded in September 1991, received favourable responses, so they went ahead, and recorded a second, 'Sundial', over two days in March this year. It contains seven songs, two of which originally appeared on the first demo and one that has been re-recorded.

Some have hailed the band as possibly the future of prog, and although I would not go quite that far, I can see what they mean. Here is a band that have managed to put together a myriad of influences and have ended up with their own peculiar brand of psychedelic progressive rock. Psychedelic? Certainly, there is little or nothing in common with bands such as Galahad or Pendragon, but far more with the alternative scene.

Of all prog bands, the one they have most in common with is probably Ozric Tentacles. It kicks off with "In The Sand", which has insistent jangling guitar. The psychedelic song builds well, with the vocals kept very much in the background. Straight from the off is the impression that the band really know what they want to achieve, and it is very well produced with stereo effects to the fore. "The Good and The Wood" starts in a far more restrained manner with a nice, gentle, opening.

This changes with strident vocals as the song gradually becomes more demented with crashing drums and screams. "Winter House" starts with a sequencer riff that is repeated throughout the song: this combines well with the gentle vocals. Nevertheless, the highlight for me is the wonderful "Insanity Fair", which starts with fairground organ-style keyboards. The song itself is very gentle and strained, but this changes into a weird drum-led entity with strange guitars and spoken vocals (employing an echo chamber), and ends with manic laughter.

Intrigued? I knew you would be. If you are more into the alternative, psychedelic side of things, then Frog are well worth discovering. They are a young band (all under twenty years old), and have a lot to offer.
#14, Jul 1992

FROG
EARTHWORKS

Way back in #14, some you may just remember me reviewing the second demo tape by young band Frog. Well, here is the third, which was recorded back in January. I think it has been available for some time, but only just have my copy. For those who were not readers back then, I described Frog as a psychedelic prog band with definite tendencies towards the prog scene. This tape seems to take this one stage further as there is even a reggae track. Frog are definitely not for the faint-hearted, as they demand listening to: this is no background or lift music. Right from the beginning and the long drawn-out intro to "Out Of The Pond" there is the very strong impression that here is something quite different. Dave has a pleasant voice, and at times, his melodic singing can sound quite strange on top of the "different" musical accompaniment. Frog produce music that can truly be said to be "prog", but they have progressed far beyond the normal Genesis clones and really have far more in common with the indie scene. There again they can produce a track that is just acoustic guitar and choral-style vocals ("Sylphen"). If you like indie, or consider yourself to have broad tastes, then this well-recorded and presented demo may be for you.

#20, Oct 1993

FROG
B AND B

This is Frog's fourth studio demo, recorded in January this year. They are a very difficult band to pin down to any particular style as sometimes they sound dreamy and very keyboard based with loads of fluidity, then at others they can be far more violent and guitar-based. Overall, 'B and B' is probably going to be their most successful demo to date, as it is definitely the easiest to listen to. Still, I find myself remembering the brilliance of the 'Sundial' demo and wishing that there were more tracks like "Insanity Fair". Very enjoyable, but it is about time they stopped messing about with demos and released a full length CD!

#22, Mar 1994

FROGFLAVOR
SPACE OF MAGIC

This is the debut album by this Japanese instrumental band comprising Hiroyuki Sekine (bass), Toru Kubota (drums) and Issei Takami (guitar). This is fusion, but at times they also bring in funk and even some King Crimson influences. According to their site there are also some heavy metal influences but I think that I must have missed those as although Issei does attack his guitar in that fashion,

sometimes it really blends into the band as a whole. The band were formed by Hiroyuki, and certainly his bass playing is a key element of the music as he has a very unfettered style and is all over the place when providing support but can also take the lead with some finger popping attack when he needs to. The overall sound is very clean, perhaps too much so, and while the music is interesting and engaging while it is playing it is only the real fusion lovers who will get a great deal out of this.
#87, Apr 2006

FROGG CAFÉ
FORTUNATE OBSERVER OF TIME
This is the third studio album from an eclectic quintet that started life as a Frank Zappa tribute outfit called Lumpy Gravy. These guys are all university trained in their music and they must be interesting to see live as this is not a regular line-up. James Guarnieri provides drums and percussion but after that it all gets a little complicated. The rest of the line-up is Bill Ayasse (electric and acoustic violins, vocals and mandolin), Steve Uh (electric and acoustic guitars, keyboards, violin), Nick Lieto (lead vocals, keyboards, piano, trumpet, flugelhorn (I have not seen one of those on a rock album for a long time!)) and Andrew Sussman who as well as providing bass and vocals is also adept on the cello. So as well as 'normal' progressive instrumentation they can add a string section or some brass to what they are performing. When these possibilities can be added to musical expertise the result can be sometimes self-indulgent but praise has to be given to these guys who have managed to avoid this trap.

The initial response on listening to the album is that they have a lot in common musically with Kansas, but it is only on proceeding further in that one realises that the comparison is not a fair one. There are times when they come across as Tull, quite a few when they come across as Zappa but they have their own style which is taking lots of bits and pieces from many different sources and putting it altogether into an album that is undeniably prog but also has more going to it that 'just' that. The use of extra instrumentation does give them a different edge to many of the bands around and this is an album that I enjoyed listening to.
#85, Nov 2005

PETER FROHMADER
ADVANCED ALCHEMY OF MUSIC
Peter has been recording since 1980, and this is his latest album, which was released last year and is an instrumental, and one that takes a lot of listening to. Although many instruments are used on this solo project, the one that takes most prominence is bass guitar, which gives the music a particular air. There is no doubt that Peter is an expert musician, but his music is not all that easy to listen to and in some ways I am reminded of The Enid as his is a very classical

approach: but The Enid never used dissonance in this way. Themes are started, sometimes repeated, and then the music goes in a very different direction. At times it could be said to be self-obsessive but is so arranged that it gives a sense of improvisation, yet is controlled, not really becoming meandering. It is an album that will be a challenge to many, and will probably appeal more to fans of Stockhausen than IQ or Genesis. Overall, this is an interesting work, but not one to listen to for pleasurable relaxation.
#31, Oct 1995

FROST*
MILLIONTOWN

This is a new band that has been put together by Jem Godfrey, and while this may appear to many to be his first foray into progressive music he has actually been around for quite a while. He formed Freefall back in 1986, and only eight weeks later they opened for IQ. Over the years they supported the likes of Galahad, Ark and Geoff Mann, but although they had three independent releases they never hit the heights and they called it a day in 1991. That did not stop his interest in music and more recently has been working on more profitable areas. So far he has successfully co-composed and co-produced pop hits, e.g. for Atomic Kitten, whose number one hit sold over two million copies alone. Apart from that he worked for Blue, Ronan Keating, Lulu and Samantha Mumba as well as scoring further chart success with Holly Vallance ("Kiss Kiss"), Atomic Kitten and Shane Ward (winner of the talent show "X-Factor"). When he decided that he needed something a little more stretching he bought a load of prog CDs and started looking for musicians. The result is that Andy Edwards and John Jowitt of IQ provide the hard-hitting rhythm section, with guitarist John Mitchell (Arena, Kino etc.) also in tow. JJ and John have always enjoyed playing together, reliving their Arena days, and it shows. Jem must have opened for JJ, either in Ark or IQ (or both), and has relived some of those Freefall days by asking John Boyes to also guest on guitars.

What I did not expect at all was the complexity and sheer brilliance of opener "Hyperventilate". It starts almost dreamily, with sounds evocative of Native American flutes before the piano tinkles in gently. Gradually Jem expands the music, playing up and down the keyboards in a gentle introduction, until a repeated sequence starts to take prominence. This builds until John comes crashing in with guitars following the same pattern then all hell breaks loose and it is off and devil take the hindmost. This is a soaring climatic instrumental with guitars and keyboards swapping roles while Andy and JJ provide total rock support. Just when you think that there can't be anymore the songs lifts, turns and then implodes on itself and falls back to piano and then it is off again. At the end of this song I was already in awe – could this be the best prog debut since Spock's Beard? The other songs show a more structured side to the band, but one that is very hard hitting and riff hungry. This is a style of music that could probably be called prog metal, but it is far removed from Threshold as the melodies are stronger and this is packed full of hooks and is totally infectious. Jem may have written all of the material but he has surrounded himself with guys that know how to deliver,

and the result is an album that may only be six songs long but this is sheer quality. If ever you doubted that the British prog scene could kick out something new and exciting, then you should know that this is just incredible. I know that they are playing some dates in Europe and are going to be at Rotherham towards the end of the year. That is a gig to miss at your peril.
#89, Sep 2006

FRUITCAKE
HOW TO MAKE IT
This is Cyclops' first overseas singing, as Fruitcake hail from Oslo. Their first album, 'Fools Tapes' sold extremely well in Norway and abroad, and on the basis of this CD I can see why. Pål Søvik (vocals, drums) and Tore Bo (bass, keyboards) are the two main songwriters, and it is obvious that they are influenced by symphonic bands like Gentle Giant, Genesis and Yes. Some linking passages are quite simplistic in their performance, yet these only highlight the complexity of others. This is an impressive album which is definitely not only enjoyable on first listen, but also improves with repeated hearing. Malcolm Parker was raving about this band to me long before I had actually got around to hearing them, and I can quite see why. If you like good music, well played, yet at the same time want relatively short songs that still have scope for great breadth and diversity (twenty-one songs on this CD) then I highly recommend Fruitcake. This is one for Pendragon, IQ fans as well as those into Pink Floyd ("Fly Away" is a dead ringer for 'Wish' period Floyd). A winner.
#26, Dec 1994

FRUITCAKE
ROOM FOR SURPRISE
Since their last album, the wonderful 'How To Make It', there have been some line-up changes in the Fruitcake camp. The two guitarists and the bassist have been replaced, and this could have interesting repercussions for their future sound. The reason for this is that departed bassist Tore Bo has co-written (with drummer Pål Søvik) all of the music except for the closing song "A Whisper". Losing a key songwriter does not always turn out to be a good idea. However, the new guitarist and bassist have slipped into position quite easily and the new album is a tasteful rendition of Floydian style prog. Guitarwork is kept to a minimum, but the usage this time seems to be better balance than before. Fruitcake is one of the top Scandinavian bands and on the basis of this album they should only get bigger and better. Three of the songs have stretched out to well over seven minutes, with "Touch The Sky" just making it to ten. Not an overly musically dramatic band, although there are some useful guitar and bass riffs in "Hunting Old Ladies", and they have managed to produce an album that is interesting and while it will not set the world alight it is a step in the right direction.
#36, Aug 1996

FRUITCAKE
A BATTLE A DAY...

The full title of this their sixth CD is 'A Battle A Day Keeps The Doctor Away', and when the opening song is called "Mopery and Dopery in Deep Space" then you could be forgiven for thinking that Fruitcake really had become as nutty as one. But, in their defence, this is actually a very accomplished classic Genesis-style album. Pål Søvik's vocals are very clear with no accent and while they appear to be happy to spend much of their time locked in the early Seventies is that really a problem? One of the joys of Fruitcake is the way that they can go from gentle acoustic-based song to blast then back again all within the space of a few bars, as can be heard on "One Night" when bass pedals dynamically change the whole feel of the music. This is music that is all about space, about letting the instruments having enough room to find their natural balance. While it is not often that they really let rip no-one can accuse Fruitcake of not having passion. This is a pleasant prog album that takes little effort to listen to.
#65, Dec 2001

FRUITCAKE
MAN OVERBOARD

This is the seventh studio album from Fruitcake, and again they have proved that they are one of the top European prog bands. Although this is very much a band of the present, their music would not have sounded out of place in the Seventies. One thing that is unusual is that within the seven-piece they have three guitarists but these guys are laying down patterns as opposed to blasting out riffs. New member Ketil Vestrum Einarsen has made an impact with some beautiful flute work, and Pål Søvik's vocals are as dramatic as ever. In some ways the music does have a Floydian bent, but in others they could be compared to Jadis in a serious mood. When these guys decide they want to take off the music is incredibly passionate and intense but they are as much at home with passages that are thoughtful and almost contemplative. Malcolm Parker has been praising this band forever, and his belief has been more than justified with this album. Apparently it is also available as a limited edition containing a second disc of rarities.
#82, Jan 2005

FUGATO ORCHESTRA
NEANDER VARIATIONS

In 2000 Balás Alpár put together the Fugato Orchestra to blend symphonic instruments with drums, bass and synths. Not bad for someone who at the time was only aged 17. Just four years later the debut album was released which brings together not only symphonic style 'classical' pieces but also brings in jazz and rock. Including Balás himself, there are 26 musicians involved in this project and the

scoring alone for someone so young is some achievement. That the music is very enjoyable indeed on top of all that is a real added bonus. While it is obvious that he has been influenced by country mates After Crying, I also feel that he has been listening to some of the orchestrations of ex-Tull keyboard player David Palmer as there is a very similar feel and deftness of touch to what he has produced here. The music is accessible and very enjoyable indeed, moving lightly through without ever being too overbearing or pompous. The result is an album that works well both in foreground and background and is well worthy of investigation. As well as the 15 songs on the CD there is also a multimedia section, which includes MP3's, photos and videos.
#88, Jun 2006

THE FUTURE KINGS OF ENGLAND
THE FUTURE KINGS…
This is the debut album by TFKOE but they have already been kicking up a storm with their demo, and anything that gets huge and massive praise from the mighty Organ is likely to be something special. The band has said that they want to bring together the likes of 'Ummagumma' period Floyd with Ash Ra Tempel: that they achieve this and more on tracks such as "10.66" is beyond debate (I love the way it climaxes and then just finishes, dead). This trio (along with producer and guest keyboard player Steve Mann) have created a progressive album that is going to be making huge waves among the progressive underground. It starts with the abdication speech of Edward VIII, but for a band that want to sound like a ghost falling down the stairs they manage to make somewhat more noise. They certainly have a presence normally accorded to the likes of early IQ, but they have brought a solid slab of rock based early Seventies prog into being in the 21st century and they ought to be getting a lot of praise for it. This is quite different instrumental music to anything else that is out there at the moment, and progheads in the UK need to get behind them so that they do not suffer the long drawn out death of pub gigs. These guys are good and the album is extremely solid.
#84, July 2005

THE FYREWORKS
THE FYREWORKS
The Fyreworks have been put together by Danny Chang (guitar, backing vocals) and Rob Reed (keyboards, guitars, backing vocals – also known as Cyan). The other musicians are Andy Edwards (lead vocals, guitar - also in Ezra), Tim Robinson (drums) and Doug Sinclair (bass). There are also some guest musicians providing flute, sax, violin, cello and oboe. They say that they are attempting to bring together the feel of classic Genesis and classic Yes, but they have also lifted huge chunks of Tull-style instrumentation and I think probably it is this that has put me off the album as a whole. During the opening song, "Master Humphries Clock", there are guitar parts that sound

as if they belong on 'Trick Of A Tail' but whole passages that belong on 'A Passion Play', or 'Thick As A Brick'. I also feel that at times Andy is definitely straining to hit notes, which has a detrimental effect on the whole. The result is that I cannot get into what is undoubtedly a very clever piece of work. I am sure that someone who has not discovered early 70's albums (and let's face it, it's twenty-five years since 'Thick'), or knows that Genesis was once a real band, will find that this album is a masterpiece. It is a real shame that I cannot say the same.
#41, Apr 1997

THE GAK OMEK
RETURN OF THE ALL-POWERFUL…

For The Gak Omek read Robert Burger, who is an incredibly talented guitarist and 'Return Of The All-Powerful Light Beings' is an "instrumental progressive interpretation of ancient and modern mysteries". Keyboard player David Cashin (who does also play on one other) and drummer Glenn Robitaille join him on the fifteen-minute-long title track, but apart from that, the whole album is just Robert on guitars, guitar synth and digital drums. The album is experimental and is challenging boundaries without being too avant-garde, it is possible to be taken into the world of The Gak Omek and question what is going to happen next and where the journey is going to lead but at all times it makes musical sense and is not a voyage into self-indulgence. Many people have been saying that this is one of the top progressive rock releases of 2004 – I am not sure if I would go that far, but that then is down to personal taste and also into the discussion of the definition of the term 'progressive rock'. What I do know is that as far as guitar instrumental albums goes this is certainly one of the most interesting and enjoyable that I have come across. While Robert can play quickly when he wants to, fluidity is stressed more highly and the result is something that can be played and listened to on many levels.
#84, July 2005

GALAHAD
IN A MOMENT OF MADNESS

GALAHAD
NOTHING IS WRITTEN

In 1986 Galahad were formed by guitarist Roy Keyworth and were originally a seven-piece with two keyboard players, playing a mix of original material and covers such as "Kayleigh", "Forgotten Sons" and "Afterglow". In July 1987, they recorded their first single, "Dreaming From The Inside" and "The Opiate", with Jennifer Rush producer Gary Jones. The line-up was now Roy Keyworth, Stu Nicholson (vocals), Nick Hodgson (keyboards), Mike Hooker (keyboards), Paddy O'Callaghan (drums) and Paul Watts (bass). They

continued gigging, supporting bands such as Haze, Ark and IQ. In 1988, the band nearly suffered a major loss as Stu was shortlisted by Marillion as replacement for Fish, but luckily, (for Galahad) he lost out. In April 1989 they released a mini-album cassette, called 'In a Moment Of Madness' with an amended line-up as Spencer Luckman had replaced Paddy on drums and Mark Andrews was now the sole keyboard player.

'In a Moment Of Madness' is one of the best prog rock albums of all time, not bad for a debut, eh? It starts with "One For The Record", which showcases the bands many talents. It is a song of many parts, but at all times driven along by Roy's guitar and Mark's great keyboards. The rhythm section is as tight as you could wish, and Stu's clear pure voice soars above it all. The song itself is about Gabriel's reunion with Genesis at Milton Keynes and contains many Genesis references such as "Rael rise from your aerosol guise, what a surprise, from your fox in a frock on the rocks". When one line finishes with words "just like a flower" a voices says "a flower?", a wonderful tongue-in-cheek reference to "Supper's Ready". Next up is "Second Life", which shows a different side of the band, and it must be said that Stu sings like Geddy Lee in this song, and it does sound as if it could have been cut by Rush. "Parade" is more keyboard dominated and shows Stu singing in yet another style. The bands strengths are that they are never content to rest with one melody and divide the songs repeatedly. Just when you are thinking how "pleasant" the song is, there is a keyboard passage that is totally dominated by some furious drumming and then it is back to the song, then another instrumental, then a new melody and finally back to the original. This is not the work of a new band, but of one very confident in their songwriting and musical ability. "Earth Rhythm" and "Lady Messiah" are yet more examples of their commercial AOR prog rock sound. In fact, I cannot see how anyone into melodic rock can fail to fall in love with this album.

The album was released on their own Avalon label, and to date has sold more than four thousand copies – not bad for a band that still plays support at the Walthamstow Standard! Kerrang! awarded the album 3K's, but it was worth far more. National gigging continued but with a far greater emphasis on original material. The band set up a free information service, 'The Ivory Tower', and a range of merchandise became available for the band's ever-increasing following. Paul Watts left to be replaced by Tim Ashton, and in August 1989 Galahad recorded a five-track session for independent radio station 2CR as well as interviews for 2CR and Radio Solent. 1990 was spent recording and writing new material, whilst continuing gigging and building on their word of mouth success. 1991 started with them supporting Pendragon at The Marquee, and in February Galahad played their first headline gig in Paris to tremendous response. Also, a song from the forthcoming CD, "The Automaton", was selected as an entry in the Friday Rock Show's "Rock Challenge". The song polled the highest number of votes ever recorded for the competition, and they sailed through winning the heat and subsequent final, which gained them a recording session at the BBC Maida Vale studios. This was recorded with new member Karl Garrett, who replaced Mark Andrews about a week before. It featured "Face To The Sun", and "Room 801" from the new album, and

"One For The Record" from 'In A Moment of Madness'. This session has just been re-broadcast by popular request.

The new and much awaited album, 'Nothing is Written' was released on Avalon in May 1991. It contains eleven songs and is more than an hour in length. The increase in time and space for ideas has certainly enabled the band to spread their songs, and while the familiar Galahad trademarks of great musicianship and diversification with Stu's clear vocals are present, there is also more depth and content. It's modern in a sense that is sadly lacking from some of the prog rock bands around, yet also harks back to the great days (well, I think they were great), when Genesis, ELP, Roxy Music, King Crimson, Jethro Tull etc. were the flavour of the day. It kicks off with "Face To The Sun", which has a beautiful keyboard-led atmospheric introduction. Stu's clear vocals take on a harsher edge as Roy's guitar kicks the song into gear. As one of the longer songs on the album (at nearly eight minutes) it gives the band the chance to spread their wings, which they do with great enthusiasm and musical skill. As with their debut album, every song has different melodies and counter melodies and such diversity of style so as to amaze the listener. "Chamber of Horrors" is a relaxing interlude, at least until Roy wraps his Gibson into overdrive and guns it like a good 'un. There is so much you can could say about this album, like "Aqaba" has a wonderful catchy hook, or that "Richelieu's Prayer" is a wonderful example of their great lyrics. I played "Motherland" to a friend who exclaimed "That sounds like a Nineties version of Uriah Heep" and I understood what he meant, as the keyboards really drive the song along: this is rock to be proud of. It ends with a wonderful over the top blast of sound: there is a small gap, and an amazed voice says "blimey". It is difficult to put into words, but it is like a pool of sound with no bottom, the more you look the more there is to see. Although it is only available on CD at present, there are also plans to release it on cassette in the near future. It has sold more than a thousand copies to date, with little or no major publicity. Galahad officially launched the album at a headline gig at the Bournemouth International Centre, and have since followed it up with gigs with both Ark and Geoff Mann as well as well as some smaller headline gigs of their own.

I hope that you will feel intrigued enough to search out material by Galahad. Prog rock hasn't received the attention from the media in recent years that it deserves and consequently many great bands have either disbanded or continued at a level that us far beneath their talents. Galahad deserve far more than this.
#10, Oct 1991

GALAHAD
DREAMING FROM THE INSIDE
Some of you have written to thank me for introducing you to the great music of Galahad. For those of you who have yet to purchase 'Nothing is Written', then all I can say is that you really are missing out on a superb album. This small piece is just to bring you up to date on happenings down in deepest Dorset. Stu and I have exchanged a few letters recently, and he even managed to dust off some copies of

their single "Dreaming From The Inside". Released in 1987, the songs were written when they first formed in 1985, but the lyrics can be traced back to 1982 when Stu was supposed to be studying Economics and History but found lyric writing more interesting. The songs were recorded when Galahad had two keyboard players and the heavy use of Mellotron and Genesis-style guitar puts the songs nearer the Seventies than the Nineties. Personally I feel that both "Dreaming…" and "The Opiate" are real gems. Sometimes it is interesting to get hold of a band's first recordings solely to see how they have improved and changed, but although Galahad have changed since these first saw the light of day they are definitely worth getting in their own right. I do not know how many copies Stu has left, but at just £2 they are well worth getting.

Moving onto more recent events, Galahad have just released a new cassette. When I say 'released' I mean that it is all planned and going ahead but unfortunately there have been technical problems in the duplicating, but it is hoped to be available soon. To give them their dues they have sent out apologies to all who have sent cheques, and have not banked them yet. The cassette contains a mixture of rare studio and live tracks so I know it is worth getting. They have just been in the studio recording four new songs to use as demo to try and get some major record label interest, and if this fails they plan to use them on their next self-financed cassette. One record company seems to have shown interest, and it looks like they have a secured a single deal, but the only problem is that it is in Belgium of all places! Finally, onto live dates, it is rumoured that Galahad are going to be supporting Pendragon on their European tour, but I have yet to have it confirmed. I do know that they are supporting Suzi Quatro (!) at the Walthamstow Standard on December 20th, and are headlining there on January 31st with Casual Affair in support.
#11, Dec 1991

GALAHAD
THE CHRISTMAS LECTURE

Long gone are the days when I could say anything constructive about Galahad. I love their music, and they are really nice guys to boot. What we have here is a tape that was recorded at the Whitchurch gig on December 12th last year, reviewed in #17. It was a very special night, being Galahad's Christmas gig, and they played some numbers that had not been aired for some years, along with a brand new song and some covers. Overall, it made for a fantastic night that was enjoyed by all present. The tape has not been edited, so if you were there that night then this is what you would have heard. It was recorded onto DAT so there was no opportunity to 'clean up' proceedings. Personally, I think the guitar could have been a little higher in the mix at times, but it still comes through with considerable force. It is always difficult to review a live tape, especially if it was recorded at a gig you were present at, but I'll try. The one major fault I noticed was the omission of "Exorcising Demons": the song has become one of the highlights of the set since its' first live airing last

April. I said this to Stu at the time, and he told me that they had to drop some songs from the set to make room for the "specials". Why not just play for two hours? As it is, this is a long tape, but it should have been longer. Galahad were on fine form that night, and I heartily recommend this tape to anyone who has yet to sample the delights of Galahad. Old, new, covers, the fourteen songs show just what is great about the current prog scene as the band move from one style to another with seeming ease. The highlight had to be the set closer, when "The Knife" segued into "One For The Record" and the crowd went mad. This tape is available for the measly sum of £5.50. Buy it! *#18, May 1993*

GALAHAD
IN A MOMENT OF COMPLETE MADNESS

Many, many moons ago, I was lent a copy of 'Nothing Is Written' by Galahad and I was so impressed that I wrote to the contact address and purchased their earlier tape 'In A Moment of Madness'. In the letter I mentioned Feedback and young Mr. Nicholson wrote back. It all seems so long ago! I reviewed the tape in a feature I wrote on Galahad back in #10, where I said it was "one of the best prog-rock albums of all-time". Now, #10 came out in October 1991 and much water has passed under the bridge since then and many more prog CDs have come to my attention. What would I feel about the album in 1993? Voiceprint Records decided to re-release the tape in CD form, and to increase the length Galahad went into the studio to record three of their older tracks, namely "Painted Lady", "Ghost of Durtal" and "Welcome To Paradise". All the tracks were then remixed for the CD by Tony Arnold. Full lyrics are included, as are the membership details because the original tape used two different bass players (neither of which played on 'Nothing Is Written') and since 'NIW' came out both the bassist and keyboard player have changed again.

The running order has stayed the same with the three 'new' tracks at the end. This means that the CD starts with "One For The Record" which tells the story of the Genesis reunion gig at Milton Keynes in the early '80's. Straight away the listener is taken into the wonderful world of Galahad. It is strange on hearing this to think that it is four years since it was recorded. It is still a firm live favourite and is often an encore where it drives along with Roy's guitar really over the top. It must be said that this is not the case here, but the band hadn't even played it live when it was recorded. Tony has done a great job, and it is difficult to believe that it was recorded on a limited budget that long ago. "Second Life" shows a different side of the band, with the riffing kept to a minimum and the guitar working well with the backdrop of swirling keyboards. "Parade" is up next, and a long build-up with a heavy dominance on keyboards is rewarded with the guitar livening up proceedings. Galahad's great strength is that they write accessible melodic rock songs, and there are many people out there who would really enjoy this if they just listened to it without the "prog" label. Spencer's drumming really comes through in this track and over the whole CD the drum sound is superb without being overbearing. "Earth Rhythm" definitely benefits from being on CD as Roy's riffing guitar goes from one speaker to another. The heaviest track on the CD, there is plenty of light and shade. “Lady Messiah” starts off very atmospherically and shows off Galahad’s pomp and majesty.

“Painted Lady”, the first of the bonus songs, is a very delicate (mostly) acoustic track, relying on Stu to provide strong yet beautiful vocals. “Ghost of Durtal” is atmospheric and lulling in the extreme and there is one part where Karl’s keyboards rose up and takes the song into a totally different area, and then provides a backdrop for Roy to place a wonderful guitar solo against. “Welcome To Paradise” brings the CD to a close, and yet again is full of atmosphere, although not as laid back as some of the others. Karl uses a totally different keyboard sound from the rest of the album, which helps transform the overall sound. The first pressing of the CD has sold out already, more than a month before it is officially launched in the UK! When it is repressed it will be available in all good record shops. It is still a brilliant album, and for those who have bought the original tape then it is still an essential purchase. What with the live tape, this CD, and hopefully a new album later in the year, this is a busy time for Galahad. Now could not be a better time for discovering the real joy and pleasure of their music.
#19, Aug 1993

GALAHAD
VOICEPRINT RADIO SESSIONS
Here at long last is the radio sessions CD from Galahad. For one reason or another it seems to have taken forever to come out; I actually heard these songs last Summer when Stu played them to me, but finally the CD has arrived. Of the three tracks, the first two are very old numbers that have been recorded for this set, while the third is an instrumental which has been re-recorded for the new album, ‘Sleepers’. “Aries” kicks off proceedings, and is one of Galahad’s longer songs at over ten minutes in length. Karl takes quite a prominent role in this, as there is a large emphasis on keyboards. Roy and Neil are certainly not as much for the fore as normal and I am sure that this is because it is such an old song. Galahad have changed a lot since they wrote this, both musically and in membership. “The Chase” is also a gentle number with acoustic guitar and long held-down keyboard chords. Even when Roy takes over proceedings with electric guitarwork the sound is fairly laid back. However, as the song develops gradually the guitar comes more to the fore. Stu’s singing is pure and clear as ever, and it is his voice that dominates these two songs for the most part. Closer “Learning Curve” could not be more different, and really shows off the newer heavier side of Galahad. From the chunky bass opening, Roy and Karl get in there with real venom: power chords underpin the melody from Karl, while Neil and Spencer nail the rhythm section to the floor. The song just builds and builds, with Roy providing some great widdly-widdly; this then leads to dynamic stuff from Karl, who is joined by Roy and the rest as they power their way through. “Learning Curve” is, in my opinion, easily the best song recorded by Galahad to date. Unfortunately, because of this the other two suffer somewhat, but on the whole this is a good album which is being sent free to members of the Galahad fan club.
#23, May 1994

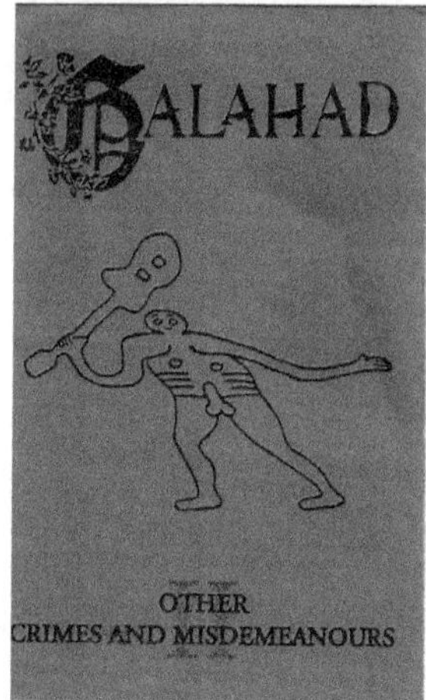

GALAHAD
OTHER CRIMES AND MISDEMEANOURS II

This cassette release is free to members of Galahad's fan club, 'Room 801', and follows on from the release three years ago of 'Other Crimes And Misdemeanours', and each is an attempt to make available recordings that previously hadn't seen the light. 'OCM II' has the results of four sessions, and background information has been provided for each. The first session resulted in their debut single, of which only 500 were pressed, and the two songs are here in slightly remixed form. They re-recorded "Dreaming From The Inside" for the Galahad Acoustic Quintet CD earlier this year. Such is the strength of the writing that some of these songs, such as "Reach Into The Flames" from the second session, just beg to be made available on CD. It blasts through with some great guitar before the more reflective bridge. This tape also includes a totally different version of "Painted Lady" to that which appeared on the 'In A Moment of Complete Madness' CD, as well as the four tracks that appeared on the 'Suffering In Silence' promo tape from four years ago. "Rollercoaster", which appeared on a free flexi from Fatea was one of these. Any Galahad fan will be happy to have these songs in their collection.

#30, Aug 1995

GALAHAD
SLEEPERS

There were times when I felt that this album would never see the light of day, and I'm sure that the band felt that way as well. The problems they had with the recording would fill the pages of an issue of Feedback all on their own. Still, that is all water under the bridge now, and at long last here is the official follow-up to their 1991 debut 'Nothing Is Written'. Back then they had won the Radio 1 Rock Show Rock War with the highest number of votes ever, and their CD had garnered a lot of acclaim. Now it is 1995 and a lot has been expected and asked of 'Sleepers'. Could it, would it, stand up to all the pressure? Many of these songs seem like old friends to me, as I have heard some of them played many times in concert, which in turn has made this one of the most difficult albums I have ever had to review. Still, it's a horrible job but someone has to do it. Kicking off with the title track, more than twelve minutes in length, Galahad manage to encapsulate what to me are all of their good points. Lyrically very strong with great vocals from Stu, the music shifts and moves in many styles and fashions. Bassist Neil Pepper is the newest member of the band, and his playing has added a certain depth to the overall sound, working well with Spencer's drumming. Roy's guitarwork is as powerful as ever, and he seems to be more content to provide power chords as well as plenty of widdly-widdly and interplay with keyboardist Karl Garrett. "Julie Anne" totally changes images, as Stu proves that he can sing gently and softly in the ballad form as well as belt it out. "Live and Learn" typifies the difference between the new and old Galahad, as it is the second part, the instrumental "Learning Curve" that proves the point as it belts along. 'NIW' is a great album to which I often return, but even by the third track in, the impression is that Galahad have really grown as a band. "Dentist Song" is a wonderfully tongue in cheek story of a visit to a dentist! Extremely catchy with a great hook, it goes to show that you really can produce great fun songs. It lightens proceedings, who says that prog can't be good time? "Pictures of Bliss" is an acoustic number, only two minutes long, which manages to transform the whole feel of what is going on. Songs do not have to be long to be beautiful.

"Before, After and Beyond" starts with a chant (which I'm sure I do not remember from gigs), but then we're up and bouncing along. This again has an extremely catchy chorus and works extremely well. Next is the highlight of the album, namely "Exorcising Demons". I was there at The Astoria countless moons ago when they played this for the first time, and I was just stunned by what I heard that night. This is Galahad at their ultimate best. It starts with moody swirling keyboards, to which are added gentle vocals. These get slightly harsher, the piano makes an entry, and then the bass starts the riff. The guitar picks this up, and as Stu gets ever more menacing, the momentum increases. Suddenly the music stops dead to let Stu shout the chorus line, and then it is back into the melee. True, it is not quite as manic as when played live, but the time changes and sheer brute force of Prog ROCK just drive it along. Every time I play it I keep turning it up just that little bit so by the time it finishes not only are the neighbours complaining, but their neighbours as well (only a slight exaggeration). "Middleground" is a lighter number, although again with hidden power, which allows the listener to recover from "Demons" and enjoy another side of Galahad. This is the one that concentrates on passion to prove the point instead of blasting violence and volume. Closing the album is "Amaranth", second in length only to "Sleepers", and is a return to Galahad's strongest areas as they play ballad against rocker and combine it with emotion and time changes to provide music of the very highest order. I, and many others, have been waiting for 'Sleepers' for a long time but the wait has definitely been worth it. If you have yet to discover the joys of the underground UK progressive rock movement then the starting point is here.
#30, Aug 1995

GALAHAD
CLASSIC ROCK LIVE

Released in conjunction with the Classic Rock Society, this is a recording of Galahad's gig at Rotherham on 22nd April 1995, and is the only Galahad live CD to date. There are no overdubs whatsoever, so what hear on the CD is what you would have got if you were there on the night. There are eight songs, and only two of these are from the latest album 'Sleepers' (wot? No "Exorcising Demons"?), although this had not been released at the time. I have said before that I feel that the sound of Galahad changed with Neil Pepper joining on bass. Just listen to the bass work on "The Automaton" and be amazed. He was badgered by the rest of the guys to provide a short bass solo and it could do with being ten times longer, as it is just phenomenal. I have always liked Stu's singing and again he proves himself a great frontman with some

wonderful emotion. He lives what he is singing and really shines on "Sleepers" and "Room 801", and with Roy doing the widdly-widdly, Karl on keyboards and Spencer keeping it all in time they provide a good show. There is no substitute to catching these guys live but if you find that difficult then the CD is worth investigating.
#35, June 1996

GALAHAD
DECADE

GALAHAD
OTHER CRIMES & MISDEMEANOURS II

'Decade' is basically a greatest hits package that has been put together by the German Bluestone label. Galahad were approached to see if they were interested in the idea, and the track listing has been agreed by the band and the label, although obviously with any compilation there are inclusions and omissions that can be argued about. No "One For The Record", no "Parade", no "Aqaba", but room has been made for some of the longer songs such as the brilliant "Exorcising Demons" and "Amaranth", while some of the earlier songs such as "Ghost Of Durtal" also make an appearance.

The lyrics to all nine songs are included and overall this is quite a good introduction to the wonderful world of Galahad. If you have yet to discover the joys of one of our top prog bands then start here. But, if you have been following their music with interest then it will be the second CD that will probably be of more interest to you.

Back in 1992, Galahad released a warts 'n' all compilation called 'Other Crimes and Misdemeanours' which included demos and live versions of songs that had never been officially released. It went so well that a decision was made to release a follow-up tape, consisting of four sessions, which duly came out in 1995. Now, two years later, 'Other Crimes and Misdemeanours II' has been released on CD. I have to confess to a somewhat biased view of this album as I have written the introduction in the booklet, but do not let that stop you from discovering some fine songs. Both numbers from their limited edition single are here in remixed form, as well as some other gems such as the three-minute prog experiment "Rollercoaster".

So, two compilations, neither featuring 'new' material but both are worth investigating all the same. If you can't wait for the new songs (writing is going well with the new keyboard player) then discover some of the older joys of Galahad.
#42, July 1997

GALAHAD
FOLLOWING GHOSTS

This is the dawn of a new era for the Galahad: it seems like an age since their last studio album, 'Sleepers', but at long last they have returned with new keyboard player Dean Baker (Karl had to leave as he no longer had the time to devote to the band). This is also the last recording to feature guitarist and founder member Roy Keyworth who has left the music business and has bought himself a jet bike instead! So, with all of the personnel changes it somehow seems fitting that Galahad have produced an album that is going to surprise a lot of people, and probably disappoint some of them as well. That is not to say that it is a bad album, far from it, as I think that it is the best thing they have ever done, but this is not the same band that produced 'Nothing Is Written' and won the Radio 1 Rock Wars. This is a band that has come of age and matured like a fine wine (although it has to be said that while I find the spoken beginning funny each time I hear it, I can imagine some people finding it juvenile). "Myopia" kicks off with some of the densest riffing they have ever attempted, and already Dean is making his presence felt. A new drummer or bassist can make some difference to the overall sound, a new guitarist even more so, a new keyboard player can put a totally different perspective on proceedings not only by what he does or does not do in the way of musical notes, but also what sounds he uses to play those notes, Each keyboard player is different, and although it is too early to say if Dean is a better musician than Karl, he has a different way of doing things. So, there is one change to the Galahad sound, but what is more noticeable is the lack of "prog" as viewed by many. This is an album that is not only extremely strong and broad-based lyrically; it is also very deep in terms of music. With guest musicians providing flute, clarinet and violin, as well as some backing vocals, along with a new way of approaching music, this is an album that I have enjoyed and found much more in every time I have played it. Some songs are short and fairly simple, with "Perfection Personified" with its upbeat tempo probably more in common with the older Galahad material than most. "Bug Eye" at fourteen minutes is about the embryo inside the mother, while closer "Shine" is also fourteen minutes long and with three parts is one of their more epic pieces. I know that some people will wish that this had more songs like "Aqaba" or "Parade" but Galahad have progressed in the truest sense of the word, with an album that hits many musical bases and is the better for it. I ought to make a special mention of the booklet, which is also outstanding. I know that my mate Artur in Poland has already made this his "Album of the Year", and who am I to disagree? *#50, Aug 1998*

GALAHAD
OTHER CRIMES.. III

This album brings together many bits and pieces, some of which have been heard before, but none easily available and are taken from four distinct sessions. The first of these contains three songs that were released on a CD EP, with the ten-minute "Aries" a real winner. How it did not appear on 'Madness' or 'Written' is a mystery, as the song is at least as strong as those that did. "The Chase" is a song that they

have often played live but not recorded before this. The use of acoustic guitar by Roy adds a quite different feel to the song that is mainly slow and keyboard based. "Learning Curve" is a different version of the instrumental that later appeared on "Sleepers" and to my ears has more power and atmosphere. When they won the Radio 1 Rock War they recorded a session of three songs, which were later played on the Friday Rock Show. Of the three the best is "One For The Record", which has always been a firm favourite of mine, telling the story of the Genesis reunion gig at Milton Keynes. "Exorcising Demons" did not make it onto 'Classic Rock Live' due to lack of room (something that I was quite upset about at the time as to my ears it is one of their finest songs ever), but at long last it makes an appearance here, recorded at the same gig in Rotherham. The last three songs are all numbers that they have recorded for various tribute albums. Of these I will always feel a special connection to their version of "The Ceiling Speaks" as I was asked to see if they were prepared to record it. A song they had played many times in concert, they were once joined by the mighty Geoff Mann to perform it, although here having the snare drum too high in the mix spoils it. If, like me, you are waiting to hear what the new Galahad album is going to be like then satiate your appetite with some rare numbers.
#65, Dec 2001

GALAHAD
YEAR ZERO

A mere four years since 'Following Ghosts' and Galahad are back with a new album. There have been a few problems in between (like losing their bassist, some people are so careless) but it has been well worth the wait as not only is this their first concept album but they have also spread their musical wings very far indeed. In fact, it takes until nearly halfway through the second track for the album to become recognisable as Galahad, as they are utilising the talents of Dean on keyboards to take the music in a new direction. When Roy starts riffing it soon becomes clear that this is the old band with many new ideas. These ideas have even allowed John Wetton to sing a few lead lines, which certainly confuses the ear as he is quite different to Stu, but is trying to sing in Stu's style. It would be easy to fall into the cliché and say that this is the album where Galahad have grown up, yet in many ways that is very true. They have decided to start with a clean palette and have brought many new styles and colours to their sound, so many that at times it is hard to think that this is the same band that brought us 'Nothing Is Written'. Except of course it is not. They have been through a few keyboard players and bassists since then, and everyone has got older, and that is reflected in the music that is far more mature and thoughtful. There is space, which allows the music to live and breathe. That is not to say that this is a sit back and relax mellowed out album, but rather one where ideas and energy have been allowed to flow and grow. "Charlotte Suite" is a short instrumental interlude and is instantly recognisable as Galahad, yet on the following "Haunted" it is only Stu's distinctive vocals that mark it out as being by them. I enjoyed this album the first time that I played it (well, I have been singing this band's praises almost as long as I have been running Feedback), yet playing it again and again I have been able to get

much more out of it. It may not be as immediate as some, but this is a prog album that cries out to be heard
#70, Oct 2002

GALAHAD ACOUSTIC QUINTET
NOT ALL THERE

This is an offshoot project of Galahad brought about by the desire of wanting to work on some old songs in a new way, and also wanting to make some product available (the problems Galahad have encountered with 'Sleepers' could fill an issue of Feedback on its own!). Stu Nicholson (vocals), Roy Keyworth (guitars) and Spencer Luckman (drums) have been joined by Mark Andrews (keyboards) and Sarah Quilter (flute, clarinet and sax). One thing that is a little unusual is that Mark used to be keyboard player with Galahad, and was with them when they recorded the mighty debut CD 'Nothing Is Written' but currently is not with the band: Neil Pepper (bass) also joins them on a few tracks. Of the thirteen songs, some are very old Galahad numbers but there are also some new ones, including instrumentals and a solo vocal ("Shrine") from Stu. Although many of the tracks are performed by GAQ, others only feature one or more members. Mark's solo "Melt", shows some wonderfully restrained piano and keyboard work that really makes one ask why he is not more active on the recording scene. "Mother Mercy" and "Through The Looking Glass" are two of the old numbers that really benefit from the different approach, as the songs seem to grow in stature with the more acoustic outlook. However, there is one real stunner on this album. Back in 1987 Galahad released a single, "Dreaming From The Inside", when they had two keyboard players, and only Stu and Roy remain from those days. It has only ever been available on the single, but it has now been re-recorded and a gem it is as well. I have always liked it, and the delicate piano and vocals are just superb. It is great to see Galahad return with such a pleasant CD although whether it will gain them any new fans I'm not sure, but anyone who likes Galahad will love the Galahad Acoustic Quintet. Buy this now and psyche yourself up ready for the release of 'Sleepers' in April.
#27, Feb 1995

GALLEON
LYNX

Galleon were formed in 1981 as KG 299, in Ljusdal, Sweden. By 1985 the band was a trio with Göran Fors (bass, vocals), Dan Fors (drums) and Micke Varn (guitar). A decision was taken by the band to bring in synthesisers to help obtain a more expressive and powerful sound: they changed their name to Aragon, and released a demo. During 1989 Micke relocated to Stockholm and the band was put on ice, but in 1990 they did some gigs to good reception. In September 1991 they went to Wavestation Studio in Ljusne to commence the recording of the debut CD.

It was delayed for four months because Dan suffered an accident at work, but 'Lynx' was eventually completed in June 1992. By the autumn, they had changed their name again, this time because of the Australian Aragon, so 1993 sees the band with a new name and a debut CD to promote. So what is it like? 'Lynx' has keyboards provided by Micke and Göran, and they are very much an integral part of the overall sound. There are eight songs, with the shortest being nearly six minutes in length, and the longest more than fourteen. They are well structured, with English lyrics, and makes me think of a proggy U2 meeting Rush. Certainly, Göran's voice sounds like Bono at times while there are enough time and mood changes to satisfy the hardened progger, with at times a good dose of electric guitar. Never a really heavy band, they manage to provide many contrasts to keep the listener interested. You can tell that it is a European as opposed to British release, and also some of the lyrics do not really stand up to close scrutiny. For example, in the opener "Untouchable" (which is one of my favourites), they use "F***ing". Now, I am no prude and also relate to many hard rock bands where swear words are used and do not sound out of place. Unfortunately, here it is used in a false manner and it makes me grate my teeth whenever I hear it. That aside, this is very listenable and I found it a very enjoyable CD.
#18, May 1993

GALLEON
HERITAGE & VISIONS

Back in #18 I reviewed Galleon's first release, 'Lynx', and they have now expanded from a trio to a four-piece with the addition of Uffe Pettersson on keyboards. I can't believe how much they have changed over the course of only a year as the Galleon on display here are totally different to the Galleon that released 'Lynx'. Here is a band in control of what they are doing as the songs have improved beyond all recognition, and at the same time, it is hard to believe that it is the same musicians: the guitarwork has taken on a new life, possibly because there are stronger keyboards to bounce off. The CD starts with a nine-minute plus "Lullaby", which manages to incorporate a rock song with loads of keyboards with, at times, a Scottish folk sound. A fiddle hasn't been credited but I am sure that there is no way that a keyboard can make that sound! Songs vary from intense and dramatic to the quite ridiculous. The shortest song on here is "Bobo The Gardener", an acoustic number telling the story of a woman who loved a gardener, then leaves him and breaks his heart. To get his revenge he broke her neck and then buried her in his garden so that they wouldn't be parted. I think the word "twee" sums it up best. It made me think back to the early Seventies when songs like this were put on albums as some sort of light relief. I'm not sure if it is tongue in cheek or if it is supposed to be taken seriously! I must admit to being very pleasantly surprised and pleased with the direction in which Galleon have moved. At times they are reminiscent of Pendragon, but the opening keyboard runs to "Permanent Vacation" (which is over sixteen minutes in length) are pure IQ. They mix and match moods and styles in a way all their own. If you tried their debut, then I can promise that you will love this.
#23, May 1994

GALLEON
THE ALL EUROPEAN HERO

So, here we have the third album from the Swedish proggers, a band I have followed with interest. I enjoyed 'Lynx', their debut, but felt that it could have been a little better (although the more I played it the more I enjoyed it), and then when 'Heritage & Visions' came out I was more than impressed as it showed a vast improvement. So, could they be better yet again? The answer to that is a resounding "Yes". 'The All European Hero' tells the story of three friends who choose different paths in a Europe that is constantly changing, and asks the question as to whether it changed their lives. While listening to the album I found that I kept being reminded of Shadowland, possibly because of the vocals and the bombastic rock nature of the music, which is combined well with the keyboards. There is so much on here to enjoy from the prog point of view, with "The Hero and the Russian Ice Princess" showing perfectly what Galleon are achieving with wonderful melodies and flowing lines that move from light to shade, twisting and melding through different styles. If you like good progressive rock, then you will just love 'The All European Hero'.
#34, Apr 1996

GALLEON
BEYOND DREAMS

Of all European prog bands that I have been dealing with over the years, I must have had more contact with Galleon than with any other. They are no longer on their own label, but have now signed to Progress Records for their most recent release. 'Beyond Dreams' seems a million miles removed from 'Lynx'; can it really be the same band? Well, actually guitarist Micke Värn has now left the fold, having been replaced by Sven Larsson, but the other three are all the same guys who were first in contact with me some eight years ago. One of Galleon's major strengths has always been their lyrics, and this album yet again shows their prowess in English, while Göran's vocals maintain enough of his Swedish accent to provide extra interest. Sven has slotted right in, and this is a very polished album, which has enough complexity to make it accessible for the progheads, but the main thrust is the songs, which are melodic and very enjoyable. Galleon is to my ears one of the best prog bands to come out of Scandinavia, not a thing I say lightly. Give your ears a treat. *#59, July 2000*

GALLEON
MIND OVER MATTER

Galleon must have been one of the first Scandinavian prog bands I heard, when I was sent their debut 'Lynx' back in 1993. They have been an ongoing outfit since the late Eighties, and Progress have just released a remastered version of their 1998 album 'Mind Over Matter'. Containing just five songs, only one is under ten minutes

long and one is well over twenty! This is symphonic prog, with great swathes of keyboards and Mellotrons as well as plenty of guitars. Göran Fors (bass, keyboards) may not be the strongest singer in the world, but he has a passion that carries it through and musically this is very powerful invoking not just the feel of older bands such as Yes and Genesis, but also the stylings of Rush, and then Pallas and IQ as well. It all goes into the melting pot to create a sound that prog fans will just love. They can do gentle when they want to, but they can also bring in pomp and presence and it is great have this album again available with a cleaned up sound.
#86, Feb 2006

GANDALF
TO OUR CHILDREN'S CHILDREN

Those of you who have been reading Feedback for a while may remember Tracy Hitchings discussing this album during her interview with me last year.

This is Austrian Gandalf's eighteenth album, and he brought in Tracy to provide vocals on five songs, the others being instrumentals. Gandalf is well-known as a multi-instrumentalist, but on this CD he has brought in some outside help for a few tracks to provide more of a band feel. "Emotion" is the watchword for this album as Gandalf builds layers of sound to quite stunning effect. I have long been a fan of Tracy, and she is called on here to provide vocals in a style not unlike her work with Clive Nolan on the Strangers On A Train project. For the most parts the album is not rock in its truest sense, but more of a coming together of mods with heavy emphasis on swirling keyboards. Definitely an album to be sat and listened to, it has some magic moments.
#27, Feb 1995

GARDEN WALL
THE SEDUCTION OF MADNESS

This is a very strange album indeed and one that I still can't make my mind up as to whether I like it or not. Having played it quite a lot, it is starting to grow on me, but I'm still not sure. There are bits that are like Red Hot Chilli Peppers, bits like Faith No More, bits of hard rock, strange organ passages that could have come from Rocky Horror, and vocals that sometimes seem to fit and sometimes do not. I do not know if it is an enormous windup or whether they are serious about this, but it makes for interesting, weird listening. There is no doubt that they are very good as a unit, and bounce off each other, but I think that this album will find that it is very limited in its' appeal. If you want to try something really unusual then search this out, but do not blame me if you do not like it.
#32, Dec 1995

GARGAMEL
WATCH FOR THE UMBLES

This is good old-fashioned prog, and none of your Genesis types here. The band only got together in 2001, comprising Jon Edmund Hansen (guitar), Bjørn Viggo Andersen (Hammond Organ, Fender Rhodes, clavinet, synthesizer), Geir Tornes (bass), Morten Tornes (drums, vocals, glockenspiel) and Tom Uglebakken (guitar, vocals, flute, saxophone). This line-up recorded two songs as an EP and then in 2002 were joined by Leif Erlend Hjlmen on cello and recorded three more songs, and it is these five that form this album. With only two under ten minutes, and one the best part of eighteen, these guys are still trying to give value for money. They have taken bits from VDGG and then thrown in some Anekdoten and krautrock together with loads of experimentation and refusal to conform to what people may view as belonging within the genre, and created something that is vibrant, exciting and definitely progressive in the truest sense of the word. There is a section within "Strayed Again" where the bass is keeping the melody going, the drums are doing a basic shuffle, and the cello and flute are having a battle. In many ways, it does not appear possible that this is a new band, yet at the same time, it is obviously not from the late Sixties, early Seventies which is where this band feel they belong. It is experimental, yet contains plenty of melody and good strong guitar and vision: they know where they are going with a song, even if the listener does not! It is a fairly dark and bleak sounding album, not one to play to get you up and going in the morning, but it certainly is interesting. If you want your prog to definitely be just that, then you need to find out more.
#86, Feb 2006

JULIAN GARNER
WAKE THE LION

Julian was previously with Kick and Rook, both bands that made an impact on the London circuit (I have pointed out to Julian that I still have a photo of him up from his days in Rook and he accused me of blackmail). This self-released album is a low budget affair (CD-R) and the opener "You Save Me From Myself" did not exactly inspire me, as the production appeared not to be so hot, and I was not too sure of the drum machine. However, I persevered, and kept the album playing while doing other things. I then realised that the problem was in expecting too much. This is an independent release, not a multi-million-pound budget, and although I would have shot the drum machine and brought in a proper drummer the album itself is quite good. The more I played it the more I have thought that my initial reservations were wrong, and actually, there is a nugget here to be discovered and enjoyed. While the opener is more in a singer-songwriter style, some of the others are reflective and soft prog. Julian has a pleasant voice and the album is an enjoyable. It would benefit from real drums, and a bigger recording budget, but for a total self-release, it is one to be proud of.
#56, Jan 2000

JULIAN GARNER
DOUBLETHINK

This is the follow-up to Julian's 'Wake The Lion' album, and shows quite a 'progression' from the last. This is a much more varied album, and while it does suffer in the production stakes has enough ideas to make it an enjoyable listen. Many of the songs feature guests so that it is not as much of a one-man band, and at times I found that I was being reminded of Go West. This is very much about shorter songs rather than prog epics, and in fact that there is very little on here that could be viewed as prog. "What Else I Can Do" features acoustic guitar, as well as electric, and is a song that is quite like Crowded House. Given improved facilities it would be interesting to see what Julian could produce.
#64, Oct 2001

JULIAN GARNER
YOUR GOOD SELF

This is Julian's most professional looking and sounding release to date (bearing in mind that he is a one-man cottage industry). It took him about 18 months to make and for the first time he used a 24-track machine. There are also more guitars on this album, with Julian showing that when he wants to he can really 'kick' it along, but there are also still plenty of keyboards. This is being referred to by some as a prog album, but that is probably quite an inaccurate description in many ways. Yes, there are some prog songs on here, such as the eleven-minute opening title cut, which even contains a healthy slice of feedback at the end, but many of the songs are musically referencing acts a long way removed from the prog scene. Take the second song, "Feet Hit The Ground" – this is a great pop song with nods to Crowded House and Sting, and could well find itself on the radio, as it has that infectious feel. Julian's music probably deserves the tag 'English' more than most as throughout the album that are obvious influences of XTC and Squeeze which gives his songs a certain style and cachet. Julian is hoping to be performing more live gigs as a solo artist using backing tapes and I look forward to that as this is a very enjoyable romp that looks as far back as the Sixties and comes right up to date. I am willing to forgive him for using a small mirror on the rear cover (I think Uriah Heep came up with the idea first over thirty years ago) and while this is a homebuilt recording, it is fun to listen to.*#83, Mar 2005*

open play

julian garner

JULIAN GARNER
OPEN PLAY

This is an interesting album from Julian, especially as he was originally seen as being a keyboard player in rock bands. This is just Julian with an acoustic guitar (sometimes twelve-string) playing and singing in a church (for the acoustics) and then recording the outcome. A choice was then made of which versions to release and the result is something that is damn fine and eminently listenable to

and enjoyable. While eight of the twelve songs are originals there are also some covers, and it is strange to go from "Three Of A Perfect Pair" into "Should I Stay Or Should I Go", which when played solo on a 12-string comes across very differently indeed to the one that Joe gave us. Julian has a fine touch on the guitar, and his singing on this album is very strong indeed, and the result is an album that is full of passion and dynamics that lovers of good music, whatever the genre, will get something out of. I found that the guitar was somewhat reminiscent at times of Steve Hackett, but that cannot be a bad thing, and this is an album that I have enjoyed playing repeatedly.
#88, Jun 2006

JERRY GASKILL
COME SOMEWHERE

With band mates Ty Tabor and Doug Pinnick being involved with extra-curricular activities, it was only a matter of time before King's X drummer Jerry Gaskill decided to release a solo album. I can't find out if this is a 'pure' solo album, but looking at the King's X site I get the impression that Ty Tabor made an appearance, but the rest is Jerry providing not only drums but guitars and keyboards as well as all of the vocals and songs. Reading the press release it seems that Doug has nothing but praise for this album, and I have to say that there is nothing wrong with it: the problem is that while it is good, it is not any more than that. I often found my attention wandering when I was listening to this album, as the songs while interesting just do not have that edge. The result is an album that obviously King's X fans will have to purchase, but it is unlikely to gain any further attention with a musical style that mixes soft rock and acoustic with prog in a way that shows promise but does not really deliver.
#79, May 2004

theGATHERING
SUPERHEAT

Following on from their success last year with their fifth studio album 'How To Measure A Planet?', Holland's theGathering have returned with a live album that was recorded at two gigs on the tour last year. This is a band with a lot of ideas, and many different musical traits, but they are let down throughout this album with some pretty poor production. If the idea is to generate the idea of how the sound may come across at times in a live gig then they have succeeded, but the listener wants some clarity to the instruments and the vocals. "Marooned" starts life as a number by Everything But The Girl while "Probably Built In The Fifties" comes across as if the band is attempting to be Hawkwind with a female singer. This is an album that is most definitely spoiled by the poor sound, which is a real shame.
#57, Mar 2000

theGATHERING
IF_THEN_ELSE

The title may sound as if it had come from one of my computer programs, but the music is much more interesting than that. In Anneke, they have one of the most interesting female rock vocalists, and they use her range to provide superb counterpoint to what is happening beneath. This is a strange album in many ways, and while all of the songs would fit under the banner 'rock', these are much more than the antics of five people from Holland left alone with amplification. Even though they sound nothing like Björk, I could see her adapting some of these songs, with "Bad Movie Scene" being a case in point. It may be under four minutes long, but it is full of melodrama and passion, and Thom Yorke would love it. They use distortion to good effect, and the impression at the end of the album is that of not fully having understood all that is going on. It means that the only course of action is to play it again, in the hope of gaining the full meaning of the music. Do that six or seven times in succession then possibly, just possibly, you may get your head inside the music. Compelling and wonderful – not an album to be taken lightly or after a big meal.

#61, Feb 2001

theGATHERING
SLEEPY BUILDINGS

The idea of a rock band presenting an acoustic or, as in this case, a semi-acoustic show is these days not that unusual. But Dutch rockers theGathering were probably not one that many people ever imagined would fall into that camp. Not all of the songs on this album are fully acoustic, but even those that are electric (such as "The Mirror Waters") are treated in a totally different fashion to how the listener would usually expect. The result is an album that is deeply emotional and atmospheric, with the whole band being tied together by the delicate yet powerful thread which is Anneke van Giersbergen's voice. It shows how much structure there is within their music and how even though they normally belt it out there is a far more evaluated side to their nature. From opener "Locked Away" to closer "Like Fountains" the listener is taken for a ride through fourteen songs that have a craggy beauty which is going to introduce them to a whole new audience. Fans of the band will just lap this up while newcomers will wonder how they have never come across this style of music before. It is often piano-based with acoustic strumming but it is Anneke that is the pin that holds it all together and she comes out of this with a lot of credit. A very interesting album.

#78, Apr 2004

theGATHERING
ACCESSORIES

TheGathering have been around for quite a while now, and like many bands they have changed their style over time, and over the years have released songs on singles that never made it onto an album. This collection of B sides and rarities is an attempt to go back and collect many of these songs together in one place so that those who have come to the band later can now hear some of their rarer material. It is an album for the collector and fan as opposed to the first timer but there are some interesting songs on here (such as their version of Talk Talk's "Life Is What You Make It") which are well worth hearing. There is out and out metal, to songs that are far dreamier and quite experimental which demonstrates why the Dutch band have such a large following. This is for fans only, but they will get a lot out of this

#86, Feb 2006

GECKO'S TEAR
CONTRADICTION

This Italian quartet (plus a few guests) are looking to America as they bring in loads of Zappa influences to create an album that is somehow both accessible while being extremely complex and off the wall. I suppose the nearest current band to compare them with would probably be Frogg Café, but somehow that does not really capture the beauty of the very complicated and definitely progressive album. That this is a guitarist's album is never in doubt, nor is the fact that this is definitely progressive as it rips themes and styles from so many different places and somehow manages to put it all back together in a different order, still making sense. There is even a small classical section in closing track "Bourgeois" which just manages to provide even more emphasis to the Talking Heads meets Zappa for a buffet where they sample everything feel of what is going on around it. This could never be termed 'neo-prog', but is again furthering the rich tradition of truly progressive bands that have come out of Italy. This is extremely complex while also maintaining a simplicity that allows the listener to get into what is going on, although it does hurt when the jaw keeps hitting the table. These are very fine musicians indeed, who know what each other is about. One that all progheads most definitely need to seek out.

#89, Sep 2006

PETER GEE
HEART OF DAVID

Peter has been extremely busy, by his standards, over the last few months. Up to this year, he had only recorded with Pendragon, with whom he is bassist and a founder member. Now after the best part of fourteen years we find him not only working with a side project, Mercy Train, but releasing a 'solo' album to boot. Usually a 'solo' album involves the artist taking on vocal duties and possibly playing instruments with which he is not usually associated. One or two (or sometimes no other) musicians are used, and often these do not usually work with the solo artist concerned: what Peter has done is turn this idea completely around. He has very strong feelings about who would be the best person for a particular song, and to this end has utilised more than thirty different musicians in his quest to get the best result for this album. The full line-up of Pendragon appears, as do ex-members Rik Carter (now keyboard player with The Mission) and Nigel Harris, Uwe D'Rose (Landmarq), Tracy Hitchings, Ian Salmon (Shadowland), Richard West (Mercy Train), Karl Groom, Tony Grinham (Threshold) and others. Taking the lead vocals on many of the tracks is Paul Wilson, brother of Damian (who used to be in Threshold and Landmarq). His voice is very similar to Damian's, but being slightly lower in pitch manages to create a quite separate identity.

Each of the songs has a biblical reference, and for the most part it is a religious album, but the music is not restrained by any pre-conceived ideas about how the message should be put across. It is an album of great depth, as it cuts across many musical reference points and should be widely enjoyed. It is one to sit and listen to, as there are many layers, and at all times is immensely enjoyable. To me one of the most pleasant songs on the album is "Heart of David" itself, which features Peter on acoustic guitar and Patrick Barrett and Clive Nolan on vocals: it really goes to prove that to create wonderful music it is not necessary to have electric guitars cranked to the max. If you are prepared to cast away any false preconceptions about what you expect this album to sound like, and instead just listen with open ears, then you will discover one of the most inspirational albums of the year.
#21, Jan 1994

GENTLE GIANT
LIVE ROME 1974

There isn't a press release, and no information in the CD sleeve either, apart from stating that it was recorded in Rome on 26/11/74. This would have been on the tour promoting their sixth album, 'The Power and The Glory', which was their biggest-selling American release. Although the harmonies and the musical interplay that made them such a hit with prog fans can just about be heard, this album does suffer from a very poor production.

This may be due to the quality of the source tapes, but at times, it is just far too quiet, a problem that is not alleviated by turning up the volume. This is an album for the fans only as it is far too much work for the casual listener, due to the poor nature of the sound quality. But if you already have the live albums that were released when the band were still going and want more, then this is a pleasant listen and a reminder of just how good this band could be. Just be wary of the fact that this is bootleg quality at best.
#61, Feb 2001

GENTLE GIANT
IN A PALESPORT HOUSE

GENTLE GIANT
INTERVIEW IN CONCERT

Before even putting it on, all I hoped for was an album that sounded better than 'Live – Rome 1974'. But '...Palesport...' also has an extremely suspect sound. It sounds as if it starts halfway through the gig and there are only seven songs from this 1973 gig, plus two from a TV in concert. The last two have a much better sound quality, but these songs are also in the first seven. With the booklet containing two photos and no information, this is another release for the desperate fan only. I had better hopes for 'Interview' as the cover at least is much improved, but all I can say in favour of this 1976 set is that the quality is better than the one from '73, but not by much. Unfortunately, it makes listening to the disc too arduous a task, and I like Gentle Giant! *#62, May 2001*

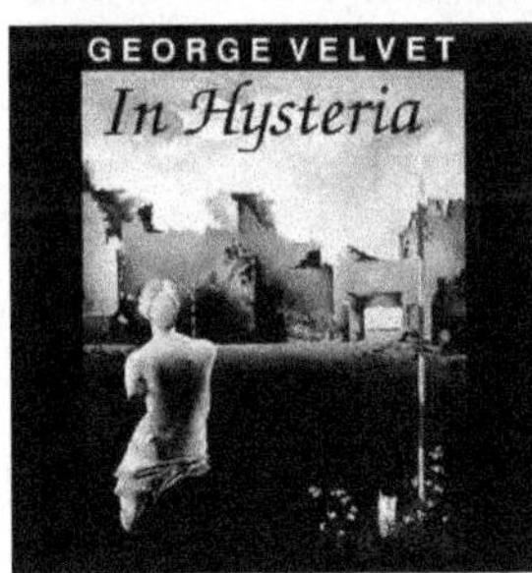

GEORGE VELVET
IN HYSTERIA

Well, here is another BJH-influenced album, but this is one that really works. George Velvet is actually Rene Broos on bass and George Knonigs on everything else. George also wrote the songs, and proves himself a very adept musician, and it surprises me a little that he did not play bass as well. Gentle music and well-constructed songs lead you into a magical world. Sure, it is yet again music to really sit and listen to, but this is really enjoyable. Some of them are more up-tempo, like the nine-minute long "Straight Through The Heart", but there is enough contrast within the album so that you do not fall get bored or fall asleep. The musicianship is of the highest order throughout, and you soon forget that you are listening to just two people, as it sounds like a full band who really know what they are doing. Multi-layered guitars give way to gentle classical, which in turn passes onto some gentle piano work. All of the songs give the impression of being very well thought out, instead of just thrown together. I found it to be one of the most enjoyable European prog albums I have heard for some time. If you like well-structured songs and melodies of bands like BJH then I urge you to discover this Dutch outfit. *#19, Aug 1993*

GERARD
SIGHS OF THE WATER

Gerard are a Japanese trio from Japan who, on the evidence given by their newest offering on Musea, are very heavily influenced by Emerson Lake & Palmer. Although the band released their debut album as long ago as 1983, they settled into the current line-up in time for their 1996 album 'The Pendulum'. The music is mostly instrumental

although drummer Masuhiro Goto provides vocals on two songs, and a guest singer on another. Whilst the drumming and bass playing is top quality, the focal point of the music is very much keyboard player Toshio Egawa. With no other melody instrument (not even a guest guitarist), it is very much in his hands to provide all of the musical styles necessary to drive the songs forward. In many ways this is music out of time as it belongs in the Seventies, long passages designed to keep the listener's jaw firmly on the floor as the speed and dexterity of Toshio is designed to amaze. It is not all frenetic stuff though, and there are dreamy interludes to counterpoint the more rampant excesses. Any fan of ELP will surely enjoy this release as much as I have. Originally released only in Japan, the Musea version contains a bonus track.
#69, Aug 2002

JIM GILMOUR
GREAT ESCAPE
Jim has been keyboard player for Saga for more than twenty-five years, yet this is only his second solo album. These ten songs are split into five instrumentals and five with vocals, and to my ears this is what lets this album down. There is no doubt that Jim is a fine keyboard player but his vocals are too weak to be sufficiently interesting as a lead singer. His voice is well suited to provide backing to Michael Sadler, but here it is laid bare. "Lost Along The Way" sounds as if it should be on a Saga album somewhere, but it is again the vocals that let it down. This is a real shame as there are some good musical ideas and songs on 'Great Escape' but while I can certainly understand why he wouldn't turn to Michael for assistance he would have been better off bringing in a more recognised vocalist to give the songs the edge that they require. Musically the album hits many bases and there is some great jazz-style piano on some, and a definite desire to move away from the prog genre at times, but for me while the music is interesting and worth discovering, I can't deal with the vocals but of course that is just my opinion.
#87, Apr 2006

GORDON GILTRAP
TROUBADOR
This album may see Gordon receive more publicity than normal as Sir Cliff makes an appearance (although it is difficult to identify his voice, it must be said). Gordon has been performing in Heathcliff for its' duration, and he has adapted a couple of the pieces he co-wrote for that musical for this album. This is Gordon at his best, normally just accompanying himself with some of the best acoustic guitar that can be currently heard in the UK. I particularly liked "Rainbow Kites" where he has used the simple device of having a one-second delay on the guitar so that it sounds like two top guitarists playing with each other. Gordon experiments with different techniques and tunings, but never moves away from the delicate beauty that is his trademark.

Buy the CD and get another free!! As well as the 'proper' album, there is another that contains purely acoustic versions of all of the songs. Gordon at his most pure. I have always rated his work, and for me this stands alongside 'Elegy' as his best album to date.
#66, Feb 02

GORDON GILTRAP
UNDER THIS BLUE SKY
'Elegy' still finds itself on my CD player regularly, and I played 'A Midnight Clear' often at work during December: there really are times when musically Gordon's guitar playing is the only thing that will do. This is a brand new album, not a reissue, and is again mostly Gordon doing what he does best, playing astounding solo acoustic guitar. He has been joined on some of these by flautist Hilary Ashe-Roy, and by Bert Jansch on the latter's "Chambertin". One of Gordon's many strengths is the way that he can take a tune and make it into something that is much more than the original. One of the numbers to benefit from this is the nursery rhyme "Sing A Song Of Sixpence", which becomes something totally different to what it was before. Sadly, there is no comment from Gordon as to why he chose this particular rhyme. One other cover that features on the album is "Here Comes The Sun", which Gordon completed in 2001 after many months of honing in an attempt to capture the right feelings and nuances. Gordon feels that there is much more poignancy now that it's composer has sadly died, and whilst I used to think that Cockney Rebel's version of this was the best I had heard I am now not so sure. While the song is instantly recognisable, it has taken on a new life, something that was not there before. One track that really benefits from the guitar and flute interplay is "Pedrolino", which is a more light-hearted piece and is named after the comic servant in Italian opera: this song was dedicated to Joe Pasquale! Yet again Gordon has produced an album that flies in the face of fickle musical fashion, and while I know that my children would much rather listen to Radio 1, I can only say that is their loss as this is an album of some majesty and grace.
#68, Jun 2002

GORDON GILTRAP
THE SYMPHONY HALL, BIRMINGHAM
This is a dual sided release, with the CD on one side and DVD on the other. It captures Gordon at the Symphony Hall in Birmingham where he was not performing just as a solo artist, and as well as having some friends helping him out (including some guy called Rick Wakeman) he also had the Sheffield Philharmonic Orchestra. The rationale was to perform his 'Eye Of The Wind' rhapsody, which was written between 1978 and 1980 to celebrate Drake's circumnavigation around the world. There is far more contained on the DVD than the CD, which in some ways is a shame as I would rather that the CD contained an audio version of the DVD (well, as

much as possible) so that I could have all of this on my iPod! There is a wonderful version of "Heartsong" which is just Gordon and Rick, and given that they hadn't been able to practise it together at all is something of a triumph! This is a wonderful album that any lover of Gordon or of acoustic guitar simply needs to have.
#89, Sep 2006

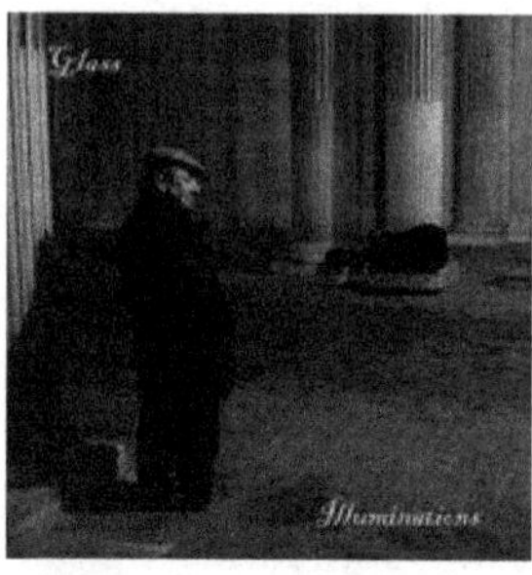

GLASS
ILLUMINATIONS
Glass formed in the early Seventies, and having made lots of friends in the US decided to decamp to the home of progressive rock, England. However, things did not go as well as had hoped and they returned home to break up in 1975. Years passed and in 1999 they wondered about releasing some of their old recordings. They were soon being asked to make festival appearances, which led to the original line-up deciding to get back into the studio and record this album which was released on Musea last year. Here is a band that had the misfortune to be American – their music shows just how much they were influenced by the Canterbury Scene, and Soft Machine in particular. Glass is an instrumental band, with Jerry Cook on drums, Greg Sherman on keyboards and his brother Jeff on bass. Mind you, there are a few noted guests with Hugh Hopper on one number and Phil Miller and Richard Sinclair on another. This is the sort of old-fashioned prog that the listener has to pay close attention to otherwise they will not get the best out of it. It is music that takes the listener into a new dimension where the world is very different indeed with strong elements. The lack of guitar is never noticed, and the music can be soaring and powerful or almost hypnotic. There is always an impression that everyone knows where he or she are going on this musical journey and there is never a sense of straying off course or taking a break on the way. It does not sound like an album that has just been recorded but rather something that has just been rediscovered from the 'golden age' and cleaned up. Very enjoyable, this should be readily available in the UK and is worth seeking out.
#88, Jun 2006

GLASS HAMMER
PERELANDRA
Glass Hammer is the brainchild of keyboard players and multi-instrumentalists Stephen DeArqe and Fred Schendel and along with some friends they have recorded their second album, following up from 'Journey Of The Dunadan', which was released in 1993. With two keyboard players at the helm it is of little surprise that keyboards play a major part on Glass Hammer's sound. What is interesting is that they are happy to produce songs such as "The Way To Her Heart" which features vocals and twelve string guitar for the most part, although an electric guitar and bass do make a fleeting appearance. They meld fairly brash rock with acoustic

guitars and powering keyboards, and the mix can go from extremely relaxing, almost new age and ambient, to overdrive at the drop of a hat. The music is well thought out and structured, with good melodies and vocals. At times there are distinct elements of Floyd while at others if it is more ELP or even Rush. One for the prog fan to savour.
#36, Aug 1996

GLASS HAMMER
LEX REX

For those with long memories, I have reviewed Glass Hammer before but it was way back in #36 (August '96) when I gave them a strong review for their second album 'Perelandra'. Now it is 2000 and this is their seventh album so what do I think now? It starts with an announcer telling invited guests about the concert that is going to take place. Later there is an intermission as well as thanks at the end where the gentlemen are invited to retire to have some brandy while the ladies have some refreshments. Each time I heard it I could not help thinking of Jethro Tull's 'A Minstrel In The Gallery' where a similar device has rather more effect. But in no way is that going to detract from what is a quite superb album. It is multi-faceted and multi-layered and given that it is basically all the work of just two people (Steve Babb and Fred Schendel) the accomplishment is even more remarkable. When I played this the first time I put it on immediately after playing The Flower Kings, and I was struck by just how different the two albums were. This also brings in many strands and musical styles but they all become part of the overall theme instead of trying to take over the piece. Both guys are strong singers, as well as good musicians and this is an album that I have really enjoyed playing. It is prog that while often based on keyboards also has a strong guitar element and manages to be all things to all progheads as those who want shorter songs can have them while those who want long instrumental passages are also catered for. It may have been six years since I last reviewed a Glass Hammer album but yet again I find myself recommending that all proggers get hold of this as soon as possible.

#70, Oct 2002

GLASS HAMMER
THE INCONSOLABLE SECRET

Glass Hammer are currently promoting themselves as America's finest progressive rock act, and one can certainly see where they are coming from. With artwork from Roger Dean, and Mellotrons and Moogs in abundance, this really is an album that is attempting to recapture those heady days of the mid-Seventies. But although there are plenty of elements from those days this is a prog album for today, with lots of time shifts and key changes as the band seamlessly switch from harmony vocals into blasting rock then down into layered keyboards. The bass can be in the background or right in your face a la Chris Squire. Although there are a few guest

musicians, Glass Hammer is a five-piece line-up with most of the music being supplied by just Fred Schendel and Steve Babb, with Matt Mendians providing the drums and Walter Moore and Susie Bogdamowicz on vocals. Of course, Fred and Steve sing as well, as well as providing the songs themselves with both of them sharing keyboards with Fred also on guitar and Steve on bass. This double CD comes in a digipak, and contains downloadable artwork, all of the lyrics and a video etc. But even if this was just released in a cardboard sleeve with no extras this would be something that all progheads would want. Switch into "The Knight Of The North" at nine minutes (it is more than 24 minutes long) and one would think that this was a long-lost ELP number if it was not for the vocals. This album contains all that a proghead could wish for if they long for the days gone by, mixed with a solid dose of the present which makes for an album that is intensely enjoyable, marvellous, glorious, (add your own superlative). I have not heard all of the output of this band by any means, but I can't believe that they have ever managed to surpass this album which is truly wonderful.
#85, Nov 2005

GONG
THE BIRTHDAY PARTY
At the end of 1994 Gong held their 25th birthday party at The Foum, London. As well as Kevin Ayres, Tim Blake, Shapeshifter Gong, Here & Now, Fluvius, Shortwave, Planet Gong, Kangaroo Moon and The Invisible Co. of Tibet, a performance was given by Gong for the first time since 1977. They played all the music from 'Flying Teapot', 'Angel's Egg' and 'You', as well as some songs from 'Camembert Electrique'. This has been captured on a double CD, which also contains a twelve-page colour booklet crammed with photographs. The whole package has been well thought out and will be an essential purchase for any lover of Gong. To anyone who does not know the music then this is an album that needs very careful playing as the world of Gong is almost like a closed shop for outsiders, a world that needs careful guidance from an expert. Play this album with an open mind and then you may find yourself surprised and delighted. If you know Gong already then you will love this and you will find it invaluable.
#31, Oct 1995

GOOD AUTHORITY
GOOD AUTHORITY
Yet another Dutch band are responsible for this twenty-minute four-track CD. They boast twin guitars, but apart from that I know nothing about them. They are not as American as Wings of Steel or Timelock, but still feature some reasonable vocals and guitarwork, so it's a shame about the songs really. Still, four songs are not really enough to form an opinion about a band. We get the obligatory ballad, and the longer tracks, but what really lets them down is "Dance To The Music". If this singalong rock song was not written to get airplay and chart position, I do not

know what is. Needless to say, as the song seems to have been written to a formula it fails miserably.
#17, Mar 1993

TADASHI GOTO
SOUNDSCAPE
This is Tadashi's debut album, and although the booklet does show him holding a guitar in one of the photos, it sounds to me as if everything has been triggered by keyboards. So let's get the bad stuff out of the way first, the 'drums' sound dire, and the bass sounds that have been triggered would be much better coming from a bass guitarist. But if Tadashi can get himself a good bassist and drummer then this is going to be someone to lookout for. He is mixing prog and fusion in a way that can be delicate and gentle, or way over the top and bombastic. He has nimble fingers, and a very strong mind for the arrangements, which results in music that is both annoying and enthralling. Annoying due to the moans I have already mentioned, enthralling because he is such a fine keyboard player who has obviously been paying attention not only to Messrs Wakeman and Emerson, but also to his fusion upbringing. There are times when he uses a keyboard to capture a sax, as on "Loveless", and while it does work there is the feeling that if only it was 'real' then it would add so much more. This is a work in progress methinks, but if he can get a band around him then I look forward to future releases with great interest indeed.
#86, Feb 2006

GRACE
POETS AND KINGS
In the late Seventies a group of art students decided to form a progressive rock band. They were heavily influenced by Genesis, Jethro Tull and The Who but even then displayed several unique features as they started to gig in the clubs and colleges of North Staffordshire. Firstly, the singer (Mac Austin) had a very powerful voice that was also delicate and melodic yet aggressive. Secondly, the band had two focal points as they had a manic flute and sax player (Harry Davies) who constantly vied with Mac for centre stage, which in turn led to an exciting and dramatic stage act. Thirdly, they put all their influences together with elements of English Folk to create a sound that was accessible but immediately recognisable as classic English prog rock. Grace's reputation for strong songs and dynamic stage presence increased, and the audiences grew. This led to record company interest and in 1977 they released their debut single "Old Stories"/"Rule Britannia" on an independent label. This received very favourable reviews and became the highlight of the set, then in 1978 they signed to MCA and released "Fire Of London"/"Beatnik". Again there were

favourable reviews and sales, and their first album 'Grace' soon followed. The reputation of the band as a top prog act was rapidly growing as both a recording outfit and a live act that used lights, projections, costumes, mime, and those two front men...1980 saw the release of another single, "Billy Boy", and their second album 'Grace Live' which featured the anthem "Molly Leigh (The Witch Of Burslem Town)" which featured mass crowd participation and hysteria. With an ever-increasing following it seemed that Grace was ready to take their place at the top of the rock tree...

Whether it was the general 'hatred' of prog rock in the early Eighties, or bickering among band members, but for whatever reason Grace suddenly broke up in 1981. A few splinter projects were carried out by individuals, but the only serious contender was the formation of the synthesiser outfit White Door which featured Mac and Harry, along with Harry's brother John. They released an album and several singles, and the established music press almost admitted to liking them. The scene now shifts to 1988, to a smoky pub in the middle of North Staffordshire. Imagine – the singer sits with a pint and a friend when the old bassist walks in, the worse for a beer or three, and laughingly it is suggested that it would be a great idea to reform the band for a one-off Christmas reunion. The reunion duly took place, and in fact they played together three times over that Christmas and the large crowds that turned up proved that no-one had forgotten who Grace were. One reunion led to another, and another, and so on, and Grace decided that they could make another go of it and started writing new material. There are still traces of their roots, but their style defies categorisation – it is melodic, delicate, powerful, emotive and it dares you to try and ignore it.

Since reforming, Grace have played many shows throughout the Midlands and Staffordshire; playing with bands such as Ark and Final Conflict and shortly will be joining Pendragon and Galahad, and there are even plans afoot to play the major clubs in Europe. Although they have had several line-up changes, Mac Austin (vocals), Harry Davies (flute, sax, whistle, vocals) and Dave Edge (guitar, vocals) have always been with the band, Dave Rushton (bass, vocals) was in the original line-up, John Davies (keyboards) was in White Door while Tony Hall (drums, vocals) used to be in Jinx. Grace are now looking to break out of the Midlands areas where they are a recognised headline band, and they have been busy in the studio recording a new album, 'Poets and Kings'. Although the album is being mixed as I write, Dave has kindly sent me a tape featuring some of the songs. What is readily apparent is the songwriting and musical ability of the band, and I was stunned to discover that the seven songs on the tape were laid down in a day just to give some idea of what the new material was going to be like. I mean, I would pay good money to have this as a completed album! The tape kicks off with "The Holy Land", which has a gentle whistle introduction that leads into a keyboard and bass led song. Mac's melodic vocals are kept high in the mix and the slower pace of the song contrasts deeply with most of the progressive rock being played today. In fact, Grace have far more in common with the Seventies prog bands than those of the Eighties or Nineties. The music is difficult to define, as there are elements of Genesis and Tull, but stamped all over it is their own style. "The Field" has a lighter folkier feel to it, with the flute and guitar more to the fore and a brighter jauntier tempo. The chorus is very strong with Mac putting a lot of power into the words, but never straining, trying to give you the impression that he really can

"see the Prince of Light". Songs have a real rocky feel, while others have driving keyboards such as "Success" which has some wonderful Tull-style screaming flute. Grace are different from the rest of the other prog rock bands around, and those wishing for a more melodic style, with great contrasts and musical ability, combined with extremely strong songs, could do far worse than discover the music of Grace.
#12, Feb 1992

GRACE
THE POET, THE PIPER & THE FOOL

In #12 I discussed the history of Grace, who are the leaders of progressive rock in the Midlands and also mentioned that the CD was due out in the first week of March. Well, it has now finally been released, albeit in the first week of July. Firstly, the band found that there were problems with the technical side of the recording, and had to re-record much of the album again, and then there were problems with the artwork, and then the lorry transporting it back from the factory in France was held up by farmers who thought that the lorry contained British lamb! For those new to the story, Grace are a band that were originally formed and recorded in the late Seventies, but broke up in '81 only to reform in '88. This history means that the band have far more in common with their Seventies counterparts than they do with the bands of today: there is far greater use of melody and less inclination to employ heavy rock.

So what is 'The Poet, The Piper & The Fool' like? It kicks off with "The Piper (Changed His Tune)" and Mac's vocals combined with the backdrop of keyboards instantly transports the listeners away. Bass and guitars play the same repetitive riff almost throughout, which means that the ear is drawn more and more to the melody created by Mac. Harry's gentle flute is heard in the almost acoustic chorus, and the use of a tin whistle leads the way into the rocky section of the songs which then reverts back to the main theme. Only at the end do you realise that this song is more than eight minutes in length, the time has flown. All of the songs contain the same hallmark of melody, often led by the keyboards with Mac's clean voice, allowing the others to add to the fabric. My favourite is easily "Success", which is their hardest-hitting song, as the keyboards and guitar drive along. This is often used by the band as their opener, and I can see why, as it's a great jumpy up and down song. Harry's flute is used sparingly, but in a more Tull-like style with breathy power. "The Poet" is also more up-tempo, with some wonderful bass playing from Dave. "Rain Dance" starts off slowly, with just long chords on the keyboards, and a shaker, with Mac's vocals clear and atmospheric. The bass joins in, then the guitar is picked, then joined by drums. After the first chorus the band are in full swing, and it is just wonderful. Of the others, special mention should be made of "Lullaby", as this song is basically just Mac and John on piano, although he does add some other keyboards as well. They are joined by a guest cellist, and the overall effect really is beautiful. For lover of Seventies progressive rock this really is a great album.
#14, Jul 1992

GRACE

PULLING STRINGS AND SHINY THINGS

Thank God for Grace and King Harry! The new album is just brilliant. Buy it!! Looking at these few words, it probably does not convey just how mind boggingly brilliant this album is (just how fast does a mind boggle?). For those of you who have never heard of Grace (buy the CD now and catch up fast) they were originally formed in the Seventies, then after two albums with MCA they split up, only to reform in the late Eighties. Original members Mac Austin (vocals), Dave Edge (guitar), Dave Rushton (bass), Harry Davies (flute, pipes, saxes and total manic behaviour) have been joined by Tony Hall (drums) and Mark Price (keyboards, ex-Final Conflict and Framework). This is the second album since Grace reformed, the other being the stunning 'The Poet, The Piper And The Fool' (where the keyboard player was John Davies), and although I never thought they could top that, this one might be better. It is very difficult to define the sound of Grace: they are "English" in the truest sense, and possibly they are close to Jethro Tull because of this, aided and abetted by the flute playing of Harry. Anyone who has seen them in concert will know that they are one of the best live acts around, with Mac and Harry vying for centre stage. The rest of the band concentrate on playing great music, while Harry becomes its' living personification (one day I will work out why he was whipping himself with a rubber chicken the last time I saw them). So, onto 'Pulling Things...' itself. Commencing with the sounds of an orchestra tuning up, "The Fool" starts with Mark repeating the same phrase repeatedly as the rest of the band join in. Gradually this gets heavier with riffing guitars, but Grace are far more than just a heavy rock outfit and the music has totally changed by the time Mac's clear vocals can be heard. Dark and shade, heavy and light, Grace are full of contrasts, bouncing them together for effect. Just when the melody seems to be settled, it changes totally, creating an edge and bite that is just waiting for… Harry!

With a driving flute that brings up images of Ian Anderson at his breathy gulping best, Harry gives the songs even more dynamism. After that the next song just has to be a touch quieter, and thankfully this is what "Mullions" delivers. The mullion is a character created by Mac and Dave Edge, who supposedly lives in lakes and has made an appearance previously. Gentle and restrained, well at least it is to begin with, as keyboard riffs combined with guitar allows Mac to turn the song into a bouncy sing-along. I've heard this number live, and it is just brilliant, but Grace have somehow managed to capture this energy in the studio. "Lean On Me" is perfect Peter Gabriel "Biko" period. Even Sara likes it (high praise indeed). "Earth Bites Back" takes things into a heavier sphere again, and it grooves along quite nicely thank you very much.

Again it is the keyboards that herald the change, and the songs twists and changes many times until it ends as a keyboard-drive rocker. I could sing the praises of this album forever and a day. There is just so much in it, the more I play it the more I enjoy it, but it is also totally accessible on first listen. Go on, give yourself a treat.

#22, Mar 1994

GRACE
POPPY

What can you possibly say about Grace that hasn't already been said before? One of the best live bands in the country? The band that reformed years after leaving MCA to produce one of THE albums of the Nineties (all proggers simply must have 'The Poet, The Piper and The Fool')? The band that is very truly progressive because they just do not sound like anyone else? The band that has two frontmen vying for centre stage all of the time? The band that very justifiably call their music English rock? Oh hell, why bother. All you really need to know is that with 'Poppy', Grace have yet again not only come up with a fairly naff cover (and I thought 'Pulling Strings and Shiny Things' was bad enough) but have musically produced a stormer. Each song has a small comment next to it, which also shows their sense of humour ("Resurrection" – "Mark Price says that he was a Gerry Anderson puppet in a previous life, hence the unique dancing style"). Bouncing rockers such as the aforementioned "Resurrection" or opener "Burglars" sit happily next to slower more thoughtful numbers such as "Oklahoma", which is about the bombing. Having lived with this for a while I have to say that not only it is immediate but it is also a grower, and for sheer depth and diversity, not to mention brilliance, it rivals 'Poet'. Grace are again showing the young whippersnappers how to do it, and do it well.

#38, Nov 1996

GRACE
GATHERING IN THE WHEAT

Over the last few years I have had the pleasure of seeing many of the so-called "underground" or 'neo-progressive' bands live in concert, some of them many times (or in the case of Credo many, many times). It is rare for me to come away having not enjoyed myself, but I think that even the members of those bands would have to say that there is something very special indeed about seeing Grace live. Very highly melodic, and managing to sound like no one else, just what has made them so good? A lot of people would point to the visual aspect of the band as with two frontmen and the rest of the band staying pretty much in the background this is a different kind of show. Vocalist Mac Austin has a very strong voice and personality, which he needs because he constantly has to fight for attention with Harry Davies. Harry, in his most basic form, provides sax, flute and backing vocals, but he far more than just a backing musician, whether it is dancing or egging the crowd on. Harry in action (especially with a rubber chicken) is a sight to be seen. Talking of chickens, this is not a young band we're talking about here, apart from second guitarist Adam Rushton whose father Dave is the bassist. Dave, Harry, Mac and guitarist Dave Edge were all in Grace some twenty years ago when they were signed to MCA, and it is no surprise that along with drummer Tony Hall and keyboard player Mark Price (whose last gig this was) they know what they are doing. After they reformed, Grace released an album on their own label before signing with Cyclops and releasing two more. It has to be said that none of these match up to the majesty of Grace in concert, something this double CD goes some way to rectify. This is a band with so much energy and passion that they put bands half their age to shame. By the time you get to the end of this album you will find yourself knackered. Penultimate song is "Rain Dance", one of the greatest audience participation numbers around. Sing, dance, go wild, the crowd did that night in December at the Wheatsheaf. Amazingly enough that was not the set closer as they came back with "Molly Leigh" (an early song that I had asked them to play in the past, having heard it on their 1980 (!) live album but had never seen them perform). The passion is so real as to be almost visual. This is a truly great album, from a truly great live band. *#50, Aug 1998*

GRAND STAND
TRICKS OF TIME

Grand Stand have changed both line-up and some of their musical direction on this follow-up to their debut album, 'In The Middle, On The Edge', which came out in 1998. While definitely a progressive rock band, they have added a more American rock flavour and vocals, something that was missing from the instrumental album with which they announced their presence to the world. That is not to say that they do not produce instrumentals any more, in fact two of the five songs do not contain lyrics (and one of these is nearly ten minutes long), but rather that now they have a singer they are making good use of him! Opener "Jurassic Spark" shows an affinity to early Genesis, yet also brings in much more modern styles and while contains many progressive themes and styles there are also sections that are much more AOR-oriented. Contrast that to "Words Are Not Enough" that sounds at times as if Camel and Jadis have jumped into bed together while at others using much more jazz-influenced piano chords to create a totally different mood. I found on playing this album the first few times that they do sound quite different on the songs, as if they have not totally settled on their own style but want to encompass everything that they like listening to. Not a bad thing for a prog band in many ways. The closing number, "Old Man's Tale", is the longest at sixteen minutes, and contains both very delicate interludes and much more powerful sections with some great guitar and keyboard interplay, as well as pieces that sound familiar but yet are not (especially if you are a Genesis fan). This is an album that is bound to find a lot of favour among the progheads. *#68, Jun 2002*

GRASS
CAFÉ CULTURE

Back in the dim times (okay, it was 1988) a band recorded their debut album 'The Dreams of Mr. Jones' but it was not until 1993 that they released a full-length CD, 'Spiritual Physics', and then there was nothing. Ark (for it was they), had built up a reputation as one of the hardest working prog bands in the UK and had even won the Radio 1 Rock Show Rock Wars but the band quietly disintegrated just as they

were on the verge of greatness. What has this to do with Grass I hear you ask (stifling the yawn)? Well, Ant Short (vocals, guitar, flute) and Pete Wheatley (guitar, backing vocals) were the main songwriters in Ark and this is the new band they have formed with Andre Ingenthron (bass) and Jason Roper (drums, backing vocals). It has been a long time since the Ark debut, and comparing the two we find that not only has Ant become more suave but also that in the photo on the rear of 'Mr Jones' John Jowitt (Mr. Bass of IQ, who was also in Ark) used to have hair! But I digress; the main difference has been the changes in the music, which has seen a leaning more towards bands like The Wonderstuff. When listening to the album the first time, I found that although I enjoyed the first five songs (of fifteen) they rather passed me by. It was not that they were poor, but just that although I enjoyed them there was nothing that really grabbed me. From there on in, it was superb song following on from masterpiece. "Café Noir" is over six minutes long, and "Why" exceeds nine, but that is the only thing preventing these from being mega hits. The mix of acoustic guitar and gentle vocals with catchy refrains and rock guitar are just right. "Hello Hello" creeps in under four minutes so that is the one that they will have to release as a single: Catchy, rocky, and in the present climate a sure-fire smash. Ark are dead, be sad. Grass are very much alive, rejoice!
#41, Apr 1997

GRATTO
ANAKIN TUMNUS

Over a period of about three years Gratto would get together and record extremely complex prog. However, the band then broke up and it was not for another two years that anything was done with the tapes. Gratto the band were Gratto (keyboards, vocals), Chris Rodler (guitars), Brett Rodler (drums) and Gary Madras (bass). I am not sure how many years Chris and I have been in contact, but it goes as far back as Drama as well as RH Factor, Leger De Main and others. I have always had a lot of respect for Chris and Brett's abilities yet here they were in an unusual setting, as Gratto co-wrote the music with Chris while providing all of the lyrics. Chris came across the tapes by accident and decided to work through them to see if there was anything that should be released and instead of going for a lengthy epic has instead released an album that is only thirty-six minutes long, containing just three numbers. But even though this album is so short (in relative terms) it contains far more ideas than many prog albums could ever hope to achieve. It is extremely complex yet retaining melody, while branching and splitting off into myriad ideas time and again. It is an album that really has to be listened to otherwise the music just washes over the top. There is so much going on that at times it conjures up images of classic Genesis but sounds absolutely nothing like them at all. I am a huge fan of Spock's Beard, as you all well know, but this album sounds far more mature with much greater depth. It definitely proves to Flower Kings that it is all about quality, not quantity. This album is already starting to make a stir in prog circles and you will kick yourself if you do not get in on the act.
#72, Feb 2003

DAVE GREENSLADE
GOING SOUTH
Dave is well known for his film work, as well as his times with the great bands Greenslade and Coliseum, but unfortunately this has much more to do with the former than the latter two. Inspired by the migration of birds, it does little to inspire me one way or another as Dave meanders instead of migrating, and the result is an album that while not dire is not exactly amazing either. If you are a huge fan of ambient, or of Dave himself, then you must get this otherwise leave well alone. *#56, Jan 2000*

GREENSLADE
LARGE AFTERNOON
It may be the best part of thirty years since the release of their superb first two albums, but Dave Greenslade and Tony Reeves are back, with 'new boys' Chris Cozens and John Young (the same John Young who features on the Qango album reviewed elsewhere). There have been few four-pieces that could boast two keyboard players, and Greenslade have been away far too long. I defy any lover of keyboard rock a la ELP not to fall in love with the opening instrumental "Cakewalk" as it drives along very nicely. John provides all of the vocals (four of the nine have lyrics), but his voice is not strong enough for this role, although for a lot of the time he just manages to get away with it. For me it is on the more expansive instrumental numbers that the guys show what we have been missing for all these years. This is an album that I would heartily recommend to any keyboard loving proggers out there.
#61, Feb 2001

GREENSLADE
THE FULL EDITION
Recorded in 2001, this is the reformed Greenslade showing that they were very much back in business. With Dave on keyboards and original bassist Tony Reeves in tow, they brought in John Young (keyboards, vocals) and John Trotter (drums) to resurrect the band that had made such an impact in the mid Seventies. Greenslade were always unusual in that they had two keyboard players and no guitarist – this gave their music a distinctive sound, often more ethereal and laid back than ELP, for example. This album opens with "Cakewalk", with the band having a blast. John takes centre stage for "Feathered Friends" but while the two keyboard players are having fun on the very Spanish sounding "Catalan" it is the fretless bass that steals the show as Tony proves that a few well-placed notes are worth a thousand played quickly with no thought as to context. Tracks are taken from throughout the band's career, mixed so that newcomers to the band wouldn't know which are new and which are nearly thirty years old. It

is nice to hear songs such as "Bedside Manners Are Extra" again after all this time, and with "Joie de Vivre" breaking eleven minutes it is safe to say that Greenslade are back and even though they may not be creating chart albums anymore there is definitely an audience of proggers that will want this CD.
#79, May 2004

GRENDEL
AU-DELÀ DU RÊVE... LA SOLITUDE

Oh well, you have to laugh don't you? Grendel is the pseudonym for Frenchman Bruno Cormand, who apparently got permission to use the name from the big Scotsman himself. The CD is split pretty much between English and French lyrics, and it is obvious that Bruno can't speak English and has had the lyrics translated for him, so he is not really happy singing them. The first song, "Midnight Call" is dreadful (can anyone explain to me what "we'll love like two licken beings" actually means?), and the next is not much better so we'll quickly pass over them. The third, "Daydream Believer" (no, not that "Daydream Believer") is actually quite good and belts along fairly well with Bruno proving himself to be a useful guitarist, if only he could sing! I would prefer Bruno to go away, find himself a proper vocalist, and really think about the songs. Apart from the first none of them are really awful, but none of them are going to stir enthusiasm either! He can play great guitar and definitely wants to rock a lot more than the other French prog I have heard, but that is all that can be really said for it.
#19, Aug 1993

GREY LADY DOWN
GREY LADY DOWN

Formed in 1990 as Shadowland, a name change took place with the arrival of the rhythm section in early 1992. The Oxford-based quintet has been gigging consistently, and have already built up a considerable live following in the area. The band comprises Julian Hunt (guitar, violin), Mark Robotham (drums), Sean Spear (fretted and fretless bass), Martin Wilson (vocals) and Louis David (keyboards). The band are currently working on their first CD, but have released a demo tape that I am currently listening to, and very fine it is too. First track is the rocking "12:02" which really sets the tone for the rest of the tape with a glorious commercial rock sound, Louis providing some driving keyboards over the top and Martin singing his heart out. After thirty seconds I knew that here was yet another undiscovered, unsigned British prog band to be proud of. Next up is "Thrill of It All" and the contrast between the two could not be more marked, as gentle guitar and violin provide the backdrop for Martin's strong clear vocals. Louis' keyboards lead the transformation in the song which turns into a swinging number with Martin still loud and clear. There are five songs on this tape, the others being "Circus of Thieves", "I Believe" and "Time & Tide". It is a tape well worth £3 of anyone's money, and I am really looking forward to hearing the CD later in the year. Grey Lady Down have captured a real pomp, prog commercial rock sound. There is not a weak link in the band, and the five songs display such diversity that I wonder what one of their gigs must be like: I can't wait to find out! If you want to discover a really great commercial rock band then I urge you to contact the band (oh, and if you have not worked it out, the name refers to a submarine). *#18, May 1993.*

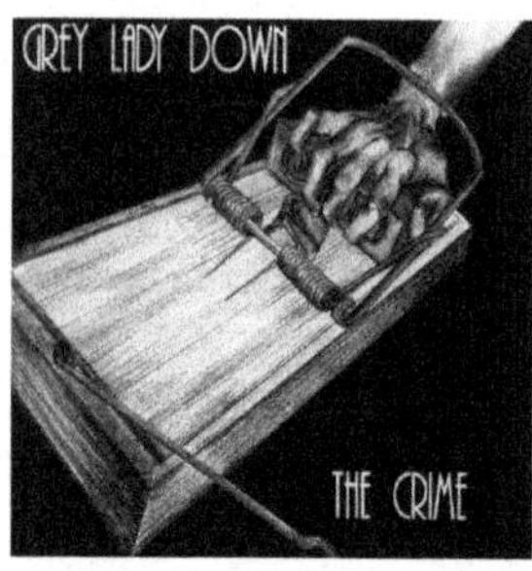

GREY LADY DOWN
THE CRIME

Last year drummer Mark Robotham came over to play me the tapes of what would be the new GLD CD. After sitting and listening (and writing copious notes) to the whole thing, I had the unpleasant task of informing Mark that I felt that there were quite a few faults with the mixing and recording. When I then heard that these tapes were going to be the first release by Cyclops I was a little wary. I mean, had they been remixed from when I had first heard them? Had any of my comments been taken on board? When the CD arrived I played the first two songs looking for faults and turned it off: I just was not being fair to GLD or 'The Crime'. The other day I put on the rugby with the sound turned down, and cranked up GLD. I am glad to say that from a tape I was not impressed with there is now a CD which is really enjoyable. I still think that the sequencers should be stronger at the beginning of "All Join Hands", but really that is a minor quibble. The songs blast out at you, stating that as I said back in #18 when I reviewed their demo tape, GLD have "captured a real pomp, prog commercial sound". GLD themselves say they play rock-prog and not prog-rock, and that is probably true with the guitars higher and more powerful than many others. Opener "12:02" starts off with the sounds and noises of the train station, and as the train rushes by the band kicks in and takes it on, dragging you along in their wake. This is a really strong opener, with repeated keyboard sections and powerful guitar. Martin Wilson has a strong voice, reminiscent at times of Steve Hogarth, and it is not only there that the Marillion similarities can be noticed, although GLD are far heavier. I wrote three pages of notes during the rugby (we lost! Can you believe it? To the Irish!) and words stand out such as "rocky", "restrained power", "transforming", riffing etc. I take back all I said about it when I originally heard it last year. GLD have arrived with a bang and a truly wonderful CD. Buy it! *#22, Mar 1994*

GREY LADY DOWN
FORCES

After the success of 'The Crime' (one of the biggest sellers on Cyclops to date), GLD were faced with the problem of the difficult second album. I am glad to report that they have easily overcome these and have produced an album that easily surpasses their earlier work. That is not to say that I did not like what they had achieved before, but 'Forces' displays more musical maturity, better songs and

much improved production. GLD are firmly based around the excellent keyboard playing of Louis David. The others are not bit players, but their particular brand of prog rock is often keyboard melody led, with everyone else playing their part. Louis has broadened his sounds and this has helped the band to become more accessible. Martin's vocals are still emotive and powerful while Julian, Mark and Sean provide the rock element. There are many highlights to this album, and I cannot see how it can fail to surpass the success of their debut. While there are brilliant blasters like "The Nail", there are longer more thought out and dramatic pieces like "Battlefield of Counterpane" (this last showing more than a hint at times of late Seventies Genesis). There is even the reappearance of an old favourite, "I Believe", which first saw the light of day on their tape which I reviewed many moons ago. All in all, 'Forces' is an album that they can rightly be proud of. I am sure that anyone who likes good melodic or prog rock will find much here to appreciate. Personally I feel that the 'bonus' piece of music long after the finish of the final track "The Flyer" is infantile and demeans much of what has gone before, but maybe I just did not get the joke.
#30, Aug 1995

GREY LADY DOWN
THE TIME OF OUR LIVES

On 11th July last year Grey Lady Down played their final gig. I was probably not one of their most vocal supporters, and this was in hindsight probably due as much to their attitude (as perceived by myself and many others) as to their music. This was not always the case, and in fact Mark came to my house aeons ago to play me the debut album long before it was released. Still, over the years I had steeled myself to the fact that they were not as good as they thought they were, and saw them a few times in concert and listened to the albums. The last time I saw them was at The Orange where Mark had the guts to sit at the same kit that had recently been vacated by Mastermind, and that did nothing to change my opinion.

Now though, and it hurts to admit this, maybe I was wrong? Knowing that they are gone it is possible to listen to the music for its' own sake and not have it coloured by personal feelings about any of the participants. The double CD is the last gig, recorded at the LA2 in front of a partisan audience, and is easily the best thing they have ever done. They mix early and later numbers, and play all that a GLD fan could wish for. Shorter songs sit happily alongside longer epics such as "Battlefields of Counterpane" and the trilogy of "The Crime", where the band has the chance to stretch their musical wings. I could have done without the long gap between the final number on CD 2 and the encore, but I seem to remember them doing something similar on their second studio CD (wasn't it a weird version of "Mull of Kintyre"?). This is an album worth hearing and if like me you have not mourned the demise of GLD then why not give this a listen and cast out long held beliefs. This is actually quite good!
#53, May 1999

THE GUARDIAN'S OFFICE
THE GUARDIAN'S OFFICE

The Guardian's Office is a new project by Fruitcake drummer and composer Päl Søvik, and sounds as if it should have been released thirty years ago, although there are some modern musical references. This is an album that finds itself deep within the world of Uriah Heep, with the odd modern tinge. Much of this is down to the melodious vocals of Tony Johannessen (who also provides the keyboards) as he does his best to evoke the power and majesty of David Byron. There is a feeling throughout of being transported back in time, and I would defy anyone listening to say that it is from a modern Scandinavian outfit. The line-up is completed by Froydis Maurtvedt (bass) and Morten Eriksen (guitars). It is an album all about melody and thoughtful tunes, guitar breaks restrained. It is an album that is full of pomp, with bass pedals being used powerfully. It is never rushed and when at times they move away from the Heep sound it is only into an area more normally associated with classic Genesis. It is timeless and sees no point in rushing to get to the end. The length of the album also hearkens back to older times as it is only about forty-five minutes long, yet contains eight songs (Flower Kings please take note – this is the way to do it!). Great artwork by Stephen Trodd yet again points back to the golden age of prog, and while this would benefit from being a 12" vinyl release with a gatefold cover that seems to be almost a churlish comment to make. A classic album that I have enjoyed immensely.

#73, Apr 2003

YNGVE GUDDAL AND ROGER MATTE
GENESIS…

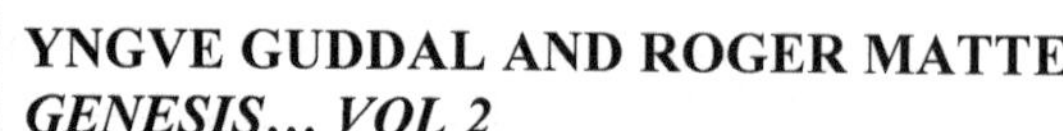

YNGVE GUDDAL AND ROGER MATTE
GENESIS… VOL 2

There is a considerable argument for saying that the only form of modern music that carries on the development of classical music is not classical itself, but rather 'progressive rock' with its complex time signatures and the mixing and melding of so many forms. Certainly there have been attempts to bring together both classical and progressive in the past, probably most notably with The Moody Blues and Deep Purple, but how about classical interpretations of progressive songs? The finest examples of this that I have heard was the series by David Palmer where he combined his experience of classical music and his time with Jethro Tull to release some superb albums in the Eighties where he arranged music of bands for the LSO, with guest musicians. Of course the first to 'benefit' from this were Tull themselves (where he turns "Fly By Night" into something incredible), while the second was Genesis 'We Know What We Like' (which featured not only Steve Hackett but also Ian Anderson). But now we have two musicians who have taken this in a slightly different direction and have produced two albums where the music has been arranged just for two grand pianos.

The first of these came out in 2002 but has only just come to my attention, and 'Genesis For Two Grand Pianos' is exactly what the name implies. This is two classically trained musicians bringing their skills and their love of Genesis together so that they somehow manage to turn the pieces into something quite different to the originals, while remaining very true indeed. This is swirling, wonderful music and I find my mind being dragged into a wonderful world where there is a beauty that sometimes is not even apparent in the original. The main problem is how to pick out a favourite combined with the issue of trying to get across to you just how glorious this is. "Mad Man Moon" contains the drama and passion, while "One For The Vine" is just awesome. The songs are mostly from the Seventies but there is also an upbeat take on "Duke's Travels". I am not surprised that it took three years to produce the follow-up as it must take quite some time to develop the arrangements (on the second album Yngve arranged two, Roger four and one joint). With classic songs such as "Lamb", "The Battle Of Epping Forest", "The Cinema Show" and "Blood On The Rooftops" on this album then it is sure to get fans very interested indeed. But for me the pick of the bunch is probably "Eleventh Earl Of Mar", which works very well indeed in this format. Of course, I am listening to all of these songs as a Genesis fan so can't possibly state how well they stand up as classical pieces in their own right but I do know that I have enjoyed playing them a great deal and that any Genesis fan in their right mind will want to investigate these further. These really are glorious albums that I have enjoyed playing a great deal and know that I will be returning to time and again.
#86, Feb 2006

THE GUITAR ORCHESTRA
INTERPRETATIONS

The Guitar Orchestra's beginnings can be traced back to early 1989 when Chris Baylis decided to record an album using only guitars to the exclusion of all other instruments apart from percussion. During the recording of the debut album Chris multi-tracked as many as forty guitars to achieve the textures and sounds he wanted. To the end of the process he brought in some other musicians, including Simon Edwards (ex-Fairground Attraction), Rickey Edwards and Hossam Ramzy (who had just been working with Peter Gabriel). The band became a seven-piece for live work, and the album was released in June 1991. Over the next few years, time was spent consolidating the success of the album with more live performances, TV and radio appearances, and the recording of the new album, which was then previewed at The Royal Festival Theatre earlier this year. 'Interpretations' was released in June, and lives up both to its' name and the name of the band as The Guitar Orchestra interpret ten classic tracks in a totally original manner. They define 'Interpretations' as "representation of an existing artwork using the original as influence or inspiration". Chris Baylis has attempted to make The Guitar Orchestra a unique outfit, taking rock instrumentation truly into the classical field and

throwing in some jazz influences for good measure. Because of this, the album may not be to everyone's particular taste as the clinical element removes the energy and immediacy that is so important for good rock, but really this album is making its own rules. My favourite track is probably "I Am The Walrus", although "Don't Fear The Reaper" is a close second. If you are interested in hearing well-known songs being played in a unique manner, or just wonder what sixty guitars can sound like when all being played at the same time, then this is for you
#25, Oct 1994

TREY GUNN
UNTUNE THE SKY

Trey is probably best-known as being a member of King Crimson for the last ten years, but as well as other bands he has also recorded six solo albums. This album is a retrospective of those albums, and features Trey on warr guitar, Chapman Stick, vocals and Bob Muller (drums), Dave Douglas (trumpet), Tony Geballe (sax, guitar) and Joe Mendelson (guitar). The warr guitar is an instrument that Trey developed with Mark Warr and is a 10-string 'touch' guitar with the range of a piano, which gives him the opportunity to play music that a conventional guitar would not be able to cope with. This is fusion music, and it is very clever. There is no doubt that Trey is a fine musician who knows exactly what he wants to achieve, but the only problem is that when experimenting with new forms and styles it can either be brilliant or can make the music very hard to listen to. No prizes for guessing which camp this falls into. I know that many people get a lot of pleasure in music that is challenging, but having struggled all the way through this album a couple of times I doubt that I will do so again.
#78, Apr 2004

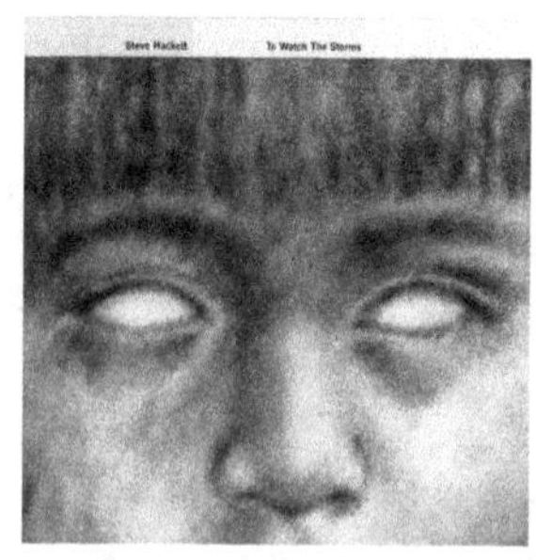

STEVE HACKETT
TO WATCH THE STORMS

This is Steve's first studio album since 1999's 'Darktown', and to old Genesis fans like me who only own 'Acolyte' and 'Spectral Mornings' it is something of an ear opener. This shows that Steve has moved far away from the musician he used to be and is now a performer of great depth who is not content to stay within any particular musical style. There are songs that are percussion based (which if I had to pick an ex-Genesis member as the instigator I would probably opt for Gabriel) while there are gentle numbers, yet also others that are far more aggressive in outlook. The drums dominate "The Silk Road", yet there is room for rock guitar, Genesis-style guitar, acoustic guitar, clarinet and a myriad of other instruments. This is music that is remarkable for clarity of vision and a determination not to be fixed into any particular genre or box. The album opens with "Strutton Ground", and the gentle guitar and multi-layered vocals lets the older Hackett fan in gently – this is the sort of music that one expects from Steve, clever and intricate yet also simple and beautiful. But then compare that

to the rock bombast that is "Mechanical Bride" which is driven along by sax before suddenly becoming a keyboard and string number, then back to the guitars. This is an album that I have enjoyed immensely and it is exciting in that within each song, let alone from one song to the next, there is a lot of change that makes the music interesting and diverse. One to return to time and again. This release is on Inside Out but it has been licensed from Camino Records which is a UK label, and I see that they are going to be offering this album as a deluxe edition with a hardback book containing a forty-page booklet with Steve's notes on each song, plus extra tracks etc. Also, if you visit the site there is an internet-only single available.
#74, Jun 2003

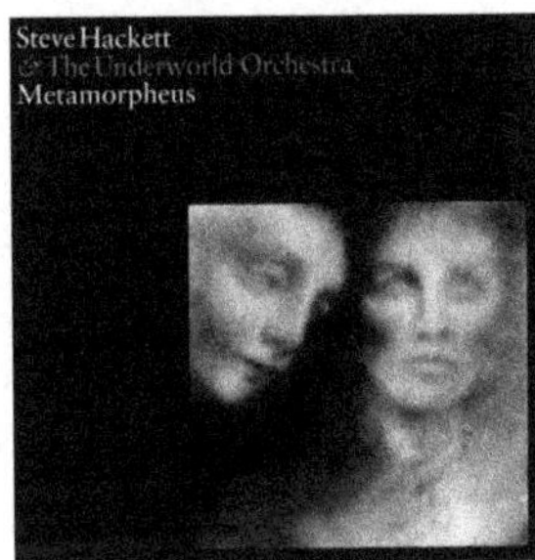

STEVE HACKETT
METAMORPHEUS

Like any other progressive rock fan, look in my collection and you will find 'Voyage Of The Acolyte' and 'Spectral Mornings'. I also remember fondly seeing Steve at Whitchurch Village Hall, where he played the complete set as a soundcheck, and then of course played it again in the evening so I witnessed the show twice in the same day! But over the years I have lost touch with much of his work (although I did review his 2003 CD 'To Watch The Storms' which is quite superb), and I was not aware that he has been embarking on a series of classical music albums. In fact, this is his fifth album in that vein and is a successor to his 1997 'A Midsummer Night's Dream', telling the story of Orpheus and the Underworld. Never have I felt so unqualified to write a review, as this features Steve on nylon guitar combining with an orchestra in a style of music that is sadly outside of my area of knowledge. It is issued in a slip sleeve, and while this is an orchestral piece, within the sixteen-page booklet there are notes as to what each song is relating to. Musically it is music that I found intriguing, and discovered that it is best listened to at night when the world is still and time can be spent drifting away 'seeing' the images that the music inspires. I have enjoyed it immensely and can see that I should not only purchase the earlier works but also start finding more about this type of music.
#83, Mar 2005

STEVE HACKETT
LIVE ARCHIVE 05

As the title suggests, 'Live Archive 05' was recorded on Steve's tour earlier this year, at London Queen Elizabeth's Hall on 3rd April. If you were there, then this is what you would have heard. The first CD comprises the first set where Steve was his own support. There he was literally on the stage on his own, just a man and his classical guitar. The last time I saw Steve in concert he was in front of an electric band but that could not be more different to this set as here there is no singing, just an explanation of what the piece is and then off into the rendition. There is a selection from the new 'Metamorpheus' album, but not a great deal as Steve does explain that it is rather hard to play with just ten fingers when it needs an orchestra. The second CD finds him joined by John Hackett on flute, and Roger King on keyboards and this allows the music to be more dramatic with more textures, yet again this is music that is much more of the classical form and shows just how far Steve has progressed with his music since the heady days of Genesis. Yes, there are a few snippets of Genesis to be heard, but Steve has moved a long way since then and he has no need to dwell on his past as his music is still changing and flowing. This is music to be absorbed, music to be relaxed to and should be thought of more as a selection of short classical or jazz pieces than the progressive rock of his younger days. Overall this is an enthralling piece of work. *#85, Nov 2005*

STEVE HACKETT
LIVE ARCHIVE 83

This was Steve's first-ever acoustic tour, and onstage only his brother John on flute joined him. Most of this concert is taken from a bootleg recorded on 4th November in Edinburgh, but there are some songs missing so these have been taken from a show two weeks later and added to the end. Although this may not have been an official recording the sound is very good indeed and for the clear majority of the time one would never realise the source. At the time Steve was known as a progressive rock electric guitarist, and although acoustic pieces had been in his repertoire for years this was a brave move for him as no other 'rock' guitarist had decided to tour an instrumental classically influenced set. Steve and John also got into the mood by appearing in full evening dress each night! The Hackett fan will be extremely interested in this as it shows early classical adaptations of songs such as "Jacuzzi" along with favourites such as "Tales Of The Riverbank". But even putting the rarity of this live recording to one side, it is something that fans will want to get just because it is so damn enjoyable. Here was a guitarist showing a very different side to what people would normally hear, and there are not many guitarists prepared to go out and just play with little or no support. There is nothing to hide behind here, no effects, just a man and his guitar. There are some rarities within the concert itself, including "The Water Wheel" which has not appeared elsewhere, but if you want to relax to some wonderful music then this is the place to be. *#87, Apr 2006*

HAMADRYAD
CONSERVATION OF MASS

In the booklet, the band basically beg the listener to play this at least a few times before coming to a judgement about it, and when placing it in the player I could hear why. However, even when playing it for the first time the sheer class and majesty shines through. This pure prog album will be loved by anyone into 'old school'. At times, they sound a bit like Genesis, or Colosseum, or Greenslade, or Yes, or Gentle

Giant, or like none of them at all. They go from one musical area to another with ease, at home with jazz or with hard rock. The result is an album that all proggers will find themselves drawn towards. In fact, the biggest problem with this album will be getting it heard by enough people. Unicorn in Canada has released it, but hopefully Cyclops or Musea will pick it up in Europe so that it can reach a wider audience. It is full of depth and passion and is the best prog album to come out of Canada by a new band that I have heard for a while.
#62, May 2001

HAPPY THE MAN
THE MUSE AWAKENS

Happy The Man released two albums in the late Seventies, but although I had heard of the band I had never encountered any of their material until now. Apparently, guitarist, vocalist Stanley Whitaker was playing with Ten Jinn at a prog festival in Mexico at the end of the Nineties when word spread that he had been a founder of HTM and many people then wanted to talk to him about it. Two promoters of NEARfest then came up to him and told him that if he could get a version of the band back together then they would guarantee them the headline spot! When he got back to the States he contacted Frank Wyatt (sax, woodwind and keyboards) and Rick Kennell (bass) and they decided to reform. Second keyboard player Kit Watkins said that while he wouldn't mind recording he was not interested in touring so they brought in ex-Rainbow keyboard player David Rosenthal and the line-up was completed by drummer Joe Bergamini. The result is the first new album from the band for 26 years, and to my ears sounds as if it comes from that age and not from the present. This is complex instrumental (just one song has vocals) music that has as much in common with the Canterbury Jazz scene as it does with Gentle Giant. It is hard to believe that this is prog from America as it belongs at home in the UK – with the way that it switches both tempo and melody reminiscent of a style of prog music that virtually no-one plays any more. Mostly it is relaxing, almost soothing, but at no time it can be said to be simple background music as there is just so much going on. I still have not heard the albums that the band released all those years ago but I think that I would like to.
#82, Jan 2005

GORDON HASKELL
HAMBLEDON HILL

For those of you who are wondering where you remember the name from, Gordon was vocalist and bassist on two King Crimson albums, 'In The Wake of Poseidon' and 'Lizard'. Since those heady days of the early Seventies he recorded his first solo album ('It Is And It Isn't) but then concentrated on playing bass for artists such as Tim Hardin, Van Morrison, Bryn Haworth, Alvin Lee and Cliff Richard. It was only after this that Gordon decided to again pursue his solo career. This has seen at least one other album, which has also been released on Voiceprint, namely 'It's Just A Plot To Drive You Crazy'. 'Hambledon Hill' has been described by Whispering Bob Harris as "...a beautiful album", and I even heard DLT play a song from this the other day so there are at least two DJ's with impeccable taste on Radio 1. "Beautiful" is probably the word that fits this album best, as it is laid back and soothing with at times a country feel. The opener is the title cut and is one of the most wonderful songs ever recorded. Indeed, my long-suffering wife asked me why I didn't listen to more music like this instead of my normal rubbish. High praise indeed. It is an album which will appeal to anyone remotely interested in the softer side of rock, such as Chris Rea or Gerry Rafferty, with eleven songs of extremely high quality: music to mellow out to. Production has been handled for the most part by Tony Arnold (who is also probably best known for his work with King Crimson), and he treats the music with great feeling and compassion, helping to give real warmth to the sound. This CD should be in every good music lover's collection. Voiceprint have national distribution so with a little bit of looking should be possible to find this CD in your local record shop. Please make the effort, otherwise this release could be appreciated by only a very few, and it deserves a helluva lot more than that. *#18, May 1993*

ANNIE HASLAM
BLESSING IN DISGUISE

ANNIE HASLAM
LIVE UNDER BRAZILIAN SKIES

Annie Haslam must have one of the most distinctive and famous voices in British popular music, and while she may not top the charts these days her voice shows no signs at all of fading. When studying the sleeve notes for 'Blessing In Disguise' I was intrigued to see that Tony Visconti, who also co-wrote five of the songs with Annie, produced it. I hadn't heard of him for years and did not even realise that he was still active in the music business. He has lost none of his touch and has captured Annie's voice perfectly. It is a delicate album and even starts with the title cut being performed a capella (which is done well and sets the mood perfectly). On some of the numbers I kept thinking of Judie Tzuke, in style although not the same vocally. Although it is a good album, it just does not compare to the live one. With just David Biglin and some backing tracks for company, Annie proves yet again that she belongs in the concert hall. Most of the songs are from her time with Renaissance, but also with some solo songs there are also some notable cover versions. The first of these is Mike Oldfield's "Moonlight Shadow" and with David providing just piano and some backing vocals it is down to Annie to totally transform the song from the upbeat pop number to a delicate ballad. More surprisingly perhaps, is her version of "Turn of the Century" where she does more than a passable Jon Anderson impression. Now does that mean that Jon sings like Annie or vice versa? One of my favourite numbers though is the hit single "Northern Lights". Slightly slower, and with just a piano this is class, sheer class.
#54, July 1999

HATFIELD AND THE NORTH
HATWISE CHOICE

This album is the first ever retrospective of Hatfield and the North, a band that brought together four top musicians and let them give vent to some music that was certainly never mainstream. This digipak contains an extensive booklet with notes by Jonathan Coe (who loved the band so much that he nicked the title of one of their albums for a book, which has recently been dramatised on TV, 'The Rotter's Club'), as well as copious notes from all four band members themselves saying how the band was formed and what it was like to be in it etc. Musically this album contains 23 songs, roughly half of them being live concert recordings and the other half being taken from the four sessions that they undertook for Radio One.

With ex-members of Gong, Egg, Matching Mole and Caravan (among others) this was always going to be a band that was eclectic to say the least. There was a jazz feeling to much of what they were doing, and what this CD captures so well is the improvisational feel of their performances. They would take the original tune and then go off and hopefully meet at the end (in the sleeve notes Dave says that they played too fast, too loud and too much but that something special often came out of it). I hadn't heard much from Hatfield and the North prior to this release, but it has made me determined to find out a great deal more. This is music that thirty years on still has a lot to say and is as valid and exciting now as it was at the time. With the amount of detail and photos in the booklet this is a great release that fans old and new should search out. *#83, Mar 2005*

HAUTEVILLE
RELIFE DATA INCOMPLETE

There do not seem to be a great many decent progressive rock bands hailing from France these days, but Hauteville seem to be bucking the trend. Fronted by Lydie Gosselin and her wonderful vocals, here is a band that are creating a bouncy exuberant style of neo prog that hits the spot.

While the guitars are high in the mix, this is not a prog metal band, just one that likes to keep the emphasis on the word 'rock' while also hitting the word 'progressive'. They can be gentle and symphonic when they want to, but there is always a great deal going on musically even if Lydie's vocals are taking a simpler, clearer route. It is interesting to find a French prog band on Lion Music as opposed to Musea, and I am sure that this must have been a conscious decision on their part as this band has musically little to do with releases on the latter as this is something that is accessible and very modern – looking forward instead of back, with little or no influences apparent from the Seventies. This is an interesting album that fans of both prog and adventurous melodic rock will enjoy and is worthy of further investigation.
#88, Jun 2006

HAWKWIND
CALIFORNIA BRAINSTORM

This album was recorded on December 16th 1990 at the Omni, Oakland, California and was originally only available in the States. It has just been released in the UK by Cyclops, together with a 176-page illustrated biography. Only 5000 of these have been issued so if you want one then you should act quickly. Recorded with the line-up of Dave Brock, Harvey Bainbridge, Richard Chadwick, Alan Davey and Bridgette Wishart, the material is very much recent with only one golden oldie, but it really is a golden one. "Brainstorm" blasts out with just as much power at it did in the Seventies! "Propaganda" is just Dave and Harvey talking to the audience, but it leads nicely into the definitively Hawkwind sound of "Reefer Madness". There is a bonus song contained, "Images", that hasn't appeared elsewhere and all in all this is a CD which is worth having but when that is added to the book then this is essential to anyone interested in Hawkwind. Oh, yes, it is a pic disc CD as well. *#27, Feb 1995*

HAWKWIND
FUTURE RECONSTRUCTIONS

'Future Reconstructions – Ritual of the Solstice' was released on July 22nd on the band's own Frequency Broadcast System label. Hawkwind have influenced a large amount of dance bands and remixers, and some of these have now been given the opportunity to remix some of the bands classic songs including "Sonic Attack", "Master of the Universe", "Spirit of the Age" and of course "Silver Machine". The result is certainly interesting and different, as some have taken the opportunity to completely rip a song to pieces and reconstruct it in a way that challenges one to recognise the original. I think that it has been a deliberate ploy to give "Silver Machine" to Utah Saints, as they are the ones most likely to have chart success. Also, to my ears it is the Saints who have done the best job with the material as they have taken the song and moved it very much into the techno or dance field, but retained enough of the original to make it instantly recognisable. However, Knights of the Occasional Table, who open proceedings with "Sonic Attack", must also be highly commended. If you like Hawkwind, or are just curious about what sacrilege has been committed, then search this out. *#36, Aug 1996*

HAWKWIND
GLASTONBURY, '90

According to the press release this is previously unreleased, and it is not hard to hear why. While collectors will always want a copy of every gig a band plays, if possible, they will avoid poor quality bootlegs, and this sounds like one of those. From the reaction of one person when they kick into "Brainstorm" this is almost definitely an audience recording, with sound quality as muddy as the fields at

Glastonbury where this was recorded at 5 am. If you are a die-hard must have everything Hawkfan then do not say you have not been warned, otherwise leave well alone.
#57, Mar 2000

HAWKWIND
IN YOUR AREA
I think that it was realising that opening song “Brainstorm” had turned into a reggae number that I first started to think to myself, “What the hell has happened to Hawkwind?” I remember seeing them in concert in the early Eighties and being blown away by their power. “Brainstorm” is a Nik Turner classic, and as such deserves some respect, surely? Yes, I know that bands should move and not stand still, but if they do not respect something why bother with it at all? My feelings about the whole album were somewhat clouded after that which is a shame as I like Hawkwind. This album contains six live and eight new studio songs, although it does not say when it was recorded. As well as the inevitable Dave Brock, the rest of the band now comprises Richard Chadwick, Ron Tree, Jerry Richards, Capt. Rizz and Crum. The introduction to “Love In Space” sounds as if it belongs on ‘Dark Side Of The Moon’ instead of an album of the band that gave us ‘Quark, Strangeness & Charm’. Thank heavens it turns into a definitive ‘Wind rocker with swirling keyboards and driving guitars. This is one of the few songs which features Dave on vocals, and one of only three that he wrote with no co-writers, so perhaps it is no surprise that it comes across eventually as true Hawkwind. The album fluctuates dramatically, with some songs coming across well, while others are just sad reflections of what Hawkwind once were. One for fans only I’m afraid.
#58, May 2000

HAWKWIND
THE WEIRD TAPES NO. 1

HAWKWIND
THE WEIRD TAPES NO. 2

HAWKWIND
THE WEIRD TAPES NO. 3

HAWKWIND

THE WEIRD TAPES NO. 4

HAWKWIND

THE WEIRD TAPES NO. 5

HAWKWIND
THE WEIRD TAPES NO. 7

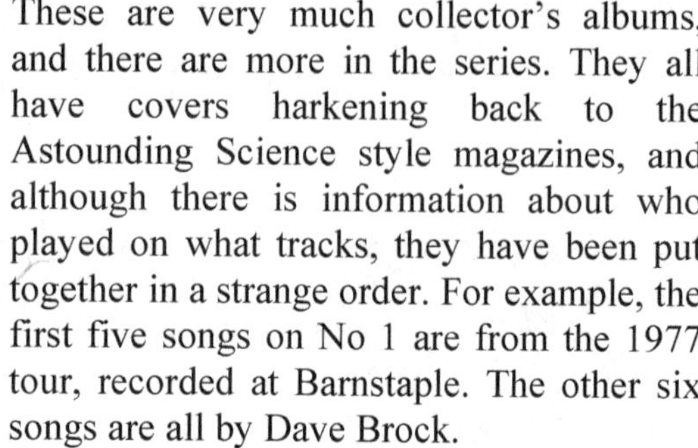

These are very much collector's albums, and there are more in the series. They all have covers harkening back to the Astounding Science style magazines, and although there is information about who played on what tracks, they have been put together in a strange order. For example, the first five songs on No 1 are from the 1977 tour, recorded at Barnstaple. The other six songs are all by Dave Brock.

Then turning to No 2 there are another five songs from 1977 (albeit a different tour with a different line-up), then three songs from Hawklords. It is No. 2 that I will be playing most, as the five songs are all pure classics: "Quark, Strangeness and Charm", "Masters Of The Universe", "Welcome To The Future", "Spirit Of The Age" and "Sonic Attack". No 3 is subtitled 'Free Festivals' and has five numbers from 1977 and three from 1975. No 4 is called 'Live '78' and manages to include "Spirit Of The Age" and "Urban Guerrilla". This is one of the few times that there is some track duplication between the CDs. No 5 switches between 1976 and 1977, while No 7 is called 'The Demoes starring Dave Brock' but again has no information at all apart from the fact that they were recorded by Dave. All in all, these have been well produced by Dave Brock, but I would have rather seen more information in the booklets, and a bit less switching from one time to another. However, to the Hawkfan these will be an invaluable addition to the collection, albeit they will not always know where the music has come from. *#61, Feb 2001*

HAWKWIND
ATOMHENGE 76

HAWKWIND
FAMILY TREE

HAWKWIND
SPACEBROCK

There are many Hawkwind records coming out now, but there appears to be some problem with quality control. 'Atomhenge 76' is a case in point. This is a double CD, with lots of great photos in the booklet, but the sound quality is not all that it should be. During "Brainstorm" the lead vocals are overpowered by the backing, and the sound levels drop and rise alarmingly. It is hard to imagine that this is a classic song, by one of the best concert acts around. Not that the problems arise here alone, it is the same throughout which is a shame as the casual fan

would like this, but as it stands it is for die-hards only.

'Family Tree' is an album of collected solo works by musicians connected in some way with Hawkwind. There are songs by The Paradogs (Jerry Richards & Alf Hardy), The Little Big Men (Richard Chadwick & Steve Bemand), Ron Tree & Vital Chi, Liz Gizzard, as well as some by Dave Brock. The '79 version of the full band also appears with "Motorway City". There are some surprisingly powerful dance tracks, with powerful keyboards and a pounding beat as well as some totally off the wall stuff which could come from the 'Wind. Some of these songs deserve to hit the clubs, where people have never heard of Hawkwind.

I think that 'Spacebrock' may be the new studio album, but do not quote me (no press releases sometimes makes life difficult). The usual suspects make appearances on the album, but the mainstay throughout is Dave Brock. He has even managed to put Shakespeare to 'music', and even gives our Will a co-credit on the track! In fact, it is like the band of old, with some great riffing guitar and spaced out keyboards. There is even "The First Landing On Medusa", which was co-written with Robert Calvert. Overall this is an intriguing album and although not as immediate as much of their work in the Seventies, this is a welcome respite to the many 'rare' CDs currently coming out and is worth hearing.
#62, May 2001

HAWKWIND
LIVE 1990
This 25-track double CD is taken from a performance given by the band for the 'Bedrock' TV show. Although this is very much a live gig it was halted during proceedings a few times by the crew so that they could adjust the lighting. It has not been released before and the line-up at this time comprised Dave Brock, Harvey Bainbridge, Alan Davey, Simon House, Richard Chadwick and Bridgett Wishart. Shortly after this gig Simon House left the group and Bridgett joined (she had previously been guesting), making her Hawkwind's first ever female vocalist. Bridgett makes her presence felt on songs such as the powerful "Ejection". Hawkwind do not sound like anybody else, they very much have their own space rock sound, with guitars and keyboards creating a melee of noise. Probably best enjoyed when not totally sober, and certainly not to be played when the listener has a headache, there are times when only Hawkwind will do. I must admit to not being totally au fait with much of the material, but this is Dave Brock yet again leading his band on a joyful jaunt through time and space. As would be expected given the circumstances surrounding the recording the sound quality is very good and while I would hesitate to point to this as a starting point to the band any established fan will like this, a lot.
#68, Jun 02

HAWKWIND

CANTERBURY FAYRE 2001

I must be honest and say that I am not sure just how many live Hawkwind albums I have listened to over the years, but this is one of the few that has been released with a strong sound quality. In fact, it is probably their best live release for many years, with a line-up of Dave Brock, Simon House, Keith Kniveton, Alan Davey, Richard Chadwick and even a special guest vocalist on "Silver Machine" of none other than Arthur Brown himself. The double CD kicks off with the gentle laid back introduction of "5th Second Of Forever" but this is just a ploy as Alan riffs his bass as if Lemmy was back in the fold and the band start to take off. It must be twenty years since I last saw them in concert, but this album brings it all back as if it was only yesterday. From here it is just a short step to a nine-minute version of "Levitation", and the band is in full swing. They have a unique sound, even after all these years, and with the space rock in full flow there is no-one to touch them. They may have replaced the sax with the violin but all this has done is give them yet another element to their sound. It may not contain "Brainstorm", but with classics such as "Spirit Of The Age", "Motorway City" and "Hurry On Sundown" as well as a full version of "Silver Machine" there is more than enough here for any Hawkfan to want to have this album. A goody. *#73, Apr 2003*

HAWKWIND

THE WEIRD TAPES NO. 8

This is the eighth release in the officially sanctioned Hawkwind rarities series, and this is subtitled 'Live 1966- 1973'. Given that this is going to be purchased only by those who are already huge fans of the band then one would have thought that a little more information on the actual songs could be forthcoming. There are ten songs, with the year of the recording given for nine of them, and of the nine there are three that are unknown as to where it was recorded. Apart from the year there is no more information, so there are no line-up details.

The result is an album that in many ways is quite confusing to listen to, but is something that Hawkfans will want to own just due to the rarity of some of the material it contains. The album starts with a strong version of "Space Is Deep" from the 1973 Space Ritual tour but most fans will probably bypass this and head straight to track five. The reason is that this is the first of two songs from 1966, which are the earliest known recordings of Dave Brock. They are in mono, and certainly sound as if they were recorded forty years ago and give no glimpse of what he would be doing soon. However, I know these details only because I read it on the web and given that Dave has produced this set I can't understand why there is so little information. I have just been onto their website and this release is not even listed yet. This is very much for Hawkwind diehards only.
#87, Apr 2006

HAWKWIND
TAKE ME TO YOUR FUTURE

This is the latest official release from Hawkwind, following on from 'Take Me To Your Leader'. What we have here is a collection of pieces that are soon to be available elsewhere, along with some that will only be available on this dual sided disc. So, if you are a fan you must get this even though most of the material will also be available elsewhere. Nice.

There are five audio tracks on one side, and seven videos on the other. Even though I think that in many ways this is an unfair release no one can doubt the care that has gone into the booklet, which is very well presented indeed.

Of the five audio, there is a reworking of "Uncle Sam On Mars" which featured on the last album, plus "The Reality Of Poverty" which not only involves ex-Hawkwind member Simon House on violin but also Arthur Brown on vocals. Of most interest to the Hawkfan will be the two songs from the Brock Calvert Project where Dave has put music to some of Robert's recitals – they work quite well. Then to finish there is a new remix of "Silver Machine" which retains the Lemmy vocals and does sound different enough. The video side contains material from four DVDs available elsewhere, but also some that is only available here. I still think that it is a bit of a cash-in, but overall it is an interesting release.
#89, Sep 2006

HAZE
IN THE END 1978 – 1988

This compilation attempts to take all the best bits of Haze and put them onto one CD: it is a well-put together package with a full history, various odd bits of info (in 1982 Haze played 30 gigs but in 1985 they played 160!) as well as complete lyrics. A full discography is provided, and copious photos show what can be done when someone who loves what they're doing handles a release. There is a great depth to the music, which makes it quite difficult to define. Is it the simplicity of songs like "For Whom" that are the attraction, or the more complex pieces like "Survive"?

All the music is provided by the Mk 5 line-up which was Paul McMahon (guitar, lead vocals), Chris McMahon (bass, keyboards and vocals) and Paul Chisnell (percussion and vocals). For the most part Haze were more laid back than many of today's bands, although "The Vice" (which starts off with some great soloing) totally disproves the case in point as it riffs and rocks along. This CD is far more than a normal release, but rather an introduction to a form of progressive rock whose demise was mourned by many. Good music, loads of information and photos, what else could you want? *#25, Oct 1994*

HAZE
C'EST LA VIE

What can you say about Haze? Certainly, one of the hardest working bands ever to get lost on the A1 (M), they are still seen as being an important influence on many of today's bands. Of course, Paul and Chris McMahon are still treading the boards as World Turtle, but back in those days they had a drummer (Paul Chisnell) and their never-ending tours (often with a young (!) Mr. Rog Patterson in attendance) have become the stuff of legend. 'C'est La Vie' was their first album, originally released on 7th April 1984. It has been combined here with the four songs from 'The Ember' twelve-inch single which was released on 21st October 1985. Side one and side two have been reversed, and all the songs have been remixed, as much as the original recordings would allow. Copious historical notes, track information and photos make this a great package for both the newcomer and the enthusiast who will probably have the originals. Progressive trios are notable by their rarity, and in this case Paul Chisnell drummed and sang some leads, Paul M provided lead vocals and guitar while Chris played bass and keyboards (yes, sometimes at the same time), with all three providing harmony vocals. Go on then, tell them about the music. Well, this is extremely well sung and played prog. Rock trios are either crap or brilliant, there is rarely any middle ground, and Haze provide complex well thought out music that is also very melodic. Yes, weird time signatures abound ("Load" is in 4/4, 6/8 and 5/4) as well as changes in moods and tempos. "The Ember" (which is still part of the World Turtle live set) has some great guitarwork and soaring vocals, "Mirage" is a riff-based rocker while "For Whom" is a delicate searching ballad. Favourite is the belting rocker "Gabadon" which is fantastic with some great riffing from Paul. Cyclops will be making the other Haze albums available when they have been remixed and I can't wait. Reissues just do not get any better than this. Buy a piece of UK progressive Rock history today, you owe it to yourself.

#38, Nov 1996

HAZE
CELLAR REPLAYED

Surely, Haze is one of the best-loved British prog bands, although I have studiously managed to miss all their gigs since they reformed: in the Eighties, they appeared to live on the road, bringing prog to the masses. Their first album release was a cassette called 'The Cellar Tapes' which came out in 1983. Having sold all the copies, and having gained a new drummer in Paul Chisnell they decided to go back into the studio in 1985 and re-record many of the songs for a new cassette, 'Cellar Replay'. Therefore, what I have in my player is a CD re-mastered reissue (with some extra tracks) of the 1985 re-recording of the 1983 album!! Confused? This is very much like going back in time. The band has moved on a great deal since 1985, and even classics such as "Dig Them Mushrooms" (which was originally recorded for a single in 1981) sound quite different today. It is not an album that I would suggest that someone new to Haze should go for (get the superb, wonderful live album instead), but is one that anyone who has

ever heard them should get immediately. Another very important point to note is that this has only been pressed in a limited club edition of 500, which is nearly sold out.
#60, Oct 2000

HEAD POP UP
TOKUSEN BURARI TABI
I have reviewed the odd Japanese prog album in my time, but I have never been sent an album direct from Japan, thanks Hiroshi. Head Pop Up are from Yokohama but apart from that I know very little about them. The press release states that they are a progressive jazz outfit, but they have more in common with ELP. This is not a totally instrumental album although there are long passages without vocals: there are two keyboard players in the band so it is not surprising that the music does focus on these. That is not to say that the bass and guitar are ignored, as they also have important parts to play, but rather that they are normally the drivers of melody. The vocals show that this is music that is a little outside of the norm, as it is here that the Eastern style shines though. The production is strong and the musicianship excellent throughout. Any fan of ELP, Floyd, or just wanting some prog that virtually no-one else in the country will have then visit the website. *#70, Oct 2002*

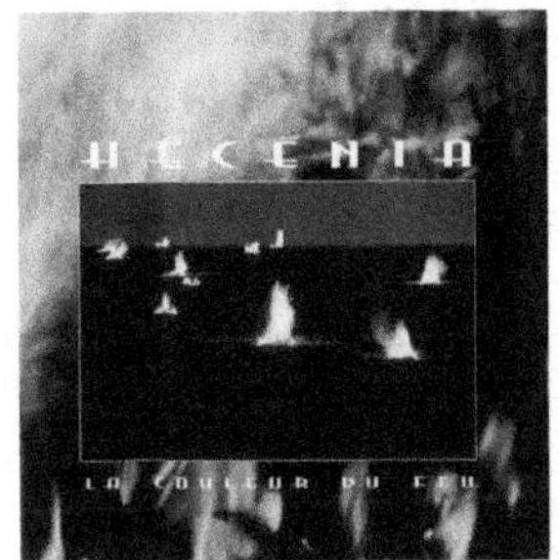

HECENIA
LA COULEUR DU FEU
Hecenia is basically a keyboard genius, Thierry Brandet, with some additional musicians (drums, bass and harp). He has been likened to Keith Emerson, and certainly his playing is very much in the classical vein, with the album starting with a solo piano piece that is both delicate and romantic. But, Hecenia is much more than that, as is shown with the next piece which is vibrant and full of fire as the piano is swapped for synths, and the bass and drums create a driving force to be reckoned with. At all times the album is interesting and full of life, as well as being crammed full of great musicianship. The last song is nearly twenty-five minutes in length, and brings together loads of different styles and influences. This is an instrumental album that works well on all levels, combining ideas from both ELP and early Genesis in a way that will appeal to followers of both bands and many more besides. *#28, Apr 1995*

HENRY FOOL
HENRY FOOL
Henry Fool is a new prog band based around Fudge Smith (Pendragon, Steve Hackett Band) and Tim Bowness (No-Man, David Torn). Along with Steve Bennet (keyboards), Peter Chilvers (bass), Michael Bearpark (additional guitar) and Myke Clifford (woodwind) they have produced one of the most interesting prog bands to come out of the UK in recent years. Fudge must find this music like a

breath of fresh air having played in Pendragon for so long. Take 60's,70's influences such as early Genesis, early Floyd, Soft Machine and VDGG and mix them with Rain Tree Crow and King Crimson then throw in some Faust and Greg Lake for good measure. The album moves from delicately sung ballads that are beautiful in the extreme to music that takes a lot of work to gain the benefit from it. This is probably too far away from what most people these days think of as 'progressive' music but in many ways, this truly is and deserves to be heard.
#65, Dec 2001

HEON
ELECTRO-ACOUSTIC REQUIEM
This album is the result of a year-long project by Martin Héon, where he has attempted to explore the acoustic range of an electric guitar. He has modified the sound using different methods but all of them have been created by him on a guitar and then multi-layered. Unlike many 'projects' where the musician has a propensity to disappear into a hole of his own making, this is a surprisingly interesting album. I do not listen to much music like this, but there are definite similarities at time with Mike Oldfield, particularly with his earlier works. It is hard to describe, as although each 'song' is recognisably very different, it should be heard to be believed. At first I did not think that I would enjoy this album but after repeated listenings, I now think that it is one of the strongest releases on Unicorn. It may not be to everyone's taste, and certainly is not in the mainstream, but for music that is pushing boundaries yet is still immensely enjoyable then this must be one of the best around.
#76, Oct 2003

STEVE HILLAGE
LIVE AT DEEPLY VALE FESTIVAL 1978
For some strange reason, I had never come across Steve Hillage prior to this CD, although even I have heard of his album 'Live Herald' which was recorded only a year before Steve's gig at the Deeply Dale Festival. Possibly it is the existence of that album which has caused these tapes to be buried for so long, but I do know that I know want to search out other things by Steve as this set is terrific! This double CD release contains the complete 77-minute set taken from the mixing desk, plus some of the songs also recorded from the audience plus some stage announcements and songs by Tractor and "Babylon's Burning" by The Ruts. But these are just extras to the thirteen numbers provided by Steve and his band Christian Boulé, John McKenzie, Miquette Giraudy and Andy 'Android' Anderson. The album starts with a stage announcement "The Radio Caroline road crew would like to thank the guy who has just blotted us all out with that acid!" Then it is off into the trip that is Steve Hillage and "Saucer Surfing" – even though the sound is from the desk, it is still is not as good as it could be but it is more than listenable and it certainly sounded good in the car! Steve was enjoying himself, as was the crowd, and it is

obvious from this performance just how much bands like Ozric Tentacles owe to Steve. Coming to this as a musical 'virgin' I was surprised at how much I enjoyed it. All I knew was that he had been in Gong, but this performance with guitars and keyboards creating a totally separate musical world is awesome. Yes, some of the recordings are not as strong as they might be and there is probably an argument for releasing this as a single CD without all the 'extras', but it is all worth hearing. This comes with two booklets, one detailing Hillage and the other the festival itself. Expect more Deeply Dale releases from Ozit soon.
#80, Jul 2004

STEVE HILLMAN
MATRIX

Steve Hillman has been around for a while, and has released ten cassettes, although this is his first CD. His early influences were Tangerine Dream and Hawkwind, and this can easily be seen in the style of music he is interested in.

Specialising in synth rock, he combines his prowess on guitar and keyboards to some great effect. Opener "Overdrive" powers along and sets the scene as the music has an exciting biting edge and Steve leads the way as guitar and keyboards vie for command. However, this is far more than a one-dimensional synth album. I find that instrumental CDs of this nature can be very boring and "background noise", but that is not the case with 'Matrix'. Here there is an air of expectancy and dynamism which is often sadly missing from much keyboard-based rock. Special mention must be made of the dark and menacing "Into Space" which manages to conjure up many images, and if you like synth rock or space rock I urge you to look out for this CD.
#25, Oct 1994

STEVE HILLMAN
RIDING THE STORM

This album has been put together from cassette albums released by Steve over the last thirteen years. This is very much electronic music, although Steve does add some bass and guitar, and Linda Hillman helps with the occasional flute. Unlike his last Cyclops release, 'Matrix', this album goes hard down the EM road and I think it unlikely that prog fans will be interested in it. True, there is quite a niche market for this sort of thing, but the question is whether Steve is sufficiently different enough to appeal. Certainly, tracks like "Earthpulse" from the 1986 album, 'Arrival' shows what he can achieve, but whether he will generate enough sales to warrant another CD release on Cyclops I have my doubts.
#36, Aug 1996

STEVE HILLMAN
CONVERGENCE

Steve has changed direction into more of a progressive rock field as opposed to his earlier Tangerine Dream style, but the best thing that can be said is that at times it is pleasant. "Wheels Within Wheels" has some interesting moments, but while the lead instrument can be interesting, the backing can be quite mundane. When an album is solely instrumental, it needs to be brilliant throughout to capture the attention, which sadly this one does not.

#59, July 2000

TRACY HITCHINGS
FROM IGNORANCE TO ECSTASY

Going back to #15, when reviewing Quasar's second album (on which she was lead singer), I said of Tracy "She has a voice that many so-called singers would die for, at times whispering, at others crying, or soaring like an angel and then coming down with a hard, rough edge. At times, pure and clear, at others harsh and secretive, she has wonderful pitch and control". 'Ignorance' is her first solo album since leaving Quasar, and the Thin Ice team are here in force with Clive Nolan writing all the material, playing keyboards and providing vocals, as well as producing it alongside Karl Groom who contributes guitars. The line-up is completed by Ian Salmon on bass and Dave Wagstaffe on drums (in other words her backing band was Shadowland apart from drummer Dave, who not only was in Quasar with her, and is now in Landmarq, is also her boyfriend). So, the songwriting and overall musicianship is of the very highest quality, and this means that all Tracy had to concern herself with was providing stunning vocals. Now, I know that some of you have either bought or searched out Quasar since I last wrote about them, and all I can say is that if you liked that then you will love this. We start with "Beauty and the Beast", which has a long atmospheric introduction, complete with tolling bell. Eventually the mood lightens and the song swings into gear, and gradually Tracy builds up to the chorus where she lets rip. Why is it that the music charts are full of female "singers" yet Tracy is unknown outside of the prog field? Anyone with half an ear, even if they do not like the music she performs, can recognise that here is someone with real talent just begging to be discovered. Am I going over the top? I do not think so, and anyone who has heard Tracy sing will agree with me. This woman should be one of our most important musical exports, but I will not hold my breath waiting for some A&R man to get his head out of the sand. I must be honest; I love this album too much to be even remotely constructive about it. The other songs are "From Ignorance To Ecstasy", "Escape", "Horizons In Your Eyes", Caamora", "Everything I Am", "Hide and Seek" and Behind The Scenes". Clive's song writing at its best, producing some wonderful rock songs, with great musicianship, and Tracy. What more could the heart desire?

#17, Mar 1993

ROGER HODGSON
RITES OF PASSAGE

It is strange to think that Roger left Supertramp in 1983 as many, myself included, feel that he was the leader of that band but they are still going after his departure. In fact, for the third time since the parting of ways, both Supertramp and Roger are releasing new albums on the same day! 'Rites of Passage' was recorded in concert last summer, and Roger's touring band was joined by Supertramp's John Helliwell as well as a guest appearance by composer Terry Riley. As Roger was one of the main writers of Supertramp, as well as being lead vocalist for many songs, the addition of John's sax has given a very definite Supertramp feel to the whole proceedings, which cannot be a bad thing. I must confess to knowing none of Roger's solo material, and the last Supertramp album I purchased was 'Breakfast In America' in 1979, but none of this has stopped me from enjoying a very fine album. There are three well-known Supertramp hits on the album, namely "Logical Song", "Take The Long Way Home" and "Give A Little Bit", but they do not stand out particularly from the rest of the album. I think it may well have benefited if they had been omitted, as the solo material is so strong on its' own, but of course it would not then have been representative of a gig (as if any live album is). Favourite is probably "In Jeopardy" although "Every Trick In The Book" is a close second. If you have ever listened to and enjoyed the lush songs and arrangements of Supertramp then you owe it to yourself to go and get this now.
#41, Apr 1997

HOLY LAMB
BENEATH THE SKIN

I should confess to not knowing many Latvian prog bands (okay, I do not know any) prior to receiving this album, but I see from their interesting web site that they have previously released an album on the Italian Mellow Records. This is a concept based on the story of God creating the earth and sending rulers for each kingdom, and the struggle for the kingdom of music. It is a shame that there was not room to print the story in the booklet as it is interesting and certainly adds to the album, but at least the link to it is printed and the album also contains all the lyrics as well as details as to which character is singing. It is a hugely impressive album from start to finish, with more than enough on here to interest the proghead. It is an album that is very cinematic in concept and in some ways, it has more in common with shows such as Jesus Christ Superstar than many other prog albums.

I found that right from the beginning I was very involved in the music as it is highly complex, bringing in not only different keyboard sounds but also moving from pop into complicated hard rock. Different vocalists have been used to assist in the telling of the story and this all adds to the theatricality of the album. Gentle flute and harp lend some passages a tranquillity

that is certainly missing from other sections! This is by far the best album that I have heard from Periferic and one that I can heartily recommend to all lovers of prog.
#73, Apr 2003

HOUSE/GOODWAY
HOUSE OF DREAMS
This is the new album by Simon House (Hawkwind, Third Ear Band) in collaboration with Rod Goodway (Ethereal Counterbalance, Magic Muscle). It is an extremely interesting album, as while the music does bring in many elements of Hawkwind there are also influences from one David Bowie. Of course, Simon did work with Bowie for a short while, and on this album, he provides all the music while Rod provides the vocals and lyrics. I get the impression from the Black Widow web site that this album has been a work in progress for many years, and the label are pleased that they have eventually been able to release it. With Simon's history, it would be hoped that people will search for this album that may not normally look for releases from an Italian Progressive Rock label, and if they do so they will be richly rewarded. This is an instantly accessible album, one that I fell in love with the first time I played it. I do not listen to perhaps as much Bowie as I should, and can never get enough of Hawkwind, so found this immediately gratifying, even more so as I did not know what to expect. There are some numbers on here that could even, he whispers, be commercially viable as singles (although there are many others that are not quite such obvious candidates). While none of the songs are very long, some seem that way as they feel quite timeless. "Waiting" is a case in point as it is under three minutes long, but the driving violin and dreamy keyboards conjure up a time long past. A superb album that needs to be investigated further.

#71, Dec 2002

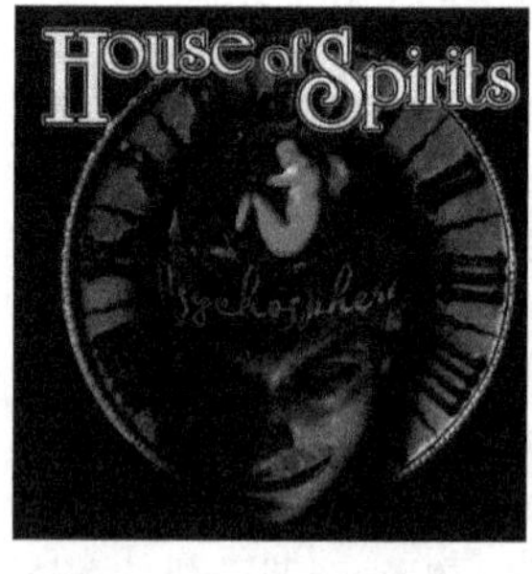

HOUSE OF SPIRITS
PSYCHOSPHERE
I looked at the cover, looked at the label, and immediately thought "another out and out metal band" but I could not have been more wrong. House of Spirits are a technical rock band with some strong progressive leanings, more Spock's Beard than Threshold. This is an album that will be enjoyed by many who are into the more technical side of prog, but unfortunately may not fulfil its' potential just because of the label on which it has been released. I have nothing against Century Media who release some bloody good records, but this album would fit much more into the output of a label such as Inside Out and I only hope they do it justice. The band broke up after the release of their debut, 'Turn The Tide' in 1995, but reformed last year after the discovery of an old demo tape. Whoever wrote the press release hit the nail right on the head when they said "with their visionary brand of Future Metal, they manage to merge catchy melodies and demanding riffs and strong vocals, creating an atmosphere loaded with a

bittersweet melancholy". Worth further investigation.
#53, May 1999

STEVE HOWE
PORTRAITS OF BOB DYLAN

One thing that strikes you immediately about the collection of songs on offer is that this is not the greatest hits of Dylan, but a personal collection, and this comes through even more when it is on the player. I have enjoyed Dylan for many years, even having the misfortune of seeing him once in concert (he was dire that night), and was interested to see not only the songs but also the guest vocalists that Steve has employed. Steve is a fair singer himself and it would have been well within him to sing all the songs, but as he says in the interview, this is a time when he saw himself more as an arranger of the music and not always the main focal point. This means that there are the sweet sounds of Annie Haslam, or Jon Anderson while Allan Clarke (The Hollies) and Max Bacon are among those who make appearances. Steve is a consummate guitarist, of that there is no doubt, and he uses many differing styles whether it is a slightly rock funky style utilising electric and slide guitars ("Lay Lady Lay") or Spanish guitars ("It's All Over Now Baby Blue"). This is an album that can be enjoyed even for those not knowledgeable about Dylan, and I am sure that Dylan fans will appreciate the music taken and treated with such care and reverence (beats Guns 'n' Roses hands down any day). A superb album.
#54, July 1999

STEVE HOWE'S REMEDY
ELEMENTS

Steve Howe needs no introduction at all, and his new band Remedy includes his sons Dylan (drums) and Virgil (keyboards) plus Gilad Atzmon (woodwind) and Derrick Taylor (bass). All the tracks were written by Steve himself, so he should shoulder the responsibility for this one. There are some good songs on here, no doubt of that at all, but there is a lot of inconsistency which makes the album very hard indeed to listen to.

It shifts styles, and Steve himself says that it is "guitar based progressive rock containing influences from blues and jazz". That the musicianship is top quality is never in doubt – Steve has been one of the most important guitarists in the rock scene for over thirty years, but that does not mean that the music itself is of the same mark.

This is not an album that many people will be approaching in its' own right; that many people will purchase it just because of the Yes connections is a shame. The fourth song is "The Clap (Where I Belong)", is Steve trying to say something? This is not the instrumental of a similar

name a la Yes but instead has a much more laid back Wishbone Ash feel. Not an album that I will often be returning to.
#78, Apr 2004

STEVE HOWE
SPECTRUM

STEVE HOWE
HOMEBREW 3

Steve is back with another solo album, I notice that this one is not credited to Steve Howe's Remedy, although his sons Dylan (drums) and Virgil (keyboards) are back with him again. This time he has been joined by Tony Levin on bass who must have felt something of an outsider given that the other musician is another keyboard player and to keep it in the Yes family it is one of Rick's sons, Oliver. This is a delight from the beginning to the end, and I was even able to keep it playing in the car when the rest of the family were there to no complaints at all! Tony can keep up with Steve whatever he is doing and often he is playing his bass almost as a second lead instrument with the keyboards and drums just there to provide the support when required.

Steve takes the band on a merry romp through loads of different styles and lots of different guitars so that he can be picking an acoustic, playing slide, gentle electric with plenty of emotion or playing complex riffs that almost defy belief. It is an instrumental album that invites the listener in to enjoy a musical journey with each new song an adventure as he spreads himself wide. I have heard a few of his solo albums over the years and this is far and away the best one that I have come across. There is plenty on here that will please fans of Yes, while those of modern guitarists such as Satriani and Vai ought to take some time out and listen to an old timer showing that there is far more to playing guitar than a thousand notes to the bar.

'Homebrew 3' is, as one might think, the third in a series of albums where Steve has opened his archives to let fans hear how some of his songs developed. Those on this collection start with his solo album, 'Turbulence', then work backwards in time through material with Yes, ABWH and all the way back to GTR. Some contain vocals, some not, and some are very close to the finished article whereas some have changed almost beyond all recognition. Only two of these are collaborations at this point, "Between Your Smiles" which was co-written with Ian Anderson and "Outlawed" with Steve Hackett. This can't be viewed in the same light as Steve's 'proper' albums and is for fans only, but is interesting all the same. I have not been playing this nearly as much as 'Spectrum'.
#85, Nov 2005

HÖYRY-KONE
HYONTESIA VOI RAKASTAA

Swedish label APM were put onto Finnish band Höyry-Kone by Anekdoten and Jan-Erik Liljestrom, who met the band in a London pub after a Daevid Allen gig. Apparently, the name means "steam engine" while the album title translates to "It's Possible To Love Insects". This is quite a strange album, with a lot going on. It owes more to classical music than it does to standard prog, as they have mixed the two together and then added a large dosage of Finnish influences. The overall impression of the music is something dark and impenetrable while having a menacing or melancholic overlook. None of the lyrics are in English, which does not help in trying to understand what is going on. It took a lot of work to listen to this, and is probably a feat I will not try to repeat again. However, if you are in to the darker and more experimental side of progressive rock then this may be for you.
#32, Dec 1995

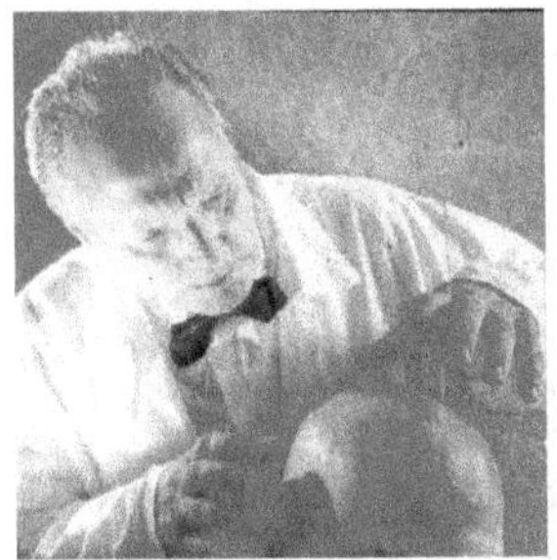

HÖYRY-KONE
HUONO PARTURI

One thing that can certainly be said about Swedish label APM is that they release music that does not fit the norm. This 1997 CD has only just been given a full release, as the label are once again planning to release new albums in the forthcoming months and this is at the forefront of the APM revival. I just can't get my head around this album at all. The first song is nearly seven minutes of classical singing. Then when guitars get going and songs start to make some sort of sense, even though there is a cello at work as well, off they go on a totally different tangent altogether. While they are going to be compared with King Crimson and Anekdoten at their most eclectic, this is an album that is a challenge to listen to, to say the least. The listener comes away somewhat baffled at what he has been listening to yet at the same time glad that he has been through the experience. This is music that will defeat even most progheads and even having played it a few times I am still not sure if I like it. It is strangely compelling, visual yet disturbing. An album to treat with great care. *#58, May 2000*

GARY HUSBAND
THE THINGS I SEE

This is an extremely interesting and challenging concept. Gary Husband is a drummer who has worked with Allan Holdsworth for many years and because of his knowledge and understanding of Allan and his music decided to release an album containing his interpretations of that music. Of course, that could not be done on drums, so Gary has instead used his talents as a pianist, and all the music has been performed by him on (or sometimes inside) that

instrument. I do not often listen to albums just of piano music, but I used to when I was younger and often these days find that I am tuned into Classic FM more often than Pulse ('The Pulse Of West Yorkshire' – the only saving grace is that it is slightly better than listening to Capital). So, I was intrigued by this album and what it would represent. What we have is a pianist interpreting music originally produced by an avant-garde guitarist and the result is something that works magnificently. John McLaughlin is quoted as saying "it has been a considerable time since I heard a truly new kind of recording. This is one of those" while Allan Holdsworth himself says, "this recording is beautiful, magic... Upon hearing it I was moved to tears". I can concur with the latter – this is a very special album and I found that listening to it in the car for the first time the miles just slipped away as I felt transported into another place, a new realm. It is music that takes the listener on a voyage, one that can have unexpected twists yet at the same time is always safe and interesting. I have not much knowledge of the original works, so am listening to these with very fresh ears and found that I got a great deal out of it. This will not be to everybody's tastes, but is a fine piece of work and with the booklet containing lots of comment is one that I heartily recommend.
#81, Dec 2004

Robert Newton Calvert: Born 9 March 1945, Died 14 August 1988 after suffering a heart attack. Contributed poetry, lyrics and vocals to legendary space rock band Hawkwind intermittently on five of their most critically acclaimed albums, including Space Ritual (1973), Quark, Strangeness & Charm (1977) and Hawklords (1978). He also recorded a number of solo albums in the mid 1970s. CENTIGRADE 232 was Robert Calvert's first collection of poems.

Hype 'And now, for all you speeding street smarties out there, the one you've all been waiting for, the one that'll pierce your laid back ears, decoke your sinuses, cut clean thru the schlock rock, MOR/crossover, techno flash mind mush. It's the new Number One with a bullet … with a bullet … It's Tom, Supernova, Mahler with a pan galactic biggie …' And the Hype goes on. And on. Hype, an amphetamine hit of a story by Hawkwind collaborator Robert Calvert. Who's been there and made it back again. The debriefing session starts here.

Rick Wakeman is the world's most unusual rock star, a genius who has pushed back the barriers of electronic rock. He has had some of the world's top orchestras perform his music, has owned eight Rolls Royces at one time, and has broken all the rules of composing and horrified his tutors at the Royal College of Music. Yet he has delighted his millions of fans. This frank book, authorised by Wakeman himself, tells the moving tale of his larger than life career.

There are nine Henrys, pur ported to be the world's first cloned cartoon charac ter. They live in a strange lo fi domestic surrealist world peopled by talking rock buns and elephants on wobbly stilts.

They mooch around in their minimalist universe suffer ing from an existential crisis with some genetically modified humour thrown in.

Marty Wilde on Terry Dene: "Whatever happened to Terry becomes a great deal more comprehensible as you read of the callous way in which he was treated by people who should have known better many of whom, frankly, will never know better   of the sad little shadows of the past who eased themselves into Terry's life, took everything they could get and, when it seemed that all was lost, quietly left him ... Dan Wood ing's book tells it all."

Rick Wakeman: "There have always been certain 'careers' that have fascinated the public, newspapers, and the media in general. Such include musicians, actors, sportsmen, police, and not surprisingly, the people who give the police their employ ment: The criminal. For the man in the street, all these careers have one thing in common: they are seemingly beyond both his reach and, in many cases, understanding and as such, his only associ ation can be through the media of newspapers or tele vision. The police, however, will always require the ser vices of the grass, the squealer, the snitch, (call him what you will), in order to assist in their investiga tions and arrests; and amaz ingly, this is the area that seldom gets written about."

Bill Harkleroad joined Captain Beefheart's Magic Band at a time when they were changing from a straight ahead blues band into something completely different. Through the vision of Don Van Vliet (Captain Beefheart) they created a new form of music which many at the time considered atonal and difficult, but which over the years has continued to exert a powerful influence. Beefheart rechristened Harkleroad as Zoot Horn Rollo, and they embarked on recording one of the classic rock albums of all time Trout Mask Replica - a work of unequalled daring and inventiveness.

Politics, paganism and .... Vlad the Impaler. Selected stories from CJ Stone from 2003 to the present. Meet Ivor Coles, a British Tommy killed in action in September 1915, lost, and then found again. Visit Mothers Club in Erdington, the best psychedelic music club in the UK in the '60s. Celebrate Robin Hood's Day and find out what a huckle duckle is. Travel to Stonehenge at the Summer Solstice and carouse with the hippies. Find out what a Ranter is, and why CJ Stone thinks that he's one. Take LSD with Dr Lilly, the psychedelic scientist. Meet a headless soldier or the ghost of Elvis Presley in Gabalfa, Cardiff. Journey to Whitstable, to New York, to Malta and to Transylvania, and to many other places, real and imagined, political and spiritual, transcendent and mundane. As The Independent says, Chris is "The best guide to the underground since Charon ferried dead souls across the Styx."

This is is the first in the highly acclaimed vampire novels of the late Mick Farren. Victor Renquist, a surprisingly urbane and likable leader of a colony of vampires which has existed for centuries in New York is faced with both administrative and emotional problems. And when you are a vampire, administration is not a thing which one takes lightly.

"The person, be it gentleman or lady, who has not pleasure in a good novel, must be intolerably stupid."

Jane Austen

Los Angeles   City of Angels, city of dreams. But sometimes the dreams become nightmares. Having fled New York, Victor Renquist and his small group of Nosferatu are striving to re establish their colony. They have become a deeper, darker part of the city's nightlife. And Hollywood's glitterati are hot on the scent of a new thrill, one that outshines all others   immortality. But someone, somewhere, is med dling with even darker powers, powers that even the Nosferatu fear. Someone is attempting to summon the entity of ancient evil known as Cthulhu. And Ren quist must overcome dissent in his own colony, solve the riddle of the Darklost (a being brought part way along the Nosferatu path and then abandoned) and combat powerful enemies to save the world   of humans!

Canadian born Corky Laing is probably best known as the drummer with Mountain. Corky joined the band shortly after Mountain played at the famous Woodstock Festival, although he did receive a gold disc for sales of the soundtrack album after over dubbing drums on Ten Years After's performance. Whilst with Mountain Corky Laing recorded three studio albums with them before the band split. Follow ing the split Corky, along with Mountain gui tarist Leslie West, formed a rock three piece with former Cream bassist Jack Bruce. West, Bruce and Laing recorded two studio albums and a live album before West and Laing re formed Mountain, along with Felix Pappalardi. Since 1974 Corky and Leslie have led Mountain through various line ups and recordings, and continue to record and perform today at numer ous concerts across the world. In addition to his work with Mountain, Corky Laing has recorded one solo album and formed the band Cork with former Spin Doctors guitarist Eric Shenkman, and recorded a further two studio albums with the band, which has also featured former Jimi Hendrix bassist Noel Redding. The stories are told in an incredibly frank, engaging and amusing manner, and will appeal also to those people who may not necessarily be fans of

To me there's no difference between Mike Scott and The Waterboys; they both mean the same thing. They mean myself and whoever are my current travel ling musical companions" Mike Scott Strange Boat charts the twisting and meandering journey of Mike Scott, describing the literary and spiritual references that inform his songwriting and explor ing the multitude of locations and cultures in which The Waterboys have assembled and reflected in their recordings. From his early forays into the music scene in Scotland at the end of the 1970s, to his creation of a 'Big Music' that peaked with the hit single 'The Whole of the Moon' and onto the Irish adventure which spawned the classic Fisher man's Blues, his constantly restless creativity has led him through a myriad of changes. With his revolving cast of troubadours at his side, he's created some of the most era defining records of the 1980s, reeled and jigged across the Celtic heartlands, reinvented himself as an electric rocker in New York, and sought out personal renewal in the spiritual calm of Findhorn's Scot tish highland retreat. Mike Scott's life has been a tale of continual musical exploration entwined with an ever evolving spirituality. "An intriguing portrait of a modern musician" (Record Collector).

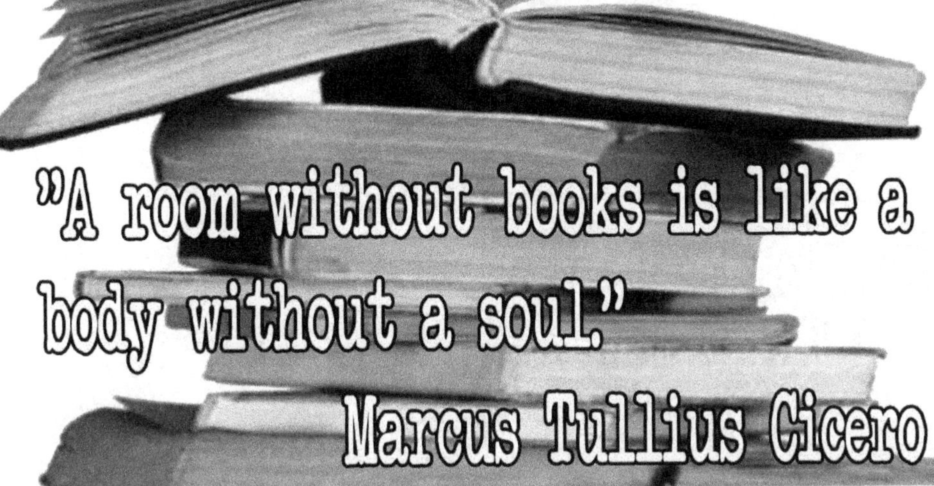

The OZ trial was the longest obscenity trial in history. It was also one of the worst reported. With minor exceptions, the Press chose to rewrite what had occurred, presumably to fit in with what seemed to them the acceptable prejudices of the times. Perhaps this was inevitable. The proceedings dragged on for nearly six weeks in the hot summer of 1971 when there were, no doubt, a great many other events more worthy of attention. Against the background of murder in Ulster, for example, the OZ affair probably fades into its proper insignificance. Even so, after the trial, when some newspapers realised that maybe something important had happened, it became more and more apparent that what was essential was for anyone who wished to be able to read what had actually been said. Trial and judgment by a badly informed press became the order of the day. This 40th Anniversary edition includes new material by all three of the original defendants, the prosecuting barrister, one of the OZ schoolkids, and even the daughters of the judge. There are also many illustrations including unseen material from Feliz Dennis' own collection...

Merrell Fankhauser has led one of the most diverse and interesting careers in music. He was born in Louisville, Kentucky, and moved to California when he was 13 years old. Merrell went on to become one of the innovators of surf music and psychedelic folk rock. His travels from Hollywood to his 15 year jungle experience on the island of Maui have been documented in numerous music books and magazines in the United States and Europe. Merrell has gained legendary international status throughout the field of rock music; his credits include over 250 songs published and released. He is a multi talented singer/songwriter and unique guitar player whose sound has delighted listeners for over 35 years. This extraordinary book tells a unique story of one of the founding fathers of surf rock, who went on to play in a succession of progressive and psychedelic bands and to meet some of the greatest names in the business, including Captain Beefheart, Randy California, The Beach Boys, Jan and Dean... and there is even a run in with the notorious Manson family.

On September 19, 1985, Frank Zappa testified before the United States Senate Commerce, Technology, and Transportation committee, attacking the Parents Music Resource Center or PMRC, a music organization co founded by Tipper Gore, wife of then senator Al Gore. The PMRC consisted of many wives of politicians, including the wives of five members of the committee, and was founded to address the issue of song lyrics with sexual or satanic content. Zappa saw their activities as on a path towards censorship, and called their proposal for voluntary labelling of records with explicit content "extortion" of the music industry. This is what happened.

"Good friends, good books, and a sleepy conscience: this is the ideal life."

Mark Twain

An erudite catalogue of some of the most peculiar records ever made. We have lined up, described and put into context 500 "albums" in the expectation that those of you who can't help yourselves when it comes to finding and collecting music will benefit from these efforts in two ways. Firstly, you'll know you are not alone. Secondly, we hope that some of the work covering the following pages leads you to new discoveries, and makes your life slightly better as a result.

Roy Weard was born in Barking, then a part of Essex, in 1948. He spent most of the mid-sixties through to the mid seventies involved first in folk music and then in the psychedelic hippie scene. He toured with many bands in various capacities from T-Shirt seller to sound engineer, production manager and tour manager. He was involved in several bands of his own, played at many of the iconic free festivals, made three full length albums and two singles, wrote for music magazines, computer magazines and produced copious MySpace blogs. He has lived all over London, spent four years in Hamburg, Germany and finally settled in Brighton where he now resides. He still sings in a rock and roll band, promotes gigs, does a weekly radio show and steadfastly refuses to act his age. This is his story.

Michael Ronald Taylor (1938 - 1969) was a British jazz composer, pianist and co-songwriter for the band Cream.

Mike Taylor drowned in the River Thames near Leigh-on-Sea, Essex in January 1969, following years of heavy drug use (principally hashish and LSD). He had been homeless for three years, and his death was almost entirely unremarked. This is the first biography written about him.

CPSIA information can be obtained
at www.ICGtesting.com
Printed in the USA
BVHW050713250719
554341BV00003B/30/P

9 781908 728845